Praise for *The Story of American Business*

"A must-read! This book is an extraordinary blend of American history, American business, and American media. Koehn guides the reader deftly through the nuances of this comprehensive survey of events, ideas, and people that have shaped our history—and our present moment—on the world stage."

—Leonard A. Schlesinger, President, Babson College

"A marvelous time machine of a book. Koehn brilliantly captures the sweep and tumult of America's entrepreneurial history, brought to vivid life through the words of *Times* reporters. A tour de force."

—Todd Park, cofounder, athenahealth, Inc.

"An exciting journey through 150 years of American innovation. Essential reading."

—Sir Ronald Cohen,
cofounder and former chairman, Apax Partners

"Business is about people chasing dreams and striving to win—from Morgan to Milken, Carnegie to Kroc, Marconi to Jobs. Koehn expertly gathers the stories to place us in their history-making moments and suggests how today's daredevil innovators evoke the risk takers of the past."

—Pattie Sellers,
Editor at Large and Chair, *Fortune* Most Powerful Women Summit

"A brilliant historical distillation of the evolution of American business. Koehn provides a vivid account of the extraordinary forces that molded the heart and soul of American entrepreneurship and capitalism."

—Jim Loehr, cofounder,
Human Performance Institute

"Koehn has created a superb framework for understanding the rich history of American business and the profound challenges that corporate America faces today."

—Tim Bennett, President, Harpo Productions, Inc.

THE STORY OF AMERICAN BUSINESS

—— FROM THE PAGES OF ——

The New York Times

NANCY F. KOEHN, EDITOR

HARVARD BUSINESS PRESS

BOSTON, MASSACHUSETTS

13 12 11 10 09   5 4 3 2

Library of Congress Cataloging-in-Publication Data

The story of American business : from the front pages of the New York Times /
Nancy F. Koehn, editor.
    p.   cm.
  ISBN 978-1-59139-683-3 (hbk. : alk. paper)
    1.   United States—Commerce—History. 2.   Industries—United States—
History. 3.   Corporations—United States—History. I.   Koehn, Nancy F. (Nancy
Fowler), 1959- II.   New York times.
  HF3021.S76 2009
  338.0973—dc22
                                                                2009004707

 The paper used in this publication meets the requirements of the American
National Standard for Permanence of Paper for Publications and Documents
in Libraries and Archives Z39.48-1992.

To all the Pilgrims at Volo Farm:

Teachers, Seekers, Leaders, Points of Light

CONTENTS

Part II: The Changing Nature of Work

Part III: Defining Moments in Technology

ACKNOWLEDGMENTS

As this book goes to press, turbulence is all around us.

A serious financial crisis has become a broader and equally serious economic crisis as equity indexes have plunged, banking systems have teetered, and business activity has slowed dramatically. In many countries, home foreclosures and unemployment have risen quickly while individual pension funds and retirement accounts have shrunk. In virtually every part of the globe, fear has mounted as individuals, families, and organizational actors have tried to make sense of what is happening: of what we have lost, of what is to come, and of what we must do to weather these storms.

At moments such as these, I am grateful for—heartened by—the perspective that history provides: a sense of what has come before and how this is relevant to our own moment, a deeper understanding of where we came from and of how others in the past—leaders, workers, consumers, companies, and other actors—traveled the roads that have led to where we walk today.

For we are not the first journeyers to know great uncertainty and stormy weather. Indeed, this book is as much about the turbulence of earlier moments as it is about smashing successes and important breakthroughs. At a more fundamental level, it is also about the connections between people and institutions: about what individuals and groups of people—organized as companies, governments, customers, unions, and more—owe to one another and how these obligations and responsibilities matter. Creating this book has been a fascinating experience of bringing such perspective to light with respect to American business.

It has also been a wonderful opportunity to look closely at a wide range of *stories*. The more information rushes at us, the faster it moves, and the more interconnected all these data and images are, the more convinced I have become of the power of stories—to inspire us, to teach us, to help us understand our world and ourselves, and to help us connect, in lasting and meaningful ways, to each other. Making this book has thus also been about coming to know, choosing, and in some instances, telling first-rate stories, working from the rich archives of the *New York Times*.

In these endeavors, I have benefitted greatly from the expertise and help of many people. At the *New York Times,* I wish to thank Alex Ward for his help in locating stories and Phyllis Collazo for her help locating photographs and obtaining permissions.

At Harvard Business Press, I have been extremely fortunate to work with Jacqueline Murphy and Ania Wieckowski. Their editorial oversight and organizational vision were invaluable in bringing this book into the world. I am grateful as well for their enthusiasm, commitment, and just plain old good sense, all of which helped bring the many moving parts of this project together.

I am also thankful to the Division of Research at the Harvard Business School for providing financial support for this project. My MBA students in two classes, The Coming of Managerial Capitalism and Entrepreneurial Leadership, have helped me test my ideas about the broad sweep of business history and entrepreneurial agency, expanding my understanding of what motivates individual leaders and why this motivation matters today. My colleagues in the Entrepreneurial Management Unit of the School have taught me much about the tools, perspectives, challenges, and rewards of the entrepreneurial journey. I am thankful as well for their good fellowship and encouragement.

I have also been privileged to work with a variety of executives from industries as diverse as advertising and cosmetics to television production and private equity. These men and women, individuals of decency and purpose, have made important contributions to how I think and write and teach about leadership, which is the underlying foundation of this book. In particular, I want to thank Tim Bennett, Phebe Farrow Port, Lynne Greene, A. G. Lafley, Leonard and William Lauder, Andy McLean, Jeanette Wagner, and Tom Watson, all of who helped me appreciate how important the *humanity* of effective leaders is.

Three women close to home helped me do the heavy lifting of making this book: Erica Helms, Katy Miller, and Rachel Wilcox. Each worked with me as a research associate. Each brought her talents, keen intelligence, and fine organizational skills to this book and the vast body of research that underlies it. And each lit up my work and world while she was with me. I thank them wholeheartedly. It has been a privilege and pleasure to have shared this project with such outstanding people.

When Harvard Business Press first approached me about doing this book some years ago, I was in the midst of a different kind of storm than that raging right now in the global economy. It took a long time before the winds and rain in my own life died down and I could begin to make sense of what had happened and—much more important—*what I was going to build of lasting value in the storm's wake*. In doing this, I leaned heavily—more heavily than I knew at the time—on a group of people (and horses) from Volo Farm, a stable outside Boston (*volo* means "I fly" in Italian). I found this place and all its journeyers almost by accident. I had never really ridden before; the only reason I found myself, one fall day four years ago, being led around a ring on a small thoroughbred with some schoolkids who were also taking their first lesson is because my sister, Alice Koehn Benson, made me promise I would try riding.

I did. I made it through that first lesson and then never looked back, soaking up the sport, the athleticism, the discipline, the suppleness, the intuition, the trust, and the astounding connections— between horse and rider and between those (two-footed creatures) who love this amazing pursuit—that come with riding seriously and with respecting horses and all they have to teach us. In all the challenges and joys of riding each day, owning horses, and showing them, I have learned a great deal about teamwork, about effective leadership, about endurance, about dealing with one's fear, about failure and forgiveness, about communicating verbally and nonverbally, about dignity and compassion, and about steering my ship toward a brilliant point on the horizon. I have always been an eager student. But I am not sure I could have learned these lessons and put them to such vital use in my own life if I had not had the good fortune to end up at Volo Farm. It is a place built on core values: respect, responsibility, connection, empathy, concern for the welfare of others, the abiding satisfaction of hard work done well, and—always, the importance of laughter. For helping me appreciate what these values mean, how they actually live day to day, and how powerful they are as we walk forward and, at times, rebuild, I want to say thank you to Linda, Hannah, Jess, Connie, Gabriel, Tucker, and all the other pilgrims at Volo Farm.

As the twenty-first century opens, business has become one of the most powerful actors on the global stage. Companies touch almost every aspect of our lives, affecting where we live, what we eat, the air we breathe, the places we live in, the work we do, the way we think about and handle our money, the technology many of us have become so reliant on, the entertainment we enjoy (and, at times, bemoan), our sense of social equity, and our perspectives on political and economic possibility. "The chief business of the American people is business," Calvin Coolidge said in 1925, describing the newfound importance of industry, finance, and commerce on the national scene. More than eighty years later, such significance is no longer novel. Americans from all walks of life think about, interact with, and follow the fate of scores of companies as a matter of course, as part and parcel of their daily routines. Our own business is, indeed, all wrapped up with business. And it is only becoming more so.

The reach and depth of business's impact show no signs of abating. As the speed of global capitalism accelerates and its impact expands, millions of people are looking to business as a driving force in this new century. We know instinctively that the economic, technological, social, and psychic shifts that inspire, frighten, and exhaust us now, as the Information Revolution gathers steam and creative destruction reshapes global financial markets, are all wrapped up with business. In Beijing, Brussels, Tokyo, New York, and other places, men, women, teenagers—even children—are watching companies with keen interest and holding them up to new standards and practices. After all, these organizations and institutions whose survival has come increasingly into question in these turbulent times are the entities upon which many have staked their careers, their finances, and their dreams. Throughout the larger crisis now unfolding, we find ourselves tracking business with an ever-more-watchful eye.

We are not the first to feel fascinated with, confused by, or wary of corporations and those who manage them. Americans have been grappling with such issues for more than a century—at least since the 1860s and 1870s, when far-reaching, disruptive innovations such as the telegraph and the railroad laid the foundations for industrialization and modern large-scale business. In these years, the country was a virtual breeding ground for new enterprises, including the *New York Times* at the center of the nation's most dynamic city. It is through this paper's pages, its real-time chronicling of companies, their leaders, and the stage on which they played, that this book takes up the still-unfolding drama of the rise of American business.

The *New York Times* was founded in 1851 as a penny paper that aimed to report the news in an objective fashion, avoiding the sensationalism (and frequently shrill tone) of other contemporary publications. The paper's in-depth reporting of the Civil War (it published the entire text of Abraham Lincoln's Gettysburg address on the front page) and its hard-hitting investigations of corruption within Tammany Hall, New York City's Democratic political machine, distinguished it from competing dailies and helped earn it a loyal, intellectual readership.

Buffeted in the early 1890s by rivals with larger circulations, the *Times* fared poorly. But in 1896, Adolph Ochs of the *Chattanooga Times* bought the floundering paper for $75,000, resolving to give New Yorkers "the news impartially without fear or favor" (he branded the front page with "All the News That's Fit to Print"). Ochs wagered that if he invested in quality—in his writers and editors, in his equipment, and in other organizational capabilities—profits would follow. Since that time, his successors have followed this path, and today the *Times* remains one of the world's preeminent newspapers. Recognized for its editorial excellence, timeliness in reporting events as they unfold, and careful analysis of breaking events, it has won a total of ninety-six Pulitzer prizes, more than any other newspaper (in 2001, for example, it won six Pulitzers for its coverage of the September 11, 2001 terrorist attacks). This book draws on such excellence to help us understand the fascinating, important history of American business and what its actors and events mean for our own important tumultuous moment.

The stories we find here are rich stuff: chock-a-block with driven, creative, restless entrepreneurs; technological breakthroughs; financial achievements, crises, and scandals; an exploding number and variety of consumer goods; and countless men and women's efforts to earn a living, care for their families, and claim their places in a shifting economic and social landscape.

In surveying these people and developments during the last 150 years, we can harness *both* the perspective that hindsight affords and the immediacy of firsthand observation and analysis as captured in the pages of the *New York Times*. These two views allow us to consider several broad themes in the sweep of U.S. business history. They also afford us some sense, inevitably selective, of how specific actors and events in this drama appeared to those around them in the midst of their respective moments.

The book is divided into three sections corresponding to three themes: the corporation, American business and the changing nature of work, and defining moments in technology. Taken together, these aspects provide us a kind of wide-angle lens on some—though by no means all—of the most important individuals and events that shaped American business history and that, in turn, did so much to give form to our own time and our possibilities in it. We will discover, for example, that financial crises with far-reaching effects are not new. Before the Federal Reserve was established and government undertook a more active role in managing the economy, the nation was buffeted by a series of financial panics, each of which gave way to a significant economic downturn. The greatest of these moments—by a long measure—was the stock market crash of 1929 that helped usher in the Great Depression. The government's response to this crisis, including the creation of the Securities Exchange Commission, Social Security, and much more, helped shape the structure of today's economy and the government's role in it. "The past," as the novelist William Faulkner once observed, "is never dead, it is not even past."

The Corporation

The modern corporation first appeared during the late nineteenth century in the thick of what many historians call the Second Industrial Revolution. During this period, lasting roughly from the 1850s until the early twentieth century, a range of supply-side innovations, including the telegraph, the railroad, and other technological developments, greatly expanded the productive capacity of the United States. These innovations helped transform the production and distribution of countless goods and services, giving birth to a host of new industries, from department stores and mass retailing to oil refining, investment banking, and automobile manufacturing.

At the same time, rising incomes, population growth, and urbanization were altering the demand side of the economy, affecting what consumers wanted and needed and how much they had to spend. The end result of these shifts on the demand and supply sides was a sea change in the American economy. By the turn of the century, the collection of scattered, loosely connected regional economies based on agriculture and mercantile commerce that had powered the country since before its independence had given way to a *national* market of unprecedented size, stretching across a continent and encompassing eighty million people. It was a market increasingly defined by widespread industrialization and mass consumption on an entirely new scale. The very term *Second Industrial Revolution* speaks to the far-reaching nature of the transformation.

At the center of all this was the corporation, or Big Business, as we think of it today. Between about 1850 and 1920, large-scale organizations emerged in many sectors. Virtually all of these companies began in an entrepreneur's garage, so to speak, as a result of the vision and drive and ingenuity of people like John Rockefeller, whose company, Standard Oil, did more than almost any other single entity to shape the oil business; or Henry Clay Frick, who, along with Andrew Carnegie, was hell-bent on conquering the young market for steel; or Lincoln Filene, whose commercial imagination helped create the modern department store.

The corporation came to many young industries during this period, but it was in the booming (and often busting) business of railroads that it came first. The vast network of railroads that had been developed by the dawn of the twentieth century demanded operational activities and budgets on an entirely new scale, and raising, investing, and managing funds on the scale of the railroads had important ripple effects. For one thing, such activity helped create the American capital markets, particularly the New York Stock Exchange, in the broad outlines we know them today. Before the railroads, a typical day on the exchange might number fifty trades, mostly in insurance company and bank stocks and government bonds. By the 1850s, hundreds of thousands of shares—mostly railroad, bank, and municipal securities—were changing hands each week. For another, the rapid growth in railroad stocks helped pave the way for the modern speculator. More than a hundred years before Ivan Boesky, Michael Milken, and Carl Icahn made their marks on the U.S. economy, men such as Jay Gould and Daniel Drew became famous for altering the structure and strategy of railroad companies by virtue of their stock dealings (some of these dealings helped fuel excessive speculation and thus contributed to a broader financial panic in 1869). The expansion of railroads also gave birth to a range of new financial instruments, accounting techniques, and oversight practices for road managers and investors.

Most of these innovations, in turn, proved central to the development of other large businesses, powering the creation of companies such as General Electric, Johnson & Johnson, Coca-Cola, Carnegie Steel (later U.S. Steel), General Motors, Campbell Soup, Eastman Kodak, Computing-Tabulating-Recording Company (later IBM), Weyerhauser, California Perfume Company (later Avon Products), and Lancaster Caramel Company (later Hershey Foods), all of which were founded between 1880 and 1920 in the midst of the Second Industrial Revolution. Some of these organizations were built from the ground up; some came about through merger and acquisition activity (which intensified in the 1890s). Regardless of their beginnings, many of these corporations are still leading players today.

American Business and the Changing Nature of Work

The coming of industrialization in the nineteenth century brought important changes to households as well as companies. Working patterns shifted. Buying habits changed. So, too, did the daily rhythms of life. Americans' sense of place and possibility altered as well. This fascinating dynamic among business activity, the changing nature of work, consumption, and national identity continues to unfold in our own time.

For centuries, most families—including Native Americans and later European immigrants and African Americans—had lived off the land as farmers, keepers of livestock, and, in the southern states, as plantation owners and slaves. During the seventeenth and eighteenth centuries, a range of mercantile businesses in major cities such as Boston, New York, Philadelphia, and Savannah grew up to service the trans-Atlantic trade. But commercial activity was a small part of the early U.S. economy. Measured in terms of today's metrics such as gross domestic product (GDP) or labor force distribution, agriculture was, far and away, the most important sector.

In 1800, for example, about three-fourths of the labor force—free and slave—worked in agriculture.

In an almost perfect flip-flop of the working patterns of the early nineteenth century, only about one-fourth of working men and women in 1920 farmed (in our time, in the early twenty-first century, the fraction is less than 2 percent). The rest earned their livelihoods in manufacturing, trade, transportation (especially the railroads), and domestic service. The productivity of the United States mirrored these long-term patterns. At the end of the Civil War, agricultural output accounted for almost 40 percent of gross private domestic product (national output exclusive of the government). In 1920, by contrast, farm output was 14 percent, while other sectors, such as manufacturing and trade, made up the remainder.

Underneath these changing numbers is the human story of industrialization. Beginning in the middle decades of the nineteenth century, Americans left their farms in growing numbers and moved into cities. So, too, did the millions of immigrants who arrived in the United States between 1880 and 1920. All of these people were trying to make a new start, to build something better for themselves and their families, in growing cities such as New York and Pittsburgh and Chicago. As they began to settle in, most found the look and feel and rhythms of their lives markedly different from what they had left behind. One important difference was speed: the pace of urban life was faster than that on the farm. It was also filled with the visible effects of rapid economic and social change: the striking contrasts between rich and poor, the ever-present allure of material advantage, the rapidity with which money was made and lost. The reporter and novelist Theodore Dreiser remembered late nineteenth-century Chicago as a place where

> the rancidity of dirt, or the stark icy bleakness of poverty fairly
> shouted, but they were never still, decaying pools of misery.
> On wide bleak stretches of prairie swept by whipping winds
> one could find men who were tanning dog or cat hides

but their wives were buying yellow plush albums or
red-silk-shaded lamps or blue and green rugs on time . . .
Such was Chicago.[1]

In this and other cities, men and women hustled to find jobs in factories, stores, and offices, where they worked under new constraints and conditions. Many now found themselves dependent on the ebb and flow of market forces, and this added uncertainty to their lives. In factories and clerical pools, millions of Americans—men, women, and children—made their livings by doing one or two specialized tasks over and over again, often under the supervision of a foreman or other manager. They worked hours and earned wages that were set by institutions—hours and wages that could change, or even end, abruptly. All of this stood in stark contrast with the flexibility and relative autonomy of farm work. Even time seemed to flow differently in the wake of industrialization. Bells, clocks, and factory whistles measured the day for industrial workers rather than the sun and the seasons.

At the same time, entrepreneurs and managers in many industries were trying to make workers more efficient and increase the productivity of their enterprises. Henry Ford's assembly line and Frederick Taylor's scientific management were two such initiatives that were widely emulated and that came to symbolize the foundations of mass production. These and other innovations helped fuel great gains in the output of American business and in average real income (adjusted for price changes, gross national product grew threefold between 1889 and 1919).

Productivity improvements did not necessarily improve the *experience* of work for most Americans, however. More often than not, assembly-line work was exhausting for the body and numbing for the soul. At Henry Ford's huge plant outside Detroit, for example, annual turnover reached 300 to 400 percent in the second decade of the twentieth century as men tried their hand—often briefly—at the monotonous, strength-sapping labor demanded by one of the nation's most efficient manufacturers. Early industrial work was often dangerous as well. Before the early twentieth century and the beginnings of government regulation, there were few safeguards for workers. As a result, men, women, and children earned their livelihoods under conditions that varied dramatically— from factory to factory and across industries. Meatpacking, steel-making, and mining were some of the most hazardous jobs.

Individually and together, working men and women tried to make sense of their experience and their stakes in the young, raw, booming industries—such as meatpacking—that were increasingly coming to define the national economy. One of the most important consequences of the collective response to industrialization was the development of the modern labor movement. In the late 1880s, the trade-union movement gathered great momentum with the formation of the American Federation of Labor (AFL). Led by the charismatic and strategic Samuel Gompers, the AFL reached across geographic lines, aiming to organize skilled workers from a range of sectors in order to achieve bread-and-butter goals such as higher wages and safer working conditions. By 1920, the AFL had more than four million members and was the largest labor association in the country. But it still represented only about 13 percent of the nation's nonagricultural workforce, a lower percentage than in most western European countries, where unions were (and still are) more powerful economically and politically.

During the 1920s and early 1930s, several AFL leaders, such as John Lewis of the United Mine Workers, tried to organize unskilled workers along industrial lines. This created ongoing tensions and conflict within the AFL, whose ranks had historically been populated by skilled workers united by their respective crafts. In 1935, the tensions concerning industrial workers boiled over, and John Lewis and his colleagues were expelled from the AFL. They established a rival federation of unions, the Congress of Industrial Organizations (CIO), and set about recruiting members. On December 30, 1936, the newly formed United Auto Workers

(UAW), acting under the umbrella of the CIO, staged a sit-down strike at a General Motors plant in Flint, Michigan. UAW members sat down at their equipment and would not resume work until GM management recognized the union as their bargaining unit. After a six-week standoff, General Motors executives agreed to negotiate with the UAW. Not long afterward, United States Steel agreed to recognize the Steel Workers Organizing Committee. Union membership grew markedly during the late 1930s, and by the end of the decade totaled nine million people. By the mid-1950s, when the AFL and the CIO reunited, Big Labor—the outgrowth of a long-term evolutionary response to Big Business—was firmly established.

The rise of Big Business and industrialization had other consequences as well. One of the most important was the mass production of countless new consumer goods: canned soups, ready-made dresses, sewing machines, soft drinks, and more. Some of the same innovations that created new things also helped make existing products—guns, gloves, locks, and china—cheaper, better, and more easily accessible. By the late nineteenth century, households encountered many of these goods in new forms and outlets. For most of the century, men and women had bought most goods from clerks in local stores, who poured, weighed, and scooped bulk items into desired quantities. In the 1880s, however, companies such as Heinz, Procter & Gamble, and Kellogg's began branding and packing their products for *national* distribution. At the same time, new distribution channels exploded onto the scene, including department stores, chain stores, and mail-order houses. Retailers such as Marshall Field's, Wanamaker's, the Great Atlantic & Pacific Tea Company, Sears & Roebuck, and Montgomery Ward offered buyers a wide assortment of new and established goods. Many of these mass marketers quickly grew national in scope.

The coming of mass distribution altered women's lives in particular. In department stores and specialty shops, urban women bought the food, clothing, and furnishings that were no longer produced at home. Consumption had become a vital component of the work of the household, and women assumed major responsibility for it, crafting new and significant public roles for themselves (a social shift that was slower in coming to remote areas, where men continued to make up the majority of customers at general stores and other retailers well into the twentieth century). By 1920, U.S. manufacturers, retailers, advertising executives, sociologists, and families understood that in most households, a woman was the chief purchaser of consumer goods. From that time on, women's purchasing power influenced marketing initiatives, social attitudes, and even relationships between the sexes.

As the twentieth century began, most American families had access to a substantially higher standard of living than that of their ancestors in 1800 or 1850. Households still spent the bulk of their incomes—an average of about two-thirds—on food, clothing, and shelter. But they had more, and often better, choices in what they bought than had earlier generations. The things that most Americans once considered luxuries, such as a clock or a bed frame and springs, had within five decades become indispensable to all but the very poor. By 1930, goods such as automobiles, washing machines, and radios, which were inconceivable on the nineteenth-century frontier, had found their way into many urban and rural middle-class families. Although vacations remained the province of wealthy households, working- and middle-class Americans spent small sums for day trips to the amusement park or a few hours at the movie theater.

The expanding choices available to most households in the early twentieth century told a cultural as well as an economic story. The same forces of industrialization, urbanization, and economic growth that had changed work for so many Americans and enlarged their sense of material possibility had also created *consumers* operating in a mass market where once there had been only *customers* interacting in local economies through personal connections. In this new world, the values of an older, preindustrial culture that emphasized spiritual as well as physical improvement began to weaken. In their stead arose a modern consumer society increasingly focused on self-fulfillment through material consumption and economic prosperity.

This society advanced markedly after World War II. Powered by increased productivity in the private sector, fiscal and monetary stabilization by the federal government, and huge international markets, real GDP in the United States rose steadily between 1946 and 1970. Americans used their rising incomes to buy new things. Some of these goods, such as big cars and phonographs, had been around for decades, but had remained beyond the reach of most families. Others, such as television, frozen foods, and birth control pills, were relatively recent.

Americans' keen interest in having "the next new thing" intensified in the early twenty-first century. From lattes to BlackBerrys to McMansions, millions of individuals continued to use consumption not only to fulfill functional needs but also to signal their values, identities, and place in a rapidly changing world. Although average real wages stagnated at the end of the twentieth century, many consumers have kept on buying, often "trading up" to microbrewery beer, plasma television screens, or high-speed Internet service from older offerings. To pay for all this stuff, Americans have relied heavily on credit—from MasterCards to home equity lines—to which earlier generations had no access. As a result, by 2006, the average household had about $20,000 in consumer credit debt, exclusive of mortgage obligations. Until late 2008, when a global financial crisis quickly spread to the larger U.S. economy, Americans kept shopping—in malls, specialty stores, on the Internet, and, increasingly, with savvy brick-and-clicks retailers that used both the Web and their stores to keep consumers interested and spending.

The workplace in which Americans earned their living and paid their bills in the later twentieth century was marked by large-scale change. One of the biggest shifts was the influx of women into the paid workforce. In the eight decades after 1920, the percentage of women in the labor force grew more than threefold. Some of this growth came in spurts: in the early part of the century, as women began to staff the new clerical and stenographic pools created in the wake of big business; during World War II, when more than three million women took temporary positions in factories and workshops that had been vacated by men in uniform; and in the 1970s and 1980s, when women from all walks of life came to claim larger social and economic roles for themselves. By the early twenty-first century, about 60 percent of all American women over age sixteen were part of the paid workforce, earning their incomes in a huge range of pursuits, from firefighting to running corporations to teaching children to scrubbing floors to owning their own businesses. On average, women continued to earn less than men. But this gap narrowed in the late twentieth century, and by 2004, women's earnings as a fraction of men's had climbed from 62 percent, where they stood in 1979, to 80 percent.

Another major transition was the nature of industrial work. In the 1950s, almost a third of the country's full-time labor force was employed in manufacturing. By contrast, only 13 percent worked in service industries. At the end of the century, these proportions had effectively reversed: about 15 percent of full-time workers were employed in manufacturing, and almost 30 percent worked in service industries. Most service workers were not represented by unions, and union membership, which had reached a high-water mark in the middle decades of the century, continued to fall (by the late 1990s, about one in eight U.S. workers belonged to a union). In expanding sectors such as health care and information technology, in call centers and fast-food restaurants, Americans in the twenty-first century earned their livelihoods in different ways and with different contracts—both stated and implicit—than those their parents and grandparents had known.

These changes were the consequences of a broader shift to a service economy, characterized by freer trade, intense global competition, increased reliance on information technology, tighter connections between financial markets and the larger economy, and new arrangements between workers and their employees. In 1960, exports and imports made up less than 10 percent of U.S. GDP. Forty years later, these goods constituted about a quarter of gross domestic product. During the same period, the flows of financial capital across national boundaries increased in frequency and magnitude. By the early twenty-first century, the United States and its economic possibilities were more tightly integrated into the world economy than perhaps at any other time in the country's history. This long-term shift had powerful effects on American business and its workforce. One such effect was the rise of outsourcing—the relocation of specific business activities overseas to low-wage countries—and the consequent decline in American manufacturing and some service jobs. A second, less direct, result of greater global exchange and competition was the advent of downsizing. Beginning in the 1980s, many large U.S. companies began shedding employees, often in sudden, large waves. For top managers, downsizing was a means to several possible ends, including keeping pace with new, lower-cost international rivals, increasing executive compensation, and, in the case of public corporations, bolstering the stock price. Downsizing was also a response to innovations in information technology—from e-mail to ATMs to telephone trees—that combined to make millions of blue-collar and white-collar positions obsolete.

At the beginning of the twenty-first century, most Americans found that keeping a job, a steady wage, and a given standard of living had become much more uncertain than a generation earlier. So, too, had the benefits that many companies had come to provide and families had come to expect in the postwar period. By 2009, it seemed clear that the social contract that had developed during much of the 1900s, in which American workers committed their time and energies to one or two companies in exchange for long-term employment and, often, some sort of health and retirement benefits, had been shattered. In its wake, millions of workers began moonlighting to support themselves and their families. Others prepared themselves for the possibility of being laid off by getting more training and developing a range of skills (and contacts) outside the company for which they worked. New questions arose—in corporate conference rooms, around the office coffeemaker, and around kitchen tables—about what working Americans and business organizations owed to each other. Perhaps not since the turn of the nineteenth century have the social role and responsibilities of business been more hotly debated.

Defining Moments in Technology

Much of the growth in American business since 1850 has been fueled, at least partially, by technological innovation. Many of the most important innovations—the railroad, telephone, radio, automobile, television, airplane, computer, and Internet—took place in transportation and communication. As such, each of these innovations affected the infrastructure of connections among people, goods, and enterprises; each created new opportunities and challenges for entrepreneurs and established companies; and each gave rise to new products, processes, organizations, and ways of competing. The powerful dynamic between technological change and business development that has done so much to shape the American economy continues into our own time. In the second and third chapters of the Information Revolution, the Internet is altering the scale, scope, and speed of business activity, much as the railroad did during the Second Industrial Revolution.

In many respects, the telegraph and railroad were behind the Second Industrial Revolution (which is also known as the Transportation and Communication Revolution). The coming of the railroads is thus one of the most significant developments in the history of American business, not only for the railroads' influence on the structure and financing of large organizations, but also for their role in enabling a new, faster, more vital economy. In 1869, the press and the public cheered the symbolic placement of the "Golden Spike" at Promontory Summit, Utah, signaling the completion of the first transcontinental railroad. Mile to mile, the locomotive had transformed travel, transport, and the shape and speed of American business.

The railroad grew up on the back of the telegraph. Pioneered in the 1830s and 1840s by inventor Samuel Morse, the telegraph used electricity to send signals—and thus coded messages—across lines stretching between locations. The speed and reliability of the telegraph quickly made it indispensable to many businesses. Railroads benefited especially from the technology, which allowed road superintendents to run their trains more efficiently and safely. By 1869, the nation's network of telegraph wire exceeded 105,000 miles, with many lines laid next to railroad tracks.

As the Second Industrial Revolution unfolded, other technologies were connecting people, organizations, and places in new ways. The telephone, patented in 1876 by Alexander Graham Bell, relied on electricity to send sounds, rather than signals, across wires. Before long, the potential benefits of instantaneous communication caught on among businesspeople and—more slowly—households. By the turn of the century, the inventor's firm, Bell Telephone (later the American Bell Telephone Company) was on its way to becoming a huge corporation. In 1885, Bell incorporated the American Telephone and Telegraph Company as a wholly owned subsidiary, which eventually became the parent company of the corporation and adopted the more familiar acronym of AT&T.

The development of radio, which began in earnest in the 1890s, was another defining moment in technology. Under the leadership of Italian inventor Guglielmo Marconi, scientists and managers commercialized a system that could send and receive signals over the spectrum of radio waves. Ships initially adopted the technology in order to communicate with points on land. Radio found much greater use during World War I, when combatants on both sides used the young technology to connect troops, ships, command centers, and supply lines. When the war ended, American congressmen, military commanders, and others set out to create a U.S. radio company that would be independent of foreign ownership. The result of these efforts was the Radio Corporation of America (RCA). David Sarnoff, a Russian immigrant who had worked in the Marconi company, led the expansion of RCA's electronics division. By the mid-1920s, Sarnoff had helped establish a network of radio stations and had begun selling radios to households and other customers. Consumers embraced both the novelty and the possibilities that radio represented. At the end of the decade, 40 percent of households had a set that broadcast weather reports, religious sermons, political speeches, music, and more.

Even as the radio was taking off, Sarnoff and others were placing bets on a technology that went much farther, sending both sounds and visual images. Invented by an electronics whiz named Philo T. Farnsworth, the television was commercialized largely through RCA's initiatives. During the Depression, when many companies curtailed spending, including that on research and development, Sarnoff continued to invest in television, building relay stations in and around New York City. When World War II ended, television production increased rapidly. In the peace and prosperity of the late 1940s and 1950s, Americans embraced this and many other products. By 1959, eight of ten households owned a television set. Men, women, and children watched news reports, soap operas, sports, and, of course, commercials as they came to live with this enormously influential technology. At the beginning of the twenty-first century, when virtually every U.S. household owned a television—and many more than one—the average set was on for more than eight hours a day.

Another technological breakthrough, the automobile, proved as important as television in shaping American business, and life more generally. In 1900, the motor vehicle was a niche product in the

United States, manufactured by thirty fledgling companies for a small number of wealthy consumers (about 2,500 cars were sold in 1899). Within three decades, the automobile industry became the largest in the country, producing more than 4.5 million cars in 1929. Two fascinating, brilliant, and driven entrepreneurs led much of this development: Henry Ford of Ford Motor Company and Alfred Sloan of General Motors. In 1908, Ford brought out the Model T, designed to be simple, reliable, and made in huge numbers. As such, it was intended to fulfill the founder's dream of building "a motor car for the multitudes." Ford went on to do just that, producing millions of standardized cars—all painted black—and harnessing the power of scale to sell these machines at declining prices. By 1925, when the ten millionth Model T rolled off the assembly line in his Michigan plant, an American family could buy a Ford for $290, about a third of what they would have paid in 1908.

At the same time that Ford was focused on making more and more standardized Model Ts and selling them more cheaply, Alfred Sloan was pursuing a very different strategy. By the mid-1920s, more than two-thirds of American households owned a car, many of them Model Ts. Going forward, as Sloan understood, the game would no longer be primarily one of selling consumers their first car. It would be one of replacement, including accepting trade-ins and satisfying consumers' growing tastes for status, comfort, and style. With as much will and focus as his rival Ford, Sloan set about transforming General Motors from a loose conglomeration of related companies into a single, tightly organized firm that could produce a variety of cars quickly and efficiently. By the end of the 1920s, General Motors was turning out cars, including Chevrolets, Pontiacs, Buicks, Oldsmobiles, and Cadillacs, for a wide range of tastes and incomes. Americans scooped these vehicles up, and by 1929, General Motors, which had had less than 13 percent of the U.S. market in 1921, claimed 32 percent. Ford's share, meanwhile, had fallen from 40 percent four years earlier to 31 percent. General Motors went on to become the largest car manufacturer and—for some time—the largest corporation in the country. And Americans' intense love affair with the automobile—and all that it made possible in terms of transportation and personal freedom—continued into the twenty-first century.

The commercialization of air travel was a second revolution in transportation. During the four decades after Wilbur and Orville Wright's 1903 flight down a beach in Kitty Hawk, North Carolina, airplane manufacture increased steadily. Both World Wars—particularly the second—were very powerful stimulants. During World War II, for example, the United States made 332,000 aircraft, more than ten times its total output in the preceding five years. The war also galvanized aeronautical research and development as the federal government and individual companies such as Boeing hustled to improve the speed and performance of military aircraft even as the engines were coming out of the factories. The development of the jet engine was perhaps the most important result of these efforts. When the war ended, Boeing, Douglas (later McDonnell-Douglas), and other manufacturers began developing jet airplanes for commercial use, laying the foundations for the sprawling U.S. airline industry and a huge increase in air travel. In 1950, American carriers logged about 8 billion passenger miles. By 1970, that number had climbed to 104 billion, and by 2007, it exceeded 835 billion.

Such magnitudes tell a story larger than the growth of an important sector; they also speak to the shifts in Americans' conceptions of time and distance. In the early twenty-first century, crossing the country meant something very different than one hundred years earlier. No doubt it was cramped and crowded at 30,000 feet, the service was often lousy, and passengers had an increasing probability of arriving late to their destination. But the trip required six hours rather than six days, and for most travelers, it was simply no big deal.

Another technological breakthrough, the computer, was also destined to remake our sense of speed, connection, and possibility.

The first digital computers, machines like the Electronic Numerical Integrator and Computer (ENIAC), were unveiled in the mid-1940s. Relative to modern PCs, these were enormous, cumbersome contrivances; the ENIAC took up almost two thousand square feet of floor space, required cables and switches and rewiring in order to program each new application, and was serviced by six full-time technicians. Used to design calculations for atomic weapons and weather applications, the ENIAC was conceived and used for governmental—particularly military—purposes. The first computers adopted for business purposes, the Selective Sequence Electronic Calculator (SSEC) and, later, the Universal Automatic Computer (UNIVAC), appeared in the late 1940s and early 1950s. Insurance companies and government agencies such as the Census Bureau initially purchased these machines, which performed calculations faster and more efficiently than their predecessors. By the early 1950s, the mainframe had become an essential piece of equipment in thousands of large corporate and governmental offices. Companies such as IBM and Remington Rand vied for market share in this growing market, and by the end of the decade, IBM had solidified its position as the leading producer.

Even as IBM was coming to dominate the increasingly important mainframe industry, researchers were hard at work trying to create smaller computers. Throughout the 1960s, companies such as Digital Equipment Corporation (DEC) began developing a series of what they called "microcomputers," each of which weighed about two hundred pounds—considerably less than a mainframe—and had specialized research uses. But the drive for small-scale computing took an even bigger leap forward in 1969 with the invention of the microprocessor. Ted Hoff, the original creator, and other engineers working for the newly formed Intel Corporation figured out how to make a silicon chip that would serve as a central processing center or headquarters for each computer. This innovation eliminated the need to build hardwired circuits for individual operations, thus laying the groundwork for radically decentralized computing capabilities.

Introduced in 1974, the first personal computer, the Altair, followed hard on the heels of the microprocessor. Three years later, Apple Computer brought out the Apple II, a personal computer that was both functionally efficient *and* user-friendly. The Apple II enjoyed enormous commercial success, opening a market that reached beyond hobbyists and nerds to include business customers and some households. In 1981, IBM responded to the growing demand for PCs by introducing its own machine and hiring a young Seattle-based company named Microsoft to supply the computer's operating system. From its first days on the market, the IBM machine was an extraordinary triumph, creating the first truly mass market for the personal computer. By the early 1990s, the PC had become a fixture in millions of businesses and in a quarter of U.S. households. In 2008, there were about 850 PCs for every 1,000 Americans—a penetration rate of 85 percent, or about the same as that for DVD players.

At the same time that engineers in the private sector were developing, commercializing, and then refining smaller computers, researchers working primarily in universities and government agencies such as the Advanced Research Projects Agency (ARPA) of the Department of Defense were envisioning a system of interconnected computers in which users around the globe could exchange information, images, and more. In the early 1990s, the first browser, called the World Wide Web, was created, and the stage was set for the explosion of the Internet. And explode it did—not just in the United States but all over the world. In 2007, more than 70 percent of adult Americans had Internet access, which they used to communicate with others at home and around the globe, research their family's health, read breaking news stories, launch their favorite videos, buy all manner of goods and services, find a date, and in some cases, even have virtual sex. As it changed our conception of connection, time, and distance, the Internet smashed through older boundaries—between friends and strangers, work and home, public and private. Some of these new, uncharted frontiers offered the possibility of greater efficiencies and previously unknown fellow-ship. For example, the 2008 presidential campaign of Barack Obama used the Internet to reach and register millions of young voters, in-volving them in the issues and process of active citizenship. At the same time, the growing power of the Internet raised important pri-vacy concerns. It also increased the pressure working people every-where felt to stay connected to their jobs—at times 24/7—and its business applications made a range of jobs obsolete and threatened to eliminate even more.

Looking back from our own moment—here in the first decade of the twenty-first century—we can appreciate the extraordinary dy-namism of American business. As we survey more than 150 years of history, we can also see several broad themes that help us make sense of what was and, at the same time, offer some hint of where business is headed in the future.

One of these large-scale changes is the power of business as a force for global change. If we think about resources, such as peo-ple, innovation, traction, money, and execution, and who has what to deal with today's pressing challenges—from global warming to income disparities across countries and regions to the opportuni-ties and challenges of financial interdependence—business is the most significant actor on the world stage. No other set of institu-tions has the resources, breadth, or on-the-ground knowledge and capabilities of business to deal with what is in front of us today. American business, which has led the world for much of the twen-tieth century, will continue to play a leading role even as the na-tion's geopolitical dominance declines.

A second theme concerns the demand side of the economy. Con-sumers have significantly more power than they did in the late nine-teenth century when the mass market first emerged. Rising real incomes, technology, and other developments have fueled this en-hanced agency, which continues to grow in our own time. There are now millions—soon to be billions—of consumers, voters, and other actors, most obviously "millennials," who want something new and distinct from business than their predecessors and who will use their power to influence business in important ways going forward.

A third theme involves the explosion in transparency. Business leaders and their organizations are increasingly operating in glass houses—with greater scrutiny and repercussions than John D. Rockefeller could have imagined when he was building Standard Oil in the 1870s and 1880s. More than a century later, a global media, giant leaps in connectivity, worldwide financial turbulence, and a generation of global citizens who demand new standards of conduct from business are reshaping not only the environment in which business operates but also the ways in which it does so. We can see this transformation unfolding in the *New York Times* Web site with its real-time input—from reporters, columnists, and readers.

Finally, though less visibly, there is a growing thirst among Americans and others around the world today for leadership that is not for sale, for men and women and organizations that are not completely defined by the transactional exigencies of the marketplace. We can see this indirectly in the populist backlash against banking executives and their compensation sparked by the 2008 financial crisis. More obviously, the enduring popularity and influence of entrepreneurial leaders such as Warren Buffett and Oprah Winfrey, individuals who have achieved enduring success partly because their vision and action transcended the next market-dictated win, testifies to the power of effective stewardship.

The importance of these themes is evident in companies such as Google, Costco, and Southwest Airlines, businesses that serve the needs of a broader set of stakeholders than shareholders. It is also evident in entrepreneurial ventures that are beginning to have an impact. Entrepreneurs have always been the foundation of American business, and they remain so today. We can look to organizations such as RED, founded by the rocker Bono and Bobby Shriver, and the online microlender Kiva, created by Matt and Jessica Jackley, as examples of where American business is going. RED brings together the power of big business, new customer priorities, and the agents of social change in the form of the Global Fund to Fight AIDS, Tuberculosis, and Malaria. The mission of RED is to harness business and consumer spending to help eradicate deadly disease in Africa. Kiva connects small lenders all over the world—many of whom lend less than $50—with promising entrepreneurs in developing countries. Three years after its founding in 2005, Kiva has helped fund more than 18,000 entrepreneurs in places such as Samoa and Ecuador.

These businesses run on innovation, dynamism, entrepreneurial conviction, and responsible leadership. Seen from the perspective of history, these forces—these sources of fuel for American business—are the same as those that did so much to shape the modern U.S. economy during the past 150 years. Although the stage on which the fascinating stories of American business take place has changed, many of the large-scale opportunities, challenges, and consequences of our time bear striking similarity to those other generations have confronted. By reading these stories of the past, we can gain a clearer understanding of the world we see changing around us today. As Mark Twain observed, "History does not repeat itself precisely, but it does rhyme."

PART I

THE CORPORATION

CHAPTER 1

THE RISE OF BIG BUSINESS

The North Chicago Rolling Mills Steel Plant—shown here in 1889—later became part of the United States Steel Corporation. By aggregating capital and other assets from smaller organizations, the big trusts of the early twentieth century paved the way for the mass distribution of goods.
(United States Steel Corporation)

AMERICA HAS ALWAYS HAD A THRIVING BUSINESS SECTOR. BUT before the mid-nineteenth century, the scale and scope of most business activity were relatively small. In the late 1700s and early 1800s, a wide range of independent merchants and manufacturers practiced their trades in bustling cities along the Atlantic seaboard, such as Boston and New York. Insurance sellers and attorneys helped facilitate domestic and international trade, working transaction by transaction at a pace that would have seemed glacially slow by modern standards. Almost all of these individuals worked from a single office or a family-owned workshop. In specialty and

1802	1826	1837	1859	1872
E. I. du Pont establishes gunpowder mill in Delaware.	Lord & Taylor founded as dry-goods store.	William Procter and James Gamble create consumer-goods company.	Great American Tea Company (later A&P) founded.	First mail-order catalog begins circulation.

general stores, urban shopkeepers offered inventories of goods that were housed and sold in one room (often in their own homes). Their rural counterparts, located some way from urban markets, often had fewer goods to ply and smaller numbers of customers to serve. A general store in the Missouri Territory, for example, served nine customers during a fourteen-hour day in 1818. These patrons bought nails, coffee, gingham, and other goods.

Although most commercial activity took place on a relatively small stage, there were some important exceptions. Two of these were part of the cotton business, which, by the-mid century, had some large enterprises in both production and manufacturing. Much of the cotton cultivated in the United States was grown on Southern plantations, owned by whites and worked by African American slaves. By 1860, many of these plantations numbered more than one hundred slaves. Further downstream in textile manufacturing, technological innovations such as the spinning jenny and the steam engine enabled entrepreneurs such as Francis Cabot Lowell to build factories that employed hundreds of workers, often young unmarried women.[1] Although large by the standards of the time, the Southern plantations and early textile mills were soon dwarfed by the magnitude, managerial hierarchies, integration, and economies of scope and scale of Big Business as it emerged after 1850.

And come it did—with a kind of low, rumbling thunder and, at times, lightning bolts in the seven decades after the Civil War. Historians have debated the key drivers behind the rise of Big Business in the late 1800s—technology, management, mass markets, and economies of scale and scope all had a role—but the fact is that large-scale business grew, and grew quickly, with long-lasting repercussions for the world of enterprise and the individual worker. It is interesting to consider that many of today's *Fortune* 500 companies were founded in the late 1800s, after railroads and the telegraph had

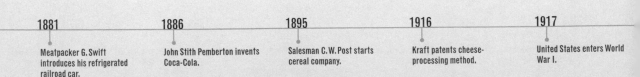

1881 Meatpacker G. Swift introduces his refrigerated railroad car.

1886 John Stith Pemberton invents Coca-Cola.

1895 Salesman C. W. Post starts cereal company.

1916 Kraft patents cheese-processing method.

1917 United States enters World War I.

transformed the transportation and communication infrastructure of the United States. Sears Roebuck (now Sears Holdings), Goodyear, PepsiCo, and Westinghouse (now part of CBS Corporation) were all founded between 1880 and 1900.[2] Ford, Boeing, United Parcel Service, McGraw-Hill, and Gillette (now part of Procter & Gamble) followed close behind.[3]

The railroads heralded a new order of business because their size and geographic reach necessitated a new kind of management. It took some time for railroad managers and investors to learn to run these complicated and far-reaching enterprises, most of which required unprecedented amounts of financial and human capital. Hundreds of railroads went bankrupt in the three decades after 1850, foundering on financial, operational, and competitive rocks. But by the 1880s, successful railroads, such as the Pennsylvania and New York Central, had adopted the corporate model, divided managerial responsibilities among different divisions, and developed ways to track and measure performance.[4]

As the large railroads expanded across the American continent, they knit people, regions, and goods together in novel ways. One of the most important changes wrought by the railroads was the opening up of national markets. These, in turn, enabled manufacturing and distribution firms to grow far beyond historical limits. For instance, railroads were essential for transporting Rockefeller's refined oil from Cleveland to the East Coast. As the scale of his business grew in the late 1800s, Rockefeller demanded—and received—significant cost reductions from specific railroads in exchange for guaranteed tonnage. This enhanced his company's competitive position and fueled still more growth. By 1878, Standard Oil controlled more than 90 percent of the nation's total refining capacity.[5] As the company expanded, it became a model of organizational efficiency as well as a giant of production. The innovative

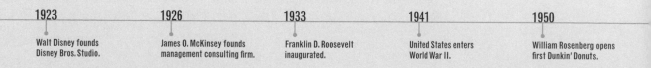

1923	1926	1933	1941	1950
Walt Disney founds Disney Bros. Studio.	James O. McKinsey founds management consulting firm.	Franklin D. Roosevelt inaugurated.	United States enters World War II.	William Rosenberg opens first Dunkin' Donuts.

moves Rockefeller and his colleagues made—buying out competitors, rationalizing production facilities, exploiting economies of
scale, integrating forward and then backward, investing in research
and development, entering foreign markets, and diversifying the
company's product line—became textbook strategies for growth.[6]
By the turn of the century, the small, independent refiners that had
dotted the first oil fields had been extinguished or swallowed by
the mammoth Standard.

The railroad and oil industries were both relatively young when
they began to consolidate. But growth began to transform established sectors, such as retailing, at around the same time. In 1859,
for example, Captain Rowland H. Macy, a former whaling skipper with tattoo-covered hands, founded the fancy-goods shop in
New York that would be the first in the celebrated department
store chain. That same year, also in New York, George Francis
Gilman opened a small shop selling hides and feathers. Within a
few years, Gilman decided to specialize in tea. He and his partner
George Huntington Hartford opened new stores, calling their
business the Great Atlantic & Pacific Tea Company (A&P) and
broadening their products to include groceries. At the turn of the
century, the chain had almost two hundred stores in twenty-eight
states. Other retailing chains followed, such as the Great Western Tea
Company of Cincinnati (later the Kroger Company) and Safeway.[7]
By 1928, a full third of the national grocery trade was controlled
by chains.[8]

In mass distribution, as in other sectors, new technologies and
processes helped make business faster and more efficient. For
example, in the 1870s, the Chicago-based entrepreneur Gustavus
Swift was anxious to expand eastern markets for his dressed beef.
He spent several years improving the refrigerated railroad car to ensure that his meat moved safely and without the heavy losses of cattle traveling on the hoof. By 1880, he had built a network of branch
offices in the Northeast to store, sell, and deliver his products, all
of which were processed in Swift's high-volume slaughterhouses

located in Chicago's stockyards. Within several years, his distribution system extended all over the country, and Americans from Boston to San Francisco increasingly ate meat killed and processed in Midwestern "disassembly lines."

Three decades later, Henry Ford pioneered a different kind of continuous operation. His moving assembly line, developed to produce his popular Model T automobile, greatly reduced manufacturing times. In 1913, it took twelve and a half hours to assemble a Model T. The next year, when the moving assembly line was fully functional, it took an hour and a half.[9] This and other improvements resulted in dramatically higher volumes and lower costs. In its first year of production, 1908, the Model T had a price tag of $850; in 1924, the car sold for $265.[10]

Although Ford remained focused on one product, the Model T, for almost twenty years, this was the exception. Most businesses that grew big in the midst of the Second Industrial Revolution diversified their offerings as they expanded (an economist would say they integrated horizontally as well as vertically). A case in point was DuPont, which during World War I saw sales of its explosives soar from $80 million to more than $300 million. Even before the conflict ended, company executives began planning for an end to what they knew was an enormous and temporary spike in demand. President Pierre du Pont and others decided to begin manufacturing paint when the war ended.[11] The former gunpowder company invested heavily in R&D and eventually developed such products as nylon and Teflon.[12] To manage a multiproduct business, du Pont and his colleagues developed a new organizational structure, the multidivisional enterprise, which gave every product its own division and divisional manager. Other companies, including the young General Motors, followed DuPont's lead and adopted the multidivisional form of organization to manage their growing business.

As the concentration of power and capital in corporations grew in the late nineteenth and early twentieth centuries, the government set some ground rules. In 1890, Congress passed the Sherman

Antitrust Act "to protect trade and commerce against unlawful restraints and monopolies."[13] The Federal Trade Commission (FTC), established in 1914, and the Clayton Act, passed the same year, aimed to regulate the growing might of Big Business. These and other government measures circumscribed managerial authority to some extent, but they did not reverse or even significantly check the larger forces driving business growth, such as globalization and merger and acquisition activity. In some cases, government even facilitated business expansion, such as the enormous increase in demand created by mobilization during World War II (adjusted for inflation, gross national product [GNP] grew 93 percent between 1939 and 1944).[14]

By the mid-twentieth century, older, seemingly insurmountable barriers that had limited firms to one nation or industry had gradually crumbled and fallen away. Corporations such as General Motors and Procter & Gamble aggressively pursued international markets, building facilities in numerous countries.[15] At the same time, the conglomerate form, exemplified in corporations such as ITT and RCA, brought completely disparate businesses under the same umbrella.[16] In most cases, whenever the stock market was on a significant upswing, mergers and acquisitions among companies rose as well. The 1990s, for instance, brought consolidation to the banking, media, and telecommunications sectors.

By the early twenty-first century, old firms, as well as some new ones, had become veritable empires, with some joining forces for even greater gains. During the 1970s and 1980s, technology and computer companies such as Microsoft, Apple, and Dell came onto the national stage. Each rose quickly to become a major—in some cases, dominant—player in its respective market.[17] IBM, founded in 1911 to sell products such as punch-card machines and meat slicers, had by 2007 grown into a high-tech product and services company with revenues of more than $91 billion.[18] The Third Industrial Revolution, like the Second Industrial Revolution one hundred years earlier, changed the way Big Business was managed, the way it communicated, and the way it produced and sold its products. At the center of all this later change was the Internet, which fueled the creation and rapid growth of companies such as eBay, Amazon, and Google. The merger in 2000 of AOL with media giant Time Warner symbolized the widespread impact of technology on business for both young and established companies.

Since the advent of large corporations in the mid-1800s, Americans have been ambivalent about the consequences of "bigness." Many have welcomed the material possibilities, including goods and jobs and rising incomes, that such growth has created. Since the late nineteenth century, countless entrepreneurs have dreamed of building enterprises that would lead markets and have great impact. But many—past and present—have also questioned the consolidation of power by large corporations. At the same time, as Big Business has grown and changed during the last 150 years, workers have had to reimagine their roles within organizations and society more generally. This has often been difficult, both practically and emotionally. Despite these and other growing pains, there was no going back. The bigness of business was here to stay.

East and West

PROMONTORY, UTAH, MONDAY, MAY 10.—The long-looked-for moment has arrived. The construction of the Pacific Railroad is *un fait accompli*. The inhabitants of the Atlantic seaboard and the dwellers on the Pacific slopes are henceforth emphatically one people. Your correspondent is writing on Promontory Summit amid the deafening shouts of the multitude, with the tick, tick, of the telegraph close to his ear. The proceedings of the day are:

1. Prayer by Rev. Dr. TODD, of Pittsfield, asking the favor of heaven upon the enterprise.

2. Laying of two rails, one opposite the other—one for the Union Pacific Railroad, and one for the Central Pacific Railroad.

3. Presentation of spikes to the two Companies on the part of California by Dr. HARKNESS, on the part of Nevada by Hon. F. A. FRITLE, and on the part of Arizona by Governor SAFFORD.

4. Response by Governor STANFORD on the part of the Central Pacific Railroad.

5. Response by General G. M. DODGE on the part of the Union Pacific Railroad.

6. Driving of the last spikes by the two Companies; telegraph to be attached to the spike of the Central Pacific Company, and the last blow to announce to the world by telegraph the completion of the Pacific Railroad.

7. Telegram to the President of the United States.

8. Telegram to the Associated Press.

Announcement in Washington of the Completion of the Road—Scene in the Telegraph Office.

WASHINGTON, MONDAY, MAY 10.—The completion of the Pacific Railroad has monopolized public attention here to-day to the exclusion of everything else. The feeling is one of hearty rejoicing at the completion of this great work. There were no public observances, but the arrangements made by the telegraph company to announce the completion of the road simultaneously with the driving of the last spike were perfect. At 2:20 this afternoon, Washington time, all the telegraph offices in the country were notified by the Omaha telegraph office to be ready to receive the signals corresponding to the blows of the hammer that drove the last spike in the last rail that united New York and San Francisco with a band of iron. Accordingly

Mr. TINKER, Manager of the Western Union Telegraph Office in this city, placed a magnetic bell-sounder in the public office of that Company, connected the same with the lines, and notified the various offices that he was ready. New-Orleans instantly responded, the answer being read from the bell-taps. New-York did the same. At 2:27 o'clock offices over the country began to make all sorts of inquiries of Omaha, to which that office replied:

"*To Everybody:* Keep quiet. When the last spike is driven at Promontory Point they will say 'Done.' Don't break the circuit, but watch for the signals of the blows of the hammer."

At 2:27 P.M., Promontory Point, 2,400 miles west of Washington, said to the people congregated in the various telegraph offices:

"Almost ready. Hats off; prayer is being offered."

A silence for the prayer ensued. At 3:40 the bell tapped again, and the office at the Point said:

"We have got done praying. The spike is about to be presented."

Chicago replied:

"We understand: all are ready in the East."

Promontory Point: "All ready now; the spike will be driven. The signal will be three dots for the commencement of the blows."

For a moment the instrument was silent; then the hammer of the magnet tapped the bell, "One, two, three," the signal; another pause of a few seconds, and the lightning came flashing eastward, vibrating over 2,400 miles between the junction of the two roads and Washington, and the blows of the hammer upon the spike were measured instantly in telegraphic accounts on the bell here. At 2:47 P.M., Promontory Point gave the signal, "Done," and the Continent was spanned with iron. The same ceremony was observed at the military telegraph office in the War Department, where were present Secretary RAWLINS, Generals SHERMAN, TOWNSEND and others. The President was unavoidably kept away by an engagement. The bell-taps here, too, repeated the blows of the hammer, and the completion of the great enterprise was known here before the echoes of the last stroke had died out of the ears of these present at the ceremonies on Promontory Point.

From the Chamber of Commerce of New-York to the Chamber of Commerce of San Francisco, on the Completion of the Pacific Railway:

Congratulatory Dispatch.

NEW-YORK, MAY 10, 1869—10 A.M.—The Chamber of Commerce of the State of New-York desires to unite at noon to-day with the Chamber of Commerce of San Francisco, in grateful thanksgiving to Almighty God, the Supreme Ruler of the Universe, on the completion of the continental line of railway spanning the territory of the American Union and commercially uniting two great oceans of the globe; and in solemn recognition of the manifold benefits and blessings, industrial and commercial, moral and political, national and international, of this great avenue of intercommunication.

The new highway thus opened to man will not only develop the resources, extend the commerce, increase the power, exalt the dignity and perpetuate the unity of our Republic, but in its broader relations, as the segment of a world-embracing circle, directly connecting the nations of Europe with those of Asia, will materially facilitate the enlightened and advancing civilization of our age.

Chicago Dressed Beef.

*The Railroads Determined to Limit
the Supply in this Market.*

Beef-eaters here were delighted to learn some time ago that arrangements had been made whereby they could get choice meat from Chicago at prices far below those that had been heretofore exacted. A bit of history is necessary. About three years ago two firms—Swift Brothers and E. C. Hammond—entered into the business of shipping beef into New-England from the Western city. One of the firms was formerly protected in its enterprise by the Grand Trunk line and the other by the New-York Central Railroad Company. The movement begun by these firms met at the start with great opposition from butchers, who declared that the quality of the meat was not equal to that which was slaughtered at near points. It was proved finally that the meat brought to the markets from Chicago in refrigerator cars was as good as that killed in neighboring slaughter-houses. After the two firms had become firmly established there was a sharp competition between them, and so strong was their opposition that they sold meat in New-England at less than cost in Chicago, sinking freight and other expenses. The rival firms, finding that each of them had backbone enough to stand loss, concluded to sell goods at regular market prices, which they

are now doing. New-York being a larger consumer of meat than any other city in the Union, the Chicago dressed meat dealers are anxious to supply the demand as far as they can possibly do so. They could undoubtedly give us good beef at reasonable prices, but they met with the opposition of City slaughterers, drovers, and commission salesmen, but above all the powerful influence of the railroad companies. The railroad companies will not allow Chicago dressed beef to come here in any great amount for reasons obvious to all close observers. It is more profitable for these corporations to bring live stock. By bringing dressed meat they will, in the first place, reduce their freight in bulk 40 per cent. All their rolling stock which is at present used for the transportation of livestock would be useless. If our own slaughterhouses were abolished and we were obliged to depend upon Chicago for our meat, killed in its slaughterhouses, the railroad companies would be forced to build refrigerator cars for the transportation of the meat. Their extensive cattle-yards in New-York and New-Jersey would soon be abandoned, and every cattle-yard along the line of the roads where cattle are unloaded, watered, and fed every 12 hours would lose its present lucrative and well-paying business.

It is understood that the number of car-loads of Chicago dressed beef brought to this City on the Erie Railroad by Swift Brothers is limited to 15 to 20 per week. If we are to have dressed meat of good quality from Chicago as cheap as the same may be bought in this City the interests of the slaughterers and the railroad companies must first be reconciled.

The firm of Swift Brothers, in West Washington Market, was visited by the TIMES reporter, but the heads of the house were out of town. Their representatives stated that a good business was being done, but that they were not authorized to make any further statement. Mr. William Ottmann, the well-known Fulton Market butcher, said that to kill cattle in Chicago and "refrigerate" them properly, so as to bring them to New-York in good condition, would make meat less expensive to the amount of ¼ cent per pound provided the odds and ends—as heads, hearts, liver, tripe, &c.—were sold at the same advantage in Chicago as in this City. As far as the quality of the meat is concerned, the shorter distance the cattle have to travel the better. In long transportation on the cars the animals become sick and feverish and buried. They have to undergo the process of preparation for the market, which is generally to feed them excessively on dry food and salt, and to keep them for 12 hours without water before they are exposed for sale, immediately previous to which they are led to a water-tank where they will consume water in such quantity as to add 100 to 150 pounds to their weight. To bring cattle to the market in good condition, Mr. Ottmann said, it was necessary, when they were undergoing long transportation, that they should be well rested before they were slaughtered. He allowed his cattle, he said, four of five days' rest in well-ventilated covered yards, where they have a free supply of water and plenty of hay, so that after the fatigues of a long journey they could be brought back to their normal condition before they were killed. So far, he said, the shipments of Chicago beef had been limited in quantity and the quality was poor.

Coca-Cola in History.

Sometime a studious historian searching for the occasions and causes of the prohibition era in the United States will pen an interesting paragraph about the "soft" drink called coca-cola during the three decades when the late ASA GRIGGS CANDLER was manufacturing it. For twenty years he and his beverage were the centre of a controversy in the South which had sociological and political as well as pharma-ceutical phases. Until the Model T Ford began to scurry about Southern roads there was no commodity of commerce so famous there as coca-cola.

After Mr. CANDLER bought the recipe and brought his fine industrial mind to its distribu-tion the business grew to a point where every little drug store put in a fountain from which to serve the aerated syrup from Atlanta. When the local-option movement became formidable, mourners for beer and whisky were advised by worthy members of the community—artfully stimulated by advertising—to find in the burgundy-colored depths of coca-cola a stimu-lant as strong as alcohol and free from harmful effects. Consumption of the drink in the South reached such a point that brewers and dis-tillers become alarmed and, spurred on by Mr. CANDLER'S public and substantial support of the prohibition movement, spread the word that his soft drink contained a harmful drug.

For years the controversy raged. Every small town was divided into two camps. The pure-food authorities took a hand. Old gentlemen, sipping their juleps, thundered against intro-ducing the Atlanta liquid into the youthful stomach. Earnest churchwomen defended it, drank it and spoke from pulpits of its innocence in contrast with beer and rum. Adventurous youths and some reformed topers discovered ways of "livening it up," and village doctors took hand in the argument. In many Southern towns there were groups of "sanctified" people who ascribed both alcohol and coca-cola to Satan. Through the late '90s and well past the first decade of this century the battle endured, and its advertising results made Mr. CANDLER a multi-millionaire. A great deal of his money he subscribed to the enemies of rum in the evangelical churches. Local and county option, and finally State-wide prohibition, came to the coca-cola belt; and then the Webb–Kenyon act forbidding the shipment of liquors into dry territory made coca-cola supreme. Foreign tourists in the South, familiar with ginger-beer, marveled at the peculiar American thirst for it.

About the year when nation-wide prohi-bition came into effect Mr. CANDLER sold his holdings in the company to an Eastern corporation, and the beverage which had so stirred the South, filled roadsides and railway rights-of-way with signboards and enriched many churches gently took its place in Big Business, where it now is. But sociologists, if so minded, can still find in the small Southern towns sad-eyed gentlemen about the Square who will ascribe to Mr. CANDLER and his soft drink chief responsibility for the outlawry of Bacchus and Gambrinus.

Henry Ford's moving assembly line powered the higher production volumes and lower prices that set the standard for American manufacturing in the decades to come. Here, in 1933, he poses in his car beside a horse and buggy—a poignant reminder of the rapid progress he helped create. (AP Images)

April 29, 1928

Uncle Sam Now World's Business Man

American Companies Have Established Their Own Factories and Branches in Every Quarter of the Globe and Have Obtained Vast Foreign Holdings to Supply Themselves With Raw Materials

BY EVANS CLARK

Eight hundred British drug stores are now owned and controlled by the same American concern, with headquarters in Boston, that runs 10,000 such stores in the United States; the familiar red signs of a well-known domestic five-and-ten-cent chain appear both on Berlin and London street corners; the laboratories of a St. Louis chemical concern turn out American mouth wash in Madrid; the plant of a Detroit manufacturer assembles American automobiles in Osaka; the tanks and filling stations of a New York oil company serve Sumatra, Straits Settlements and Siam; fifty-four theatres in Brazil are now linked in a continuous chain of management with the movie palaces of Manhattan, Brooklyn and Queens. The evidence accumulates that Uncle Sam has now become the world's leading business man.

A little more than ten years ago, a company was formed in New York called the American International Corporation. The name and its purpose to foster American business on a world-wide scale attracted instant attention. The idea seemed a novel one. But today practically every big concern in the United States is an American international corporation. American business jumped the boundaries of States with the trusts of the past generation. The super-trust of today, following the same inexorable economic destiny, oversteps the boundaries of the nation. Paris, Rio, Berlin, Buenos Aires, Melbourne or Calcutta are included by the American corporation of 1928, with Chicago, New Orleans or Philadelphia in the field of its active operations.

Change Is Swift.

That American business is selling its products in the markets of the world is no new development, although the volume has made gigantic expansion since the World War broke. Apart from a few pioneers, however, most of our exporters formerly employed foreign concerns as distributors. But in the past few years American companies have set up business for themselves on a vast scale in other lands—either through branch houses and plants or through subsidiary companies owned in this country but incorporated under foreign laws. The ever-present Boots signs on British drug stores disguise the United Drug Company ownership. Compagnie Case de France is the Case Threshing Machine Company in its European incarnation. Mergenthaler-Setzmaschinen Fabrik, G. M. B. H., is the well-known American linotype company as it does business in Germany; even the famous Dunhill of London is really a Schulte cigar store.

Like a great many phases of our fantastic industrial development the sweep of this movement has been more swift than is comprehended by the public, let alone economists and Government statisticians. That America is the world's banker has been generally recognized. The implications of our new position in the society of nations are giving serious concern in high places both here and abroad. But the fact and the consequences of our new status as business man for the world at large have hardly entered public consciousness.

As Others See Us.

As a matter of fact, the foreigner knows much more about America's position than the average American himself; he sees evidence of American penetration on every hand. The billboards of London proclaim the presence in the land of Palmolive soap, Sun-Maid raisins, Underwood typewriters, Kodaks, Ford cars, Gillette safety razors, Wrigley's chewing gum and the goods of the United States Rubber Company. Shaftesbury Avenue is known as New York Avenue— out of seven theatres along that thoroughfare

six were recently showing American pictures and plays. One can stand on a near-by street and see within a few blocks the "Pen Corner" with the Waterman fountain pen and Dixon pencil stores; American Art Metal furniture in another window; and the offices of Armour & Co., the Ingersoll Watch Company, Kodak, Ltd., the Dennison Manufacturing Company, F. W. Woolworth & Co., Texas Oil and six other American concerns. On London news stands American magazines, published in England, are displayed along with British publications.

That the United States should be business man to the world is in some ways more important than its role as banker. Like the spider who leaves his trail of silk behind him, every American dollar that has gone abroad—and the number is almost 15,000,000,000 exclusive of war loans—has tied the United States with the other nations of the world in an intricate and sensitive web of mutual interest and obligation. A pull here, a break there, sets up stresses and strains at every other point. But the migration of business has double-tied the strands. Not only are dollars at stake, but property and lives as well: land, buildings, factory and office staffs and the whole complicated structure of dealings that make up the going concern.

Films the Latest to Conquer.

Oil and machinery have been America's greatest contributions to the commerce of the world. They do not loom quite as large as farm products, it is true, but they embody in their production that inventive genius and passion for organization that are America's peculiar gifts. American oil and agricultural machinery companies were the great pioneers in international business. Even at the turn of the century they had flung their branches around the globe and back again. And now American automobiles meet and pass at the cross-roads of the world. American electrical equipment is the standard everywhere; American office machinery dominates the world market; American sewing machines, elevators, talking machines, shoe machinery, printing presses, air brakes, pneumatic tools and railway signals are sold across the seven seas. Films are the latest American conquest; in no other field is American supremacy—at least in bulk—more completely established.

The business of the oil companies is typical of the American expansion abroad. When the United States Army fliers made their famous trip around the world they found Vacuum oil supplied wherever they landed—Seattle, Chignik, Yokohama, Baghdad, Belgrade, Paris, Scapa Flow. The Standard Oil Company of New York owns subsidiary companies in Great Britain, China and Australia; operates a large candle factory at Tientsin; controls over 3,000 storage and distributing stations in Japan, China, Dutch East Indies, Siam Straits Settlements, Burma, India, Ceylon, Syria, Turkey, Bulgaria, Greece, Australasia and South Africa.

Twenty-three years ago the Texas Company had no foreign marketing subsidiaries. Today it has twelve of them—in Belgium, England, New South Wales, Brazil, South Africa, Porto Rico, Cuba, Denmark, France, Italy, Philippine Islands and Sweden—representing a total investment of $27,000,000 and handling about one-quarter of the company's entire business. The company has fourteen bulk storage and distributing terminals in foreign countries and an overseas payroll containing more than 3,000 employees.

Over on the other side of the globe—at Sydney and Melbourne in Australia, and at Auckland and Wellington in New Zealand—the Atlantic Refining Company and the Union Oil Company are erecting modern ocean terminals from which tank cars will eventually run to all parts of the two countries to feed the companies' tank wagons and service stations, and eventually the carburetors of cars which are mostly American.

Our Omnipresent Motors.

American automobile plants operate in every populous nation in the world. The salesrooms of American automobile companies can be found along the boulevards of the leading cities of five continents. General Motors operates no less than five assembly plants in Australia—at Adelaide, Brisbane, Melbourne, Perth and Sydney; besides others at London, Stockholm, Copenhagen, Antwerp, Berlin, Buenos Aires, Montevideo, Port Elizabeth (South Africa), Wellington (New Zealand), Osaka (Japan), and Batavia (Java).

The Ford Motor Company also has a far-flung chain of branch offices and factories in all parts of the world. Its foreign plants, which put together parts shipped from the United States or bought locally, are located in Alexandria (Egypt), Antwerp, Barcelona, Berlin, Buenos Aires, Copenhagen, Cork, Manchester, Mexico City, Rotterdam, Santiago de Chile, Sao Paulo (Brazil) and Yokohama. Sales branches are located in Cristobal (Canal Zone), Havana, Helsingfors (Finland), Lima (Peru), Montevideo, Pernambuco (Brazil), Porto Alegre (Brazil), Rio de Janeiro, Shanghai, Stockholm and Trieste.

Machines and Tools.

The farm machinery corporations—especially the International Harvester Company—are among the chief cosmopolitan concerns. The International has large manufacturing plants at Croix (France), Neuss (Germany) and Norkoping (Sweden), with warehouses and stores in eighteen cities of these four countries and manufacturing and sales subsidiaries in Argentina, Brazil, Australia, Denmark, Italy, Great Britain, Latvia, New Zealand, Norway, Spain and Switzerland.

The "Big Five" packers—now the Big Four since the merger of the Armour and Morris interests—are purveyors of meat to the entire world, and have found it necessary in the process to draw their supplies largely from South America. One out of every four animals slaughtered in Brazil belongs to subsidiaries of the Chicago packers. They also control half the meat trade of Argentina, and operate packing plants in Uruguay. Armour & Co. alone controls 100 subsidiary companies in twelve different countries of the world and, with Swift & Co., supplies about 45 per cent of the entire meat supply of Great Britain.

Dominion Over Electricity.

The main typewriting companies lead our overseas business in the distinctly American field of office machinery and equipment. The Remington Interests have combined with the Rand and Kardex companies in an international corporation to supply the whole range of office equipment. The typewriting company alone has 1,000 salesrooms throughout the world and selling subsidiaries in ten countries including India,

Ceylon and Burmah. The Underwood typewriter and the Elliott–Fisher bookkeeping machinery companies have effected a similar merger with international ramifications.

The four great rubber companies—Goodyear, Goodrich, United States and Firestone—have widespread overseas holdings both to supply themselves with raw material and to market their finished products. The Goodyear company, using by itself one-seventh of the entire rubber output of the world, has branches and subsidiaries in 135 countries and colonies; Goodrich owns directly or through subsidiary companies, factories in Canada, Great Britain, France and Germany; the United States owns vast plantations in Sumatra and the Malay Peninsula, and the Firestone Liberia concession is a small nation in itself.

Telephones in Spain.

In the public utility field the International Telephone and Telegraph Company has by all odds the largest holdings abroad. Through its controlled and associated companies it operates national systems in Spain, Mexico, Chile and Puerto Rico, serves one of the Brazilian States and the city of Montevideo, runs the telephones of Cuba, and since last month controls the system in Buenos Aires. In addition to it owns three cables and radio services with international connections and fourteen foreign electrical equipment companies with factories in Paris, London, Shanghai, Tokio, Madrid, Milan and Budapest. On the overseas payroll of this great empire of business are 50,000 employees or more.

In a few highly specialized fields American companies have practically monopolized world output and sales. The Singer Sewing Machine and National Cash Register companies and the two leading talking machine companies have covered the globe with chains of branches, factories and agencies. The Victor Company alone has a $9,000,000 investment abroad with plants under construction or in operation in Argentina, Brazil and Chile and a substantial interest in the British Gramophone Company, Europe's largest manufacturer, with plants in France, Spain, Czechoslovakia, Germany, Italy, Australia and India.

The great railroads opened up transportation and communication possibilities for other industries, but the roads became big businesses themselves as well. Distinct operating divisions like that of the Northern Pacific Railway, shown here in 1900, became the standard of large modern corporations of the time. (Northern Pacific Railway)

February 12, 1933

The City Department Store: The Evolution of 75 Years

The Macy Anniversary Directs Attention to the Development of The Great Institutions That Serve the American Shopper

BY L. H. ROBBINS

From small and relatively recent beginnings, the department stores have become institutions of vast importance in present-day life. Hence the seventy-fifth anniversary this week of R. H. Macy & Co. has interest for the historian and for the students of business and social trends.

For long after Captain Rowland H. Macy opened a fancy-goods shop in Sixth Avenue just below Fourteenth Street in 1858, seventy-five years ago, there was no department store in all the world. There were already merchant princes in New York, but they were specialists. The most illustrious of them sold dress goods and dress accessories only.

Historians are a little hazy as to the actual beginning of department stores. They mention the Bon Marché of Paris. But in the New York chapter they speak of the day in 1874 when the rising young firm of L. Straus & Son rented space in the basement of the little Macy store for a display of china, glassware and crockery. That was the first time in this country, they say, that dry goods and house furnishings were sold under one roof.

Before that year, Captain Macy had acquired two small buildings adjoining his shop and had added stocks of haberdashery and toys. For a while he sold groceries also. He was a sturdy, bearded, picturesque figure. Someone has said that he resembled the poet Longfellow, except that he had tattoo designs on the backs of his hands; except also that he sometimes waited on customers in his shirtsleeves, with a black cigar in his mouth. He had been a Nantucket whaling skipper; hence the tattooing, hence also the handle to his name, and the red star, his good-luck symbol, above his door. At first his family lived over the shop, in the time-honored way of merchant families.

The City of 1858.

In 1858 Manhattan town was mostly below Forty-second Street. Horse cars crept along the avenues and brought in the suburbanites from around Central Park, competing with half a thousand rumbling omnibuses. The El roads, with their smoky, puffy engines, and the cable-car lines had still to come. The trains of the Hudson River Railroad ran down the west side to Chambers Street. The New York & Harlem road and the New York & New Haven delivered their passengers near City Hall. Commuters from Newark and Elizabeth came all the way by boat.

The woman shopper of 1858 visited almost as many stores as she had purchases to make. She bought gloves in one, perfume in another, bombazine [a twill fabric] in a third, a broom in a fourth. Her shopping list led her all over town. Wherever she went she was waited upon by men clerks. A little later hundreds of the men marched away to the Civil War, and women clerks replaced them. The department stores today have few men behind the counters, and that circumstance dates back to the crisis of the 1860s.

Bargaining was the accepted rule in mercantile life. If the merchant asked a shilling and sixpence for cambric, the shopper bid a shilling and perhaps got the goods at her price after much haggling. Discounts were common, credit was demanded as a right by all respectable citizens, and cash was long in coming forth. Captain Macy didn't care for that method. His system was to price-mark goods plainly, to hold to those prices and to insist on "terms strictly cash."

Another Innovation.

Captain Macy started also the custom of pricing goods in odd figures—$1.98 instead of $2,

for instance. The world smiled, voiced the 1858 equivalent of "Oh, yeah?" and supposed that the object of such price-marking was illusion. Research shows, however, that the innovation was meant to be a check on the clerks, not all of whom in those days were above the suspicion of a Yankee shopkeeper. He reasoned that sales had a better chance of being recorded, and that the temptation to pocket a coin or a bill was less when the clerk had to visit the cashier's cage to make change.

Clerks in New York stores in 1858 served long hours for little pay, standing up from dawn till dark. The store was a dignified place, and their duty a solemn one. Conversation behind the counters was forbidden. Talk of what was on at the Eden Musée or at Barnum's had to wait until the sales force limped home on flat feet at night. There was no giggling among the little cash girls, red-ginghamed and pigtailed, who ran errands all day. Their lot was too serious for humor. There were no rest-rooms for weary helpers, no lockers for their coats, no hospital nurses for their ills.

There were no elevators, no escalators, naturally, when a store consisted only of ground floor and basement. Gas jets served for lighting. Arc lamps came in later, around 1878, and the first one was more a curiosity than a means of illumination. The first store telephone was a nuisance; so many customers flocked to use it for the exciting novelty of the thing. City delivery was a simple problem; a pushcart answered. Captain Macy's hand-cart is still in existence, and the boy who pushed it about town in 1874 is still with the firm.

From such modest beginnings of long ago rose the department store of R. H. Macy & Co., which will observe, this week, its seventy-fifth anniversary. From such a beginning have raised all the great department stores, the most conspicuous mercantile phenomena of today.

Modern Developments.

They cover whole city blocks. They tower often to twenty stories in air and descend three or four levels below the street. They measure their floor space in millions of square feet. They count their employees in thousands. There are stores that can boast 150 departments. Such a store buys from 35,000 producers, uses the services, in the holiday season, of 14,000 persons and may do a yearly business running close to $80,000,000.

In variety they outrival the infinite Cleopatra. They sell motorboats, and they sell rose-bushes. Any one of a dozen of the great New York stores deals in anagrams, aquariums, barometers, Bibles, cameras, clocks, divans, dolls, dumb-waiters, easels, flags, furs, golf clubs, gazing balls, humidors, hose for gardens and hose for legs, ice bags, ironing-boards, jar rings, jewelry, kapok, khaki, lingerie, lorgnettes, mail boxes, music, needles, nose masks, overalls, overnight bags, ponchos, punchbowls, road maps, rugs, samovars, spurs, tapestry, typewriters, ukuleles, umbrellas, vacuum bottles, Venetian blinds, weather vanes, window panes, yardsticks, lace yokes, young men's clothing, zwieback and perhaps 800 other general classes of merchandise.

The separate items they carry need higher mathematics to enumerate. A typical New York store has made as many as 160,000 deliveries in a day. Its own trucks range over a territory 100 miles wide. Its mail delivery covers the earth and reaches even to Istanbul, Aden, Manila, Hong Kong, Buenos Aires and Tanganyika.

The Crowds of Patrons.

Psychologists and sociologists wishing to study the largest cross-section of the American population possible to assemble in one spot would proceed to the metropolitan department store. On a dull day 125,000 people enter the doors, people enough to fill the Yale Bowl twice. In the holiday season their number approaches a quarter-million. More than one store in New York on an ordinary day is a city in itself as populous as Albany, Syracuse, Paterson or Hartford. The department store can claim the honor of being the biggest social centre of these times.

To prepare for this rush of trade requires a vast organism, a relatively small part of which is visible to the customers. On floor after floor which the public seldom sees the work of the sales force is thought out, planned, ordered and supported. The stock room that supplies a department is as ample and as active as the department itself. There is an air of aliveness and alertness in these important quarters behind the scenes, just as in the showiest of the show floors.

Store owners were their own buyers seventy-five years ago. Now they entrust that part of the work to highly paid experts, any one of them equipped with knowledge enough to be a complete merchant in his or her own right, but, drafted by modern organization to play specialized parts. A store may have 100 buyers, and more than half of them will likely be women. Outside their offices the manufacturers' salesmen with sample cases sit waiting for audience, fifty at a time, like boys in a schoolroom. The total of salesmen calling in a day may reach to 600.

The old-time merchant depended on his five senses in selecting goods. The department store enlists science, and a busy testing laboratory takes the guess out of buying. Ingenious machines grind and rub and pull and twist at the materials which the buyers have under consideration. They determine the tensile strength of paper, thread, cloth and clothesline, the bursting point of knitted and woven goods, the heat transmission of garments and blankets, the resistance of textiles to fading in sunlight and shrinking in laundry tub.

They find out the wearing qualities of a hundred substances, from sole leather to silk; the bounciness of tennis balls and motor tires, the toughness of golf balls. There is even an incubator where moths are propagated to serve as living sacrifices in tests of the efficacy of moth-proofing products. One store laboratory in this city has made 79,000 tests in six years.

Those are but sketchy outlines of a few of the details of the great thing that has come into the world within the memory of people not yet very old. The effects of the department-store movement on shopping are familiar enough. The stores draw crowds, and because people are gregarious by nature, the crowds draw greater crowds.

Throngs come not alone to buy, but also to see. The late John Cotton Dana called the department store the greatest of museums of modern art. He meant not the art that hangs in a golden frame on the wall, but the art that produces the things that life uses—chairs and carpets, dress fabrics, tableware, kitchenware, wallpaper, shoes—there is art, he said, in all things that man makes well.

Contrasts With Early Days.

The merchants of the 1860s would hardly know what to make of many things common in department store conduct today. They would find continuation schools for junior clerks; dances, revues, summer camps and rest farms for employees; linguists to act as interpreters for customers from foreign lands; special delivery hourly for travelers at hotels; personal service for people in haste; and psychology examinations for the drivers of the store trucks.

They would marvel at the air refrigeration on summer days; at the ateliers of design in which skillful craftsmen create beauty while the crowd watches; at the trout pools in fishing-goods season, with brook and brown and rainbow trout at home in them. They would discover, somewhere on the premises, life-size dwellings completely and admirably furnished from cellar to attic. They would wonder at finding, in one large store, 400 college graduates in careers of merchandising.

No doubt they would be thunderstruck by it all. But the present-day public takes the department store for granted.

The Great Oil Monopoly

How the Standard Company Robs the Public.

The Views of an Experienced Observer on the Situation—a Brief Review of the

Operations of Mr. Rockefeller's Corporation—How It Grew and Prospered.

CLEVELAND, NOV. 17.—Very few men will ever know how much money was made by the Standard Oil Company in the recent flurry in the oil market, and the stockholder himself who obtains full knowledge of all the deals that have been made, and their results, must stand close to the inner door, of which John D. Rockefeller alone holds the key. While the Standard is, in the real meaning of the word, the greatest monopoly in America, as powerful in its own field as the Government itself, and holding the entire refined and crude oil market of the world in the hollow of its President's hand, its methods and dealings are the most securely covered up and hidden from the public eye of any corporation that anywhere approaches it in size or ramifications. It fears nothing in the world so much as to be talked about, and the last thing desired by its managers is the advertisement of the public press.

A shrewd and experienced observer gives an opinion of the situation and the operation of the Standard as regards the present market. "In July last," said he, "crude oil was at 49 ¾ cents. Suppose the Standard then—as they no doubt did—bought 3,000,000 or 4,000,000 barrels, and had, we will say, 8,000,000 or 10,000,000 barrels by the time it had reached 65 cents. Then they turn in and commence to sell at that figure. They buy and sell, making a profit every time. With their inside knowledge, and their control of the market, I have no doubt that by the time oil reached 96 cents, the Standard manipulators had cleared for the company no less than $8,000,000.

"When the Standard was first incorporated as a company under the laws of Ohio its capital stock was placed at $1,000,000. In 1879 that stock was increased to $3,500,000. Within the last four months it has been expanded to $70,000,000, and the stock allowed to go into the market, although it has never got into the Street. It is now worth about 80 cents, which would give the company a value of some $56,000,000. When this increase of stock was made all the possessions and branches were turned into the common stock—the various works, pipelines, and oil.

"When one measures this great monopoly as to wealth, power, and resources, it does not seem possible that the beginning was so small. In 1864–5, when the Pennsylvania oil excitement first commenced, the firm of Clark & Rocke-feller was doing a commission business in the river section of Cleveland. The two partners were Morris P. Clark, a big Englishman, and John D. Rockefeller; a medium sized long-headed and cool Scotchman. Among thousands of others these gentlemen became interested in oil, and went into Pennsylvania and bought some territory. I do not know how they made out with it, but soon afterward their speculation took a new turn. Sam Andrews was a ware-house man who was shrewd and skillful in vari-ous ways, and Clark and Rockefeller made a deal with him by which the experiment of refin-ing oil in Cleveland was to be tried. A still was erected and Andrews put in charge. He fur-nished the management and did the work while the firm put up the cash, and looked after the buying and the selling. All was at first done in a small way. After a time Andrews went to exper-imenting, and found a way by which oil could be refined better, and at less cost than by the old method. The business grew bit by bit, and some suggestions as to its possibilities began to dawn not only on these refining pioneers, but on other men whose minds had seen turned toward the subject of oil. About this time Messrs. Clark and Rockefeller had some difficulty as to a question about land, and the former sold out. Rockefeller and Andrews went on together, ex-panding their business and improving it. After a time Mr. H. M. Flagler, the present Secretary of the Standard, was taken into the partnership, and the firm became Rockefeller, Flagler & Co. Clark had seen enough of the business to know there was money in it, and a new firm was formed under the name of Clark, Payne & Co., the second partner being Col. Oliver H. Payne, the present Treasurer of the Standard.

"It is not known in whose mind first dawned the possibility of the scheme that has been so successfully put into operation, but Mr. Rocke-feller has always been credited with its parent-age. If he did not suggest it, his was the hand that put it into execution. Clark, Payne & Co. were approached by Rockefeller, Flagler & Co., and the idea that soon blossomed into the Stan-dard was unfolded. These two went in on an equal footing. This combination gave them an advantage over any other one firm, and they were not the men to throw away that advantage. The next largest Cleveland firm was approached and allowed to come in, but on terms not quite so good as the two original firms had given each other. Then other firms were approached in turn, each one receiving less consideration than its predecessor at the hands of the then strong and determined combination. By the time the little fellows were reached the negotiation became practically a dictation: 'Here, your works are worth so much, your trade so much. We will allow you a share based thereon if you come in quietly, but if you don't agree to our terms we will knife you.' This is what their argument amounted to, and the careful outsiders who could see danger from afar accepted the terms and gained shelter. The foolish passed on and were punished with ruinous competition against odds that were too much for them, and under which they eventually went down. The Standard Oil Company was chartered into life, and its career was thus formally opened."

Big Business Now Sweeps Retail Trade

Huge Corporations, Serving the Nation Through Country-Wide Chains,

Are Displacing the Neighborhood Store—The New Age of Mass Distribution

Is Working a Revolution in American Sales Methods

BY EVANS CLARK

Yesterday the corner tobacconist's was just a tobacco store and nothing more. Today the chances are it is one link in a chain of tobacco stores whose length is the breadth of the continent, and tied in with it, through the ownership of a super-trust, may be other chains with a sweep as vast—drug stores, candy shops, quick lunch counters, even hotels.

Yesterday was the age of mass production. Out of a welter of small competing factories strong hands welded together the trusts of today. Steel, oil, meat, automobiles, copper—most of the necessities of this complex civilization—are now produced by huge aggregations of capital that operate on a national, even an international, scale.

Now comes the age of mass distribution. One-third of the grocery business of the nation has already been wrested from the independent store around the corner which serves the neighborhood and is now in the hands of great corporations which claim the nation as their customer. And the same process that has made trusts out of groceries sweeps through the entire field of retail trade. Drug and shoe stores, restaurants, clothing, candy, furniture and general merchandise shops are being caught up and carried along by the seemingly irresistible tide of amalgamation and combination. Out of every dollar spent in retail stores today 17 cents goes into the treasury of chain corporations.

Where it will end can only be guessed. E. A. Filene, one of the best-known merchants in the country, predicts a super-chain super-trust that will serve the entire country with every kind of merchandise through a giant merger of general stores in the nation's leading cities and towns.

The chain store movement, however, is but the obvious and visible sign of an economic revolution, which is changing the whole industrial structure. The retail store is only one cog in the machinery of distribution. But the whole machine is being overhauled today. For generations the best minds in the nation's business world have been intent on perfecting our system of production. The job has been largely accomplished—to the wonder of the entire world. Now the brains of American industry are concentrated with the same passionate attention on perfecting our system of distribution.

$8,000,000,000 Marketing Waste.

The American business man of today is counting the cost of waste in distribution much as his father before him counted the cost of waste in production. According to Herbert Hoover, Secretary of Commerce, no less than $8,000,000,000 is thrown away every year through inefficient marketing—more than our entire export trade. So great, in fact, have these losses become that they threaten to cancel the savings made through our more efficient production. Intent on lowering the cost of making things, Americans have failed until recently to grasp the fact that the cost of selling them has been going steadily up. In a way mass production itself has created the necessity for mass distribution. With mass production has come a realization of the need of low prices—for low prices make possible the mass buying upon which it is premised. But the ultimate consumer—in the price he pays for the finished product—must meet the cost of selling as well as the cost of making. As the expense of distribution goes up it prevents prices from failing, mitigates the principal advantage of mass production and undermines the dizzy structure of our prosperity.

It is no wonder that the unmistakable tendency in this direction has aroused the industrial world.

The business of selling is in much the same state today as was the business of manufacturing when the first great trusts were being formed—except, of course, for those larger corporations, which now market their products themselves. Like the fly-by-night operators before the days of the Standard Oil, or the multitude of small steel and iron works before the United States Steel Corporation was formed, hundreds of retail stores in every town have elbowed each other for a place in the fitful sun of business success—each operating largely by rule of thumb of its owner, with little buying power, no control over prices, no capital to finance labor-saving devices, and one chance out of ten of avoiding failure in the end. And, standing between them and the manufacturer, have been scores of wholesalers and jobbers, each vying with the other in a desperate struggle to keep afloat. Most of the waste in distribution, the chain store backers believe, is the product of small scale operation and cut-throat competition and they have set out to prove their contention by making a big business out of small trade.

Even the national manufacturers who sell their own products are charged with sins of waste by critics of our present system of distribution.

Costs Are Being Cut.

But American industry has seen the light. As the chain store strategists begin to remold the very structure of our distributive machinery the chief manufacturing executives are in full cry to reform the methods by which their own selling is carried on. Stirred by critics who have pointed out the growing proportion of selling expense that goes for advertising and super-salesmanship, they are beginning to check up results against the cost. Even the main advertising firms and publishing houses themselves have begun to help their clients make marketing a science.

The McGraw-Hill Publishing Company, for example, owner of a string of fifteen technical magazines, has built up a corps of market counselors who advise their advertisers as to market conditions and the way to reach the largest number of buyers with the least possible expense. The Crowell and Curtis publishing companies have made statistical studies of the buying power of cities with figures on retail stores, banks, automobile ownership, electric lighting and other market indices. Such advertising agencies as the J. Walter Thompson Company and George Batten have compiled censuses of wholesale and retail firms in various selling areas and ratings of purchasing power based on income tax returns.

The Department of Commerce, which also is doing pioneering work along these lines on its own account through a nation-wide survey of market methods, has compiled a catalogue of agencies engaged in research into more efficient selling. The listings in it have reached the astonishing total of 544.

Far more spectacular than this patient research and its application—most of which goes on in inner offices hidden from the sight of the average man—are the achievements of the chain store strategists.

By all odds the largest retail trade trust in the world is the Great Atlantic and Pacific Tea Company. This amazing concern has organized no less than 17,500 stores in almost every city, town and hamlet in the country, through which it will do a business in 1928 estimated by the editor of a grocery journal at $750,000,000. Out of every 100 grocery stores in the United States today five now belong to this one company.

Began in New York.

Its growth illustrates the peculiarly rapid expansion of chain stores in the past few years. New York City was the birthplace of the chain grocery as well as the chain tobacco store. George H. Hartford, founder of the A. and P., was the great pioneer in the field of mass distribution. He began business in charge of Gilman's red-front spice and tea store back in 1859. When he died in 1917 he was a mass-storekeeper with 3,200 units in his string. But since his death his work has marched on—in more than double-quick time.

Seven years ago the A. and P. chain had 4,500 links—built up, slowly, but surely, during the preceding sixty-two years; but since then the number has jumped to the present prodigious total of 17,500.

Independent Grocer Passes.

Other leading concerns in the grocery field are the Kroger Grocery and Baking Company, with 3,765 stores located mainly in the Middle West and doing a business of $161,000,000 a year; the American Stores—in Pennsylvania and New Jersey, 2,000 in number—with gross receipts of $120,000,000, and the Safeway Stores of the Pacific Coast, operating 916 outlets selling $76,000,000 worth of goods a year. Other chains, well known in the East, are making rapid headway, even though they have not broken into the ranks of the half-dozen leaders.

The Piggly-Wiggly Corporation originated the idea of self-service stores. Over 2,500 stores of this type are in operation today, 540 owned and operated by this company directly and the balance paying a license fee to it for the use of its name and the patented equipment. Another company—the Roly Poly—conceived the idea of taking the store to the customer rather than waiting for the customer to come to the store: grocery stores on wheels are the modern edition of the old-fashioned huckster touring the country roads with his vegetable cart. H. C. Bohack, James Butler, Economy Stores and other names now stare at the public from many hundred store fronts.

So great has been the growth of such stores in the big cities that in New York and Philadelphia 70 cents out of every dollar spent by the public for groceries goes to some company operating a chain. Competition is no longer between the chains and the independents—the independent grocer has ceased to exist as a real factor in the market—but between the chains themselves. Over half the grocery business is done by chains in Boston, Baltimore, Washington, Chicago, Kansas City, Los Angeles, San Francisco and eight other leading American cities. The total number of chain grocery companies in the country is now more than 850, operating no less than 64,000 stores and doing a business of $2,356,000,000 a year—exceeding one-third of the entire grocery trade of the United States.

The United Drug Company leads all other chains in the drug field and has the largest foreign holdings of any of the big retail corporations. Besides owning and operating a chain of 465 stores in this country and 37 in Canada, it holds also the 800 Boots stores in the leading cities and towns of Great Britain. More than 27 per cent of America's chain drug sales are made by this concern—$58,000,000 a year. Its ownership, it is interesting to note, is vested in the hands of 9,500 drug store proprietors who have united for common action in the Rexall stores. It is said that one-quarter of the nation's population is served by the Rexall-United group.

Vast Expansion Followed.

Woolworth laid the first stone in a structure that today does a business of $272,000,000 a year through 1,600 stores in the United States and Canada, 300 in Great Britain, 20 or more in Germany and half a dozen in Cuba.

The Woolworth is more than twice the size of any other variety chain, but the Kresge, Kress and McCrory firms are each of them in the class of big business themselves. The Kresge Company alone operates 440 stores, doing a business of $123,000,000 a year; McCrory and Kress own chains of about 200 outlets each, with gross sales of from $40,000,000 to $80,000,000 a year. Starting in a small way under an individual proprietor, a dozen of these concerns have now achieved the stature of great corporations, the stock of which, along with railroads, steel companies and oil concerns, is held by the public and actively traded in on Wall Street.

Following the lead of the great grocery, drug and variety chains the mass distribution idea has spread through the field of retail trade in every direction. Thom McAn, John Ward, Rambler and other familiar store-front names testify to the rapid growth of shoe chains; the number of such stores has jumped from 1,600 to over 7,000 in the past three years. Restaurants and tea rooms are now being gathered into combinations that turn out meals in quantities that rival those of the shoe factory or the rubber tire plant. The Childs chain alone now serve 50,000,000 meals a year in thirty-four different cities from the Atlantic to the Pacific. Candy corporations, graced by dainty feminine names like Fanny Farmer, Mary Lee or Lydia Darrah, break out with stores all over the country like a mushroom field after a summer rain. The seventy-five Happiness stores (United Cigars) alone sell $7,000,000 worth of sweets a year.

That mass distribution is upon us these figures amply demonstrate. Chain stores are no longer a novelty. They begin to etch what may prove to be a new pattern for the entire structure of retail trade.

What the Future Holds.

What the ultimate course of mass distribution may be is hidden from our eyes; but one effect of it, already noticeable, may have sensational results. Not only does the great chain store corporation of today assume the functions of the middleman but it is reaching into the field of the manufacturer as well. The A. and P. Company makes its own cans and bakes its own bread; the United Drug Company produces a large part of its own stock in trade; meat for the Kroger stores is slaughtered in their own plants—much to the discomfiture of Chicago packers. Executives of even the biggest retail corporation are reluctant to take on the duties of manufacturing, and the tendency has not gone far as yet; but the issue has at least been raised.

The fate of the independent store-keeper is also a matter for concern. His welfare will obviously affect the course of economic evolution

TABLE 1-1

Field	Number of Chain Companies	Number of Units
Groceries	800	64,000
Variety chains (30 to 81)	780	8,100
Shoes	596	6,402
Drugs	415	3,475
Cigars and tobacco	30	2,850
Department stores	180	2,489
Women's clothing	215	2,036
Restaurants and tea rooms	166	2,000
Hotels	400	1,500
Candy	33	731
Meat	52	598
Millinery	46	596
Clothing	29	531
Bakeries	12	523
Hardware and sporting goods	52	511
Men's hats	24	465
Music and radios	46	435
Stationery and books	17	356
Furniture	18	179

not a whit, but there are those who look with dismay upon the social effects of the change that is upon him. Apologists for the new dispensation, however, point out that while his independence may be sacrificed he will gain in financial return and in security. It is better, they say—at least from the economic point of view—to be employee–manager of one link in a chain backed by millions than the harried monarch of a precarious business of your own.

February 12, 1905

In Business and Out, Morals Just the Same

National Biscuit Company Declares Against Two Standards.

Employees as Stockholders

Big Corporation's Men Own 6,666 Shares, According to Its Unusual Report, Just Issued.

The National Biscuit Company's annual report, which was made public yesterday, contains an unusual reference to the management of great corporations and morality among their officers. The report says:

"The inevitable tendency of business in this age is toward corporate life. Through corporations only can the great resources of this country of ours be properly developed. In that respect we believe they have a great mission to fulfill. If this be true, then the future welfare of this country must depend, in large measure, upon the manner in which these corporations shall be conducted, and we believe that every officer of a corporation should endeavor to so manage its affairs that it shall commend itself to the people of the country, to the end that the attitude of the people toward these corporations shall be not hostile, but friendly. To accomplish this, the vital point, it seems to us, is that the corporation must not be separated from the individuals who manage its affairs, and that these individuals must carry into the management of the corporations the same rules of conduct that they apply to their private lives.

"They must not have one standard of morality as officers of a corporation and another as private individuals. They must not only obey the law, but must actively support the law. Such are the ideals which the officers of this corporation have set up for the conduct of its affairs."

February 28, 1971

134 Years of Growth

Brothers-In-Law Put Ivory Company Afloat

Procter & Gamble was founded in 1837 when two brothers-in-law, William Procter, an English candlemaker, and James Gamble, an Irish soapmaker, signed a partnership agreement in Cincinnati. Each contributed $3,596.47 and P. & G. was afloat.

Both partners had sons and by the mid-eighteen-hundreds the second generation was in charge. Sales spurted in the Civil War when the Federal Government chose P. & G. to supply all the soap and candles for the Armies of the West. In 1879 Ivory soap was introduced and a few years later the slogan "99 44/100 per cent pure—it floats" was coined.

In 1911 P. & G. branched out from the soap business with Crisco, its first food product. By 1930 company sales had passed $200 million and in that same decade P. & G. began marketing Dreft, the first synthetic detergent, and Drene, the first synthetic shampoo.

Tide was brought onto the market in 1946 and the company started to build factories to produce the heavy-duty synthetic detergent around the world.

In the early nineteen-fifties the company began marketing toothpaste, home permanents, shortening and peanut butter. They were soon followed by baking mixes, paper products and bleach, as P. & G. acquired the assets of Duncan Hines, Charmin Paper mills and Clorox.

By 1965, the company's sales exceeded $2-billion and were spread over 14 operating divisions. In 1967, after a Supreme Court ruling, P. & G. had to divest itself of Clorox.

In the late nineteen-sixties enzymes were introduced into detergents and pre-soaks. The company began phasing them out in 1971 under pressure from consumer groups and public opinion.

Last year P. & G. had net sales of $2,978,750,000 and earnings of $211,907,000. It has 42,000 employees and 85,000 shareholders.

The company reached a milestone of sorts just 19 days ago when for one of the few times in its 134-year history it was left without the services of either a Procter or a Gamble on its board of directors or in top management.

David G. Gamble, 56, a Cincinnati lawyer and great-grandson of the founder, was replaced on the P. & G. board by John Harper, chairman of the Aluminum Company of America.

CHAPTER 2

WALL STREET: ITS ORIGINS, INFLUENCE, AND EVOLUTION

On October 29, 1979, the New York Stock Exchange
commemorated the fiftieth anniversary of Black Tuesday,
celebrating the financial system's resurgence from the day
over 16 million shares were sold in the great crash.
(*New York Times*/D. Gorton)

THROUGH BEAR AND BULL MARKETS, HOSTILE TAKEOVERS AND ANGEL investors, the rise of robber barons and the phenomenon of corporate raiders, Wall Street—that is, American securities markets and the investment firms that support them—has exercised a powerful influence on U.S. business and the broader economy.

1791	1873	1882	1893	1913
Congress charters the First Bank of the United States	Bankruptcy of Jay Cooke & Company	Dow, Jones & Company founded.	Foreign investors sell U.S. securities for gold. Panic of 1893 ensues.	Federal Reserve System created.

The earliest activity in the capital markets dates back to the nation's independence in the late 1700s. But the Street really began to assume its modern form and importance in the mid-nineteenth century, developing in tandem with the railroads and the country's first large corporations. In the intervening 170 years, Wall Street has also affected the national psyche. Its players have been lauded for creating wealth and despised for instigating financial ruin. The story of the public market, its financiers and critics, and its effect on a variety of stakeholders is inseparable from that of American history as a whole.

The first real securities trading in the United States centered on bonds issued to finance the Revolutionary War and, later, to fund the young U.S. government.[1] The American merchants who began to trade stocks and bonds during this time were building on a tradition already established in Europe, where securities markets, especially those in London and Amsterdam, had been in business for decades and had developed into sophisticated exchanges.[2] In the late 1700s and early 1800s, exchanges were established in the eastern port cities of Philadelphia, Boston, New York, and Baltimore.[3]

New York's exchange soon emerged as a stronghold for banking, insurance, and some newly incorporated business ventures.[4] Early traders congregated in coffeehouses and other meeting places in the Wall Street area of lower Manhattan.[5] In 1792, in the wake of a speculative bubble and its subsequent collapse, stock auctioneers and traders attempted to impose a more regulated structure on the young market and to institute membership policies.[6] The contract they signed under a buttonwood tree at what is today 68 Wall Street became known as the Buttonwood Agreement.[7] In 1817, this agreement was renegotiated, and the original association of traders reorganized.[8] The resulting group, established as the

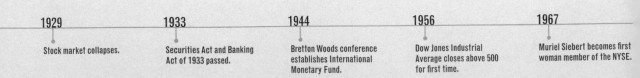

1929	1933	1944	1956	1967
Stock market collapses.	Securities Act and Banking Act of 1933 passed.	Bretton Woods conference establishes International Monetary Fund.	Dow Jones Industrial Average closes above 500 for first time.	Muriel Siebert becomes first woman member of the NYSE.

New York Stock and Exchange Board, or the NYSE, operated with nineteen brokers who participated in morning auctions.[9]

In the early decades of the nineteenth century, the exchange was dominated by government bonds and bank and insurance company securities.[10] This activity was on an altogether different scale and occurred at very different speeds from the volume and pace of today's capital markets. A modern time traveler sent back to the exchange during the 1820s or 1830s would likely find the whole thing a very sleepy affair. On one March day in 1830, for example, only thirty-one shares were traded on the NYSE.

Beginning in the 1840s, however, the emergence of railroads revolutionized American capital markets along with the nation's transport. The enormous financial demands of building, maintaining, and managing regional and, later, cross-country lines dwarfed the resources of individual or small groups of investors. Railroad promoters and executives had no choice but to turn to institutional markets for the money they needed. And turn they did, seeking millions and millions of dollars in funds on the NYSE during the middle decades of the nineteenth century (by 1860, investment in privately owned railroads totaled more than $1 billion, or about $21 billion today). The enormous increase in railroad securities floated and sold fueled corresponding growth in the exchange. By the 1850s, monthly transactions on the NYSE totaled over a million shares, or about 50,000 shares a day. The financial needs of the railroads also gave rise to a range of speculative techniques. Players on Wall Street learned to buy long and short, to trade on the margin, and to use puts and calls. Along with these techniques came speculators themselves, men—and a few women—who hoped to make fortunes buying and selling securities in a booming, largely unregulated market.[11] Sisters Tennessee Claflin and Victoria Claflin Woodhull, the first female stockbrokers, opened their firm with the support of

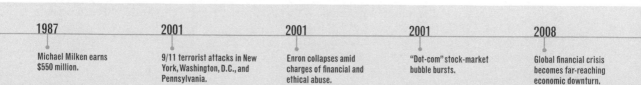

1987	2001	2001	2001	2008
Michael Milken earns $550 million.	9/11 terrorist attacks in New York, Washington, D.C., and Pennsylvania.	Enron collapses amid charges of financial and ethical abuse.	"Dot-com" stock-market bubble bursts.	Global financial crisis becomes far-reaching economic downturn.

Cornelius Vanderbilt in 1870. It took nearly one hundred years, however, for the first woman—Muriel Siebert—to obtain a seat on the NYSE.

In the years after the Civil War, several financial titans used the market to land enormous personal windfalls. Some of these men's actions had far-reaching results for the national economy. For example, Jay Gould, a scrawny farmer's son who became known as the "Mephistopheles of Wall Street," effectively restructured the railroad industry through the manipulation of stocks. As he wrested control from major railroads, Gould forced competitors to consolidate and expand while at the same time initiating fierce price wars.[12] In 1869, Gould engineered a plot to corner the national gold market that brought about a stunning, if short-lived, stock market crash.[13] More than twenty years later, financier J. P. Morgan, who was a major investor in railroads and other young industries, manipulated a shaken financial market in a different way in order to defuse the gold panic of 1893-1895 and maintain stability for the value of U.S. greenbacks.[14] At the turn of the century, Morgan orchestrated the creation of the world's first billion-dollar corporation, U.S. Steel, which was formed from the merger of a number of firms, including Andrew Carnegie's steel company. When another money panic caught hold in 1907, Morgan organized the lending of $19 million by stable banks to help stabilize institutions in trouble.[15] In the years before the Federal Reserve System or substantial government regulation, Morgan served as a kind of one-man central bank, exercising great influence over the national economy.[16]

Such power did not go unchallenged. Many Americans distrusted the authority that financiers wielded and the wealth they controlled. The most powerful bankers, such as Morgan, were accused of comprising a "money trust," or a monopoly on national credit.[17] In response to public opinion and other pressures, Congress, acting under President Woodrow Wilson's urging, passed the Federal Reserve Act in 1913. The act established a central bank, created a system of regional Reserve Banks, and gave members of the Federal Reserve Board power over currency and credit. The legislation brought flexibility and stability to the nation's financial system, aspects that proved critical to a growing nation and its economy.

In the 1920s, more and more Americans began to participate in the capital markets. They bought and sold securities issued by a wide range of institutions—not only government bonds and railroad stocks, but also paper issued by utilities, manufacturers, financial service firms, and communications companies. Many people began to invest their savings in stocks, and by the late 1920s a great bull market had developed, one that attracted large amounts of foreign investment as well as domestic funds.[18] Stock prices rose steadily during the decade and then took flight in 1928 and the first half of 1929. With the advantage of hindsight, it appears that a bubble had developed in the market by early 1928, with securities prices rising faster than expected earnings and other economic indicators. During the ensuing eighteen months, many investors paid scant heed to various warning signs such as increasing business inventories, slowing consumer spending, and declining industrial production. The market roared on. By September 1929, the *New York Times* average of specific industrial stocks had reached 452, an increase of over 200 points since early 1928.[19]

In October 1929, the market began to waver and move downward. October 24 was a day of panic selling. Still, financial experts remained outwardly confident, and President Herbert Hoover pronounced the basis of the nation's business as "sound and prosperous." On October 29, 1929, the stock-dumping rush that had begun the previous week culminated in the spectacular crash of Black Tuesday, when more than 16 million shares were sold (3 million was the normal number of transactions at the time). The market continued to decline for two weeks. By mid-November, stock prices had fallen to about half their value two months earlier, and the *New York Times* average stood at 224 (this average would reach its lowest point—58—in July 1932).

The stock market crash and the Great Depression that followed on its heels shattered public confidence in capital markets and in the financial system more generally. "An entire generation of Americans," historian Robert Sobel noted, "had learned to distrust securities in general."[20] Demands for heightened regulation on Wall Street mounted. Responding to these calls, Congress passed a series of landmark laws in the early 1930s designed to reshape the securities markets. The Securities Act of 1933, along with the Securities Exchange Act of 1934, required companies to disclose detailed, independently certified financial information to the government and stockholders in the form of annual reports.[21] The latter act also established the Securities and Exchange Commission, with which all stock exchanges now had to register.[22] The Glass–Steagall Act, passed in 1933, aimed to end speculative activity by financial institutions by separating commercial and investment banking. For the first time, Wall Street was accountable to federal oversight.[23]

World War II stimulated U.S. industries and the economy more generally, but for the most part, Americans in the early 1940s remained wary of Wall Street.[24] In the postwar years, however, stock market activity picked up significantly. Exchanges throughout the United States saw increased trades, and regional exchanges, such as the Pacific Coast Stock Exchange, were created by mergers between local ones.[25] Employee benefits, such as health care and pension plans, expanded with the growth and increasing bargaining power of organized labor.[26] With a growing middle class, more small investors began to put their savings in the market, and sales of specialized financial products, such as mutual funds, proliferated.[27] Between 1940 and 1961, annual trading volume on the NYSE, the nation's most important exchange, rose from 208 million shares to more than one billion (table 2-1).[28]

In 1974, Congress passed the Employee Retirement Income Security Act (ERISA), which was designed to regulate the growing investment of pension funds.[29] The new law required all companies that sponsored retirement plans to create trust funds—separate

TABLE 2-1

NYSE Average Daily Share Volume (millions)

1900	102.4
1910	161.1
1920	227.6
1930	810.6
1940	207.6
1950	524.8
1960	766.7
1970	3,122.79
1980	11,700.27
1990	39,748.32
2000	260,265.80
2006	402,116.40

Source: NYSE Euronext, NYSE Statistics Archive, http://www.nyse.com/marketinfo/datalib/1022221393023.html.

from the firm's assets—that would meet pension obligations to all retirees, current and future.[30] One of the most important consequences of the legislation was the formation of huge capital pools that needed to be invested in bonds and, increasingly, in stocks. Another consequence was the vast proliferation of mutual funds, which offered workers in participating companies an opportunity to invest funds set aside for retirement benefits in a range of securities. This, in turn, vastly expanded stock ownership as Americans from many walks of life found their finances and futures affected by what happened on Wall Street. At the end of the 1990s, more than 100 million Americans—more than a third of the population—owned stocks.[31] In 2005, the assets held by American mutual funds totaled $8.9 trillion dollars.[32]

Much as the financial demands of the railroads had helped transform Wall Street in the mid-1800s, so the growth in mutual funds and the availability of capital altered securities markets in the later twentieth century. For most of the 1960s and 1970s, institutional and large individual investors generally had sought steady, modest gains from relatively low-risk, "investment-grade" bonds.[33] But as the amounts in mutual funds rose rapidly, money managers found themselves with an embarrassment of riches—with more money than they could possibly invest in low-risk, low-return securities.

Against this backdrop, new players, risk patterns, and financial instruments emerged. During the late 1970s and 1980s, Michael Milken, a brilliant, driven trader, created a huge market for non-investment-grade bonds, or "junk bonds." As the high-yield market grew, the high-risk but potentially high-return bonds that Milken issued, bought, and sold came to be used for a range of activities, including financing entrepreneurs such as Ted Turner of Turner Broadcasting and restructuring established and often distressed companies such as Mattel. Junk bonds were also used for— and indeed, enabled—hostile takeovers in which corporate raiders, such as Carl Icahn, and private equity firms, such as Kohlberg Kravis Roberts (KKR), that specialized in leveraged buyouts (LBOs) sought control of large companies. One of the largest of these transactions was the $25 billion leveraged buyout of RJR Nabisco in 1988. Milken's high-yield department at his firm, Drexel Burnham Lambert, raised $5 billion of the total amount.[34]

By the late 1980s, Milken was one of the most powerful individuals in the U.S. capital markets. Some of his actions—buying and selling securities, interacting with money managers—took place in the gray area of the law where established statutes had not yet caught up to new instruments and practices. Beginning in the late 1980s, Milken and others were indicted under existing securities laws, and in 1990, Milken pled guilty to six felony charges. He was fined $600 million, barred from working in the securities industry, and sentenced to ten years in prison.[35] Drexel Burnham, which had risen to prominence on Milken's abilities and power, fell with him and was liquidated in 1990.[36]

As the twentieth century drew to a close, the Internet was coming into widespread use, and technology start-ups had the Street abuzz with excitement. Many of these young companies were financed by venture capitalists and private equity firms that channeled money into young companies before they went public.[37] With a successful initial public offering (IPO), these investors and the founding entrepreneurs stood to gain millions.[38] In the headiness of the late 1990s, some new technology companies with a compelling concept came to be more highly valued than established industrial companies with long balance sheets of tangible assets.[39] Some of these high-tech stocks turned out to be overvalued, and at the end of the century, the Internet bubble burst. Around the same time, in 2001, the Houston-based energy company Enron collapsed—almost overnight—a victim of unscrupulous and misguided leadership. In the wake of these high-profile falls, the press, the public, and the federal government showed a renewed interest in accounting practices, executive compensation, and the ethics of the Street.[40]

Exchange That Brought Fame to Buttonwood Tree Will Mark 175th Anniversary

BY ALEXANDER R. HAMMER

It all started on May 17, 1792, when 24 merchants and auctioneers agreed to meet daily under a buttonwood tree on Wall Street to buy and sell securities among themselves.

This laid the foundation for the birth of the New York Stock Exchange, the world's largest securities market place. This year the exchange is celebrating the 175th anniversary of the "buttonwood agreement."

The 24 original members of the exchange traded in a mere handful of issues, including an $80-million bond issue that consolidated the nation's Revolutionary War debts. Among the other traded issues were shares of insurance companies, Alexander Hamilton's First United States Bank, the Bank of North America and the Bank of New York.

Before the "buttonwood agreement," stock trading in New York was carried on in various coffee houses, auction rooms and offices, but it was mostly unorganized. People were hesitant to invest because they had no assurance they could sell their securities readily.

The exchange changed locations frequently during its early life. But by 1865 the exchange had settled on part of the site of its present building at Broad and Wall Streets.

It is doubtful whether trading in securities kept the brokers of the exchange very busy during the first two decades of its existence. The economy was basically a mercantile-agrarian one and there were few enterprises large enough to permit public financing.

It was not until after the War of 1812 that the United States really started to flex its economic muscles. The tempo of business quickened as the country headed into a post-war boom. Commercial activity thrived, new enterprises multiplied and speculation was in the air.

New York State bonds, issued to pay for the Erie Canal and other canal stocks, joined the new issues traded on the exchange in the 1820's, and railroad issues began trading in the 1830's. The rails dominated the list until well past the turn of the century. Today railroad stocks make up only 2.2 per cent of the 11 billion listed shares traded on the exchange, a telling indication of their decline as an economic force.

Regulation Stiffened

To keep pace with the industrial revolution, the exchange between 1860 and 1875 inaugurated significant moves in self-regulation. The call system of trading, whereby each stock on the list was called for bids and offers by brokers at set times during the day, proved no longer adequate and was abandoned for a continuous auction.

Early in 1869 the exchange began to take a more vigorous stand in listing standards. In January of that year, the exchange delisted the shares of the Erie Railroad when the carrier failed to comply with a regulation requiring the registration of all outstanding shares.

Late that year a committee on stock listing was established by the exchange and rules providing for transfer agents, registrars, engraving and printing standards were written.

At the same time, the exchange began formulating its policy of asking for fiscal information about the companies whose securities were traded.

Today, any corporation that seeks to list its securities on the exchange knows that this will involve public disclosure of pertinent financial information.

The First Tickers

The appearance of the first stock tickers in 1867 and the installation of telephones 11 years later were the added impetus to the exchange's position as the nation's central securities marketplace.

In the 1890's a new outgrowth of the industrial revolution began to make itself felt on the exchange—the trading of shares of modern corporations. The turn of the century also brought the formation of the nation's first billion-dollar enterprise, the United States Steel Corporation.

Volume on the exchange continued to increase as a result, and in 1903 the present exchange building was erected. By 1906 average daily volume exceeded a million shares. This was not equaled again until after World War I.

The postwar period again increased activity on the exchange because of heavy demands for capital to finance economic expansion. At the end of 1924, 433.4 million shares were listed on the exchange with a market value of $27 billion.

However, by the close of 1929, 1.1 billion shares were listed with a market value of $64.7 billion. In that year an exchange seat sold for $625,000, a figure that has not been equaled since. The latest seat sale on the exchange was made for $330,000 on April 14.

The exchange faced its most critical test in the fall of 1929. On Tuesday, Oct. 29, the worst price crash in the exchange's history occurred as more than 16 million shares were traded, an all-time record.

The market upheaval, part of a worldwide economic depression, helped pave the way for passage by Congress of the Securities Acts of 1933 and 1934, which increased controls over the securities markets.

April 24, 1960

Statistics House Thrives on Facts

The 100-Year History of Standard & Poor's Mirrors Rise of Financial Information

Standard & Poor's Helps Make Corporate Reports Everybody's Business

BY RICHARD RUTTER

"This company makes no reports and publishes no statements—and has not done anything of the kind for the last five years."

Such was the reply made a little more than a century ago by one of the nation's largest railroads to the New York Stock Exchange when the Big Board made the first tentative efforts to obtain information about the operations of the companies whose securities it listed for trading. That was an era when corporations took the attitude that their business was nobody's business but their own and when securities investment was considered sort of a private gambling game. As one observer wrote later: "That is why all brokers' offices, like all saloons, had a back door."

Attitudes Change

But times and attitudes have changed. Today, corporation business is just about everybody's business, and the front door is the main means of entry and exit for investors. In a very real way, the history of Standard & Poor's Corporation is the history of that change.

Standard & Poor's, marking its 100th anniversary this month, is probably the largest financial publisher in the world and offers one of the most extensive investment advisory services. It issues more than thirty daily, weekly and monthly publications. The New York headquarters is said to contain the largest private collection of financial information in the world.

It took the better part of a century to amass that information and for a long time it was an odds-on, torturous task. In fact, not until 1935 were many companies required by Federal law to make annual and public reports on their financial conditions to the Securities and Exchange Commission.

Henry Varnum Poor was about seventy-five years or more ahead of his time. A lawyer by training, he became editor of The American Railroad Journal, in 1849. Railroads at that time were the nation's leading corporations engaged in public financing. Mr. Poor had the idea, naïve for then, that if the public was to invest its money in a company, it had the right to know what was going on. Corporate records often were sketchy, reports issued irregularly, if at all.

Henry Poor thereupon started a one-man crusade to lift the curtain of secrecy closing off management from ownership. He fired off questionnaires to railroads asking officials for pertinent financial and other operating data. In many instances—as in the case of the reply to the New York Stock Exchange—the answer was an irate brush-off. But the persistent Mr. Poor persisted enough to publish in 1860 a "History of the Railroads and Canals of the United States." This is often referred to as the grandfather of all investment publications.

After a hiatus during the Civil War, there followed in 1868 the "Manual of the Railroads of the United States." Henry V. Poor and his son Henry William later brought out annuals, "Poor's Directory of American Officials" (1886–95) and "Poor's Handbook of Investment Securities" (1890–92). The latter broadened the scope of financial analysis from railroads to various industrial activities.

Age of Mergers

The Twentieth Century ushered in the age of mergers and the trend prevailed also in the investment publishing and advisory field.

The Standard half of Standard & Poor's stemmed from the Standard Statistics Bureau founded in 1906 by Luther Lee Blake, a one-time telegraph operator. Luther Blake began his operation from a room in the old Calumet Hotel in New York. There he compiled data about 100 corporations on separate cards and distributed them by a bellhop for a fee of $5 a month to banks and brokerage houses. In 1913 Luther Blake acquired Babson's Stock and Bond Card system and in 1914 he incorporated the Standard Statistics Company.

It is noteworthy that both Poor's and Standard Statistics foresaw the Great Crash of October 1929. In March of that year, Poor's advised all of its clients to liquidate their entire holdings. Over a period of weeks, Standard warned its subscribers to dispose of not only stocks of dubious merit but also "such blue chip issues as have, in their current fantastic prices, already discounted reasonable long-term possibilities."

Came the Crash, the Depression and World War II. In 1941, Standard Statistics merged with Poor's Publishing Company.

Last year, more than 23,000 corporate financial reports and 4,895 municipal reports cleared the company's library. The library received some 33,000 requests for information and sent out 19,800 letters to companies in regard to their statements. The news clipping department snipped 2,000 items every day from a seemingly endless flood of newspapers, magazines and various periodicals.

About 25 per cent of Standard & Poor's $11,000,000 business each year comes from its advisory service, handled by a Planned Investments department. The company estimates that securities under its supervision have a value of some $3,000,000,000.

Not so long ago, the editor of Poor's Register of Directors and Executives received an inquiry from an African tribal chief. His tribe carved figures from elephant tusks and needed a sales mailing list to build up exports. The Register, which lists 73,000-odd officers and directors, with their business affiliations and addresses, proved just the answer.

Gould's Eventful Life

The Story of a Remarkable Business Career

Enters Wall Street

[GOULD was born on May 27, 1836, in Roxbury, New York. His father was a farmer, and as a boy, Jay had limited schooling. In his mid-teens, he took up surveying and later, tanning. In 1859, at the age of twenty-three, he moved to New York in search of bigger opportunities. There he met and married Helen Miller, the daughter of a successful merchant. Within a few years, Gould became interested in the young burgeoning stock market.]

Jay Gould was twenty-three years old when he went into Wall Street as a broker. Gould had considerable money of his own when he began speculating in securities, and had the confidence of two or three large capitalists. He started on his Wall Street career in a small office, and frequently took his stand with the curbstone brokers. He made money right along. In 1860 he became intimately acquainted with Mr. Henry N. Smith, who was then one of the big men in Wall Street. Soon the firm of Smith, Gould & Martin was formed, and it was prosperous from the start.

Daniel Drew was one of the heaviest customers of Smith, Gould & Martin, and through him the attention of Gould was drawn to the Erie Railway. That company was embarrassed for money, and its stock was selling cheaply. Gould bought as much of it as he could carry, and when the bitter fight came on between Daniel Drew and Commodore Vanderbilt for the possession of the Erie, Gould, being one of the largest stockholders, was taken into the Directory by Mr. Drew. He helped Drew issue millions of dollars worth of new stock in the place of convertible bonds and when Commodore Vanderbilt tried to get up a corner in Erie in the Spring of 1867, the millions of dollars' worth of unauthorized stock with which Drew and Gould fed the market not only broke the corner, but nearly ruined Vanderbilt.

Suits and injunctions began to spring up, and after a while it became so warm for Drew and Gould in this city that they, together with most of the other Directors of the Erie Company, fled to Jersey City on the night of March 11, 1867. Gould carried with him about $7,000,000 in currency. A few days afterward the Erie was changed into a New Jersey corporation, with headquarters in Jersey City.

Gould's Erie Career

Early in July, 1867, Gould and James Fisk, Jr., were in absolute control of the Erie Road. They had crowded Drew out, and Mr. Gould was made President of the road. The books of the company about this time showed that the company owed Mr. Gould $4,000,000, mostly moneys said to have been advanced by him from time to time.

Mr. Gould soon saw the advantage to Erie—which was being constantly assailed by litigation—of an alliance with Tammany Hall [the Democratic Party machine that exercised powerful influence on New York city politics] and he induced William M. Tweed and Peter B. Sweeney [who were leaders in the machine] to become Directors of the company. The "Erie printing press" was then started up and millions of dollars more of new stock was issued. Erie became the leading speculative feature of the stock market.

[Gould] maintained that it was his duty to issue as much new Erie stock as was necessary to keep him in control of the property and to thwart the efforts of Commodore Vanderbilt to get possession of the property. It was about this period that Mr. Gould made his famous declaration before a legislative body. "When I am dealing with Republicans I am a Republican; when dealing with Democrats I am a Democrat; but at all times I am an Erie Railroad man."

In due course of time Gould was sued for $11,000,000, which it was claimed he had wrongfully taken from the Erie Company. After considerable delay, and when driven into a corner, he offered to make restitution. The Erie Company never got the express company stock, and the "restitution account" did not realize anywhere near its face value. Mr. Gould was credited with having made a large sum on the rise in Erie stock which followed his "restitution."

The Gold Panic.

Probably the boldest and most stupendous undertaking that is associated with Jay Gould's name was the attempt made in 1869 to lock up all of the gold in this country in a speculative "corner."

In March, 1869, the price of gold touched 120¼, which was the lowest figure that it had reached in three years. Jay Gould, as President of the Erie Railway and the principal owner of the Tenth National Bank, had the command of large sums of money. He proposed to [speculator Jim] Fisk that they take advantage of the low price of gold and "corner" it. Fisk did not think the scheme practicable, and declined at first to go in. Subsequently he reconsidered his determination and joined in the undertaking zealously. Gould bought $7,000,000 of gold at 132 and put up the price to 140. He induced other brokers to buy heavily, and within a few days gold advanced to 144. It soon dropped back to 136. The element of uncertainty in Mr. Gould's plan was the policy of the Government with reference to gold sales. Should the Government at any time release some of the millions stored in the Sub-Treasury bars, no "corner" could be successful.

According to the testimony elicited by a committee of the House of Representatives appointed to investigate the cause of the gold panic, Gould and his associates caused articles to be published falsely representing that it was the policy of the Administration to advance the price of gold. The price began to advance and the situation took on an exciting aspect. Public interest was aroused and the efforts to force up the price of gold were denounced. Some of Gould's associates got frightened and dumped their holdings on the market. Mr. Gould was obliged to keep buying to protect himself.

The gold-buying operations of the Gould clique assumed monstrous proportions on Thursday, Sept. 23—the day before the famous "Black Friday." On Friday morning [alerted by Abel Corbin, President Ulysses S. Grant's brother-in-law that the Administration would not tolerate his scheme], Gould went down town with his mind made up to one thing, and that was to get rid of his tremendous holdings of gold as quickly as possible. He did not take Fisk or any of the others into his confidence, but while they were carrying out the pre-arranged plan and buying all of the gold within reach, Gould fed the boiling, seething market from his own abundant store.

The scene in the gold room on that memorable morning was intensely exciting—chaotic, in fact.

A little before noon an order came from Washington directing Assistant United States Treasurer [Daniel] Butterfield to sell $4,000,000 of gold. Almost simultaneously James Brown, an influential Scotch banker, who had been stirring around among the reputable capitalists, entered the gold room and offered to sell several millions of gold. The "corner" was broken then and there, and within fifteen minutes the price fell from 160 to 133. The Gold Board suspended, and nearly half of Wall Street was involved in ruin . . . Gould and his associates escaped from "the Street" with difficulty and took refuge in the Grand Opera House. Gould had saved himself from financial disaster by his secret selling of gold. Fisk, however, repudiated all of the losing contracts that he had made. There was a feeling of extreme bitterness in Wall Street against the gold cornerers for many a day thereafter.

In the Pacific Railways

When Mr. Gould began to take an interest in the Pacific railroads he found, as he subsequently expressed it, that they had been "badly financed." He took hold of some of them, notably the Union Pacific, the Kansas Pacific, the Denver Pacific, and the Missouri Pacific, and "financed" them with conspicuous results.

Mr. Gould's policy while in control of the Union Pacific was such as greatly to curtail the earning power of the Kansas Pacific Road, which was a natural dependent on the Union Pacific. Consequently the marketable value of Kansas Pacific stock went down to almost nothing. Gould bought much of it. It was then that the consolidation of the Kansas Pacific and the Denver Pacific with the Union Pacific was suggested. Mr. Gould was committed to the scheme. Before it was completed Gould had got control of the Missouri Pacific, and although still in the Union Pacific Directory, he threatened to build a short line connecting the Kansas Pacific with the Colorado Central, and thus, with the Missouri Pacific, forming a strong competing line to the Pacific coast. This frightened the Boston Directors of the Union Pacific and they hastened to Gould's house and insisted upon his standing by the consolidation agreement. Gould subsequently testified that he offered the Boston people his check for $1,000,000 to let him out of the agreement, but they declined and remained with him until he signed a binding contract to stand by the agreement. In his testimony before the Pacific Railway Commission in 1887 Mr. Gould ruefully remarked that he lost a good thing when he abandoned his Missouri Pacific extension scheme and at the same time frankly admitted that the success of that scheme would have resulted in wiping out the Government's claim of $17,000,000 against the Union Pacific.

When the Union Pacific consolidation was completed Gould was found to be the largest holder of the securities of all the subordinate roads.

Turns to Telegraphy

There is a tinge of sentiment about Mr. Gould's obtaining control of the Western Union Telegraph Company, if his own statement of how it happened may be accepted as a fact. He declared under oath before a United States Senate investigating committee in 1888 that he acquired the control of Western Union in order that he might give his friend Gen. Thomas T. Robert the position of General Manager.

As rapidly as opportunities offered, Mr. Gould increased his holdings of Western Union Stock until he became by far the largest holder. He used to say that his large railroad interests made it necessary for him to have a controlling voice in the telegraph system of the country, because the railroads and the telegraph naturally go hand in hand in developing the country. After the Western Union had absorbed the Mutual Union and the Baltimore and Ohio telegraph companies, the stock of the Western Union Company was doubled, making the total $80,000,000.

Of that amount Mr. Gould is believed to have held for many years between $16,000,000 and $20,000,000.

Mr. Gould's Wealth

Jay Gould's wealth has been variously estimated in recent years. The most conservative calculations put it at between $40,000,000 and $50,000,000, but persons who were closely associated with Mr. Gould in business put it at nearer $100,000,000. [Financier] Russell Sage has frequently remarked that Mr. Gould was a much richer man than most people had any idea of. It was only a few months ago that a well-informed Wall Street man figured out that Mr. Gould owned $28,000,000 of Western Union Stock, about $18,000,000 of Manhattan Railway Stock, between $12,000,000 and $15,000,000 of Missouri Pacific Railroad Stock, and upward of $40,000,000 of bonds and miscellaneous securities.

Mr. Gould has not been active in speculative ventures for the past few years. When he withdrew from the firm of W. E. Connor & Co. in 1886 he announced his formal retirement from the "Street" and, although his name was frequently used in connection with Wall Street ventures subsequently, there never was any proof that Mr. Gould was doing more than was necessary to protect his interests.

Ladies as Stock Speculators

A Circular That Made a Flurry in Good Society

Considerable comment, not always of a favorable tenor, was occasioned yesterday in the highest social circles in this City, in consequence of a circular purporting to emanate from a private Stock Exchange for the exclusive use of ladies, which has recently been opened by Mrs. M. E. Favor, at her residence, No. 40 West Twenty-fourth-street. The circulars were addressed to prominent ladies, many of them the wives of gentlemen whose names are familiar in finance and in the professions, and set forth that the Exchange was "under the immediate management of a lady of standing, who had had a long and successful experience in stock speculation," and did business in Wall-street "through a widely-known house of bankers and brokers of large capital and unquestionable solidity." "Many a woman," said a gentleman, speaking of the document, "may be led to pledge her diamonds, or to compromise her settlements or her husband's financial standing, with the vague promise of a fortune thus held out to her."

To a reporter of THE TIMES, who called at her residence, Mrs. Favor said that she had merely issued a business circular, not differing materially from those usually issued by such establishments to parties likely to become their patrons. The Exchange, she said, was opened a few weeks ago at the urgent solicitation of ladies of large and independent means, who had speculated in Wall-Street for years, and had often met with losses because their facilities for information were not equal to those of men. She [Mrs. Favor] was simply the salaried manager of the concern, and had no share in its profits or responsibility for its expenditures. Ladies of the highest standing—married and unmarried—some with fortunes in their own right, and others the wives of prominent lawyers, doctors, and even bankers—dropped in during business hours, and gave orders to buy or sell according to the state of the market. The transactions were conducted upon strictly business principles, and new customers were admitted only on introduction or when guaranteed by parties with whom they were acquainted. They took no orders for less than 100 shares, and consequently, poor women could not speculate through them if they would. Mrs. Favor declined to give the names of the ladies interested in the concern, or those of any of its customers, and said that speculation in stocks was a very common thing with women of fortune. She attributes the unfavorable criticism to the jealousy of down-town brokers who find a large and profitable set of customers giving their orders elsewhere.

J.P. Morgan, At Seventy, Believes In Keeping At It

"MORGAN has retired from Wall Street"—so the bears have said on the Stock Exchange times innumerable within the last five years when the speculative necessity has demanded something in the news line on which they could base their selling of the day or hour.

"It is said in well-informed circles that there is no truth in reports that Mr. J. P. Morgan has retired," the opposition bulletin has gone out, and in the absence of developments supporting either hypothesis the market community has quite forgotten the disquieting gossip and given its attention to new rumors, some with, some without, tangible foundation. Such is the way of the Street.

It would, none the less, be quite as inaccurate to announce to-day or to-morrow that the "Old Man," as he is traditionally known in the market, had retired, as at any time since the retirement rumors were first put into circulation.

Yet there is a material difference between the life that Morgan leads to-day and that which he followed in the boom times that heralded the opening of a century. The desk by the Broad Street window sees him no more. Sitting there in his place is another Morgan, large as his father physically, who has demonstrated an inheritance of financial ability and all of the parent's capacity for hard work. This is "Young J. P.," as contrasted with the "Old Man" of the Street, and while the son receives his business callers at the familiar desk, the father meets his in that wonderful library of the Madison Avenue home, among his books and his pictures and his rare manuscripts.

All this personal detail might be related of many a man in New York without substantial variance save as to incidentals, and there would attach to it no significance whatever. Its interest lies in the fact that the man of whom it is told has been and is considered by most judges the largest individual figure in the recent history of American finance—a creator of values, and hence of wealth, for himself and for many others.

More Than a Mere Money Getter.

The question comes naturally enough: how and why he has done it—what was the motive that led to the tremendous and continuing expenditure of effort, even presupposing an original equipment of financial genius that would not admit of a narrow field of activity. This is the question that was asked not long ago at a dinner where financial men were in the majority. The conversation had drifted to the early careers of the men who have been associated in American finance for the last generation or so, and it was recalled that John D. Rockefeller began business as a grocer's clerk, that Andrew Carnegie was a messenger boy in Pittsburg, that James J. Hill was carpenter in a Canadian village, that Levi P. Morton was a dry goods clerk, that Henry C. Frick was a clerk in a country store. One after another the ambitions of these men were traced as they developed in the later life, and the conclusion drawn reasonably enough that a combination of inherent ability of a high order, energy unflagging, and ambition to achieve more than others, has led them into their present positions.

But what was to be said of Morgan? He was not born poor; on the contrary, he was heir to a fortune estimated at from $5,000,000 to $10,000,000. It was one of the notable fortunes of the country in the fifties, and when John Pierpont Morgan went into business here in the early sixties there was open to him a career entirely honorable and very comfortable, that would have carried him to an inconsequential old age and an unhistorical grave. He did not choose this career, but rather chose to work as few men have worked in the last half century, only to convince himself when he reached the stated threescore years and ten that a man must keep on working or he will straightway die.

Start of the Morgan Fortunes.

For the purposes of this examination it may be interesting to go back even to 1835, when Joseph Morgan, the proprietor of the City Hotel in Hartford Conn., pulled the Aetna Fire Insurance Company out of the financial difficulties into which it had fallen after the great fire in New York two years before, reorganized it, and made a matter of $150,000 in the process. Of this he gave $50,000 to his son, Junius Spencer

Morgan, to buy a share in a mercantile business. The son cleared up to $300,000 as his part of the profits inside of fifteen years, and then bought an interest in a Boston mercantile house. So it happened that John Pierpont Morgan, who was born two years after his father had made his first business start in Hartford, came to be a Boston schoolboy, and was graduated from the English High School there in 1854.

Young J. P. Morgan, "Pip," as he was called by his schoolmates, was sent from the English High School to the University of Goettingen, and upon his graduation there was dispatched back to Wall Street in 1859, and obtained a position in the firm of Duncan, Sherman & Co. A few years later came the initial venture into business on his own account, in the firm of Dabney, Morgan & Co.

His First Railroad Deal.

But it developed that during all the year in question [1869] Morgan had been figuring out a campaign to rescue the old Albany & Susquehanna Railroad from the hands of Jay Gould and Fisk, by whom it had been used as an appendage to their Erie operations, and the rescue was eventually accomplished. Then came the first of the Morgan railroad reorganizations, which resulted, in February 1870, in the lease of the Albany & Susquehanna to the Delaware & Hudson, in which system it still remains.

The firm of Dabney, Morgan & Co. received a handsome sum in the reorganization, and was then dissolved, while the Drexels of Philadelphia, a historic banking concern of Swiss extraction and conservatism, took young Morgan into partnership and placed him at the head of their New York house under the firm name of Drexel, Morgan & Co. Furthermore, the attention of William H. Vanderbilt was attracted to the young financier, and soon afterward were made the beginnings of one of the most notable alliances in the history of American finance.

It is a matter of ordinary financial knowledge that the decade from 1880 to 1890 was characterized by most extensive and most destructive competition between the various railroad systems of the country, and it was during this period that J. P. Morgan had occasion to develop publicly the policy regarding railroad affairs that he has stood for ever since. It found its concrete expression in the famous West Shore deal in 1885, which ended a period of warfare between the New York Central and West Shore Railroads almost without parallel for its severity even in those days of rate cutting and kindred devices.

The West Shore was the only route connecting the Cities of New York, Albany, and Buffalo that was not preempted by the Central, and the Vanderbilts undertook, straightway upon it opening in the early eighties, to crush it. By 1885 things had reached the point where the only question at issue was as to which road would go into a receiver's hands in the end, and it was at this point that J. P. Morgan stepped in. It was not an easy task, for the Vanderbilt family of that day were fighters, and concessions from them were out of the question. Mr. Morgan's proposition—the only one to which he could gain their assent—was that he should acquire the West Shore in the interest of the New York Central without compensation for himself, and it was on Dec. 5, 1885, that the West Shore Railroad was incorporated to succeed the New York, West Shore & Buffalo, and leased to the Central for 475 years, with a renewal option at a rental of the interest on its $50,000,000 of bonds.

The entire capital stock of $10,000,000 was taken by the Central. Mr. Vanderbilt was so pleased that he gave his banker a famous silver service, which cost $300,000, and then had the dies broken, so that it never could be replaced.

But Mr. Morgan's activities in the suppression of destructive competition were by no means confined to the railroads in which he had a direct banking interest. The records of railroading from 1884 to 1889 are replete with "gentlemen's agreements" between the Presidents of roads all over the country, and in these negotiations Mr. Morgan played always a prominent part.

To the Treasury's Relief.

From causes growing out of the depression of 1803, the situation of the National Treasury at the opening of 1895 was worse, according to competent authority, than at any time since the resumption of gold payments in 1879.

Then came the contract with the Morgan-Belmont syndicate to supply to the Government $65,117,500 in gold in return for $62,317,500 thirty-year 3 per cent bonds. The syndicate undertook to import the gold, where necessary, to pay for the bonds, and had its payments to the Government in progress by Feb. 15. Almost instantly there was a change for the better in conditions, and by March the syndicate, in complete control of the foreign exchange situation, had stopped the gold exports entirely. By June the syndicate had completed, in advance of the time set, payment for the foreign half of the loan, and before the close of that month the free gold in the Treasury had reached the $107,000,000 mark.

The year 1899 marked an epoch in American finance in which J. P. Morgan had a pretty large part, for then it was that he negotiated the first foreign loan of any size ever placed in this country. This was to take up and refund the entire National debt of Mexico, and the amount of the loan was $110,000,000. It was followed the next year by an American participation of $25,000,000 in the British war loan, which was handled on this side of the water by J. P. Morgan in connection with Baring, Magoun & Co.

The Chief and His Cabinet.

So at the opening of the new century Mr. Morgan was easily the largest financial figure on this side of the water, if not in the world.

Big things began to happen with the opening of 1901. In January it was announced that he had bought the Jersey Central Railroad and turned it over, with its valuable coal properties, to the Reading. Soon after came word that the Pennsylvania Coal Company, the Hillside Coal Company, and others had been bought and turned over to the Erie, two acquisitions which brought the control of the anthracite traffic practically within the Morgan sphere of influence. Then went forth into the Street rumors that a consolidation of Northern Pacific, Great Northern, and the St. Paul Roads, was imminent, but these were forgotten when in the latter part of the month came news that Mr. Carnegie was going to start a steel plant at Conneaut, Ohio, to manufacture "merchant pipe" in competition with Mr. Morgan's Federal Steel Company and John W. Gates's American Steel and Wire Company.

Launching of the Steel Corporation.

Here was denial of the very principle, in the case of the most important industrial enterprise in the country which Mr. Morgan had been working for in the railroad field for twenty years, and if one must needs wonder how he found the time to give the matter attention, it is easy enough to conceive the motive that led to the formation of the United States Steel Corporation. That great institution, with its initial capitalization of $154,000,000, was launched in February to take over the Carnegie Steel Company, the Federal Street, the American Steel and Wire, the American Tin Plate, the American Steel Hood, the American Sheet Steel, and various smaller steel companies.

The Steel Corporation had achieved the greatest success in its flotation that had ever been known, and despite an increase in its capitalization in the Summer of 1901 and the strike of the steel workers in that Summer, by May of the following year there was a profit of $10,000,000 to be distributed to the members of the original syndicate, who stood ready in the beginning to put up $200,000,000 if called upon. The amount actually advanced had been $25,000,000.

This United States Steel enterprise is perhaps as notable an example of J. P. Morgan's persistent optimism as anything in his whole life. It was capitalized on the expectation that the conditions of the most prosperous year in the history of the country up to that time would continue indefinitely. When the depression of 1903 came along, and the Street stocks dropped off until the preferred, with its 7 per cent dividend, was quoted at under 50, and the common dividendless, down to 8¾, a banker went to Mr. Morgan to ask him how [he felt] about it.

"I'm not concerned with the stock market conditions of the Steel stocks," was the gruff reply, "but I can tell you that the possibilities of the steel business are just as great as they ever were."

This is a fair statement of the principle that J. P. Morgan applies to all enterprises having to do primarily with the potential energy of this country.

The Past Year in Financial History

Achievements of 1928 in the Field of American Trade and Industry,

in the Credit Market and on the Stock Exchange

Undoubtedly the place of 1928 in American financial history will be fixed primarily by the year's extraordinary stock speculation. Other years have witnessed abnormal excitement on the Stock Exchange; notably, in the more recent economic period, 1925, 1919 and 1916; but the excitement in stocks on those occasions was caused and accompanied by equally spectacular movements in other branches of finance and industry. The stock market of 1928 was wholly exceptional for the scope, magnitude and violence of a speculative movement which appeared to pervade the entire American community, and which was discussed in Wall Street as a financial phenomenon standing entirely by itself and ignoring all rule, precedent and warning signals which had been recognized in the past.

Transactions on the New York Stock Exchange reached approximately 900,000,000 shares for the year, whereas the 520,000,000 of 1927 was the previous high record. Sales in a single day rose to 6,954,000 on one day of November, whereas the highest daily record prior to 1928 was 3,786,000, in 1926, and the largest figure prior to 1925 was 3,270,000, in 1901. Some stocks on which speculation particularly converged increased four or five times in quoted value during 1928; at the year's top prices THE TIMES averages of selected stocks had risen 32 per cent from last February and 61 per cent above the highest average ever reached before 1927.

To equip and conduct this wholly unprecedented speculation, brokers' borrowings on the New York Stock Exchange increased between February and November $2,069,000,000, or 48 per cent, and the increase during the three Autumn months [was] $1,353,000,000, or nearly 27 per cent. Not the least striking aspect of this immensely expanded credit was the fact, reported by the Federal Reserve, that $1,416,000,000 of the increase from February to November was in the form of loans not made by reporting banks, but mainly by individuals and corporations whose advances of credit were not protected by a cash reserve.

If it were not for the year's stock speculation, 1928 would be mainly associated with the complete change in the money market.

These were the highest rates reached since the deflation of 1920–21. They were accompanied by an advance in the Reserve Bank rate, and by borrowings on rediscount by private banks from the Federal Reserve. In July and in December the reserve ratio of the Federal system fell to the lowest percentage since the middle of 1921.

The year's tight money did not handicap trade, as it has frequently done in other years.

Production of steel for the year exceeded all previous records, and three or four months in Spring and Autumn far surpassed the best performance for their respective periods. Recovery in the metal industries was general, copper output was at high record, and slow but distinct improvement came to the textile trade. The motor-car industry, which in 1927 had fallen 904,000 cars below 1926, to the smallest yearly output since 1922, began to increase in February of the present year. By March it was exceeding even 1926, and it reached in August the largest monthly production ever recorded. The Reserve Bank's computation placed the net profits of 210 selected manufacturing corporations during the first nine months of 1928 at a figure 18 per cent above 1927 and 11 per cent above 1926. Numerous extra dividends and "stock split-ups" were announced through the year by the specially fortunate companies.

PREMIER ISSUES HARD HIT

Unexpected Torrent of Liquidation Again Rocks Markets.

DAY'S   SALES   9,212,800

Nearly 3,000,000 Shares Are Traded In Final Hour—The Tickers Lag 167 Minutes.

NEW RALLY SOON BROKEN

Selling by Europeans and "Mob Psychology" Big Factors in Second Big Break.

The *New York Times* front page announces yet another day of widespread selling in the stock market in late October 1929. (*New York Times*)

October 29, 1929

Premier Issues Hard Hit

Unexpected Torrent of Liquidation Again Rocks Markets.

Day's Sales 9,212,800

Nearly 3,000,000 Shares Are Traded In Final Hour—The Tickers Lag 167 Minutes.

New Rally Soon Broken

Selling by Europeans and "Mob Psychology" Big Factors in Second Big Break.

The second hurricane of liquidation within four days hit the stock market yesterday. It came suddenly, and violently, after holders of stocks had been lulled into a sense of security by the rallies of Friday and Saturday. It was a country-wide collapse of open-market security values in which the declines established and the actual losses taken in dollars and cents were probably the most disastrous and far-reaching in the history of the Stock Exchange.

Although total estimates of the losses on securities are difficult to make, because of the large number of them not listed on any exchange, it was calculated last night that the total shrinkage in American securities on all exchanges yesterday had aggregated some $14,000,000,000, with a decline of about $10,000,000,000 in New York Stock Exchange securities. The figure is necessarily a rough one, but nevertheless gives an idea of the dollars and cents recessions in one of the most extraordinary declines in the history of American markets.

Market Leaders Hard Hit.

Shares of the best known American industrial and railroad corporations smashed through their old lows of Thursday, and most of them to the lowest level for many years, as wave after wave of liquidation swept the market, during its day of utter confusion and rout. As bid after bid was filled for stocks and more and more offered, stocks of the best grade dropped almost perpendicularly, with 2, 3, 5 and even 10 points between sales under probably the most demoralized conditions of trading in the history of the Stock Exchange and the Curb. United States Steel declined 17½, General Electric lost 47½, United States Industrial Alcohol, 39½; Standard Gas, 40½; Columbia Gas, 22; Air Reduction, 48⅞; Allied Chemical & Dye, 36; Baltimore & Ohio, 13⅞; A. M. Byers Company, 30¾; Chesapeake & Ohio, 23½; New York Central, 22⅝; Peoples Gas, 40½; Westinghouse Electric, 34¼; Western Union, 39½; and Worthington Pump, 29.

Drastic SEC Curbs Placed on Brokers to Protect Public

Commission Announces New Rules Five Days After Their Acceptance by Exchange

Central Securities Depository in Prospect—Nation-Wide Program Is Proposed

SPECIAL TO THE NEW YORK TIMES. WASHINGTON, OCT. 31.—The most comprehensive revision of Stock Exchange practices in the history of the New York Stock Exchange, a revision which will fundamentally alter the conduct of brokerage businesses throughout the country, was announced today by the Securities and Exchange Commission in the second of three reports on the case of Richard Whitney, former President of the New York Stock Exchange, now serving a Sing Sing term for grand larceny.

The basic object of the new procedures is to protect the money and securities of the public.

Summary of Exchange Rules

The principal provisions of the new Stock Exchange rules were announced as follows:

1. Increase in the capital requirements so that a member firm's indebtedness bears no more than a 15-1 ratio to his net capital, exclusive of underwriting capital. The present ratio limit is 20 to 1.

2. Prohibition of any Governor or officer or employee of the Exchange from making a loan of money or securities from any Exchange member, except under special conditions.

3. Disqualification of Governors or members of the Exchange committees from participating in an investigation of any member of a firm indebted to the Governor or committee member.

4. New quarterly short term reports on the financial conditions of member firms as against the semiannual long-term reports now in effect.

5. A system of surprise audits and inspections of member firm offices.

6. Members must immediately report all loans over $2,500 by members, member firms and general partners, whether in cash or securities, with certain exceptions.

7. Prohibition of margin transactions in the accounts of Exchange member firms and their partners if the firms carry margin accounts for customers.

8. No member shall carry an account for a general partner of another firm without the prior written consent of another general partner of such other firm.

Weekly Statement Required

9. Every member firm will be required to submit to the Exchange weekly statements of their obligations in respect of underwritings and net positions resulting therefrom.

10. The segregation of brokerage capital from capital used in incurring commitments as an underwriter or a dealer through the formation of affiliated firms to handle underwriting and dealer activities.

Among the new rules are also a prohibition of members who do business as individuals from carrying securities accounts for customers, a rule which will affect very few members; more intensive control of personnel of Exchange members, and greater supervision and enforcement of the Exchange rules relating to business practices.

The commission urged other national securities exchanges, as well as brokers and dealers organizing into national securities associations, to consider the new rules of the New York Stock Exchange for adoption, saying it desired some sort of national standardization so far as that may be practical.

April 2, 1989

Michael Milken Is Indicted

BY WILLIAM S. NIEDERKORN

Michael R. Milken was indicted last week by a Federal grand jury on charges of violating the Federal racketeering law. Prosecutors are seeking the unprecedented financial penalty of $1.8 billion in the case against Mr. Milken, the Drexel Burnham Lambert executive who pioneered the use of "junk bonds" to finance corporate takeovers. Two others are also charged in the criminal action, the largest ever undertaken against Wall Street figures: Lowell Milken, a senior Drexel executive and brother of Michael Milken, and Bruce L. Newberg, a former trader in Drexel's high-yield, high-risk bonds. All three pleaded not guilty. Arthur L. Liman, who was Senate counsel during the Iran-Contra hearings, will lead the defense team. If there is no out-of-court settlement, the trial may begin as early as the end of the year.

As one of the creators of high-yield "junk" bonds, Michael Milken became one of the most powerful American financiers in the 1980s. At the end of the decade, however, he was indicted on ninety-eight counts of securities law violations; here he arrives at the court for his sentencing in 1990. (Chester Higgins/*New York Times*)

The Benefit of the Doubt

BY FLOYD NORRIS

HIGHLY CONFIDENT. *The Crime and Punishment of Michael Milken. By Jesse Kornbluth. Illustrated. 384 pp. New York: William Morrow & Company. $23.*

Michael Milken was the most important financier in the United States since the first J. P. Morgan. Like Morgan's, his efforts resulted in a restructuring of much of American business, and like Morgan he had the power to direct capital to favored customers. Both men used that power to become phenomenally rich. Unlike Morgan, Mr. Milken wound up in prison.

"Highly Confident" is, in many ways, Mr. Milken's story from his point of view. The author, Jesse Kornbluth, writes that he spent hundreds of hours with the secretive financier, both before and after he entered the Federal prison at Pleasanton, Calif., from which he is expected to be released in March. In 1990, he pleaded guilty to securities law violations, and would not have been eligible for release until 1994 had his sentence not been reduced earlier this month. It is clear that the author has been given access to every negative thing that Mr. Milken's defense team could find about his accusers and prosecutors, whose motives and ethics are questioned at every opportunity. Mr. Milken gets the benefit of the doubt on almost every factual question.

But the book nonetheless cannot gloss over the fact that Mr. Milken clearly was guilty of some crimes. A series of transactions with Ivan F. Boesky, the takeover-stock speculator and inside trader who got a reduced sentence by fingering Mr. Milken, "was a clear violation of the securities laws," Mr. Kornbluth concludes.

In the furor that followed the publication of a previous book on Mr. Milken, "Den of Thieves," by James Stewart, much attention was focused on whether Mr. Milken had been guilty of insider trading himself in a case involving an abortive merger of the Occidental Petroleum Corporation and Diamond Shamrock; Mr. Stewart concluded that he was. In part, the evidence turns on contradictory statements by James Dahl, a onetime Milken aide who received immunity for testifying against him.

Mr. Kornbluth, unfortunately, chooses not to go into the details of the Occidental deal, evidently believing that the failure of the prosecutors to bring a charge exonerated Mr. Milken. He doesn't even seem to have bothered to ask Mr. Milken about the key telephone call Mr. Stewart claims Mr. Milken made to Mr. Boesky, tipping him about plans for the merger.

But while insider trading was the Wall Street crime du jour of the 1980's, Mr. Milken's commission of it, or lack thereof, is not what made

him a major figure. It was his vigorous and successful advocacy of bonds rated below investment grade—high-yield bonds to Mr. Milken
and "junk bonds" to his critics—that transformed American finance. At the peak of power
for Mr. Milken and the firm he dominated,
Drexel Burnham Lambert, he was the most
feared and the most courted financier in the
land. Many a company went deeply into debt
simply because it feared that if it did not,
Drexel would effectively use the company's unused borrowing capacity to finance a raider.

Mr. Kornbluth, a contributing editor at Van-
ity Fair, appears to be uncertain about just what
role Mr. Milken played at Drexel. He quotes an
unnamed Milken lawyer as viewing him as a
"control freak" who tried to run his own defense just as he had run his department, but
Mr. Kornbluth elsewhere paints a picture of a
very detached manager. When Mr. Milken
learned of ethical violations by his aides, "he
told himself that these practices were unfortunate" and should be stopped, but did nothing.
"For a so-called visionary, he didn't seem to
mind sitting back and letting those closest to
him act like sharpies," Mr. Kornbluth writes.

Mr. Milken was for a time perceived as a genius, and it is that reputation that Mr. Kornbluth
does the most to reinforce. We are told that he
saw the 1987 stock market crash coming (rather

than warn his clients, he advanced the closing
date of an investment fund Drexel was raising,
fearing that investors would not bankroll it after
the crash). And we are told that Mr. Milken
warned others at Drexel that the firm's customers
were getting too deeply into debt, although he
oddly did nothing to stop the flow of deals.

It is true that Drexel's most outrageous
deals, which led to huge losses for customers
and eventually to Drexel's own bankruptcy,
were done after Mr. Milken's departure. But a
reader of "Highly Confident" could get the in-
correct impression that Mr. Milken's own deals
were all brilliant. Mr. Kornbluth's only mention
of Selig Zises, the former chairman of Integrated Resources, is to praise him for organizing a "We Believe in You" advertisement
signed by Drexel clients after Mr. Milken was
indicted. Mr. Kornbluth does not bother to note
that Integrated Resources later proved to be a
house of cards, costing Drexel customers many
millions when it collapsed.

In the end, Mr. Kornbluth fails to explain
why a man as decent as he believes Mr. Milken
to be would have allowed "indisputably sleazy"
activities to go on at Drexel. He concludes that
Mr. Milken's failure had something to do with
not wanting to examine his own psyche, but the
argument is unpersuasive. Mr. Milken remains
as much a mystery as ever.

With Enron's Fall, Many Dominoes Tremble

BY ALLEN R. MYERSON

The Enron Corporation, despite its origins as a gas pipeline business, was no mere energy company. Its ambition, its passion for innovation and its boundless appetite for risk gave it a far greater reach than that of competitors, even those that control many more power plants or far larger reserves of natural gas.

In the last decade, it became not only the world's largest trader of electricity and natural gas, but also a telecommunications company, an investment firm, a paper and lumber producer and an insurer. It was, with more than $100 billion in revenue last year, the nation's seventh-largest company.

Its collapse last week reverberated through not just the nation's energy industry, but also through retailing, real estate, insurance, banking, Internet services, newspaper publishing, even the manufacturing of plastics and glass.

Most other energy companies were content to provide electricity or natural gas. Enron signed contracts with 28,500 customers worldwide, including J. C. Penney and Owens-Illinois, to manage all their energy needs, usually promising that it would absorb the risks of volatile prices and fluctuating supplies itself. Now those customers fear that the risks are once again all their own.

Houston, where Enron keeps as high a profile as its 50-story downtown headquarters, is bearing the greatest burden. There, the Trammell Crow Company immediately cited Enron's collapse in halting the planned groundbreaking last month on a 34-story office, apartment and shopping complex next to Enron Field, the new home of the Houston Astros.

At the end of last week, those who did business with Enron, or depended on it in other ways, were still trying to puzzle through all the consequences of its ruin. No easy task, this, considering that Enron's own finances, more convoluted than anything even a Max Bialystock could imagine, proved beyond the grasp of its chief executive, Kenneth L. Lay.

CHAPTER 3

MERGER MANIA

When AT&T merged with other major independent
telephone carriers in 1913, it became
a government-sanctioned monopoly. The company
became the largest corporation in the world before
the Bell System was broken up in 1984.
(*New York Times*/Sara Krulwich)

N THE CENTURY AFTER THE NATION'S FOUNDING, PRIVATE ENTERPRISES
were often family-owned affairs, and mergers, when they
occurred, were sometimes the result of actual marriages.[1] Toward the end of the nineteenth century, however, business consolidation began to take place on a larger scale and for much greater

1882	1890	1890	1901	1901
Standard Oil Trust is formed.	American Tobacco Company is created.	Sherman Antitrust Act passed.	Teddy Roosevelt becomes president, promising a "Square Deal."	J. P. Morgan creates U.S. Steel, world's first billion-dollar corporation.

financial stakes. At first, this growth was largely horizontal, joining companies that produced the same product.[2] Later, companies began to integrate vertically, acquiring businesses that supplied the raw materials for their products, transported them to market, or marketed them to the end consumer.[3] Finally, to serve strategic or financial ends, firms that engaged in very different businesses joined forces or were taken over in a bout of aggressive market activity.[4]

Beginning in the late 1890s, five great waves of merger activity have swept through American financial markets: the first at the end of the 1800s; the second at the close of the Roaring Twenties; the third in the late 1960s; the fourth in the early 1980s; and the fifth, which contributed to a worldwide, cross-border phase of combination, at the end of the twentieth century.[5]

Until the 1840s, most American businesses were still owned and operated by the same individual or small group of people and were run on a local scale.[6] Family companies and partnerships were common—Procter & Gamble, one of the largest consumer goods manufacturers of the modern era, was formed by a partnership between immigrant candle- and soap-makers William Procter and James Gamble in 1837.[7] But mergers and acquisitions as we think of them today were still uncommon affairs.[8] "Big Business" as such did not exist until the mid- and later nineteenth century when the railroads became an important part of the national landscape.[9] Once railroads became established, rivalry between competing lines was intense, and consolidation came hard on the heels of stock market speculation by men such as financier Jay Gould.[10]

Consolidation of other types of firms followed. John D. Rockefeller gained both strategic and cost advantages in the 1860s and 1870s by buying out competing refiners in his hometown of Cleveland and in other cities. By the early 1880s, Standard Oil was far

1908	1911	1914	1933	1960's
General Motors formed from a merger of Cadillac, Oldsmobile, and other auto companies.	Supreme Court breaks Standard Oil Trust into 34 separate companies.	The Federal Trade Commission established, Clayton Act passed.	Glass-Steagall Act passed to separate commercial and investment banking.	Federal government adapts antitrust policy to allow for conglomerate mergers.

and away the largest oil refiner in the nation.[11] In a move that would be copied widely by corporations in other industries, Rockefeller organized his firm's various holdings as a trust. This allowed him to circumvent regulations that made doing business across state lines difficult and expensive.[12] As the demand for oil escalated in the late nineteenth and early twentieth centuries—first for lighting and later for automobiles—the power of the industry that Rockefeller had done so much to build and organize grew as well.

By the turn of the century, the business environment in America was ripe for large-scale combination. The expansion of markets made possible by railroad transport, along with increased tariffs on foreign goods, created the potential for national monopoly and oligopoly in certain sectors.[13] New technologies, such as the modern Fourdrinier papermaking machine, gave birth to new industries. Many of these young industries underwent "ruinous competition" in which deadly cycles set in: temporary scarcities were followed by waves of new entrants and ensuing price wars, which resulted in mass bankruptcies.[14] In this environment, which characterized the early railroad business and steel manufacturing, as well as oil refining and papermaking, combining forces with another firm seemed an appealing alternative to many managers. Between 1898 and 1902, more than 2,600 companies were swallowed by merger.[15]

Perhaps the most famous deal of this period was financier J. P. Morgan's 1901 buyout of Carnegie Company, the steel manufacturer founded and managed by Andrew Carnegie. By 1899, Morgan had already consolidated numerous makers of finished steel products, including 85 percent of U.S. steel tube and pipe makers, and he paid a premium—$480 million—to acquire Carnegie's enterprise, the largest, most powerful player in the steel business.[16] The resulting company, comprising several other major steelmakers and related concerns, was named U.S. Steel. It was capitalized at $1.4 billion

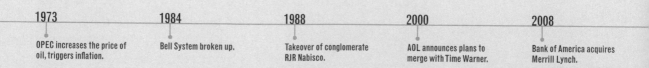

1973	1984	1988	2000	2008
OPEC increases the price of oil, triggers inflation.	Bell System broken up.	Takeover of conglomerate RJR Nabisco.	AOL announces plans to merge with Time Warner.	Bank of America acquires Merrill Lynch.

(or about $25 billion in today's dollars), making it, in real terms, the biggest merger to date—a position it would maintain until the merger wave of the 1980s.[17] In steelmaking, as in other industries, the flurry of merger and acquisition activity led to growing concentration of resources and, in many instances, market power. By 1906, for example, the one hundred largest American companies controlled 40 percent of the nation's industrial capital.[18]

Throughout the late nineteenth and early twentieth centuries, Americans grew increasingly anxious about the number and size of big companies. The federal government responded. In 1887, Congress passed the Interstate Commerce Act, designed to regulate the railroad industry. Three years later, it enacted the Sherman Antitrust Act, which outlawed "[e]very contract, combination in the form of trust or otherwise, or conspiracy, in restraint of trade or commerce among the several States, or with foreign nations." In 1911, antitrust litigation against Standard Oil and the American Tobacco Company forced both firms to break up; Standard was split into thirty-four separate companies, including the Standard Oil Company of New Jersey, which later became the Exxon Corporation, and the Standard Oil Company of New York, which later became Mobil.[19] (In 1999, in another wave of mergers, Exxon and Mobil combined to create the Exxon Mobil Corporation.) The Clayton Act of 1914 further strengthened the existing legislation by prohibiting, among other things, horizontal mergers deemed harmful to competition.[20] That same year, Congress established the Federal Trade Commission (FTC) to help investigate and pursue antitrust cases.

The second wave of mergers in American business took off during World War I and continued to swell, with brief downturns in 1918 and 1921, before cresting in 1929.[21] The acquisitions that took place during this period were more gradual than the rush of the 1890s, and the federal government generally took a more relaxed, even favorable, view of the activity and its effect on the economy.[22] Cars, trucks, telephones, and radio fashioned new connections among people, places, and goods, enhancing the national marketing possibilities created by the railroads and telegraph in the previous century.[23] Partly in response to this, firms began to diversify their offerings by crafting lines of related products: National Dairy acquired ice cream and milk producers and Kraft–Phoenix cheese; the DuPont chemical company's portfolio included paint and artificial leather in addition to explosives; and General Electric began to produce electrical appliances in addition to electrical equipment.[24]

The year 1929 marked the collapse of the stock market, the onset of what would become the Great Depression, and an end to the ten-year wave of merger and acquisition activity. These events, in turn, called forth a new burst of federal regulations intent on reining in the financial abuses of banks and businesses and addressing the shattered prospects of many American workers. Before it was declared unconstitutional in 1935, the National Industrial Recovery Act of 1933 allowed firms to form associations and fix prices in exchange for worker benefits such as a minimum wage and maximum workday.[25] Alongside these popularly acclaimed protections for workers in traditional industries such as manufacturing, support grew for the regulation of businesses dealing with new technologies. In 1934, the Federal Communications Commission was established to regulate telecommunications firms, including the monolithic American Telephone and Telegraph Corporation.[26] In 1938, the Civil Aeronautics Act expanded the safety and certification mandates of the Air Commerce Act of 1926, giving the government the power to regulate air lines' fares and flight paths.[27]

As American business and the broader economy recovered in the years following World War II, a third wave of merger activity gathered steam. This wave was distinguished from earlier ones by a shift toward conglomerate mergers, or the acquisition by one firm of businesses that were related loosely or not at all to the core enterprise.[28] Between 1926 and 1930, for example, almost two-thirds of all mergers were horizontal, meaning they were combinations of similar businesses; less than one-fifth were conglomerate.[29] By the early 1960s, in contrast, these percentages had flip-flopped: only one-eighth of mergers were horizontal, whereas almost two-thirds involved conglomerates.[30] Many managers favored conglomerates because of the potential stability conferred by size and diversification.[31] However, not all conglomerates formed in the 1960s survived the following recession, and not all leveraged their diversification successfully.[32] In the longer term, vertically integrated, multidivisional enterprises with related product lines and active research and development units often proved more durable.[33]

Because conglomerates, although powerful, did not concentrate their power through monopoly, they were often better able to elude the strictures imposed by antitrust regulation.[34] The government still sought to prevent many high-profile mergers in this period, however. In 1962, for instance, the Supreme Court struck down a proposed vertical merger between a shoe manufacturer and retailer in *Brown Shoe Co., Inc. v. United States*, ruling that even a small increase in market concentration could constitute an illegal concentration of power.[35] In 1967, the court ruled against a decade-old merger between Procter & Gamble and the Clorox Chemical Company based on the advantage conferred by P&G's television marketing capabilities (at the time of the acquisition, Clorox already controlled the largest share of the national market for household bleach).[36]

The potential of multinational conglomerates to influence the domestic political affairs of foreign nations also became a point of contention. In 1973, the assassination of Salvador Allende, a Chilean president unpopular with U.S. conglomerates such as ITT and Anaconda Copper, incensed many in the international community and thrust a public spotlight on the largely unregulated power of conglomerates.[37] Of course, powerful multinationals were not always based in the United States. The 1973 oil crisis, which had a deep and lasting effect on the American economy, was the result of price-fixing by the Organization of Petroleum Exporting Countries (OPEC) and the embargo imposed by its Arab members on the United States and other Western countries.[38] In the economic slowdown of the mid–1970s, merger and acquisition activity fell off considerably. In 1975, the value of annual mergers and acquisitions, adjusted for inflation, was $45 billion; seven years earlier, in 1968, it had totaled $257 billion in real terms.[39]

In the early 1980s, however, depressed values—in both goods and securities markets—led enterprising financiers or, sometimes, internal managers to acquire other businesses that they believed would appreciate.[40] At Drexel Burnham Lambert, Michael Milken used the young market for high-yield or "junk" bonds to help entrepreneurs and executives finance a range of merger and acquisition activity, including hostile takeovers. With the explosion in debt-financed acquisitions in the mid–1980s, merger activity intensified, eventually reaching a new peak of $247 billion in 1988 (or about $429 billion in today's dollars).[41] The most publicized deal that year, the leveraged buyout of RJR Nabisco by the merchant bank Kohlberg Kravis Roberts, was valued at $24.7 billion (about $43 billion in real terms), making it the biggest merger in U.S. history at that point.[42] Merger activity cooled in the late 1980s; by 1991, the real dollar value of such transactions had dropped to $107 billion, slightly less than the inflation-adjusted level in 1980.[43]

Beginning in the mid–1990s, mergers again increased steadily and eventually dwarfed even the activity at the height of the 1980s mania. After the fall of the Soviet Union, American companies such as Timken, an Ohio-based ball-bearing company, hustled to buy facilities in Asia and Eastern Europe.[44] The cross-border merger wave late in the decade was five times larger—adjusted for price changes—than that of the previous decade.[45] Within the United States, mergers between giants such as J.P. Morgan and Chase Manhattan and between U.S. Air and America West followed deregulation in the banking and airline industries.[46] The federal government intervened selectively, pursuing an antitrust case against Microsoft that ended in a 2001 settlement, and blocking the proposed merger between Staples and Office Depot.[47] However, many more deals between industry leaders were completed without federal interference. In 2000, for instance, the Internet company AOL acquired the media giant Time Warner. That same year, merger deals topped $1 trillion for the third time in a row.[48]

Mergers and acquisition fell off after the Internet bubble burst. The terrorist attacks on September 11, 2001, further dampened activity. But by 2007, merger mania was—once again—alive and well.[49] The trend toward global acquisitions continued, with corporations from emerging economies such as India increasingly taking part in the play.[50] Other new actors included private equity firms, which were involved in more and more buyouts of public companies. By 2006, private equity accounted for 25 percent of U.S. mergers and acquisitions (compared with 10 percent the year before).[51] At the same time, the value of attempted hostile takeovers, or buyouts not solicited by the acquisition target, rose to $351 billion, up from a previous high of $117 billion in 2000.[52] The latest swell in mergers brought public and media attention to the benefits reaped by CEOs of the acquired companies, who sometimes left with "golden parachutes" worth tens of millions of dollars. Was the value created for shareholders in these deals commensurate? Was more regulation needed to oversee the surge in cross-border alliances and the increasing role of private equity? Was this wave, too, bound for steep descent? These were some of the questions facing executives, investors, and other stakeholders of public companies in the early twenty-first century.

Quiet But Very Effective

The Business Methods of the Copper Manufacturers' Trust.

Among the numerous associations of manufacturers and producers for the putting up and maintenance of prices to dealers and consumers since the Standard Oil Company set the fashion, one that has not thus far been ventilated and that seems to have made the most of its opportunities is the Association of Copper Manufacturers of the United States. In it are included all of the manufacturers in this country of sheet copper and copper bolts, circles, segments, and special patterns, used in manufacturing. There are 14 mills in the country, included in the association, situated principally in Connecticut and New-York, but there are also mills in Pennsylvania, Maryland, Massachusetts, Michigan, Illinois, and other States.

The association has been in existence many years, the earlier of which were rather turbulent, for, like other combinations of a similar character, it included some who, having little confidence in their associates, either secretly or openly broke loose from the combination at their earliest convenience and made prices to suit themselves regardless of the schedule they had agreed to when they entered the association. Discipline was administered to such by abandoning the price schedule for a season, while all the members "went for" the trade of the offender as best they could, cutting under

his prices until his trade was crippled and he had received punishment enough and was ready to give bail to keep the peace.

When the war had been carried on until it had accomplished its purpose and the offending manufacturers had been whipped into submission, the association celebrated the event with a banquet and a meeting, at which the price schedule was again established, and the process of "milking" the public was again resumed. This was about six years ago.

Since then the lines of the association have fallen in peaceful places, all the members maintaining prices with a zeal proportioned to the horror with which they recalled the dark days of the free competition. The price list of the association adopted at its last meeting, Dec. 10, 1887, shows the association to be one of the most effective in the country, and the industry, at present prices, to be one of the most prosperous. The syndicate taxes the members of the association 16½ cents a pound for ingot copper and compels them to buy in quantities sufficient to last them for three months. Between this and the lowest price stated in the list for sheet copper is a margin of 8½ cents, showing, if 4 cents represents the cost of rolling this grade, a very comfortable profit. Comparisons with English prices for the same classes of goods show that the prices exacted for rolling in this country are from two to three times as high as they are abroad.

Members of the association defend their action by declaring that they are in the business to make money, and that if anybody believes there is any too great a profit made upon their goods there is nothing to prevent his building a rolling mill and trying it on for himself. But this is said in a tone of voice which conveys the intimation that if any one should have the temerity to do such a thing the association would jump on him collectively and individually, and make his infant years as a manufacturer years of peculiar and impressive adversity, which, if he survived them, would make him eligible to membership in the association; and by this time, it is thought, he would be quite willing to help maintain the association schedule of prices.

Telephone Merger Coming

Plans Laid to Bring Principal Independents Into the Bell System.

Preliminary steps for a merger of the principal independent telephone systems with the American Telephone and Telegraph Company have been taken by banking interests allied with the Bell system. This was made known yesterday through an announcement from St. Louis which told of proposals to the Kinloch and other independent systems in the Middle West.

The plan does not involve the immediate purchase of the independents, but, as it was explained yesterday, is an arrangement by which the various "outside" systems may be got into shape for a combination with the Bell companies should a consolidation be found possible under the Sherman law.

Within the last several years the independent telephone companies have developed widely, particularly in the farming communities, and the aggregate of mileage outside of the Bell system is large. Various attempts at consolidation have been made. The independents have had financial difficulties in many sections. Within the past two years several of the companies in the lake States passed into the hands of J. P. Morgan & Co.

The negotiations now under way, it was explained yesterday, are entirely of a tentative character and are dependent on the clearing of legal difficulties, as well as an agreement upon valuations.

The Bell system is capitalized at $500,000,000, of which about $260,000,000 is outstanding. It controls the leading telephone companies throughout the United States from coast to coast.

Roosevelt Won't Drop Trust War

Pledges Remainder of Administration to Obtaining Honest

Observance of Law.

Voices Determination to "Punish Certain Malefactors of Great Wealth."

PROVINCETOWN, MASS., AUG. 20.—President [Theodore] Roosevelt spoke here to-day at the laying of the cornerstone of the Cape Cod Pilgrims Memorial Monument, and his utterance marked the climax of the most notable celebration the town has ever held.

His speech, which was a consideration of the policies of his administration with regard to the trusts, and a eulogy of the Puritan character, was received with the greatest enthusiasm, the crowds standing patiently till the very end. The speech took about an hour to deliver, and was frequently interrupted with applause.

President Roosevelt's speech was as follows:

An Event of World Importance.
Must Not Lose Puritan Spirit.

There is no use in our coming here to pay homage to the men who founded this Nation unless we first of all come in the spirit of trying to do our work to-day as they did

their work in the yesterdays that have vanished. The problems shift from generation to generation, but the spirit in which they must be approached, if they are to be successfully solved, remains ever the same. The Puritan tamed the wilderness, and built up a free government on the stump-dotted clearings, amid the primeval forest. His descendants must try to shape the life of our complex industrial civilization by new devices, by new methods, so as to achieve in the end the same results of justice and fair dealing toward all. He cast aside nothing old merely for the sake of innovation, yet he did not hesitate to adopt anything new that would serve his purpose. When he planted his commonwealths on this rugged coast he faced wholly new conditions, and he had to devise new methods of meeting them. So we of to-day face wholly new conditions in our social and industrial life. We should certainly not adopt any new scheme for grappling with them merely because it is new and untried; but we cannot afford to shrink from grappling with them because they can only be grappled with by some new scheme.

The utterly changed conditions of our National life necessitate changes in certain of our laws, of our governmental methods. Our Federal system of government is based upon the theory of leaving to each community, to each State, the control over those things which affect only its own members and which the people of the locality themselves can best grapple with, while providing for National regulation in those matters which necessarily affect the Nation as a whole. It seems to me that such questions as national sovereignty and State's rights need to be treated not empirically or academically, but from the standpoint of the interests of the people as a whole. National sovereignty is to be upheld in so far as it means the sovereignty of the people used for the real and ultimate good of the people; and State's rights are to be upheld in so far as they mean the people's rights. Especially is this true in dealing with the relations of the people as a whole to the great corporations, which are the distinguishing feature of modern business conditions.

More Efficient Control Needed.

Experience has shown that it is necessary to exercise a far more efficient control than at present [exists] over the business use of those vast fortunes, chiefly corporate, which are used (as under modern conditions they almost invariably are) in inter-State business. When the Constitution was created none of the conditions of modern business existed. They are wholly new, and we must create new agencies to deal effectively with them. There is no objection in the minds of this people to any man's earning any amount of money if he does it honestly and fairly, if he gets it as the result of special skill and enterprise, as a reward of ample service actually rendered.

But there is a growing determination that no man shall amass a great fortune by special privilege, by chicanery and wrongdoing, so far as it is in the power of legislation to prevent, and that the fortune when amassed shall not have a business use that is anti-social. Most large corporations do a business that is not confined to any one State. Experience has shown that the effort to control these corporations by mere State action cannot produce wholesome results. In most cases such effort fails to correct the real abuses of which the corporation is or may be guilty, while in other cases the effort is apt to cause either hardship to the corporation itself, or else hardship to neighboring States which have not tried to grapple with the problem in the same manner; and, of course, we must be as scrupulous to safeguard the rights of the corporations as to exact from them in return a full measure of justice to the public.

I believe in a National incorporation law for corporations engaged in inter-State business. I believe, furthermore, that the need for action is most pressing as regards those corporations which, because they are common carriers, exercise a quasi-public function, and which can be completely controlled, in all respects, by the Federal Government, by the exercise of the power conferred under the inter-State commerce clause, and, if necessary, under the post-road clause, of the Constitution. During the last few years we have taken marked strides in advance along the road of proper regulation of these railroad corporations; but we must not stop in the work. The National Government should exercise over them a similar supervision and control to that which it exercises over National banks. We can do this only by proceeding further along the lines marked out by the recent National legislation.

Experiment at First.

In dealing with any totally new set of conditions there must at the outset be hesitation and experiment. Such has been our experience in dealing with the enormous concentration of capital employed in inter-State business. Not only the Legislatures, but the courts and the people, need gradually to be educated so that they may see what the real wrongs are and what [are] the real remedies. Almost every big business concern is engaged in inter-State commerce, and such a concern must not be allowed by a dexterous shifting of position, as has been too often the case in the past, to escape thereby all responsibility either to State or to Nation. The American people became firmly convinced of the need of control over these great aggregations of capital, especially where they had a monopolistic tendency, before they became quite clear as to the proper way of achieving the control.

Through their Representatives in Congress they tried two remedies, which were to a large degree, at least as interpreted by the courts, contradictory.

On the one hand, under the anti-trust law, the effort was made to prohibit all combination, whether it was or was not hurtful or beneficial to the public. On the other hand, through the inter-State commerce law, a beginning was made in exercising such supervision and control over combinations as to prevent their doing anything harmful to the body politic.

The first law, the so-called Sherman law, has filled a useful place, for it bridges over the transition period until the American people shall definitely make up its mind that it will exercise over the great corporations that thoroughgoing and radical control which it is certain ultimately to find necessary. The principle of the Sherman law so far as it prohibits combinations which, whether because of their extent or of their character, are harmful to the public must always be preserved. Ultimately, and I hope with reasonable speed, the National Government must pass laws which, while increasing the supervisory and regulatory power of the Government, also permit such useful combinations as are made with absolute openness and as the representatives of the Government may previously approve. But it will not be possible to permit such combinations save as the second stage in a course of proceedings of which the first stage must be the exercise of a far more complete control by the National Government.

Many Rich Men Criminal.

Many men of large wealth have been guilty of conduct which from the moral standpoint is criminal, and their misdeeds are to peculiar degree reprehensible, because those committing them have no excuse of want, of poverty, of weakness, and ignorance to offer as partial atonement. When in addition to moral responsibility these men have a legal responsibility which can be proved so as to impress a Judge and jury, then the department will strain every nerve to reach them criminally. Where this is impossible, then it will take whatever action will be most effective under the actual conditions.

In the last six years we have shown that there is no individual and no corporation so powerful that he or it stands above the possibility of punishment under the law.

No individual, no corporation, obeying the law, has anything to fear from this Administration.

Will Prosecute All Criminals.

I wish there to be no mistake on this point. It is idle to ask me not to prosecute criminals, rich or poor. But I desire no less emphatically to have it understood that we have undertaken and will undertake no action of a vindictive type, and above all, no action which shall inflict great or unmerited suffering upon the innocent stockholders and upon the public as a whole.

Our purpose is to act with the minimum of harshness compatible with obtaining our ends. In the man of great wealth who has earned his wealth honestly and used it wisely, we recognize a good citizen worthy of all praise and respect. Business can only be done under modern conditions through corporations, and our purpose is to heartily favor the corporations that do well.

Laws for the Wageworkers.

I very earnestly hope that the legislation which deals with the regulation of corporations engaged in inter-State business will also deal with the rights and interests of the wageworkers employed by those corporations. Action was taken by the Congress last year limiting the number of hours that railway employees should be employed. The law is a good one; but if in practice it proves necessary to strengthen it, it must be strengthened. We have now secured a national employers' liability law; but ultimately a more far-reaching and thoroughgoing law must be passed. It is monstrous that a man or woman who is crippled in an industry, even as the result of taking what are the necessary risks of the occupation, should be required to bear the whole burden of the loss. That burden should be distributed and not placed solely upon the weakest individual, the one least able to carry it. By making the employer liable the loss will ultimately be distributed among all the beneficiaries of the business.

The Importance of Character.

I have spoken of but one or two laws which, in my judgment, it is advisable to enact as part of the general scheme for making the interference of the National Government more effective in securing justice and fair dealing as between man and man here in the United States. Let me add, however, that while it is necessary to have legislation when conditions arise where we can only cope with evils through the joint action of all of us, yet that we can never afford to forget that in the last analysis the all-important factor for each of us must be his own individual character. It is a necessary thing to have good laws, good institutions; but the most necessary of all things is to have a high quality of individual citizenship.

Shown here in 1904, Theodore Roosevelt led the charge in the trust busting of the early twentieth century, asserting that federal government had a vital role to play in regulating multistate corporations. (*New York Times*)

June 14, 1925

Trade Board Will Play a New Role in Business

Commission's Wish to Bring About More Informal Adjustments and Interpret Real Spirit of Anti-Trust Laws.

BY GILBERT H. MONTAGUE

The author of this article has had large experience with the procedure of the Federal Trade Commission. At the time the law was framed he appeared before Congress as a representative of the Merchants Association of New York City, and he writes from the standpoint of support of the recent changes in the personnel and spirit of the commission.

Shall the Federal Trade Commission be abolished? Or can the commission, under its new policies and procedure, render a service in the handling of anti-trust problems which no other branch of the Government can accomplish?

Less sensationalism, more adjustments through informal conferences, more sympathetic cooperation with business men and fuller opportunity for parties investigated to be heard before any adverse public action is taken—these are the commission's new policies.

Under such procedure the commission plans to throw out all cases involving purely private controversies that are redressable in the courts and to confine its attention strictly to cases where the public interest is clear and unmistakable; to speed up its investigating machinery so as to keep always abreast of the increasing flood of complaints which it is receiving, and to dispose of all except extraordinary cases or cases of fraud by taking from the party investigated, without publicity and without formal proceedings, an agreement to discontinue the practice complained of and a stipulation of facts which will insure a prompt and drastic formal order should the party later break his agreement.

Discord Within and Without.

Within the commission the majority members, who favor the new plan, are sharply opposed by the minority members, who prefer the commission's old policy. Outside the commission, radical Senators, who for years have sustained its former procedure, are now raising the same cry for the abolition of the commission that for years has been voiced by some of the business men who have most suffered from old methods.

In all this conflict and realignment of the critics of the commission there is real danger that the high significance of the very interesting experiment in anti-trust law administration in which the Federal Trade Commission is now engaged may be entirely obscured.

When the commission was created in 1914 both the radicals and the business community were distrustful of the Supreme Court's handling of anti-trust cases. Both believed that a commission could deal more competently with such problems than could any court.

Only a few years before the Supreme Court had adopted the "rule of reason" in applying the Sherman act to antitrust cases. By what now seems to have been a curious perversity this action convinced the radicals that the Supreme Court was unjustifiably restricting the anti-trust law, and convinced the business community that the Supreme Court was committed to a hopelessly indefinite application of the anti-trust law.

What Is "Reasonable"?

Radicals and business community alike in 1914 were misinterpreting the "rule of reason" to mean that this court had unwarrantedly assumed the power to declare which trusts and monopolies were "reasonable" and which were "unreasonable"; to confer immunity upon those which the Supreme Court considered "reasonable," although the Sherman act apparently forbade all trusts and monopolies, whether "reasonable" or "unreasonable." The Supreme Court's standards of "reasonableness," from the business community's standpoint, seemed vague and unpredictable.

Temporarily, then, so far as the handling of trust problems was concerned, the Supreme Court in 1914 was in deep disfavor. When, therefore, President Wilson proposed the creation of a Federal Trade Commission the suggestion that these problems, in the first instance at least, should be handled by a commission instead of a court was eagerly endorsed not only by the radicals but also by the overwhelming vote of the business men of the country as expressed in the referendum then taken by the Chamber of Commerce of the United States.

The radicals hoped that a commission would be more rigorous and the business men hoped that a commission would be more sympathetic than the courts. To insure its having the fullest possible discretion to accomplish one or other of these absolutely contradictory purposes the Federal Trade Commission act vested the commission with sweeping powers to prevent everything comprehended within the undefined limits of "unfair methods of competition in commerce."

Since 1914 full opportunity has been afforded to compare the courts and the Federal Trade Commission in their handling of anti-trust problems. Thus far the popular verdict upon this comparison appears strongly in favor of the courts and against the commission.

In 1920 the Supreme Court finally decided what was meant by the words "unfair methods of competition in commerce" of the Federal Trade Commission act, and held that these included only such practices as are "opposed to good morals because characterized by deception, bad faith, fraud or oppression," or such as are "against public policy because of their dangerous tendency unduly to hinder competition or create monopoly."

From 1920 to 1925, notwithstanding the Supreme Court decision in 1920, the commission continued, in a series of unsuccessful proceedings, to beat its wings against that decision in a vain effort to enlarge its jurisdiction and powers beyond the limits which the Supreme Court had prescribed, all of which terminated in repeated defeats for the commission in the Supreme Court and the other Federal courts. By 1925 it was manifest that there must be some change in the Federal Trade Commission's policies and procedure. Every year the commission had been falling more and more into arrears in its preliminary investigations, its drafting and issuance of complaints and its prosecution and final disposition of proceedings. To meet the situation to which all these various causes had contributed the commission last March determined to avail itself of the provision of the Federal Trade Commission act which expressly authorized withholding of prosecution, even when the law had been technically violated, unless "it shall appear to the commission that a proceeding by it in respect thereof would be to the interest of the public."

This authority, which wholly differentiates the Federal Trade Commission from every other Federal or State official charged with the administration of any of the anti-trust laws, vests the commission with uncontrolled discretion to determine whether it shall withhold prosecution even when the law has been technically violated.

This unique power and this extraordinary discretion were expressly conferred by Congress in the Federal Trade Commission act,

1924. Herein the commission, in March, 1925, found the most ample authority for the adoption of its new polices and procedure.

Saving Time and Money.

Intentionally or unintentionally, the commission is now embarked upon an entirely novel experiment in the administration of the anti-trust laws. If it succeeds in this experiment, the commission will have demonstrated that it possesses a power and a discretion which not the courts, not the Department of Justice, not the Department of Commerce nor any other branch of the Government can possibly have in the handling of anti-trust problems.

From the standpoint of economy, this will enormously enhance the commission's efficiency and capacity for handling the increasing flood of complaints which every year is pouring in upon it. Time and money previously expended in preparing complicated pleadings and trying long proceedings—lasting months and even years, and requiring the taking of testimony in many cities throughout the country—may now for the most part be wholly saved, except in extraordinary cases or cases involving actual fraud or cases in which the party investigated insists upon litigating.

If this experiment proves to be both effective and acceptable, it will be demonstrated that the Federal Trade Commission can render an entirely new type of service, bringing the rank and file of American business into readier conformity with the real spirit of the anti-trust laws.

December 5, 1909

What Is To Be Done With the Trusts?

BY FRANK FAYANT

All the Government now needs to do is to prepare bills of complaint against the hundreds of trusts that have sprung up in recent years, and the courts will send to the financial scrap heap some $10,000,000,000 worth of big businesses. But is this going to happen? The wise men of old burned much midnight oil studying the problem: What happens when an irresistible force meets an immovable body? We have just such a problem now in this country. The Sherman Anti-Trust act of 1890 is an irresistible force: the big businesses of this country are an immovable body. That nearly a fifth of all the wealth of the country is in the form of corporate combinations is evidence that the Sherman act cannot be enforced.

The Standard Oil lawyers . . . wasted much time telling the court of the varied economic benefits resulting from the combination—increased wealth production, command of the world's foreign trade, and low prices. But these things were of as little interest to the court as the catalogue of the company's crimes. If the Standard Oil Company had given all its profits to the poor it would have made no difference. The law denounced it for the crime of being big, and that was all there was to be said . . . all its badness was in its bigness.

A mere list of all the corporation "law breakers" in this country would fill several columns of THE TIMES, for nearly all the industrial companies that have been formed in recent years are combinations of competing companies. They have been organized for the purpose of restraining trade. A score of the largest of these combinations are appraised in the security markets at $3,000,000,000 and their yearly profits are running close to $500,000,000 (table 3-1).

Free competition was the very cornerstone of English industry when the factory system began to take the place of hand labor, with the introduction of steam power. It is this idea of free competition that runs through our common law, inherited from England, and which is the basis on which anti-trust legislation like the Sherman act is formed. In this country today we have four principal varieties of capitalistic monopoly—patents and copyrights; natural monopolies, due to the wealth or favorable location of lands, mines or waters; franchises, as railroads, telegraphs, and telephones; and industrial monopolies.

A few years ago a few thousand men owned the big industries of the country. Now they are owned, as THE TIMES recently showed, by hundreds of thousands. The transition from partnerships to great public companies has given every thrifty American opportunity to become a capitalist. Where three-score rich men owned the Carnegie Steel Works, a hundred thousand capitalists, big and little, now share in the profits of the industry.

Bigness in American industry and commerce is coming to be popularly associated with honest American progress. The Steel Trust has done much to educate the public to the new view that it isn't a crime to be big. When the Steel Trust, with its unprecedented billion-dollar capital, was launched, it was the target of all the anti-trust attacks, but it weathered the storm, and a panic or two besides, and it now goes along as peacefully as a country bank. The thinking American is coming more and more to distinguish between right and wrong in trade, irrespective of the wealth of an individual or corporation.

TABLE 3-1

	Market Value	Yearly Products
Steel	$1,500,000,000	$100,000,000
Telephone	$700,000,000	$45,000,000
Oil	$650,000,000	$85,000,000
Tobacco	$500,000,000	$40,000,000
Pullman Car	$110,000,000	$11,000,000
Broilers	$170,000,000	$12,000,000
Copper	$140,000,000	$6,000,000
Harvester	$150,000,000	$13,000,000
Electric (General)	$130,000,000	$11,000,000
Telegraph (Western Union)	$120,000,000	$10,000,000
Sugar	$100,000,000	$8,000,000
Rubber	$90,000,000	$4,000,000
Leather	$90,000,000	$5,000,000
Meat Packing (Swifts)	$80,000,000	$18,000,000
Powder	$75,000,000	$5,000,000
Electric (Westinghouse)	$70,000,000	$4,000,000
Telegraph (Mackay)	$70,000,000	$7,000,000
Mercantile Marine	$70,000,000	$7,000,000
Biscuit	$60,000,000	$4,000,000
Car and Foundry	$60,000,000	$8,000,000
Total	$5,000,000,000	$403,000,000

Conglomerate Mergers Get Spotlight

BY JOHN J. ABELE

Are conglomerate companies a bold new form of economic enterprise, infusing companies they acquire with a new sense of purpose, efficiency and productivity?

Or are they a new form of economic monopoly, concentrating control of key industrial organizations in the hands of a few aggressively managed corporations with an apparently insatiable appetite for acquiring other companies?

These are two of the questions in the air after Monday's announcement by the Federal Trade Commission of a broad study of the ramifications of the rapidly accelerating trend toward conglomerate mergers.

The number of conglomerate mergers, in which companies acquire other companies in completely different fields of business, has been increasing at a bewildering pace in recent years.

The trend has produced a whole new crop of corporate giants that compare in size with the mammoth corporations that developed in the first half of this century.

It also has spawned a host of smaller companies that hope to emulate the success of the larger conglomerate companies by carrying out a series of acquisitions in a variety of fields.

Five years ago, Ling-Temco-Vought, Inc., was a relatively modest Dallas aircraft and electronics company with sales of $325-million a year.

Last year, L-T-V recorded sales of $1.8-billion. Its business has been expanded to include interests in meat-packing, sporting goods, chemicals and pharmaceuticals, metal products, and an airline. Earlier this year, the company acquired a 63 per cent interest in the Jones & Laughlin Steel Corporation, one of the nation's largest steel producers.

Gulf & Western Industries, Inc., is another prime example of a fast-growing conglomerate company. Five years ago, it was an unheralded producer and distributor of auto parts, with sales of $107-million a year.

Last year, Gulf & Western had sales of $1.3-billion. Its volume in the current fiscal year is expected to reach $2-billion.

The company's rapid-fire acquisition program has carried it into such fields as motion pictures and television, sugar, cigars, metalworking machinery, tools, bearings, consumer finance, insurance and paper.

The company is currently bidding for a controlling interest in the Allis-Chalmers Manufacturing Company, a big producer of farm, electrical and construction equipment that was unsuccessfully wooed last year by Ling-Temco-Vought and several other companies.

In one of the first challenges to a conglomerate take-over, the F.T.C. has given notice of its plans to oppose the Gulf & Western bid for Allis-Chalmers. Gulf and Western has said it will fight the F.T.C. on the issue.

Early precursors of the conglomerate movement included Textron, Inc., whose operations now range from helicopters to zippers, and Litton Industries, Inc., whose foundation in electronics has been expanded to include shipbuilding, business machines, restaurants and industrial construction and engineering.

A crisis of sorts developed in the conglomerate companies earlier this year when Litton, widely regarded as one of the most successful practitioners of the conglomerate merger, reported a sharp decline in earnings, the first decline in the history of the company.

Part of the problem was ascribed to management difficulties which struck hard at one of the key concepts of the conglomerates, the idea that they are able to instill a heightened degree of management skill in the companies they take over.

Litton's problems also dealt a heavy blow to the popular idea that earnings of conglomerate companies are able to proceed on an ever-upward course.

Supporters of the conglomerate concept argue that progress in profits is made possible by the superior skills and resources that are available to an acquired company through alliance with a larger company with experience in a variety of different fields.

Skeptics wonder if the interchangeability of management skills from one industry to another truly exists. They also question whether earnings growth is due primarily to improvement of existing operations or to a welter of acquisitions, whose earnings are piled on top of those of previously acquired companies.

The skeptics also wonder about some of the complicated financial maneuvers that often accompany a conglomerate merger. They see "paper pyramids" being constructed on a variety of stock-oriented deals involving convertible preferred stocks, convertible and nonconvertible debentures, warrants and the like. They worry that one weak spot could cause the whole structure to tumble.

The basic reason for a conglomerate company is diversification, with assets scattered in a number of fields.

The reasoning is that corporate sales and profits will continue on an even keel despite downturns in one or more fields.

"All our acquisitions have been made according to a well defined plan of strategy," declares the officer of one conglomerate. "We're seeking to build up solid operating entities that will be able to rely on their own internal growth. Right now, we're trying to [g]et ready for the economy of the mid-1970's."

Other observers, however, detect traces of megalomonia on the part of some conglomerate managers, seeking to build huge corporate empires in a hurry.

"There are good conglomerates and there are bad conglomerates," says a Wall Street security analyst. "Some have high-quality, soundly conceived acquisition programs. Others display an unhealthy tendency. They're trying to go too far too fast."

Pro or con, financial observers do not believe the trend toward conglomerate mergers will slow down because of the F.T.C. study. They expect the study to take a long time to complete and question whether any legislation will result from the facts on economic concentration developed by the study.

One Wall Street source suggested that one effect of the study might be to speed up the flow of mergers. "This could set off a flurry of more mergers as companies try to get their acquisitions before any legislation develops," he said.

The Giant Target of Trustbusting '74

BY GENE SMITH

The Justice Department having filed its biggest antitrust action ever—against the American Telephone and Telegraph Corporation, the biggest corporation the world has to offer—it should come as no surprise that just about everything on the subject comes out in superlatives.

For example, on Friday, Nov. 22 the company withdrew its $600-million debt issue "because of unsettled market conditions following the antitrust action against A.T.&T." Having been the largest fixed-income financing ever attempted by any company, the cancellation was certainly the biggest ever.

And A.T.&T. can also lay claim to the following superlatives:

Assets—$67-billion at the end of 1973.
Earnings—$2.99-billion in 1973.
Employees—1,010,000 (more than anyone except the Federal Government).
Stockholders—2.93-million.
Shares outstanding—558-million.
Private vehicle fleet—175,560 cars and trucks.
Dividends paid—$2-billion in 1973.
Uncollectables—$152-million.

In fact, "Ma Bell," as it is called in the financial community, may just be so big that many think the Government may back off from its attempt to break up the giant. The Justice Department is trying to get A.T.&T. to get rid of the Western Electric Company, its manufacturing subsidiary, and either divest itself of its long distance telephone business or some or all of the 23 operating companies. It has indicated it would like Bell Telephone Laboratories, Inc., to be split into several companies.

John D. de Butts, chairman of A.T.&T., vowed at a news conference on Nov. 21 to fight the antitrust suit "to the end."

"We will not seek a consent decree," he stated emphatically.

The target of the Justice Department's suit is actually the Bell System, which is divided into four major parts.

A.T.&T. itself provides services to the telephone companies under license contracts, operates long-distance lines and provides the interconnections between the companies.

The Western Electric Company, the manufacturing and purchasing subsidiary for the entire Bell System, appears to be the central target of the suit.

TABLE 3-2

The Bell System

Operating companies (telephones in millions)

New York Telephone	11.7
New Jersey Bell	5.3
Bell of Pennsylvania	7.2
Diamond State Telephone	0.4
Chesapeake & Potomac Tel.	1.0
C. & P. of Maryland	2.8
C. & P. of Virginia	2.3
C. & P. of West Virginia	0.7
Southern Bell	9.0
South Central Bell	7.6
Ohio Bell	4.4
Michigan Bell	5.1
Indiana Bell	1.9
Illinois Bell	6.7
Wisconsin Tel.	1.9
Northwestern Bell	4.6
Southwestern Bell	12.2
Pacific Telephone	12.0
Pacific Northwest Bell	2.8
Mountain States Telephone	5.2
New England Telephone	5.7
Cincinnati Bell	1.0
Southern New England Tel.	2.2

Western Electric Company: 31 factories in 20 states, plus distribution and data centers; 207,000 employees

Bell Telephone Laboratories: 20 laboratories in 10 states; 17,000 employees

Long Lines Department: 7 regional divisions; 35,000 employees

Other Units include Teletype Corporation, Sandia Corporation, Empire City Subway Company

Bell Laboratories is the research and development arm for the system, including Western Electric.

The total plant value of the Bell System, according to the United States Independent Telephone Association, was $75.5-billion as of last Jan. 1 against $17.7-billion for the independents.

Bell System construction outlays are expected to total $9.5-billion for this year against $2.3-billion for all the independent companies.

Western Electric by itself ranks as one of the largest companies in the nation. Its 1973 sales of just over $7-billion gave it the 12th spot in the latest Fortune magazine listing of the 500 largest industrial companies in America.

Its assets, of more than $4.8-billion, placed it 19th in that listing while net income of $315.3-million made it the 18th best profit producer in the nation. Its 206,608 employees gave it seventh place of all industrial operations.

Another operation little known by the public is the long lines department of A.T.&T., which is responsible for managing the nationwide telephone network. It does not actually operate telephones but it does provide the facilities that connect the various companies, both Bell and independent, to form the telephone network.

On a typical day, long lines handles more than 20 million long distance calls, over a third of which are interstate. It also transmits radio and television broadcasts and handles news stories and wirephotos as well as computer and other data.

Long lines also provides the circuits for international calls, by percentage the fastest growing segment of the telephone business. It is now possible to reach more than 245 countries or places from any telephone in this country.

Overseas calling has more than tripled in the last five years, to about 50 million calls last year. The company expects this volume to exceed 200 million by 1980 and likes to point out that when overseas service was introduced in 1927 a three-minute call from here to London cost $75. Today, it is as low as $4.05.

The annual report for 1973 showed that A.T.&T.'s record $23.5-billion of revenues came from: $9.6-billion in service and equipment charges; $9.2-billion in toll messages; $1.3-billion in local message charges; $1.09-billion in private line toll services; $983-million in miscellaneous sources, principally directory advertising (Yellow Pages); $940-million in Wide Area Telecommunications Service (wats) tolls; $316-million from coin telephones across the nation; and $159-million from local private line services.

All of this amounted to a monthly average of $18.18 for each telephone on A.T.&T.'s lines. The Bell System handled an average of 432 million calls a day—5.36 for each phone excluding residential extensions—and a total of 9.5 billion long distance calls during 1973.

December 29, 1985

The Peril Behind the Takeover Boom

BY LEONARD SILK

The biggest wave of corporate acquisitions and buyouts in American history is beginning to cause widespread alarm. The merger mania has sent stock prices to levels no one ever envisioned for 1985. But in the process, American business has gone heavily into debt to pay for its multi-billion dollar takeovers. And this boom in corporate debt, particularly with its use of high-yielding, less-than investment grade "junk bonds," is bringing warnings even from those involved in financing the megadeals.

The situation has so troubled Paul A. Volcker, chairman of the Federal Reserve Board, that he now wants to restrict the use of junk bonds, a step that would thwart many highly-leveraged takeovers.

"We spend our days issuing debt and retiring equity, both in record volumes," said Mr. Volcker, "and then we spend our evenings raising each other's eyebrows with gossip about signs of stress in the financial system."

Mr. Volcker's position, however, has raised a cry from free-market proponents, led by the Reagan White House. Last week, the Administration, with the backing of a host of Government departments and agencies, argued that such borrowing restraints, if put into effect next month, would constitute a troublesome interference in the marketplace. The vehemence of the attack on the Fed came as a surprise, but not the free-market philosophy behind it. Many economists have long argued that Reagan Administration policies, particularly those that downplay antitrust issues, have strongly encouraged this wave of mergers.

"The board's proposal would destroy the market for corporate control, which disciplines inefficient management and enables stockholders to maximize returns on their investment," said Douglas H. Ginsburg, Assistant Attorney General and head of the Justice Department's antitrust division.

Even as the debate intensifies, so do the big mergers—the most recent being General Electric's announced agreement this month to acquire R.C.A. for $6.3 billion. Some of the biggest names in corporate America—from chemicals to broadcasting—have been in the spotlight in this year's deals, in sharp contrast to the situation only a few years ago when $1 billion-plus deals occurred only in oil.

Among the 1985 deals radically changing America's corporate landscape: R.J. Reynolds bought Nabisco; Philip Morris took over General Foods; ABC was taken over by Capital

Cities Communications, and Beatrice is going private in a leveraged buyout. General Motors bought Hughes Aircraft and Union Carbide is in a battle that pits its management against the GAF Corporation.

Indeed, there were at least 24 mergers in 1985 with $1 billion-plus pricetags, and these megadeals have helped fuel the rally that drove the Dow Jones Industrial average above 1,500. According to Goldman Sachs, the investment bank, 70 percent of the market's rise since the beginning of 1984 is a result of the merger wave.

That wave has burdened corporate balance sheets with vast quantities of debt. Salomon Brothers, the investment house, estimates that the debt of non-financial corporations rose by $145 billion in 1985, to a total of $1.6 trillion—a situation that many critics fear will leave the companies vulnerable if the economy were to go into a slump. The big concern is that many companies might not be able to afford the payments on their new debt if the economy weakens, pushing down corporate profits, and stock prices drop, undermining the equity that backs up much of the debt.

According to the journal Mergers and Acquisitions, there were 2,999 deals worth $124.8 billion in 1984. During the first three quarters of 1985 there have been 2,295 deals amounting to $88.5 billion. At the current rate, with General Electric's acquisition of RCA for $6.3 billion giving extra thrust to the fourth quarter, the 1985 total will reach $125 billion, matching 1984's, according to Mergers and Acquisitions.

Companies and corporate raiders—among them T. Boone Pickens, Carl C. Icahn and Irwin L. Jacobs—are financing some of these deals through the sale of junk bonds to wealthy individuals and savings and loans, pension funds, insurance companies and other institutional lenders. Shell corporations are often used to float these bonds. Since the shell companies have no other assets than the stock acquired, that stock, in effect, becomes the collateral for the bonds—a practice Mr. Volcker wants to curb. He would require a 50 percent down payment on any acquisition involving a loan collateralized with the stock of the acquired company.

Junk bonds have been used by corporations to acquire other, larger companies, and by executives to buy out shareholders using little or none of their own money. And they have changed the takeover game by encouraging more mergers than might otherwise have taken place.

The Federal Reserve says that the ratio between the market value of corporate debt and equity now stands at 71.4 percent, a high level historically although by no means a record. What makes this ratio alarming, economists say, is that both equity and debt levels are extraordinarily high. Although there has been a vast accumulation of debt since 1981, when the current merger wave began, the rise in equity values has roughly kept pace with the increase in debt, thanks largely to the rise in the stock market and the economy's general expansion.

Many fear that the burden of servicing the heavy debt could hurt corporate America if the economy goes into a deep recession and profits fall.

Felix Rohatyn, a senior partner in the investment banking house of Lazard Freres, who helped to arrange General Electric's recent purchase of RCA, says he considers the big risk in the current takeover wave to be "in the credit area, in the financial structure, in the speculative frenzy in the stock market." Even the most worried experts, including Mr. Rohatyn, stress that they are not against all mergers and acquisitions, but only certain kinds.

"Mergers and acquisitions have been with us a long time, and there is nothing inherently wrong with them under the free-market economic system we have," said Martin Lipton, an attorney of Wachtell Lipton, Rosen & Katz, who has counseled both acquiring and defending companies. But, he said, a "new kind of takeover activity" surfaced about five years ago—"takeovers not for the purpose of expansion or diversification but for liquidating a company and making an immediate profit."

As a result, he said, "we have ended up with unlimited junk bond financing, with no limit to the size of the takeover."

But the current merger wave has its strong defenders. Most free-market economists see the takeovers and the consequent bidding up of stock prices as healthy and desirable. They say the merger wave will be self-limiting as the remaining corporations grow leaner and tougher, with stock prices readjusted to their appropriate levels.

"I have the unscientific suspicion that there are a lot of mergers when the market is at either of two extremes," said Prof. Lawrence White of New York University. "You had waves at the end of the 1920's and the 1960's, when a buoyant stock market made it easy to float a lot of securities to buy out other companies. And you've got it in the 1980's, when stock prices of many companies were perceived to be too low and you could pick up bargains."

Prof. Michael C. Jensen of the University of Rochester and the Harvard Business School holds that takeovers actually encourage the productive use of assets. He says they do not siphon commercial credit from its uses in financing plant and equipment or create monopoly power. He even maintains that "golden parachutes"—lucrative financial deals made by existing management if a takeover occurs and they lose their jobs—are good because "they deter managers" from blocking a takeover.

"The takeover market," he says, "provides a unique, powerful and impersonal mechanism to accomplish the major restructuring and redeployment of assets continually required by changes in technology and consumer preferences."

The evidence for this assertedly positive effect of takeovers comes from several sources. Mr. Jensen and others who see the current wave as improving economic efficiency, base their conclusions on stock-market studies analyzing how the prices of acquired and acquiring company shares performed shortly before and after a takeover. Their assumption is that the stock market is "efficient," and rationally processes all available information; hence, when it marks up a stock after a merger, the market demonstrates its confidence in the superior performance of the new management team. However, Prof. F. M. Scherer of Swarthmore College, now a visiting fellow at the Brookings Institution, says that such studies fail to consider an alternative explanation: that the stock market had undervalued the acquired company's shares, which is what made it an attractive takeover candidate, even when a premium had to be paid. The takeover act sends a signal to the market to upgrade its valuation. "It is the stock market, not management of the target firm, which has erred and needs disciplining," says Mr. Scherer.

Further, he holds that conclusions like those of the Reagan economists rest on observations of short-time periods and do not take account of studies that have taken a longer perspective. Those studies, he said, show systematic declines in the stock prices of acquiring companies in the year following the takeover.

[A] number of leading financial experts are worried about the debt expansion, especially if the rapid run-up of equity prices should go into reverse. James J. O'Leary, economic consultant to the United States Trust Company of New York, warns that total private debt—corporate and consumer—has been "exploding" at an annual rate of 12 to 13 percent, while nominal gross national product grew by less than 7 percent in 1985.

The business failure rate, says Mr. O'Leary, is already four-fifths as high as it was during the worst years of the Depression. What is remarkable now, he adds, is that so high a rate of failures has taken place during a period of cyclical expansion; he fears that it could foreshadow a still more serious wave of bankruptcies if the business cycle turns down.

What can be done to stem takeovers leading to a massive increase of debt? One solution would be through the tax laws, by encouraging more equity. By encouraging debt and discouraging equity, the tax laws have helped fuel takeovers.

In addition to changing the tax laws, there are other possible remedies suggested by those close to the takeover game:

- Change the attitude of institutional investors, to reward management for long-term performance;
- Alter accounting conventions so as not to discriminate in favor of acquisitions over research and development and capital expenditures;
- Impose greater restraint on financial institutions, which have so great an impact on the economy of the United States and the world;
- Avoid excessive money and credit creation, which fuels merger mania by encouraging flight from cash to assets and high leverage;
- Prevent "abusive" takeovers in which companies with a history of good and responsible management are taken over for the sake of "busting them up" and extracting immediate financial gain;
- Let the Securities and Exchange Commission write better rules for mergers and acquisitions to insure greater openness and fairness.

RJR Nabisco, An Epilogue

BY BRYAN BURROUGH

Like Stanley Kubrick and Joe DiMaggio, RJR Nabisco died this week. The 14-year-old company, formed in 1985 by the ill-conceived merger of the R. J. Reynolds tobacco conglomerate and the Nabisco food corporation, is to be broken up, its foreign cigarette company sold to the Japanese so that Nabisco can once more go its own way, alone.

It is a story that, were it not for the furious 1988 bidding battle that culminated in the company's $25 billion leveraged buyout, the largest in history, would never have escaped the business pages. But the events of that autumn 11 years ago insure that RJR Nabisco will rank high in the century's pantheon of financial ignominy.

The pundits are saying it is the end of an era, and so it is. How raw it all seems today, now that hostile takeovers are passe and Michael Milken campaigns against prostate cancer, that the nation's 19th-largest company became a piece of meat for the leading investment bankers to snarl over.

First into the fray was Peter Cohen, the chairman of Shearson Lehman, itself now divided and long forgotten. Mr. Cohen, working with RJR's flamboyant president, F. Ross Johnson, was determined to grab a piece of Wall Street's exploding buyout business for himself.

This outraged the acknowledged prince of the buyout business, Henry Kravis, of Kohlberg Kravis Roberts & Company, who summoned Mr. Cohen to his midtown Manhattan office and sought a portion, on the order of 100 percent, of the brewing deal. This bit of incivility, and the multibillion-dollar takeover offer Mr. Kravis made in its wake, ignited a fire that within days consumed all of Wall Street.

When business historians look back at the 1980's, they will no doubt point to the numbers, to the weaknesses in its core businesses, to explain why RJR Nabisco failed. And they will be right. As a platform on which to pile several billion dollars of debt, the tobacco business, soon to be beset by pricing wars and an avalanche of litigation during the 1990's, was never sufficiently stable.

But the real story of RJR Nabisco was and always will be the people who made it fail. Business journalists are sometimes criticized for "personalizing" their subjects, and, yes, it's not terribly relevant whether Bill Gates likes his martinis shaken or stirred. But RJR stands as a reminder, if we need one, that it is human beings and not computers or balance sheets who make the decisions on which corporations live or die.

It was Ross Johnson who, annoyed in part by Nabisco's lagging stock price, spearheaded the original plan to merge with R. J. Reynolds, a company in the same plight. This reasoning was not unlike marrying two lepers in hopes of somehow curing their disease. Prodded by the fee-hungry investment bankers who buzzed about him like horseflies, he seemed willing to try almost anything.

If a merger or restructuring failed, he famously reasoned, it just meant a few hundred people would lose their "portable" jobs or the company would lose a few million dollars. And "a few million dollars," Mr. Johnson said at the time, "are lost in the sands of time." When the merger failed to goose the combined companies' stock, Mr. Johnson came up with the idea for a leveraged buyout, which would have paid off all the public shareholders and taken the company private—in effect, eliminating the stock problem.

Despite warnings that RJR was not fit for a leveraged buyout, Mr. Kravis began his blitzkrieg. The Cassandra-like speeches of his archrival, Theodore Forstmann, a general partner at the buyout firm of Forstmann, Little & Company, have stayed with me for years. As the bidding escalated that fall, Mr. Forstmann bowed out early, telling everyone who would listen that the deal just didn't make financial sense. And he was right. But in its overweening need to anoint a "winner," to treat a financial transaction as if it were the Stanley Cup, the business press, and here I include myself, didn't want to hear Mr. Forstmann's tiresome jeremiads.

RJR's demise is not without its ironies. Its chief executive today is Steven Goldstone— Mr. Kravis bailed out in 1994—who was Mr. Johnson's primary legal adviser during his bid for the company in 1988. It was Mr. Goldstone who, during an afternoon at Mr. Johnson's Florida condo, tried in vain to persuade Mr. Johnson against attempting the buyout.

Mr. Goldstone is the author of the final chapter of the tale he never wanted written in the first place. Others may get a wry smile out of Carl Icahn's role in RJR's death. Like most of his fellow corporate raiders, Mr. Icahn has all but disappeared from the public eye since the 1980's. In fact, his success in pressuring Mr. Goldstone to split up the company is probably the most notable achievement by a raider this decade. It's fitting, as if RJR is being led into the darkness by the Ghost of Takeovers Past himself.

The legacy of RJR Nabisco was immediate and lasts to this day. It was the deal that was too big, too loud, too out of control. It was the one event that more than any other, more than Mr. Milken's jailing, more than the government investigations, ended the Roaring 80's, and for a simple reason that had nothing to do with balance sheets and everything to do with human beings.

RJR scared people, especially chief executives. While no one will shed tears for Mr. Johnson—he did, after all, walk away from the company with a $50 million severance package—his very public immolation persuaded hundreds of chief executives to tread more carefully where their companies' futures were concerned.

Of even greater significance was its effect on corporate boardrooms across the country. For the first time corporate directors began seriously questioning the harebrained schemes investment bankers brought before them. Until RJR, too many boards allowed Wall Street deal-makers to lead them by the noses. The diminution of this power was a turning point in the drive toward greater corporate accountability, which, economic arguments aside, remains the most enduring lesson of Wall Street's decade of excess.

June 7, 1995

A New Test Of Antitrust Hard Line

News Analysis

BY EDMUND L. ANDREWS

WASHINGTON, JUNE 6—Which is the greater threat to competition, a $5 billion company that buys another that is pre-eminent in its field, or a $64 billion company that buys one with no competitor at all?

In Federal antitrust circles these days, the answer depends largely on which company is the MICROSOFT Corporation and which is I.B.M. At a time when the Justice Department has made it clear that it wants to be an aggressive antitrust cop, the uninvited bid by I.B.M. to acquire the LOTUS DEVELOPMENT Corporation, announced on Monday, puts the Government under pressure to draw meaningful distinctions about perceived competitive threats to the technology marketplace.

Only three weeks ago, antitrust officials at the Justice Department were crowing about their success in blocking Microsoft from buying INTUIT INC., a small company that makes the most popular software on the market for writing checks and managing household budgets.

In the Government's view, the acquisition threatened more than check-writing programs. Microsoft, with $5 billion in revenues, was in danger of choking competition in future markets for electronic home banking and electronic commerce, officials said.

Yet now comes the International Business Machines Corporation, which during the 1970's and early 1980's was involved in one of the longest antitrust investigations in history, and is now a company with revenues of $64 billion. I.B.M. is trying to buy Lotus, the owner of a protean software program called Notes that has no direct competitor.

A casual observer might expect that the Justice Department would immediately saddle up a new posse and prepare to shoot down this deal as well. But the casual observer would very likely be wrong.

The conventional wisdom among antitrust experts is that the Justice Department will not try to block I.B.M., and they say the reasons are almost self-evident. Despite its size, I.B.M., they say, is a relative weakling in the personal computer software industry and the Lotus software programs represent an entirely separate market.

But many industry experts say the hostile takeover attempt by I.B.M. invites new questions about the assumptions governing Federal antitrust policy. Can Microsoft really be that dangerous, with I.B.M. gunning for part of its market? Does a takeover pose a threat to competition if the acquired company dominates a market that is only starting to emerge?

For all their differences, the two deals share many similarities. Both Microsoft and I.B.M. had fumbled in their own attempts to enter lucrative niches within the computer market. Both companies were far less interested in the current market than in those still in their infancy: markets that meld computers and communications, in which the product is not a software program but a whole array of services that go along with it.

But the most important similarity—and one that will show up time after time in the software arena—is that the target companies for both Microsoft and I.B.M. were companies that enjoyed something close to monopolies in their markets.

The Biggest Media Merger Yet

Everything about the $165 billion takeover of Time Warner by America Online is big. AOL is the largest Internet company. Time Warner is the largest media and entertainment company. Their proposed marriage will be the largest corporate merger in history. The implications of this merger are big too, for the way stocks are valued, for the way information services reach consumers, and perhaps for the way entertainment, politics and journalism evolve in a 21st-century corporate environment.

Some parts of the picture are clearer than others. The Internet stock boom looks less ephemeral today. For the consumer the deal poses no grave threat, because the companies operate in separate businesses. With or without the merger, consumers will eventually get a broad range of Internet services over high-speed cable wires. They will now get these services more quickly and probably more cheaply, and with a broader choice.

That is one result of a potent delivery-content marriage like this one. AOL serves about 20 million Internet subscribers. Time Warner serves 13 million cable subscribers and owns magazines, movie and music studios and cable channels with powerful brand names. AOL wants to expand its services to include Time Warner's news and entertainment programs and to provide Internet service over Time Warner's high-speed cable wires rather than slow-speed telephone wires. Time Warner wants to tap AOL's Internet customers, a market that advertisers crave but that Time Warner has been unable to create on its own.

Because the companies do not compete for the same customers, the merger is not expected to encounter antitrust problems. Yet there is a consumer threat that, to their credit, Steve Case, AOL's chairman, and Gerald Levin, Time Warner's chairman, flagged at yesterday's news conference and promised to solve. The issue is known as open access. By law, customers who tap into the Internet over telephone wires are provided nondiscriminatory access to the Internet service provider of their choice. But cable companies are under no legal obligation to provide nondiscriminatory access, posing the danger that they will control the content of the news and information that flows into homes by controlling the Internet service provider.

Mr. Case has lobbied the federal government to require cable companies to provide open access. But until now he was on the outside of the cable world looking in. Now he will own the cable wires himself, and he promised yesterday to commit the new company to open access. That is an important pledge that regulatory authorities need to monitor closely.

With open access, there is little economic reason to fear the merger. But there remains a gnawing anxiety about the societal impact of these huge media mergers. Continued consolidation among companies the size of Disney and ABC, Time Warner and AOL, MCI and Worldcom does not have to monopolize broadcasting, entertainment or Internet service markets to pose a serious threat. The mere creation of corporate behemoths is a danger in a country whose laws permit companies to buy political influence. The remedy to this political threat is not to scuttle mergers, but rather to fix campaign contribution laws.

The challenges that these big, multifaceted companies represent for journalism are just now coming into focus. For decades journalists, readers and viewers have been coming to grips with the concentration of ownership in newspaper chains and networks. In that environment, maintaining a wall between advertising and news departments has worked well. But building walls among the multiple compartments of these new information, entertainment and marketing giants may not be so simple. Yesterday Mr. Case said he was teaching Mr. Levin about "Internet time" and Mr. Levin was teaching him about journalistic tradition. That is an interchange that will have to take place not just in their company, but all across a media world that is being reshaped more rapidly than anyone could have predicted.

The acquisition of Time Warner by AOL in 2000 was at the time the largest corporate merger in history, creating the biggest media company in the world. Here Steve Case, CEO of AOL, takes the stage at the press conference to discuss the announcement. (Ruby Washington/*New York Times*)

CHAPTER 4

LEADERSHIP, PAST AND PRESENT

Ray Kroc, the founder and chairman of McDonald's, munches a Big Mac at a restaurant near company headquarters in Oak Brook, IL in 1971. A former milkshake-machine salesman, Kroc helped create an industry when he bought the McDonald brothers' small restaurant franchise. (*New York Times Pictures*/George Tames)

E VERY BUSINESS BEGAN ITS LIFE AS AN IDEA OR INKLING OR DREAM of an entrepreneur. Entrepreneurship has been defined as the relentless pursuit of opportunity without regard to resources currently controlled, a definition that succinctly captures the imagination, energy, and determination of countless American business visionaries, past and present.[1] But only a small number of these individuals created and sustained large-scale, successful organizations that outlived their founders, and only a fraction of these

1810	1848	1870	1871	1906
Cornelius Vanderbilt begins ferry business between NYC and Staten Island.	John Jacob Astor dies.	John D. Rockefeller incorporated Standard Oil.	J. P. Morgan establishes Drexel, Morgan & Company.	Sarah Breedlove develops hair product for African American women.

enterprises endured beyond a generation or two. In the early years of industrialization—as today—most new businesses failed, and most entrepreneurs did not make the transition from creative visionary to institution builder.

No wonder we are interested in the men and women who defied such odds.[2] Through insight, charisma, diligence, and extraordinary drive, some individuals harnessed the economic and social trends of their times to construct lasting businesses in a range of industries.[3] John D. Rockefeller, whose young life was dominated by the whims of a huckster father, grew up to make a spectacular fortune and build one of the world's most successful companies by imposing order on the chaos of the Pennsylvania oil fields. Madam C. J. Walker, born to former slaves in Mississippi, left her career as a laundress in middle age to create a hair-care empire that employed thousands of African American women and made her the first African American woman to become a self-made millionaire. In the late twentieth century, the Information Revolution gave the United States a new class of entrepreneurial leaders with new skills and visions, including Bill Gates and Steve Jobs. At the same time, corporations that had long outlived their founding entrepreneurs paid steep premiums for executive leadership (or at least the perception of it), as compensation for CEOs and other top management soared. In the twenty-first century, business is still personal. As these portraits of its leaders attest, it always was.

The men who emerged at the head of the first truly big companies in the late 1800s—men such as Rockefeller, Andrew Carnegie, and Jay Gould—both fascinated and repelled the American public (the term *robber barons* speaks to the schism in popular sentiment). Steel, oil refining, and even the railroads had existed before these men created their far-flung enterprises. But the skills they had and developed—in the promotion of new technologies, the ceaseless pursuit of

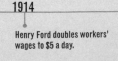
1914
Henry Ford doubles workers' wages to $5 a day.

1923
Alfred Sloan is named president of General Motors.

1954
Ray Kroc becomes general franchise agent for McDonald's.

1956
Warren Buffett founds an investment firm.

1962
Sam Walton opens the first Wal-Mart discount store.

competitors, the development of new management structures, and the manipulation of financial markets—transformed entire industries by creating firms of unparalleled scale and scope.

This growth fueled an unprecedented and rapid accumulation of personal wealth. For example, Carnegie, a first-generation Scottish immigrant, was worth half a million dollars (about $6.5 million in today's dollars) by 1863, when he was in his late twenties, and he commanded a price of $480 million (about $12 billion today) for the buyout of his enormously successful steel business in 1901.[4] His story, like those of some of his Pittsburgh neighbors, such as Henry Clay Frick, Andrew Mellon, and Henry Heinz, was one of rags to riches. So too was the story of Rockefeller, whose drive to bring stability and control to the young, boom-and-bust business of oil refining helped make him one of the richest Americans in history.[5]

On the one hand, the rapid rise of these new fortunes seemed gold-plated proof of the American promise of opportunity: a brass ring for millions to try to grab. On the other, the large corporations that fueled such gains in personal wealth and status wielded increasing power over potential competitors as well as the men and women who worked for them. Business practices viewed as unfair and anti-competitive brought scathing criticism from the press and triggered government action in the form of antitrust and labor legislation. Meanwhile, the families of wealthy business leaders often turned—generously, and very publicly—to philanthropy.

But the industrial managers and financial speculators were not the only leaders building big companies and amassing fortunes during the late nineteenth and early twentieth centuries. The national mass market also opened the door for entrepreneurs who were as passionate about their products as Rockefeller was about efficiency and control. Elizabeth Arden, née Florence Nightingale Graham, translated makeup and makeovers into a national brand

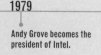

1979

Andy Grove becomes the president of Intel.

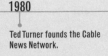

1980

Ted Turner founds the Cable News Network.

1987

Howard Schultz acquires Starbucks.

2003

Oprah Winfrey appears on *Forbes* list of billionaires.

2008

Steve Jobs takes leave of absence from his CEO position at Apple.

and a million-dollar company.[6] George Eastman, inventor of the Kodak camera, democratized photography and founded a business that dominated the industry for decades. And Henry Heinz, who as a teenager sold garden vegetables and his mother's bottled horseradish from a cart, triumphed over several big setbacks to turn his childhood hobby into an enduring enterprise.[7] Like Arden, Heinz understood that economic change—including rapid urbanization, industrialization, and rising incomes—was increasing the demand for consumer goods. At the same time, women were beginning to play important roles in deciding what households bought and what such decisions meant. Heinz used these insights and his passion for producing high-quality condiments to help create a mass market for processed foods and one of the largest companies in the industry.

Milton Hershey's passion was candy making. So strong was his commitment to the sweets business that even after two of his companies failed, he kept trying to find a way to make creamier, tastier caramels.[8] After more false starts and enormous effort, he built this business into a million-dollar venture, only to sell it in 1900 in order to pursue a fascination with milk chocolate. At the time, milk chocolate was a new, largely untested product, and techniques for producing it were guarded jealously by European chocolatiers.[9] But when Hershey developed his own recipe and began selling it in 5¢ bars, chocolate suddenly took the nation by storm. In 1911, Hershey's company racked up more than $5 million in sales (about $100 million today).[10] An unstoppable tinkerer, Hershey then focused his energy and idealism on building a factory town— Hershey, Pennsylvania—of utopian proportions. By the 1920s, the young town included a park with a roller coaster, a zoo, and well-funded schools for the families of town residents, most of whom were company employees.[11]

By the third decade of the twentieth century, the landscape that business leaders played on had become much more complicated. For one thing, labor unions became prominent, and executives had to learn to work with their constituents. For another, government's role in the economy had expanded greatly since the late nineteenth century. The early years of the 1900s saw the passage of a range of legislation—from the Pure Food and Drug Act to new securities regulation—designed to impose new rules and greater transparency on what business did. As mass consumerism took hold, households also began to play new roles, voting not only with their ballots but also with their dollars. By midcentury, entrepreneurs confronted a very different, and in some ways more restricted, market than their predecessors had two generations earlier.

Although the opportunities in America had changed since the late nineteenth century, they were greater than ever for enterprising individuals who could recognize them. Ray Kroc was one of these people. Kroc, a milkshake-machine salesman, was in his fifties when he first visited a hamburger joint in California run by the McDonald brothers. Although the brothers weren't interested in running a chain, they eventually allowed Kroc to bring their burgers, along with their assembly-line food preparation and golden arches, to other states. In 1961, Kroc bought out the business and continued building more outlets across the country, tapping into the mass appeal of quick, inexpensive meals of consistent quality. By the time he died in 1984, the 8,000 restaurants nationwide were bringing in more than $8 billion annually in sales, and McDonald's was well on its way to becoming an American icon.[12] In the 1980s, a vast majority of Americans ate at McDonald's at least once a year, and more young people found their first jobs at one of the chain's restaurants than anywhere else.[13] Although these jobs were largely minimum wage, McDonald's also offered lucrative franchise opportunities for eager entrepreneurs. In the 1990s, African Americans made up about 12 percent of these franchisees.[14] No other establishment of the time, perhaps in the nation's history, had such an effect on what Americans ate and how they experienced the workplace.

Chains of all kinds found their footing in the late twentieth century, from Sam Walton's Wal-Mart, which brought discounted goods of all kinds to rural communities and small towns, to Howard

Schultz's Starbucks, which helped introduce a high-end coffee culture to urban and suburban locales. Although both became ubiquitous fixtures of American commerce, their business philosophies contrasted sharply. Walton used everyday low prices to appeal to lower- and middle-class Americans, whereas Schultz created a powerful brand and experience that turned a cup o' joe into a $3 made-to-order specialty coffee drink. Whereas Wal-Mart relentlessly drove suppliers' prices down and drew criticism for its low wages and lack of benefits, Starbucks paid coffee growers premium prices and offered health insurance to part-time employees. Yet both firms became targets for social activists and lightning rods for a larger debate about the ethics of global trade. By the early twenty-first century, the power of labor unions had waned, and the government was generally friendly to business interests, but activists and consumers held corporations and their leaders to increasingly high standards regarding the conditions of workers around the world and the environmental impact of their operations.

From Wal-Mart and Starbucks to Apple and General Electric, many big businesses were infused with their leaders' values and personalities. But few firms were as closely linked to an individual personality as Harpo Productions, the company that television host Oprah Winfrey founded in 1986. In many respects, Winfrey *was* the business. Her talent and personality created the flagship product, *The Oprah Winfrey Show*. Her relationship with millions of viewers built a very powerful brand with a reach far beyond television, and her values fueled Harpo's other projects. By 2005, Winfrey had expanded her media empire to film projects, radio, and magazines. Her endorsement—of a book, a product, a person—had become a ticket to instantaneous, ardent, and widespread popularity (the term *Oprah Effect* spoke to Winfrey's impact). Winfrey's own wealth climbed with the ongoing success of Harpo. In 2003, she was the first African American woman to break onto *Forbes*'s annual list of billionaires. At the same time, she continued to make a series of important decisions about how to use her wealth—decisions that affected Harpo's future direction. One of the most important of these was her pledge in 2000 to build the Oprah Winfrey Leadership Academy for Girls in South Africa. Like her other community-based philanthropic endeavors, including her foundation and the scholarships she funded for students in the United States, these were both personal and business choices. They were also high-profile examples of the increasingly important concept of corporate social responsibility.

As the twenty-first century took root, Americans were holding corporations and their leaders to new benchmarks. Some of these involved the social and environmental impact of specific companies. Some involved the way particular companies did business or kept house (the Enron, Tyco, and Worldcom scandals of the late 1990s and early 2000s shone high-voltage spotlights on this issue). Still others involved executive pay and its relation to company performance. All of this translated into American's growing disenchantment with corporate leadership and into more volatility in the top ranks of American business; by 2005, the average tenure of a CEO had been halved to about five years from the long-term average of ten.[15] Yet viewed from the wide-angle lens of history, the fluctuations in the executive sphere of the early twenty-first century—from heroic corporate turnarounds and social initiatives to rampant fraud and disastrous falls from grace—were nothing new. America had always had a love/hate relationship with Big Business, and the corporate world had always counted both villains and heroes among its players. The heads of industry who transformed the work and life of a nation attracted some of the nation's most bitter criticism along with its greatest, most treasured expectations.

Carnegie, the Genius of Steel

BY JOHN CHAMBERLAIN

Burton Hendrick Makes an Absorbing Story of His Life

THE LIFE OF ANDREW CARNEGIE. *By Burton J. Hendrick. Two volumes. 434 and 425 pp. New York: Doubleday, Doran & Co. $7.50.*

In this sumptuous two-volume life of Andrew Carnegie Burton J. Hendrick, who became famous as the historian of American life insurance, has done two things: he has told the story of steel, with all that it has portended for the United States, and he has pursued, a patient and admiring Boswell, the quicksilver character of the "little white-haired Scotch devil" whose canny recognition of the value of inside information laid the foundations of one of the greatest of the American fortunes. The volumes, constructed out of a plethora of detail and written with an accomplished smoothness, have the virtues—which are undeniably many—of the "official" job, and the usual vice of partiality as well. Perhaps the virtues and the vice are inseparable; in any case they are welcome, for they provide the meat upon which our Stracheys feed. In failing to write the really definitive biography of the steelmaster Mr. Hendrick has nevertheless carried through an absorbing job.

Carnegie, whom Mr. Hendrick visualizes as a genius in the art of living, is a perplexing character. But Mr. Hendrick is perplexed by the perplexity his hero has caused in others. As the builder of America's first vertical trust, as the industrial wizard who was the most successful exponent of competition in a period that was leading John D. Rockefeller to seize upon the opportunities offered by combination, Carnegie was undeniably a superior man. There are those, like Allan Nevins, who exalt him because he stuck to the tenets of the Manchester economists, abstaining (as far as possible) from pools, always trying to give the best quality of steel, in times of depression, for the lowest price. To believers in competition, Carnegie shines as an honest business man where Rockefeller seems black as the ace of spades. But from the point of view of the elder Morgan, echoed so recently as a year ago by John Winkler, Carnegie was a menace to the "community of interest" that meant a stable financial community. Champions of Carnegie's indispensable partner, Henry Clay Frick, have been quick to call the steelmaster cowardly and insincere because he hid himself away in Scotland during the terrible days of the

Homestead strike of 1892, leaving Frick to break the Amalgamated Association of Iron and Steel Workers. Carnegie had formulated the golden rule of labor in a Forum article: "Thou shalt not take thy neighbor's job." Yet when Frick smashed the union in the Homestead plant Carnegie approved the hiring of nonunion men. But somehow Mr. Hendrick, in the face of the Frick admirers, absolves Carnegie: Frick becomes the misguided person who betrayed the Scotchman's better instincts. Just where the balance will rest in any definitive biography we do not know. But there are two sides to the question which Mr. Hendrick does not present as a choice. Carnegie being quicksilver, he takes different shape in the hands of different commentators. It is really amazing how diversely he can affect men who are agreed on most subjects.

Perhaps the answer to all jockeying for position [between his admirers and detractors] is that it is thoroughly mistaken: there is no need to take a man out of his functional position. It is, or should be, greatness enough for Carnegie that he domesticated the Bessemer converter in the American steel industry; that he picked men who know their way about the steel mills and could produce the best product for the least money; that he built the first vertical trust in America; that, in short, he was, with Rockefeller and Morgan, one of the outstanding builders of industrialized America. There is no necessity for claiming more.

Carnegie became a financier of steel by a process of brilliant opportunism. His eminence cannot be put down to luck, for his persistence would have made him great one way or another. As an employee of the Pennsylvania Railroad during and after the Civil War, the young Scotchman who had left Dunfermline with his father, mother and brother in the "hungry" '40s, was on the spot at the very moment that was propitious for an advance in the iron industry. The young Carnegie had made money by getting in on the organization of the first sleeping car manufacturing company, which was the work of Theodore T. Woodruff, not Pullman. His connection with the Pennsylvania enabled him to do this. As an inhabitant of Pittsburgh, Carnegie was on the spot when Drake's well opened up infinite vistas for the pioneers in oil. He made a small fortune in crude oil before Rockefeller was in the business. After the Civil War he worked his way into the iron industry. By the time he was 30 years old he had a wide variety of interests. Four companies—the Union Iron Mills, the Keystone Bridge Company, the superior Rail Mill and the Pittsburgh Locomotive Works—were largely dependent on his personal oversight. And besides, he was interested in the Columbia Oil Company, in Woodruff Sleeping Cars, in Adams Express, in several banks and insurance companies, and, here and there, in a street railway line. His income for 1863 was $47,860.67—this at the age of 27. And, as Mr. Hendrick says, the age of "swollen fortunes" was far in the future.

The result of Carnegie's canniness as an investor was that he had capital to finance his adventure in steel. Step by step the "little Scotch devil" of Tom Scott's characterization built his vertical trust—a trust that eventually controlled its product from the Lake Superior ore bed to the salesmen's order book. The vertical trust is not, of course, to be confused with a monopoly such as Rockefeller achieved in the business of selling refined oil, for it leaves room by its side for other competitive geniuses to build other vertical trusts. But no one could build as thoroughly as Carnegie; he could always undersell his rivals, for he kept scrapping his old machinery and made use of the best processes. The vertical trust of the Carnegie Company of the '90s owned or leased its own iron deposits in the Northwest, owned its own fleet of lake ore boats, operated its own harbor at Conneaut on Lake Erie, owned its own railroad to Pittsburgh, ran its own mills, had its own supply of coke (gotten by taking Frick of Connellsville in as a partner) and sold its own product to tube factories, nail factories and the like. When the time came, in 1901, for the "stabilization" of the industry with the formation of the United States Steel Corporation, which put an end to the brilliant competition provided by Carnegie methods, Carnegie and his associates were in a position to sell out at a tremendous sum to Morgan. And from 1901 on to the time of death the Carnegie story is one of a series of benefactions made possible by the huge profits derived from the sale.

Andrew Carnegie's steel fortune was derived from his development of steel
rails for the railways and from a fierce devotion to driving down costs.
He became a prolific philanthropist later in life. (Davis and Sanford)

Millionaires of Pittsburg— Twenty Years Ago and Now

Remarkable Material Prosperity Which Has Followed the Development

of the Steel, Oil and Coal Industries.

Pittsburg: Coal—Steel—Oil—and three hundred millionaires in little more than half a century. In 1850 the residents of the city did not think in millions, and those among them who used more than six figures in the estimates of their fortunes could be told off with the fingers of one hand. Twenty-five years later, with the oil excitement at its height, finds twenty, perhaps twenty-five men in the city in control of one or more millions of dollars. The last quarter of the century witnesses the first real fruits of the steel development, and the year nineteen hundred finds Pittsburg the home of one hundred and fifty millionaires, a number which has been doubled, approximately, since the new century began. Men of great wealth have sprung from obscurity like mushrooms, and the tales of their sudden acquisitions of fortunes read like chapters from the Arabian Nights. On this page are recounted, in brief form, the stories of [some] of the men who have come to the front in Pittsburg during the past twenty-five years, every one of whom has made his fortune either by his own foresight or by being rightly located at the right

time, and the stories of these men form, in large degree, the story of Pittsburg.

H. J. Heinz descended from one of the poorest families in Allegheny. His mother used to make excellent [horseradish], and when young Henry was old enough she would send him around to the neighbors to sell it. In that manner the family was kept alive. The demand for the [horseradish] grew, and Mrs. Heinz found that her friends would buy jelly from her as well as [horseradish]. It was not long until her entire time was taken up in making [horseradish], which her son peddled. Finally they converted their kitchen into a regular workshop, and in the Winter, when there was no fruit, Mrs. Heinz would make mincemeat for pies. Now there are "57 varieties," and Mr. Heinz is worth $20,000,000. From the modest little shop in the kitchen the plant has developed into one which employs several thousand persons, besides which Mr. Heinz has scores of farms upon which hundreds of farmhands are employed. Practically all of Mr. Heinz's immense fortune has been made within the past fifteen years, for it was not until that time that he began to branch out. Mr. Heinz, who is about 60 years of age, lives almost as modestly today as he did when he was a poor lad. He is much interested in Sunday school work, and all of his spare time and much of his money are devoted to advancing this work.

Henry C. Frick, without whose name any story of Pittsburg wealth would be incomplete, is in a class by himself. Born as the poorest of the poor, he has now reached the age of 60 years, and he has $1,250,000 to show now for every year he has lived, or $75,000,000 all told. Cold as an iceberg to the outside world, and as retiring as the most confirmed recluse is Mr. Frick, and he was made all the more retiring when Berkman, the Anarchist, almost killed him with a bullet and knife in his Pittsburg office many years ago. And yet Mr. Frick worked unceasingly and fruitlessly for the liberation of Berkman from his twenty-two year sentence, always insisting that he was but the ignorant tool, and should not have been punished so much. The world knows the story of Frick's finance and his victories. But few know, however, that it was his own cold courage and nerve that won him a position in the fight for the world's millions. Less than forty years ago the head of the famous banking house of Mellons in Pittsburg received a letter from one signing his name H. C. Frick, written from the coke country in the vicinity of Mount Pleasant, Penn. He asked the loan of $20,000 for a short time, and made no pretense at having much to offer as security. The nerve of the writer so impressed the head of the house that he instructed James B. Corey, relative of the now head of the Steel Corporation, to make a quiet trip into the wilds and look over this H. C Frick. Mr. Corey found the young man, a beardless lad, living in a little shack, which was divided into an office and a living room. Frick was not at home when Corey called, and Corey had time to look over the little place of living and business combined. Everything was so much in order that the Mellon messenger thought he would like to see more of the young man with the cast-iron nerve. He came. He conquered Corey. He outlined his idea to carry out which he would need $20,0000 in cash, and he wanted it at once.

"Give him the money," was the report of Corey on his return to Pittsburg, and the big banking firm did, and for that they have received many times the Biblical hundredfold, for from that time until now H. C. Frick's banking has in the main been done by the Mellon interests. It is unnecessary to remark that Frick made good on his first big move, which was buying some coking lands.

W. P. Snyder, who is talked of as the next President of the United States Steel Corporation, is one of the really self-made rich men of the city. He is worth possibly $15,000,000, and has cleared $1,500,000 on pig iron alone within the past twelve months. He began life the poorest of the poor, being the eldest son of a Methodist minister of Allegheny. His fortune has been made in the last twenty-five years. He is not more than 50 years of age, and owns lake steamship lines, coke ovens, coal mines, ore fields, and blast furnaces. The ability of Snyder always to stand on his own feet and his iron nerve are what brought him to the front. He was one of the very few who refused point blank to deal with those who formed the Steel Corporation many years ago, though his best friends told him time and again that his refusal would be his undoing. Snyder simply smiled and continued at his work, making pig iron, and to-day he is considered the king of all in this line of business. He alone has fought the steel corporation to a standstill, and, to-day the United States Steel Corporation is paying very heavy prices for its outside pig iron, prices it would never have thought of paying were it not Snyder who controls the market. Mr. Snyder is much of a home man, and one of the hardest men to obtain an audience with in Pittsburg.

Alex. R. Peacock perhaps holds the palm for picturesqueness among the many youthful millionaires of Pittsburg. His fortune is in the neighborhood of $15,000,000. His flight to wealth was somewhat rapid. Much less than twenty years ago, he was a poorly paid employee of a Broadway dry goods house. The now Mrs. Andrew Carnegie, on her shopping tour for a wedding trousseau, went into this house to buy, and became confidential with the trim little woman clerk who waited on her. There was a certain piece of goods which the lady wanted but which could not be found in the store. The girl called the floor manager, whose name was Peacock, and the difficulty was explained to him. Without knowing who the customer was or who she was to be, Peacock said:

"I will send to Europe, lady, and, have the goods made for you, if you wish." And he did. Mrs. Carnegie later spoke to her husband about the young man who had been so quick to grasp a condition. Mr. Carnegie looked in on Peacock, and soon had him in Pittsburg, where he afterward became a member of the Carnegie Steel Company. Peacock soon showed that he could sell other things than silks. He sold one order of 600,000 tons of steel rails to one customer, the biggest order ever sold by any one.

Standard Oil Men Celebrate Jubilee

Original Company Incorporated by Rockefeller and Associates Fifty Years Ago.

The fiftieth birthday of the original Standard Oil Company, incorporated at Cleveland, Ohio, on Jan. 10, 1870, by John D. Rockefeller, Henry M. Flager, Samuel Andrews, Stephen V. Harkness, and William Rockefeller, was celebrated yesterday with a luncheon and a dinner at which 135 officers of oil companies and heads of the departments were the guests. Many of the visitors came from refineries and oil fields in far parts of the country.

The oil men were welcomed at 26 Broadway in the forenoon by A. C. Bedford, Chairman, and W. C. Teagle, President of the Standard Oil Company of New Jersey, and after luncheon in the company's dining room viewed the first complete showing of the "Story of Oil," a nine-reel film depicting the process of producing petroleum and its by-products.

Last night the guests had dinner in the Council Room of the University Club. The speakers included John D. Rockefeller, Jr., E. T. Bedford, J. G. Milburn and W. C. Teagle. A. C. Bedford was toastmaster. Mr. Rockefeller read a letter from his father, founder of the original Standard Oil Company, in which the elder Rockefeller declared that in spite of all the controversy that has surrounded the company, he believed the public instinctively felt that no company could grow and prosper over a period of fifty years, as the Standard Oil Company has done, "unless its business was based upon scrupulous regard for its obligations as a great servant of the public."

Praising the character of the men who founded the company, Mr. Bedford gave that character as the primary reason for the greatness and success of the organization. John D. Rockefeller, he added, brought heat and light within the reach of the poorest, for his was the guiding hand from the very beginning.

"But now a great measure of his possessions are at the service of humanity, regardless of country, race or creed," said Mr. Bedford. "He seeks to advance the education that develops men's minds and he fights the disease that kills men's bodies. No man, living or dead, has given such vast sums to improve the fundamental conditions which make life worth living."

Mr. Rockefeller's Letter.

In his letter written from Ormond, Fla., John D. Rockefeller, Sr., said that he and his brother

William were the only persons alive of those who were present at the organization of the company. He traced the struggle of the early days when modern methods of financing had not been so fully developed.

"And here I may be pardoned for saying that the Standard Oil Company made a record without precedent in the history of commercial enterprises in turning to its weaker and bankrupt competitors," he continued, "and offering them a chance to recoup their waning fortunes without any risk on their part excepting the putting in of their plants, many of which were superannuated and illy equipped to cope with the more up-to-date refineries even of that time.

"I am happy that all who took stock prospered and did much better than they could have done under any other circumstances. I regret that some, from fear that this organization, strong and prosperous as it was, could not succeed, sold their stock."

Opposition was to be expected, the letter said, as the methods of economizing in every step "brought about an economic revolution, accompanied, as such great movements always are, by more or less antagonism from those who continued to prefer the old and obsolete methods."

Although he had not been active in the company for twenty-five years, said Mr. Rockefeller, he had followed its progress. He added that he believed it "not only commands but deserves the confidence of the general public."

Lincoln Filene, Merchant, Dead

Noted Retailer Who Headed Boston Specialty Store Built a Sales Empire

Advocate of Employees' Role in Management Was Civic Leader, Philanthropist

MARSTONS MILLS, MASS., AUG. 27—Lincoln Filene, a merchant who was born during the Administration of Abraham Lincoln, died today at his summer home. He was 92 years old.

Mr. Filene and his late brother, Edward, joined in building William Filenes's Sons Company, a store founded by their father, into an establishment that calls itself the world's largest specialty store.

Formed National Network

Mr. Filene helped build a $600,000,000-a-year national retail sales empire. His social consciousness caused him also to share benefits with his employees and the community at large.

He wrote a book in 1924, "A Merchant's Horizon," to urge wider adoption of the policies by which employees at Filene's in Boston took part in management.

"Every release of the worker to more use of his mind, every addition to his skill," he wrote, "means steadily better wages. We should have them. Society can well afford to pay a steadily rising wage bill so long as it is steadily enriched by new intelligence."

The Filene's store had long before set up an employee organization with power to arbitrate disputes on working conditions. In 1903, it introduced a profit-sharing plan. It was a pioneer in a minimum wage for women.

In 1912, it started Saturday summer closings, and in 1924 it added paid winter vacations to the usual summer holiday. It was an early organizer of a health clinic, insurance, credit union and retirement plans.

Beyond his own store's horizons, Mr. Filene helped found the American Arbitration Association, worked for codes of fair business dealings and aided in bringing about state systems of unemployment insurance.

Son of Immigrant

William Filene, his father, an immigrant from Prussia, had started a Boston store about 1849, and went on to other ventures in New York and Salem and Lynn, Mass. Lincoln Filene—he dropped his first name, Abraham, in 1933—was born in Boston April 5, 1865.

William Filene came back to Boston in 1881, and in 1890 turned over a growing store to his sons. They rapidly made it part of a national trend toward enlarging enterprises.

Edward, as president, in 1909, started an automatic bargain basement policy, in which quality goods were bought and sold at low prices, cut periodically and then given away to charity if still on hand after thirty days.

Lincoln, as chairman, a post he held at his death, handled personnel. In 1916, he got other merchants together to form a cooperative Retail Research Association and then an Associated Merchandising Corporation, a worldwide buying organization.

In 1929, he led a merger of Filene's—despite opposition by Edward—with Abraham & Straus, of Brooklyn, and F. & R. Lazarus & Co., of Columbus, Ohio, into the Federated Department Stores. Lincoln Filene served as chairman until last June 12.

The Federated network now comprises thirty-eight stores and branches in eleven states. In the year ended last Feb. 2, it achieved its record volume of $601,491,511 in sales. The net income was $23,510,924.

One of Thomas Edison's great competitors, George Westinghouse was a pioneer in the electrical industry. Westinghouse Electric's development of the U.S. electrical system fueled the company's success. (*New York Times*)

Ray A. Kroc Dies at 81; Built McDonald's Chain

BY ERIC PACE

Ray A. Kroc, the builder of the McDonald's hamburger empire, who helped change American business and eating habits by deftly orchestrating the purveying of billions of small beef patties, died yesterday in San Diego. He was 81 years old and lived in La Jolla, Calif.

Mr. Kroc, who also owned the San Diego Padres baseball team, died of a heart ailment at Scripps Memorial Hospital in San Diego, a McDonald's spokesman said. At his death he was senior chairman of McDonald's.

Mr. Kroc, a former piano player and salesman of paper cups and milkshake machines, built up a family fortune worth $500 million or more through his tireless, inspired tinkering with the management of the McDonald's drive-ins and restaurants, which specialize in hamburgers and other fast-food items.

He was a pioneer in automating and standardizing operations in the fiercely competitive, multibillion-dollar fast-food industry. He concentrated on swiftly growing suburban areas, where family visits to the local McDonald's became something like tribal rituals.

First McDonald's in 1955

He started his first McDonald's in Chicago in 1955 and the chain now has 7,500 outlets in the United States and 31 other countries and territories. The total systemwide sales of its restaurants were more than $8 billion in 1983. Three-quarters of its outlets are run by franchise-holders.

Richard G. Starmann, a vice president and spokesman, said at McDonald's headquarters in Oak Brook, Ill., that 1983 was a profitable year for the company, which is the United States' largest food service organization in sales and number of outlets.

What made Mr. Kroc so successful was the variety of virtuoso refinements he brought to fast-food retailing. He carefully chose the recipients of his McDonald's franchises, seeking managers who were skilled at personal relations; he relentlessly stressed quality, banning from his hamburgers such filler materials as soybeans.

Mr. Kroc also made extensive, innovative use of part-time teen-age help; he struggled to keep operating costs down to make McDonald's perennially low prices possible, and he applied complex team techniques to food preparation that were reminiscent of professional football.

In the major leagues of American business, Mr. Kroc's career was unusual because its enormous success was so late in coming. He was in his 50's when he went into the hamburger business, making himself president of the McDonald's Corporation in 1955. In 1968 he became chairman, and he took the title of senior chairman in 1977, when McDonald's purveyed more than $3.7 billion worth of fast-food fare, outselling its archcompetitor, the Pillsbury-owned Burger King, by 4 to 1.

McDonald's shares were a Wall Street favorite in the early 70's, before the bear market took hold. They reached a peak in January 1973 of around 77; investors who bought them when first offered in the mid-1960's had seen their wealth multiply more than sixtyfold.

Over the years, Mr. Kroc was repeatedly involved in controversy. The authors Max Boas and Steve Chain charged in a 1976 book, "Big Mac: The Unauthorized Story of McDonald's," that McDonald's had exploited its employees by forcing them to take lie-detector tests and by appropriating their tips. The architecture of McDonald's outlets was sometimes criticized, as was the nutritional content of the food. But one critic, the nutritionist Jean Mayer, once said: "I am nonfanatical about McDonald's; as a weekend treat, it is clean and fast."

A Commanding Figure

Mr. Kroc cut a commanding figure, his thin hair brushed straight back, his custom-made blazers impeccable, his eyes constantly check-ing his restaurants for cleanliness. The bulky rings on his fingers glinted as he ate his hamburgers with both hands.

"I guess to be an entrepreneur you have to have a large ego, enormous pride and an ability to inspire others to follow your lead," he once said.

But his leadership entailed a wish that his followers be, like him, driven by an unending urge to build and to excel.

Mr. Kroc established the McDonald's headquarters in Oak Brook, a few miles from the Chicago suburb of Oak Park, where he was born Oct. 5, 1902, the son of an unsuccessful real estate man whose family came from Bohemia in what is now Czechoslovakia.

Sold Milkshake Machines

Ray Albert Kroc went to public schools in Oak Park, but did not graduate from high school. In World War I, like his fellow Oak Parker, Ernest Hemingway, he served as an ambulance driver. Then, after holding various jobs, he spent 17 years with the Lily Tulip Cup Company, becoming sales manager for the Middle West.

But by 1941, "I felt it was time I was on my own," Mr. Kroc once recalled, and he became the exclusive sales agent for a machine that could prepare five milkshakes at a time.

Then, in 1954, Mr. Kroc heard about Richard and Maurice McDonald, the owners of a fast-food emporium in San Bernardino, Calif., that was using several of his mixers. As a milkshake specialist, Mr. Kroc later explained, "I had to see what kind of an operation was making 40 at one time."

"I went to see the McDonald operation," Mr. Kroc went on in a memoir published in The

New York Times, and suddenly insights gained during his years in the paper-cup business and the milkshake machine business mingled fruitfully in his mind.

"I can't pretend to know what it is—certainly, it's not some divine vision," he continued. "Perhaps it's a combination of your background and experience, your instincts, your dreams. Whatever it was, I saw it in the McDonald operation, and in that moment, I suppose, I became an entrepreneur. I decided to go for broke."

Franchise Is Initiated

Mr. Kroc talked to the McDonald brothers about opening franchise outlets patterned on their restaurant, which sold hamburgers for 15 cents, french fries for 10 cents and milkshakes for 20 cents.

Eventually, the McDonalds and Mr. Kroc worked out a deal whereby he was to give them a small percentage of the gross of his operation. In due course the first of Mr. Kroc's restaurants was opened in Des Plaines, another Chicago suburb, long famous as the site of an annual Methodist encampment.

Business proved excellent, and Mr. Kroc soon set about opening other restaurants. The second and third, both in California, opened later in 1955; in five years there were 228, and in 1961 he bought out the McDonald brothers.

In choosing franchise owners to manage the new outlets, Mr. Kroc and his associates looked, as he explained it in 1971, "for somebody who's good with people; we'd rather get a salesman than an accountant or even a chef."

Mr. Kroc's survivors include his wife, Joan, of La Jolla; a brother, Dr. Robert Kroc of Santa Ynez, Calif.; a sister, Lorraine Groh of Lafayette, Ind.; a stepdaughter, Mrs. Linda Smith of San Diego, and four granddaughters. A memorial service is planned for Friday in Oak Brook.

April 26, 2004

Estée Lauder, Pursuer of Beauty and Cosmetics Titan, Dies at 97

BY RICHARD SEVERO

Estée Lauder, the last great independent titan of the cosmetics industry, who convinced generations of women that her beauty creams were "jars of hope" in their quest for the eternal look of youth, died on Saturday at her home on the Upper East Side of Manhattan. Her family, in announcing her death, said she was 97.

"The pursuit of beauty is honorable," Mrs. Lauder used to say. And she clearly believed that the business of beauty was just as honorable. No one but a believer could have given so much of herself in becoming an internationally respected strategist in the age-old struggle against wrinkles, sags, bags and blemishes. Her weapons in that effort were creams, powders, ointments, potions and muds, many containing top-secret emollients. And if they didn't do the trick, she had an array of scents, equally secret in their constitution, that might befog man's vision of woman aging.

Her efforts resulted in the establishment of a company estimated to be worth about $5 billion when it went public in 1995 and she was given the title of founding chairwoman. In 2003, it had 21,500 employees and an estimated worth of about $10 billion. Its products are sold in more than 130 countries across five continents.

Estée Lauder Companies was not formally established until 1946 but its roots go back to the 1920's with facial creams concocted over a gas stove in a modest kitchen by Mrs. Lauder's uncle, John Schotz. It was nurtured financially and technically years later by Arnold L. van Ameringen, a Dutch-born industrialist. The company grew exponentially in the 1950's with the introduction of a bath oil called Youth-Dew, the creation of which is variously attributed to Mrs. Lauder and Mr. van Ameringen.

"I love my product," Mrs. Lauder once said. "I love to touch the creams, smell them, look at them, carry them with me. A person has to love her harvest if she's to expect others to love it."

Mrs. Lauder also loved to touch her customers. During the period when she was building her business, she invariably showed up at stores where her products were being introduced and, with no provocation at all, whip out a jar and rub its contents on the wrist or face of a prospective customer so that her skin would acquire "a gentle glow."

She also understood the rewards that come from generosity and she was known in the industry for her free samples and particularly for the concept of "gift with purchase." She introduced these creative marketing measures when her company was in its infancy and she was advised by an agency that the $50,000 she had available for advertising was not enough to have any effect.

Although she was protective toward those who trusted her to create effective products, she used stark candor to describe her competitors, all of them ferocious and all of whom she outlived by many years. She referred to Charles Revson as "my arch and implacable enemy" and she said that Elizabeth Arden was "not a nice woman, not a generous woman." She said that Sam Rubin of Fabergé was "patronizing even for those prefeminist days" and that although Helena Rubenstein may have looked like a czarina, "the skin on her neck was less than perfect."

Perfection in the face of woman consumed Mrs. Lauder, and so did her desire to make a lot of money and leave the conditions of her childhood behind her. "Someday, I will have whatever I want," she is said to have predicted many years ago. By the late 1980's, with personal assets of $233 million and a listing in Forbes's gallery of the 400 richest Americans, it was clear that she had made her prediction come true.

Although the mythmaking that is so much of the magic of the beauty industry led many women to believe that Estée Lauder was born in Europe to an aristocratic family, she was a New Yorker and not an aristocrat at all. Josephine Esther Mentzer was born at home in Corona, Queens, on July 1, 1908, according to several biographies, although her family believes it may have been two years earlier. She was the daughter of Max Mentzer, a hardware man who was the proprietor of a hay and seed store, and Rose Schotz Rosenthal Mentzer, a woman who was much interested in beauty regimens.

The Mentzers were hard-working immigrants and Esther, destined to become known to the world by the diminutive of Estée, recalled well the Christmastime wrapping of gifts of hammers and nails, her father's gifts to his customers.

In her 1985 autobiography, "Estée, A Success Story," Mrs. Lauder recalled her mother as "a Hungarian beauty whose mother was a French Catholic and whose father was a Hungarian Jew." She described her father as "an elegant, dapper monarchist in Europe, who, when transported to a new country, still carried a cane and gloves on Sundays."

In interviews conducted over the years with various journalists, Mrs. Lauder said much that indicated her beginnings were quite genteel and comfortable. But Lee Israel, whose unauthorized biography, "Estée Lauder, Beyond the Magic," was published in 1985, maintained that the Lauder family's life in a working-class Italian neighborhood was much more modest than Mrs. Lauder would acknowledge.

Whatever her circumstances, there was no quarrel about the suggestion that as a young girl, Estée, a petite blonde, was known for her lovely skin and her determination to always look good. This determination was heightened when, as a student at Newtown High School in Queens, she became interested in the work of her uncle, John Schotz.

He had come to the United States from Hungary in 1900 with considerable training in chemistry. People referred to him as Dr. Schotz, although it is not clear that he had a doctorate. Whatever his background, he created a number of beauty products, including Six-in-One Cold Cream, Dr. Schotz Viennese Cream and a number of fragrances.

Estée studied his homemade products closely and, since Dr. Schotz was no businessman, helped him to sell them. Estée said little about her past and it is not clear that she even graduated from Newtown High. But in school or out, she remained fascinated with his beauty aids and was still promoting them in 1930 when she married Joseph Lauter, whom she had been dating for about three years. He was the son of William and Lillian Lauter, who had come to the United States from the part of Austria known as Galicia. Mr. Lauter had tried his hand without much success in both the silk and button businesses. The name was changed to "Lauder" later in the decade.

Their marriage foundered and they were divorced in 1939. Their separation lasted until 1942, when Estée told her friends that Mr. Lauter was a very nice man and that "I don't know why I broke off with him." They remarried that December and remained together until his death in 1982.

In 1982, [Mrs. Lauder] demonstrated her approach to life. When she felt that her ruby and diamond tiara clashed horribly with her turquoise dress, she immediately switched to a more suitable gold and diamond crown. "You know how it is," she told Charlotte Curtis of The New York Times. "You have to wear something."

July 1, 1984

The Hot Ticket in Retailing

BY ISADORE BARMASH

BENTONVILLE, ARK.—Sam M. Walton, founder of Wal-Mart Stores Inc. and reputedly one of America's richest men, played the crowd last month at the company's annual meeting.

In the gymnasium of the local high school here, he greeted old friends, hugged women and roused 1,800 shareholders, employees and guests in song—from "The Star Spangled Banner" to the company cheer. "Give me a W," he intoned, and cheers and whistles reverberated off the red, white and blue-hung rafters.

And it didn't stop there. That afternoon the 66-year-old Mr. Walton and his wife were hosts at a barbecue for 700 at their home. In the evening, country singer Tammy Wynette crooned to the crowd at the Waltons' and lured Mr. Walton to join her at the microphone. The next day, in this small town tucked away in the northwestern-most corner of Arkansas, there were sports competitions, a boating trip and a forum for local and national politicians.

But if the ambiance of Wal-Mart's annual gathering was down-home and light-hearted, the balance sheet presented by company executives was pure sophistication. It told a tale of striking success in retailing, one that few of Mr. Walton's Northern brethren in the business could duplicate.

The 22-year-old discount chain, which operates largely in rural communities of 5,000 to 15,000 people in an ever-widening tier of 19 states in the South and Southwest, is the nation's fastest-growing retailer. The Bentonville-based company's growth rates in sales, profits, return on equity and other corporate barometers have been the highest in the industry since the late 1970's—a fact that did much to spark the cheers from employees who benefit from a generous profit-sharing plan.

"Wal-Mart is one of the very few general merchandising companies that are astutely managed, highly profitable and well positioned for the future," says Cathleen W. Mackey, analyst for the First Manhattan Company in New York. Adds Stanley H. Iverson, analyst for Duff & Phelps Inc., Chicago: "Wal-Mart is the fastest-growing major retailer in the United States and the No. 2 discount merchant behind K Mart. Its management, motivation, communications and responsiveness to change are unique in the retailing industry."

Much of the company's success has been laid to Sam Walton, its chairman and chief executive. Born in Kingfisher, Okla., Mr. Walton is a country boy who struck it rich by peddling discounted products to rural America—and struck it very rich, indeed. Last fall, Forbes magazine identified him as one of the wealthiest men in America, in the good company of Rockefellers, Hunts and Gettys. It is an achievement, however, that Mr. Walton, a wiry bundle of energy, company boosterism and general enthusiasm, is loath to discuss. He'd rather talk retailing and give credit to his employees.

There are, he says, not many secrets in the industry. "Anyone willing to work hard, study the business and apply the best principles can do well," he says. "I worked at it. I walked into competitors' stores. And I wandered into more stores than anyone else. I was fortunate in getting some smart people to work for me and we avoided mistakes that the others made. We learned from everyone else's book and added a few pages of our own."

Mr. Walton's stamp is everywhere on the company—just as it was at the annual meeting. But, analysts say, this very dominance by the company founder could develop into a problem for Wal-Mart as it moves forward. The silver-haired Mr. Walton insists he has no plans "to quit now nor at any other time" and insiders deny any potential problems with succession. But analysts worry that the high-flying company could be brought down by a new hand at the controls. There are concerns in the industry that Mr. Walton's departure could wound Wal-Mart in much the same way that Harry Cunningham's retirement hurt K Mart and Fred Lazarus Jr.'s death set back Federated Department Stores.

Another question stems from whether Wal-Mart can sustain its huge growth plans, which call for doubling sales every two to three years, opening between 100 and 125 stores a year and moving into new territories and businesses.

So far, Wal-Mart's rapid growth has been managed with remarkable vision. Its strategy combines an aggressive expansion program with a state-of-the art computerized merchandise information system, a tight rein on expenses, a strong distribution network and a progressive employee relations program.

In the last five years, according to the First Manhattan Corporation, a brokerage firm, Wal-Mart's annual sales grew by an average of 39 percent, higher than K Mart's 10 percent and Target's 29 percent. Wal-Mart, which is about one-third the size of K Mart, had $4.6 billion in sales for the 1984 fiscal year, which ended Jan. 31.

Margaret A. Gilliam, analyst for the First Boston Corporation, New York, estimates that sales will be $6.5 billion this year and is optimistic that its strong growth can be sustained. "We believe that Wal-Mart, with its highly motivated organization, lowest costs in the industry, commitment to planning for the future and a desire to be the very best will continue to forge ahead," she said.

Mr. Walton and his top team project sales of $12 billion in four or five years—three is more likely, analysts say—and a net income of about $300 million or more by then.

Wal-Mart's strategy is simple: It combines low operating costs, an emphasis on providing national brands at discount prices and an effort to dominate its market wherever it bases its stores. Unlike most retailers who justify rising prices and markups as a reflection of inflation, Wal-Mart trims prices by cutting distribution costs and putting pressure on suppliers to lower prices.

Its operations have given it competitive clout that has hurt its competitors. K Mart, its biggest competitor, may have inadvertently helped Wal-Mart.

"Sam Walton watched K Mart closely and learned from its mistakes," said John Ternes, a former K Mart district manager who now manages Wal-Mart's North Fayetteville, Ark., store. K Mart, he said, uses "too many imports and letters of credit that may have run up against the Southern stigma on imports and didn't let them take advantage of domestic opportunities.

And K Mart went too heavily into private labels when customers around here are very national-brand conscious."

Sam Walton knows his market as only a native to that circle of states would. His family moved from Oklahoma to Columbia, Mo., when he was young. In 1940, the University of Missouri awarded him a baccalaureate degree in business administration and he later spent two and a half years in Des Moines working as a trainee at J.C. Penney. His lessons learned, he bought a Ben Franklin franchise store in 1945. With his brother, James, a co-founder of Wal-Mart and now a senior vice president, he operated a franchised chain of 17 Ben Franklin Variety Stores, turning them into the largest regional variety store franchise in the country. In 1962, the brothers began Wal-Mart.

Not unlike Harry Cunningham, K Mart's former chairman, Sam Walton sensed the potential for discount stores, particularly in rural areas.

"We had a variety-store background," said Mr. Walton, interviewed in an office filled with mementos of his love of quail hunting, tennis and dogs. "The big discount entrepreneurs were in the East and hadn't come here yet. Even so, we were latecomers because there were already Woolco discount stores here, K Mart and Kuhn-Big K stores, along with small regional chains like ours. Later other discounters came. I had no vision of the scope of what I would start. But I always had confidence that as long as we did our work well and were good to our customers, there would be no limit to us."

Sam Walton has a cool intensity about him. He walks fast, plays a good, hard game of tennis and periodically takes off to hunt quail. At work, he usually spends the first four days of the week visiting Wal-Mart stores and comes to headquarters on Fridays for staff meetings.

Those who work closest with Mr. Walton say he has boundless energy and "an extremely positive attitude." Perhaps one reason is that his lifelong efforts have made him one of America's richest men, with assets of $260 million and more, mostly from company stock, according to the Forbes article. The Walton family owns about 40 percent of the stock, insiders another 8 percent.

And analysts are now high on the stock's potential. Although retail stocks will likely remain out of favor with investors in coming months, says Mr. Iverson of Duff & Phelps, Wal-Mart "is our first choice among all general merchandisers for the longer term." It has recently sold at $38 a share.

For workers, the profit-sharing plan is a boon. Wal-Mart last year contributed 8.2 percent of employees' salaries into the plan, which has a current, accumulated $158 million in its portfolio. Employees who have been with the company at least a year participate and a long-time employee's stake can be sizable.

As a visitor toured the headquarters with Mr. Walton, the chairman greeted a merchandise manager and asked what he figured his profit-sharing was worth. "Oh, about a million dollars or so, I guess," the long-time employee replied. He was serious.

But without the strong influence exerted by Mr. Walton, can Wal-Mart sustain its growth? Insiders say the lines of succession have already been drawn. Mr. Walton is said to have at least three or four likely candidates: The most likely may be Mr. Shewmaker, the 46-year-old president, followed by David Glass, 48, vice chairman, Donald G. Soderquist, 50, executive vice president for administration and distribution, and Alvin L. Johnson, 49, executive vice president for merchandise and sales.

Talking Business with Grove of Intel

New Approach to Hierarchy

The Intel Corporation has been an exceptional innovator. Organized and run by scientists, Intel developed the preliminary design that put a computer's brain on a single silicon chip. In a decade, the company has soared from a $1.9 million loss on $600,000 in revenues for 1969 to $77.8 million in earnings on sales of $662.9 million in 1979.

Intel has also earned a reputation as one of America's best-run companies—as original in management as in its product. Andrew S. Grove, Intel's 44-year-old president, talked about Intel's "corporate culture" in a recent interview with New York Times editors and reporters.

Q. We're struck by the open-shirt, casual approach at Intel. Is that essential? Or does it say more about California than about your business?

A. The "open-shirt" syndrome, golden chains and things—that is a very minor part. It's not so much that we advocate an informal approach—we don't care about the approach. The point is to eliminate a lot of the formality, the protocol, the symbols of management hierarchy; to make sure that we concentrate on the essence rather than on the form.

Q. Are you eliminating the symbols of hierarchy because you have no hierarchy?

A. Our approach to hierarchy is that we expect people to do different jobs. People obviously have different degrees of influence, and we pay people whatever a particular level demands in the marketplace.

Beyond that, though, we really try to make no further value judgment as communicated by appearances, parking spaces, offices, titles, the formality of titles. We try to beat into people that their work is very important for what it is.

Q. One has the impression that it is a sort of cliché within the California electronics business. Or is Intel unique?

A. Yes and no. There are other companies that are like us, but I don't think microelectronics is necessarily like this.

Q. If it's not a cliché, then what's the idea?

A. Do you know Alvin Toffler's notion that future organization is going to be "ad-hoc-racy"? The particular thing he says is that hierarchical management, hierarchically distributed power, will be unable to cope with the rapidity of change in environment and business conditions and technology. Therefore a very fluid movement of power will have to move back and forth from a hierarchical distribution to knowledge-based distribution, and back and forth.

One of the most difficult tasks is to make sure decisions are made by the most appropriate people to make decisions. Wait a minute, somebody says; decisions get made by a management chain. They really are not; you may go through the motions of making decisions, but you really aren't.

Q: Well, who does make the decisions?

A. The people coming in the door tend to be very young, very timid, very inexperienced. Somehow the notion that they have to decide the architecture of the next generation of microcomputers—they can't cope with that. They would dearly love to go to someone who looks like a manager, acts like a manager and exudes all the confidence in the world and have him make the decision.

Somehow we have to force them to cope with issues like this, and boy, the future of the company depends on some of these choices. You make a mistake on that one, and it's 10 years gone. And 10 years in this business is everything.

We made choices in the early years which were equally crucial; but if somebody had said, hey, you better watch out because the choice of silicon gate technology versus metal gate technology is going to mean the survival of this corporation, I would have been incapable of opening my mouth.

Q. But in short, this manager, this authority figure, who may be all of 30 years old, is already too out of touch with new technology to make the decision himself?

A. Not 30 years. Make it 40 years, and it's correct. That's where the person is that we are talking about. A few years out of school, a second-level engineering supervisor.

We are sitting around, about eight people, and we don't agree of course, that's the other thing. They are not timid in arguing about it; but somehow, sooner or later, they have to come out of that room with an architecture. And I can't help them. The only thing I can do is to make sure that when they beat each other up, nobody gets overwhelmed by one person being more vocal than the other, and to make sure they understand they have to make a decision.

Now this is where washing out some of the old symbols is useful. The more competent these people feel in this role, the more they accept that they really are expected to make a decision. It's kind of like we leave our stripes outside when we go into the meeting.

The Richest Man and How He Grew (and Grew His Company, Too)

BY JANET MASLIN

Review of Alice Schroeder's The Snowball: Warren Buffett and the Business of Life, *Bloomsbury, 2008.*

In 1940, 10-year-old Warren Buffett was taken to New York as a birthday gift from his father. Some kids yearn to see the circus and the zoo. Little Warren wanted to visit Wall Street.

While at the New York Stock Exchange he managed to meet Sidney Weinberg, senior partner of the investment bank Goldman Sachs, and engage him in conversation. At the end of their talk, Weinberg put his arm around the boy and asked, "What stock do you like, Warren?" People have been asking that question ever since.

Sixty-eight years later Mr. Buffett is said by Forbes to be the richest man in the world. He just announced a $5 billion investment in Goldman Sachs that should keep the company afloat and boost his own net worth. And his opinions are so hotly sought that "The Snowball," a biography with which he has enthusiastically cooperated, would be of interest even if it answered only softball questions. It approaches him seriously, covers vast terrain and tells a fascinating story.

Mr. Buffett made a smart choice when he chose Alice Schroeder as his Boswell. Yes, he found an appreciative biographer with whom he seems to have a warm rapport. But he also found a writer able to keep pace with the wild swerves in the Buffett story and the intricacies of Mr. Buffett's Berkshire Hathaway business empire.

He began dreaming up money-making endeavors from the time he was 6, and he hoarded his earnings. He would look at a dollar, but see the $10 it would eventually become when compounded. (He held off on major philanthropy until late in his life, ostensibly for that reason.) At 14, he made enough money delivering newspapers to file a $7 tax return. He deducted his watch and bicycle as business expenses.

Surely Mr. Buffett was the only student at his high school to own a tenant farm and earn more money than his teachers did. After that, "college was only going to slow me down," he recalls. Nevertheless he attended Wharton business school at the University of Pennsylvania and was as notable for goofy pranks and slovenly habits as for precocity.

A turning point came when he was rejected by Harvard Business School and decided to attend Columbia. One professor there was Benjamin Graham, author of "The Intelligent Investor." Graham became his mentor and role model. Exposed to Graham's idea of security analysis, "Warren's reaction was that of a man emerging from the cave in which he had been living all his life, blinking in the sunlight as he perceived reality for the first time."

The superhuman tenacity that he brought to sniffing out undervalued companies also served him well in his personal life. Unable to win the interest of Susan Thompson, he chased her father instead; eventually, she became Susie Buffett. They had three children, to whom a distant yet manipulative Dad was "the disengaged, silent presence, feet up in his stringy bathrobe, eyes fixed on The Wall Street Journal at the breakfast table." But Dad was putting his research to amazingly lucrative use. Only when Susie accidentally put dividend checks down an incinerator and scurried to retrieve them did she realize how much money her husband was making.

The story of Mr. Buffett's business rise is also a social climb of sorts, despite his cultivated folksy air. The book details his eyebrow-raising friendship with Katharine Graham of The Washington Post, an anomalous liaison since he claims that Daisy Mae of the "Li'l Abner" comics was his feminine ideal. In any case, Mr. Buffett required a constant supply of hamburgers and motherly care. He surrounded himself with Susie, a surrogate wife (Astrid Menks, whom he later married) and a close circle of other women.

Then there are the business stories that make it shockingly timely. Ms. Schroeder reports in depth on Mr. Buffett's reluctant involvement in the 1991 near-meltdown of Salomon Brothers with lessons on the risks of deregulation, the precariousness of derivatives and the dangers of involving government in bailing out financial institutions.

In shaping its definitive portrait of Mr. Buffett, "The Snowball" need not make excessive claims of his importance. With story after story, Ms. Schroeder makes that self-evident. "No group of shareholders in history," she writes, with one eye on her subject's life history and the other on his legacy, "had ever missed their C.E.O. as much as Berkshire's shareholders would miss Buffett when he was finally gone."

How to Stay a Titan

BY RON CHERNOW

On May 15, 1911, in a soft voice that belied the supreme drama of the moment, Chief Justice Edward White read aloud a 20,000-word opinion, ordering the breakup of Standard Oil for violating the antitrust laws. Thus ended a morality play that had riveted America for five years, ever since Teddy Roosevelt's trustbusters decided to teach the trust and its founder, John D. Rockefeller, a lesson in corporate citizenship.

Amid the current wave of corporate mergers, the specter of Standard Oil now hovers over a swelling antitrust debate. On Tuesday, the appeals hearing in the Justice Department's antitrust probe of Microsoft is scheduled to begin. Many critics have noted the often eerie parallels between Rockefeller and Bill Gates.

Standard Oil was the most feared and admired monopoly of its day, refining, distributing and marketing nearly 90 percent of America's oil. Microsoft produces 90 percent of the operating systems in new personal computers, prompting similar public ambivalence, for computers are now as indispensable to the economy as oil.

The saga of John D. Rockefeller abounds in cautionary tales for Bill Gates. Like Mr. Gates, Rockefeller earned his fortune in a new industry where the rules of the game had to be improvised. He invested in his first Cleveland refinery in 1863, just four years after oil was discovered in Pennsylvania. In 1870, he established Standard Oil to bring this chaotic industry under his control. While skeptics wondered whether the oil would last, Rockefeller exhibited a fierce, messianic faith in its future. As he coped with a chronic surplus of refining capacity, he lost all trust in competition and began to champion a new economic dispensation: cooperation, his euphemism for monopoly.

In building his empire, Rockefeller patented many tactics that would be outlawed by the Sherman Antitrust Act in 1890. He colluded with railroads to win lucrative freight rates, secretly bought out rivals, throttled oil producers by controlling the pipelines, and monopolized oil sales by slashing prices when interlopers appeared. Like Mr. Gates, he adhered to the gospel of high-volume, low-cost production, believing that he had vouchsafed something precious to humanity: cheap illumination by kerosene.

Mr. Gates, of course, is no less evangelical about computers. He stoutly denies that Microsoft is a monopoly because it has lowered prices and improved products. Yet falling prices for personal computers and constant upgrades of Windows technology don't really acquit him of being a monopolist; they simply affirm that he is a very smart monopolist. Many people assume that the trust kings of the Gilded Age simply gouged consumers and sold shoddy products. But Rockefeller was an enterprising businessman who boasted that, in its first 20 years, Standard Oil lowered retail kerosene prices to 7.5 cents per gallon from 23.5 cents— a drop only partly explained by sinking crude oil prices. The trust blanketed oil fields with efficient pipelines and pioneered marketing by tank wagons. It was dreaded more for its low, predatory pricing than for fleecing consumers. Incessant innovation and relatively cheap prices may be necessary conditions for maintaining a monopoly.

Rockefeller never construed his monopoly as an unlimited license to mint money. If he got too greedy, consumers could switch to substitutes— say, coal instead of fuel oil. Indeed, Edison's light bulb finally doomed the kerosene business that first formed Rockefeller's fortune, though he and Standard Oil were then rescued by the automobile. Rockefeller set prices high enough to guarantee substantial profits but never so high as to lure competitors back into the field. And he refrained from achieving a 100 percent monopoly, later confessing that he allowed a few dozen refiners to eke out a meager existence so he could cite competition in the industry.

The same qualities that make people like Rockefeller and Bill Gates matchless businessmen—a single-minded intensity, an implacable attitude toward competitors—prepare them poorly for the delicate art of public relations. Almost from Standard Oil's inception, Rockefeller was hounded by courts and legislators, yet he never conceded any legitimacy to public inquiry. He seldom granted interviews or allowed himself to be photographed. When Ida

Tarbell exposed his methods in McClure's Magazine from 1902 to 1905, making him America's most hated mogul, he didn't dignify her serial with a response. By the time Standard Oil hired its first publicist, in 1906, it had already lost the battle for public opinion.

Under fire from the Justice Department, Mr. Gates has awakened belatedly to the need to burnish his image, fielding a small army of aggressive public relations people. He now pops up in golf advertisements and on talk shows. The change in persona, if often cosmetic and unconvincing, at least acknowledges the need for greater accountability and the decisive role of public opinion in antitrust cases.

As Rockefeller's story illustrates, antitrust prosecutions tend to be highly political. Major cases are long, expensive and hard to win; trustbusters resort to them as weapons of last resort. Because Standard Oil adopted a strident, antagonistic tone toward investigators, it bore the brunt of Teddy Roosevelt's wrath. Some Standard Oil executives thought that U. S. Steel, International Harvester and other trusts forged by J. P. Morgan escaped prosecution by taking a more conciliatory approach.

In defying the Government's 1995 consent decree that prevented it from "bundling" its Windows operating system with its Internet Explorer browser—the fear being that Microsoft would unfairly parlay dominance in desktop computers into Internet control— Microsoft gambled on a hard-line approach. Yet, in refusing to make concessions, it has only invited wider scrutiny—as the Standard Oil precedent would have predicted.

If Microsoft seems an all-powerful colossus, it is actually far more vulnerable than Standard Oil. The oil trust was 20 times the size of its nearest competitor, the puny Pure Oil. Except for production, where its market share never exceeded 35 percent, Standard Oil owned the entire industry. The antitrust crusade against it was spearheaded by a ragtag band of maverick refiners, muckraking journalists and reform-minded attorneys general, supported by small oil producers from new fields in Texas, California and Kansas.

By contrast, Microsoft faces a phalanx of formidable competitors, including Netscape, Oracle, I.B.M. and Sun Microsystems. These powerful companies deploy hordes of lawyers, publicists and politicians to keep Microsoft on the defensive.

Even so, Mr. Gates remains popular, even heroic, among many Americans. The move to block him will succeed only if his competitors can convince the public that they aren't trying to win in the political arena what they have failed to achieve in the marketplace. So far, there are only glimmers of a mass popular revolt against Mr. Gates of the sort that Ida Tarbell and Teddy Roosevelt managed to engineer against Rockefeller.

If Standard Oil's fate argues for Microsoft to take a more cooperative approach, it also suggests that the Justice Department should avoid broad antitrust action against the company. Standard Oil presided over a comparatively static industry, with big technological shifts—like the advent of long-distance pipelines or oil tankers—occurring only two or three times a decade. The core products remained remarkably unchanged.

By contrast, the computer industry thrives on perpetual revolutions in the design, power and even purposes of its products. New technologies, like network computers or the Java programming language, have the potential to reshape the industry and subvert Microsoft's domination. The panicky, almost paranoid reaction of Bill Gates to his competitors is perhaps the strongest testimony to his underlying anxiety about his monopoly—an anxiety that seldom ruffled the sleep of John D. Rockefeller.

The Justice Department should insure that Mr. Gates doesn't abuse his operating system monopoly as he expands into new areas. At the same time, it should recognize that he can never rule his industry as absolutely as Rockefeller did the oil business. There's no need to re-enact the agony of the Standard Oil breakup.

Oprah Winfrey's Odyssey: Talk-Show Host to Mogul

BY PAT COLANDER

Here is a typical story from the pages of the improbable career of Oprah Winfrey: It's 1984, the 30-year-old host of a Chicago morning talk show is in North Carolina, on the set of Steven Spielberg's film "The Color Purple." Though she has no previous acting experience, she has been cast in an important supporting role in a lavish production of Alice Walker's Pulitzer Prize-winning novel.

Between takes, Ms. Winfrey is reading "The Women of Brewster Place," a novel by Gloria Naylor that describes the lives of seven black women living in a slum building in a place that sounds much like Boston or Philadelphia but could be just about any urban ghetto. Ms. Winfrey decides that she will try to secure the rights to the property.

Now it's April 1988, on a street-facade back lot at Universal Studios. Filming is being completed on a four-hour, two-part ABC made-for-TV movie. Not only does Ms. Winfrey star in the production, she is executive co-producer of it; Harpo (Oprah spelled backwards) Productions, the company of which she is chief executive officer and major stockholder, is in charge of what has become a multimillion-dollar enterprise.

"I had gone from a situation where I was totally intimidated [on the set of 'The Color Purple'] and had no control, to a situation where I had all of it," Miss Winfrey said in a recent interview in her office at Harpo Productions in Chicago.

This kind of turnabout is not a novelty to Ms. Winfrey; her rise from supporting player to executive producer reflects her dramatic transformation from television personality to media mogul. "The Women of Brewster Place," which begins next Sunday evening at 9, with the conclusion on Monday, March 20, at the same hour, is but the first of a number of full-scale feature-film productions Harpo has planned. Ms. Winfrey and Harpo have acquired the rights to Toni Morrison's "Beloved," a post-Civil War novel about a young, black woman haunted by slavery, and to "Kaffir Boy," the autobiography of Mark Mathabane, a black man who grew up amid the poverty and degradation of apartheid South Africa. (Quincy Jones owns the rights to the 1937 novel by the folklorist Zola Neale Hurston, "Their Eyes Were Watching God," along with Harpo. Many consider the book to be the definitive work about a black woman's coming of age in America.)

In fact, most Harpo projects are stalled at the moment. Of Ms. Winfrey's 40 employees—the majority are women in their 30's—18 work for "The Oprah Winfrey Show" and 21 work at Harpo Productions, most of them in public-relations. (At present, the film production and prime-time specials area has two full-time employees.) The small company will not be going ahead with any feature film making until the renovation of an 88,000-square-foot film and television production facility that will be Harpo's studios is completed early next year.

Harpo Studios, which will fill an entire square block just west of downtown Chicago, will be the largest film and television production house in the Middle West. It will also be the permanent home of "The Oprah Winfrey Show"—which Ms. Winfrey was able to gain ownership of from Cap Cities/ABC last November—along with several movie and television production studios and Harpo's corporate offices. Ms. Winfrey, whose net worth is estimated at upwards of $40 million, signs every check and makes all major decisions about Harpo projects. "If you're not taking responsibility for what you've earned, you could lose it," Ms. Winfrey said, adding with a laugh, "It would be easier to just go shopping."

She finds the power—her talk show is seen by approximately 10 million people each weekday—and the money "humbling," she said, and the more successful she is, the stronger she feels about her commitment to important work.

"You can never lose sight of the work," she said. Ms. Winfrey sees her mission as education and her medium as the black experience. "I really want to bring people closer to knowing themselves," she said. "In a society that is so media controlled, doing good film is one of the best ways to raise consciousness. You present the story and then you let people choose to change the way things are or not. I want to make a difference. I want that on my tombstone."

Ms. Winfrey viewed the making of "The Women of Brewster Place" as a learning experience for her and for Harpo. There hadn't been this kind of an assembly of black actors for any TV production since "Roots." The cast of "The Women of Brewster Place" includes Cicely Tyson, Olivia Cole, Robin Givens, Moses Gunn, Jackee, Paula Kelly, Lonette McKee, Barbara Montgomery, Phyllis Yvonne Stickney, Douglas Turner Ward, Lynn Whitfield and Paul Winfield.

Ms. Winfrey was determined to not abuse her authority—something she thinks is easy to do. She was the first one on the set every morning. "You can work 18 hours a day and still be pleasant," she said. "I made sure I knew everybody's name so there was no one thinking I was Miss Mightier-Than-Thou."

Ironically, it was Ms. Winfrey's movie work that provided the impetus as well as the means for her to take control of her talk show. "I wanted an extra week off," she said jokingly, as a simple explanation of what prompted her takeover of the program. Though she had a contract with ABC that she considered "perfectly good," she needed some balance in her life, she said. It was the clear viability of her opportunities as an actress that may have finally provided the necessary wedge for Cap Cities/ABC to agree to her gaining ownership of the program.

The evolution of the deal was, of course, much longer and more complex than Ms. Winfrey's comments would indicate. It started in September 1984. The name of the program had been changed from "AM Chicago" to "The Oprah Winfrey Show" and the format had been expanded from a half-hour to an hour. Ms. Winfrey had by then joined forces with [attorney Jeffrey] Jacobs, who began a search for a syndication contract. (The networks are prohibited by law from syndicating their own shows, making inevitable the introduction of a third party, such as King World, a giant in the syndication arena. In this instance, it may have tipped the balance in a critical way.) "It's always been my philosophy to try and control as much of your own destiny as possible," Mr. Jacobs explained in a recent interview. In mid-1986, an agreement was made with King World, which was already distributing "Wheel of Fortune" and "Jeopardy" in the Chicago market through WLS-TV—the local Cap Cities/ABC affiliate—to distribute "The Oprah Winfrey Show" across the nation (eventually through 198 outlets and in 90 percent of the country's markets).

At her instigation, part of the agreement stipulated that Ms. Winfrey would handle her own public relations. The primary function of the newly created Harpo Productions was to answer her fan mail (at present, the program receives about 2,000 letters each week).

The syndication of "The Oprah Winfrey Show," said Stephen W. Palley, chief operating officer of King World, was "a historic success, and a success of greater proportions than we had seen before. The show has huge household ratings and the kind of demographic advertisers like very much." The original syndication agreement made Ms. Winfrey a multimillionaire, but it was the combination of her personal appeal and King World's shrewd marketing that assured her future.

Within six months, the program became the highest-rated talk show in syndication—the third-highest-rated program overall behind "Jeopardy" and "Wheel of Fortune."

Projected revenues from licensing fees for the current season of the program are estimated at more than $100 million, and it's widely believed that Harpo collects at least half that. Ms. Winfrey is an industry phenomenon reminiscent of Lucille Ball.

The end of the ownership struggle marked another situation that had come full circle. In this case, it took five years.

Ms. Winfrey says that she was never more frightened than she was when she came to Chicago in January 1984 to be the solo host of a morning show with a reputation for failure. "Everybody, with the exception of my best friend, told me it wouldn't work. They said I was black, female and overweight. They said Chicago is a racist city" (all true, Ms. Winfrey acknowledges). She was also told the talk-show formula was on its way out.

When Dennis Swanson, then vice president and general manager of WLS-TV, and now president of ABC-TV Sports, came across Ms. Winfrey on an audition tape, he knew he had found the alternative to Phil Donahue. "When you've looked at as many audition tapes as I have, hers just jumped out of the stack," he said in a recent phone interview from his New York office. Within two months of her debut, she was beating Mr. Donahue in the local ratings.

Ms. Winfrey has been called a classic American success story. She was born in 1954—"the year the schools were desegregated," she said—in Kosciusko, Miss., where she lived on a farm with her grandmother. At age 13, she ran away and was finally sent to live with her father in Nashville. After five years of his strict discipline, she became a student at Tennessee State

University, with a job at a radio station in Nashville. Soon she was hired as a reporter/anchor for Nashville television station WTVF.

In 1976, Ms. Winfrey left Tennessee to be a co-anchor at WJZ-TV in Baltimore; two years later, she was made co-host of a morning talk show. Ms. Winfrey knew right away that she had found her niche. It was that job that led to "AM Chicago."

Ned Zachar, a media analyst with the Chicago investment research firm of Duff and Phelps, said in a recent telephone interview that he sees no reason why the "The Oprah Winfrey Show" would not continue to be an economic success. "It doesn't cost very much to produce. It's just Oprah in her studio talking about entertaining topics. People like to watch, and therefore advertisers like to advertise."

'Neutron Jack' Exits

Jack Welch vacated the executive suite last week after a two-decade run at the helm of General Electric, one of America's most successful companies, leaving behind a remarkable record of achievement and upheaval. Mr. Welch was a white-collar revolutionary, bent throughout his career at G.E. on championing radical change and smashing the complacency of the established order. His legacy is not only a changed G.E., but a changed American corporate ethos, one that prizes nimbleness, speed and regeneration over older ideals like stability, loyalty and permanence.

The General Electric Mr. Welch took over when he became chief executive in 1981 was the iconic corporation of the American century, the descendant of Thomas Edison's ingenuity. It had a hand in inventing the light bulb, the electric locomotive, steam turbines, the refrigerator, electric meters and motors, the jet engine, Silly Putty and synthetic diamonds. It was also an unflappable supertanker, unfamiliar with speedy change.

"Fix it, close it or sell it" was Mr. Welch's favorite slogan as he ordered his colleagues to get out of businesses in which G.E. could not be a market leader. He sold off and bought hundreds of companies as he sought to refocus on high-growth opportunities, mainly by expanding the company's reach into delivering financial and consulting services.

By not hesitating to get rid of slower performing operations, Mr. Welch engaged in what the economic philosopher Joseph Schumpeter called capitalism's "creative destruction." He earned the nickname "Neutron Jack" for dismissing 100,000 employees in his early days as chief executive. Rather than dwell on the human cost of such downsizing, Mr. Welch recalls the challenge with relish in his memoir, "Straight From The Gut," which will be published this week. One of his bequests to G.E. is the "vitality curve," which makes managers each year identify their top 20 percent of performers, who are to be nurtured, and the 10 percent who are the least productive employees, to be dismissed.

In making the company more like himself—brash and impetuous—Mr. Welch also courted trouble at times. He calls the 1986 acquisition of Kidder Peabody his worst mistake. The brokerage firm, sold in 1994, was embroiled in a series of insider-trading and false-accounting scandals. More recently, G.E. has stubbornly refused to clean the Hudson River of PCB's, and the company was unable to close its $45 billion merger with Honeywell because of European antitrust concerns.

Still, the insistence by Mr. Welch and his disciples on a more decentralized, leaner approach to business is credited with helping American companies outpace foreign competitors throughout the 1990's in adapting to rapid technological change. Indeed, Mr. Welch may have an even more impassioned following in Korea and Japan, societies that still need to overcome the complacency of entrenched corporations. The management revolution he started has not ended with his retirement.

PART II

THE CHANGING NATURE OF WORK

CHAPTER 5

FROM FARM TO FACTORY

Workers change shifts at the Detroit plant of the Chevrolet Motor Company in 1934
as an auto industry strike approaches. The oppressive conditions
of the Great Depression provided a powerful stimulus to organized labor.
(World Wide Photos)

N ITS BROAD OUTLINES, THE EVOLUTION OF WORK IN THE UNITED States has mirrored that of business—with profound implications for how Americans experience their everyday lives, economic possibilities, social place, and individual identities. Striking changes to the nature of work and the workplace began to take place in the later nineteenth century, with the shift from agriculture to manufacturing, and continue today as manufacturing increasingly gives way to service and knowledge work. Some of

1793	1823	1834	1836	1882
Eli Whitney develops cotton gin.	Merrimack Manufacturing Company begins textile production.	Cyrus McCormick patents horse-drawn mechanical reaper.	Massachusetts is first state to pass child labor law.	Frederick W. Taylor lays foundations of scientific management.

these changes have been material. For example, in almost all sectors, real (price-adjusted) wages and incomes have surged upward during the last 140 years. At the same time, the average workday in the early twenty-first century is shorter than that in 1850.[1] In fits and starts, women have poured into the workplace since the dawn of the First Industrial Revolution. But only in the past fifty years have women and minorities been able to claim an increasing range of professional roles. Other shifts have been intangible, such as our ideas about what companies and the government owe workers—in terms of a safe environment, job security, health care, and retirement benefits—and our sense of connection to others doing similar work. Through all this, the forces and pressures of economy, technology, government, and society have all had a hand in shaping our individual answers to a powerful question: *What do you do?*

In the colonial period and the early years of the republic, most Americans worked the land and tended livestock. Some were landowners, and farmers, themselves; some worked as day laborers or journeymen; and still others served under contract, as indentured servants pledged to work a certain number of years in exchange for passage to the New World. By 1800, about 30 percent of the men, women, and children of the nation's labor force were slaves.[2] The overwhelming majority of these people were African American (or Negro in nineteenth-century parlance), and most of them worked on farms or plantations, primarily in the southern states.[3] Ironically, it was around the same time, against the backdrop of a growing slave population, that the concept of free labor, or workers who could enter and leave a job of their own free will—without fear of retribution by the employer—took root among white Americans.[4] This arrangement gave workers more freedom in their relationship with employers. However, because

1886
AFL is founded in
Columbus, Ohio.

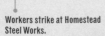

1892
Workers strike at Homestead
Steel Works.

1903
Milton Hershey begins
building factory town.

1908
Henry Ford introduces the
Model T car.

1910
AFL membership tops
1.5 million.

indentured servants had traditionally been supplied with room and board for the length of their service, it also gave employers the freedom to release workers when they could no longer afford to support them.[5]

Sixty years later, on the eve of the Civil War, more than half of the free labor force and most slaves still worked in agriculture. But many farms, especially in the North, had become more specialized, and some part-time subsistence farmers had turned full-time to other pursuits, including professional trades, in order to support their families.[6] At the same time, the First Industrial Revolution, in the form of textile factories, had arrived. In New England and other parts of the Northeast, entrepreneurs such as Francis Cabot Lowell sought women and, later, immigrants to staff their growing enterprises. Both groups responded, pouring into young mill towns in search of work. The first tremors of urban industrialization, which would soon transform the economy, were beginning to shake the scene.

First, though, Americans would fight their way through a bloody, wrenching conflict that tore the country apart for almost five years. Afterward, as the manufacturing sector expanded and new technologies—such as the mechanical reaper—reduced the demand for human labor on farms, the landscape of opportunity changed. Millions of immigrants and native-born workers still headed west to clear land for cultivation, as they had for more than a century. But many other Americans now turned to the cities, where the quickening tempo of industrialization was creating brand new jobs and livelihoods. In 1790, 95 percent of Americans had lived in rural areas; almost one hundred years later, in 1880, 72 percent did.[7] But by 1920, the share of Americans still living outside the cities had shrunk to less than half.[8]

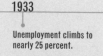
1933
Unemployment climbs to nearly 25 percent.

1936
UAW and CIO initiate strike against General Motors.

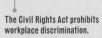
1964
The Civil Rights Act prohibits workplace discrimination.

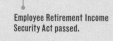
1974
Employee Retirement Income Security Act passed.

2000
Share of Americans working in manufacturing falls to 15 percent.

For most workers, the shift from farm to factory was not easy. Men, women, and children accustomed to working by the sun and the seasons found themselves measuring their days (and paychecks) by bells and clocks. The relative autonomy of farm work was replaced by the supervision and regulations of a foreman. Instead of the vagaries and grace of nature, factory laborers encountered the monotony of machine work and the caprice of the business cycle that could alter their hours and wages without warning. The rise of industrial production also disrupted the lives of artisans, once the primary sources of clothing and tools, prompting them to organize the first craft labor unions.[9] As workers and management tried to come to terms—economically and psychologically—with the imperatives of large-scale industrialization, conflicts erupted. The late nineteenth and early twentieth centuries witnessed frequent strikes, some of them—such as the Haymarket Riot in 1886—turning violent. In these ways and countless others, the Second Industrial Revolution affected the lives of millions of Americans.

Not all workers at the turn of the century experienced the benefits or shocks of industrialization directly, however. In 1900, more than 40 percent of the entire labor force still worked for themselves, as independent farmers, mom-and-pop storekeepers, craftsmen, doctors, and entrepreneurs.[10] And until World War I, African Americans remained largely in the South, engaged primarily in agricultural and domestic work. The transformation of work that began in the later 1800s, though ultimately inescapable, was not clear-cut—for individual Americans or for society as a whole.

Early in the twentieth century, the machine technology that had enabled the first factories was supplemented by a mechanical breakdown of *human* activity. Henry Ford's assembly line, fully operational in 1914, slashed dramatically the time it took to produce an automobile and the price a consumer paid for it. That year, Ford factory employees saw their labor reduced to the repetition of a single task, but they also saw their pay jump to $5 per day (nearly $100 today). Around the same time, an ambitious and exacting engineer named Frederick Winslow Taylor began advocating the analysis and measurement of a worker's activity in order to determine an optimal routine resulting in maximum productivity. Once this routine was established, Taylor believed, workers should be paid according to their individual output.[11] He called his system "scientific management," contending that it involved a complete "mental revolution" on the part of workers and management toward their roles and each other.[12] Scientific management proved enormously influential, not only in the early 1900s when it was introduced but across the twentieth century and into our own time.[13] The result, for generations of workers, was a workplace driven by single tasks; intense, ongoing scrutiny; and, often, mind-numbing monotony.[14] The result, for generations of managers, was a consistent focus on measured output as a proxy for employee performance, the creation and maintenance of safeguards against employee indolence (what Taylor called "soldiering"), and a subtle but pervasive distrust of industrial workers.

As scientific management was taking hold in the early 1900s, the power and numbers of organized labor were growing. Unions such as the Knights of Labor, the AFL (American Federation of Labor), and later the CIO (the Committee for Industrial Organization, renamed the Congress of Industrial Organizations in 1938) had attempted to organize laboring men and women, using strikes and other tactics to raise wages and improve working conditions.[15] Incidents such as the 1911 fire at the Triangle Waist Company in New York City, in which 146 trapped workers perished, stirred public sentiment and served as a grim reminder of how desperate these conditions could be.[16] In 1919 alone, more than four million workers participated in strikes.[17] By the end of the decade, 20 percent of the labor force was organized.[18]

The onset of the Great Depression in the early 1930s was marked by unprecedented levels of unemployment, increased poverty, and—at times—collective despair. For hundreds of thousands of people, joblessness was compounded by homelessness. "Hoovervilles," nicknamed for former President Herbert Hoover and his perceived inability to prevent the unprecedented down-turn, were groups of improvised dwellings made from cardboard and other debris. These makeshift shanty towns appeared on the outskirts of major cities across the country.[19] Hunger drove millions of people to soup kitchens and bread lines. In several cases, it also drove the desperate to converge on grocery stores and loot the shelves for food.[20] In part because of the severity of these conditions, the Depression years saw greater potential for large-scale social and political action than at any time since the Civil War.[21] In this environment, the 1937 sit-down strike staged by members of the young United Auto Workers (UAW) and the CIO against General Motors was a smashing victory for organized labor, making the UAW a force to be reckoned with in its own right and enhancing the broader importance and appeal of unions.

The Depression also provided the context for increased government involvement in and regulation of workplace issues. In 1935, Franklin D. Roosevelt signed the Social Security Act, establishing compensation for the retired and the unemployed. The same year, the Wagner Act guaranteed most workers the right of self-organization, that is, to form, join, or assist labor organizations, and outlawed unfair labor practices, including employer interference with union activity.[22] As the country rushed to meet the production challenges of World War II, union membership climbed steeply (table 5-1). By 1950, the share of union workers in nonagricultural sectors was more than 30 percent.[23] The era of Big Labor had arrived.

The new postwar work environment reflected a variety of trends and influences. Some were economic: since the late 1800s, the portion of workers in the agricultural sector had fallen steadily, from about half of all workers in 1870 to less than 10 percent in 1960.[24] Blue-collar work still dominated the economy, claiming about 50 percent of the workforce, but white-collar work was on a continuous rise.[25] By 1960, the vast majority of the labor force—at least 84 percent—consisted of hired workers; fewer and fewer, as a percentage of the whole, were self-employed.[26] Other changes in

TABLE 5-1

World War II by the Numbers

U.S. Military Production, 1941–1945

Tanks	86,000
Army trucks	2,000,000
Handguns and rifles	17,000,000
Rounds of ammunition	41,000,000,000
Aircraft	300,000
Aircraft engines	813,000

In Uniform, 1941–1945

Service men and women	16,000,000
Dead	405,000
Wounded	671,000

Economic output	1939	1945
Real GNP	$209 billion	$355 billion
GNP per capita	$1,598	$2,538
Government expenditures	$35.2 billion	$158.4 billion
Manufacturing	$18.1 billion	$52 billion

Labor force	1939	1945
Civilian employment	45,700,000	52,800,000
Armed forces	370,000	11,400,000
Women in the labor force	12,000,000	19,490,000
Unemployment	17.2%	1.9%

Consumption	1939	1945
Alcoholic beer	$3.4 billion	$7.5 billion
Food	$15.7 billion	$33 billion
Radios, TVs, records, and musical instruments	$420 million	$311 million
New and used cars	$1.6 billion	$357 million
Tobacco	$1.8 billion	$2.8 billion
Housing	$9.1 billion	$12.4 billion

Sources: *Historical Statistics of the United States, Colonial Times to 1970,* vol. 2 (Washington, DC: U.S. Dept. of Commerce, Bureau of the Census, 1975).

Thomas K. McCraw, *American Business 1920–2000: How It Worked* (Wheeling, IL: Harland Davidson, Inc., 2000).

the workplace and its conditions reflected shifts in societal attitudes and public policy, some propelled by union influence. From 1900 to 1960, for instance, the average weekly work hours for non-farm workers had fallen from nearly sixty hours to about forty.[27] Increasing government involvement at the state and national levels during these decades included regulation that required employers to pay workers overtime rates and contribute to compensation programs for work-related illness or injury.[28] In addition, many companies in the postwar period began offering pension plans, health insurance, and other benefits. In the space of a few generations, the kind of work most Americans did, and the terms on which it was done, had undergone a radical transformation.

Even more significant than these changes to the workplace, however, were the changes in the labor force itself. This was especially evident in the positions occupied by women and minorities. The young, single female labor force that staffed the New England mills in the early 1800s had set an important precedent. But most of these women had worked in the paid labor force only temporarily.[29] Much more important were the consequences of war in creating new opportunities for women. For example, labor shortages during the Civil War allowed women to replace male teachers; during World War II, the government encouraged women to take up jobs in factories and offices formerly considered "men's work," although most of these women (personified by the fictional "Rosie the Riveter") were expected to vacate these positions when the men returned.[30]

War and social action also opened doors for minority workers during the twentieth century. During World War I, the demand for factory work together with a temporary halt to European immigration opened new jobs—with better wages and positions—to African Americans. In what came to be called the "Great Migration," more than a million African Americans left the South for northern cities between 1910 and 1950. Finally, the movements and legislation of the Civil Rights era helped spur institutional change. The Civil Rights Act of 1964 made it illegal for employers to discriminate against workers on the basis of race, sex, or religion and established the Equal Employment Opportunity Commission.[31] In practice, however, equal representation in all professions, and thus equal earning power, was harder to achieve. In 2004, the median income of an African American household was just over $30,000, whereas the median income of a white household was nearly $47,000.[32] In 2005, only 3 percent of chief executives and 5.3 percent of physicians and surgeons were African American.[33]

By the late 1990s, the broad outlines as well as the look and feel of the American workplace were once again in flux. Union membership and influence, which had reached a kind of zenith in the 1940s and 1950s, continued to erode, as they had for some time in the late twentieth century. The proportion of workers engaged in agriculture reached an all-time historical low at less than 2 percent. Since the 1970s and 1980s, the fraction of Americans earning a living in manufacturing had been declining, as corporations moved many of their labor-intensive operations overseas. By 2000, the share of workers employed in manufacturing had shrunk to just 15 percent.[34]

As these aspects of the Second Industrial Revolution waned in relative importance, another revolution—this involving information processing and science-based production—was getting under way. The Third Industrial Revolution, or Information Revolution, necessitated different skills than its predecessors and placed a premium on knowledge work, including accounting, engineering, and management. This widespread transformation involved huge growth in the number of service jobs, and by the mid-1990s, more Americans worked in white-collar occupations such as service and sales than in all other sectors put together.[35] Not all service work was created equal, however. Growing disparities appeared in what people earned and what their career prospects were, many of these gaps based—more heavily than in the past—on educational attainment. In 2003, for example, the median income for families in which the householder had a high school education was $45,000.[36] With a bachelor's degree or more, this increased to $81,000; with a professional or doctoral degree, median income reached $100,000.[37]

For knowledge workers who enjoyed higher incomes and greater possibilities than many other Americans, the personal computer and the Internet had revolutionized the workplace and altered irrevocably the rhythms and contours of their days. On the one hand, e-mail, the BlackBerry, and other technologies had made communication faster, easier, and cheaper than it had ever been before. An executive in New York could log onto the company intranet and see up-to-the-minute productivity statistics from a call center in Bangalore. (Two decades earlier, this task would have taken weeks and involved much higher time and financial costs.) On the other hand, the same innovations that saved so much time and money for many knowledge workers made it possible to move white-collar positions overseas in a shift not unlike the earlier off-shoring of manufacturing jobs.

These facets of the Information Revolution, combined with the increasing integration of the global economy and the white-hot speed at which business moved, provoked both optimism and anxiety. Decades of union activism had helped make the modern workplace safer and had prompted many private-sector firms to grant health and retirement benefits to employees. Yet most service workers, who made up the fastest-growing sector of the economy, were not organized. And even unions could not shelter workers from the winds of globalization. Under these new conditions, the debate surrounding the mutual obligations of corporations, workers, and the government continued into the twenty-first century.

The Federation of Labor

Trades Unionists Form a New Organization.

COLUMBUS, OHIO, DEC. 11.—It will doubtless prove a trifle galling to Terence Vincent Powderly and his old Executive Board to learn that the trades unionists, who have been in session here for the best part of a week, have elected as President of their new organization, the American Federation of Labor, Samuel Gompers, the man he so vilified in the "secret" circular that was printed in to-day's TIMES. The fact that Mr. Gompers was elected without opposition may give Mr. Powderly an idea of the estimation in which he is held by trades unionists. The new organization has no fear of the Knights, for its membership was in existence long before they were thought of. It begins life with 25 trades unions as a nucleus. There is reason to suppose that as many more will join the fold before another convention is held. Its primary object is to secure as members every trade and labor union in the country, and some of the steps it has taken to attain this object show the shrewdness of the builders.

The salient points in the constitution of the new organization are as follows:

This association shall be known as the American Federation of Labor, and it shall consist of such trades unions as shall conform to the rules and regulations.

The objects of the Federation shall be the encouragement and formation of local trades and labor unions and the closer federation of such societies throughout the organization, of central trades and labor unions in every city, and the further combination of such bodies into State, Territorial, and provincial organizations, to secure State legislation in the interests of the workingmen.

The establishment of national and international trades unions based upon a strict recognition of the autonomy of each trade.

To secure national legislation in the interests of the working people and influence public opinion by peaceful and legal methods.

The basis of representation in the convention shall be from national and international unions of less than 4,000 members, one delegate; 4,000 or more, two delegates; 8,000 or more, three delegates; 16,000 or more, four delegates, and so on, and from each local trade district or union not connected with a national head, one delegate.

No organization which has seceded from any local, national, or international organization shall be allowed representation or recognition in the Federation.

The officers shall be an Executive Council, with power to watch legislative measures directly affecting the interests of working people and to initiate, whenever necessary, such legislative action as the convention may direct.

This council shall use all possible means to organize new national and international and local trades unions, and to connect them with the Federation.

While we recognize the right of each trade to manage its own affairs, it shall be the duty of the Executive Council to secure the unification of all labor organizations so far as to assist each other in any justifiable boycott, and with voluntary financial help in the event of a strike or boycott duly approved by the Executive Council. When a strike has been approved by the latter, the particulars of a difficulty, even if it be a lockout, shall be explained in a circular issued by the President of the Federation. It shall then be the duty of all affiliated societies to urge their local unions and members to make liberal financial donation in aid of the working people involved.

The revenue of the Federation shall be derived from a per capita tax of ½ cent. per month from each member in good standing.

The Federation elected as its President Samuel Gompers, of New York. He is Vice-President of the International Cigarmakers' Union, and is considered one of the cleverest leaders in the trades unions of the country. He was born in London of Dutch parents. He has been a resident of this country since his thirteenth year, and worked at his trade, cigarmaking, since he was 10 years old. He is now 37, and has been a member of his union since its organization in 1864.

Adolph Strasser, President of the International Cigarmakers' Union, expressed himself as follows, after adjournment:

"Our work will result in amalgamating all national and international trades unions. The Knights of Labor are defunct; it's no use talking about a corpse. They have lost 75 per cent. of the order in Massachusetts since Oct. 1 through the collapse of the Peabody strike."

Henry Emerich, of the National Furniture Makers, said:

"We have laid the foundation of a great labor movement."

George Block, National Bakers' Union, said:

"We will soon have all the trade and labor unions of the country in the Federation."

Christopher Evans, President of the federation of Miners and Mine Laborers, said:

"The convention could not have accomplished more."

The unions which favor the Federation have a membership of 350,000. Letters expressive of sympathy with the cause were received from unions having an almost equal membership. All the delegates took night trains for their homes. They seemed certain of having accomplished a good bit of work.

A Question Often Asked: "How About the Tariff and Homestead!"

Desperate Situation Brought About by Frick at the Carnegie Steel Works—It Has Cost Two Million Dollars Already and the End Is Not in Sight.

PITTSBURG, SEPT. 20.—It is three months to-day since H. C. Frick, Chairman of the Carnegie Steel Company, Limited, closed down the Homestead Steel Works and locked the doors of the plant against the 3,800 old employees unless they consented to work at his terms. That order, competent persons estimate, has cost the Carnegie Company $2,000,000, as the battle stands to-day. The end of this most sensational struggle between capital and labor is not yet in sight. The future is as threatening as it was on June 29.

The inception of the lock-out, the fight with the Pinkerton [detective agents] and sacrifice of ten lives, the reign of terror and defiance of civil authority, the calling out of the entire State militia, the attempted assassination of Mr. Frick, the introduction of thousands of new men from all over the country, the arrest and indictment of 167 of the strikers, and the sentence of Anarchist Berkman to twenty-two years in the Riverside Penitentiary—these are all familiar incidents to newspaper readers.

But with the situation of to-day it is different. The Carnegie Company claims to have about 22 men at work at Homestead. The strikers do not concede this, and well-informed reporters who visit the town daily say it is not so. The company is certainly not making armor plate, but it is turning out steel beams and such other lighter shapes as do not require either a large force or the highest order of skill.

It is also admitted that the present force of employees is not a satisfactory one. The personnel of the men is constantly changing, a score or two coming and going daily. There is dissatisfaction among those who are there. Compelled by their environment to live within the works, to put up with practically the same food day after day, with no opportunity for exercise or recreation, no entertainment, no friends, no society, it will be seen that their lot is not a happy one.

Until last Monday the company had been maintaining the new men at its own expense—an outlay of over $1,200 a day. Now the employees, while receiving their supplies from a common source, are compelled to pay their way. Naturally this has not contributed to their contentment. On the streets, where they venture frequently, but always in groups, [they] are hooted at by the children and the women, who hail them as black sheep and scabs.

Boarding-house keepers dare not entertain them on pain of boycott and persecution, and merchants and saloonkeepers, for the same reason, prefer their room to their patronage. So it is that, while Homestead is not marked by the personal violence which characterized it before the troops came, the feeling to-day is more bitter than ever.

Neither the general officers of the Amalgamated Association of Iron and Steel Workers nor the strikers themselves will admit that they are defeated. They persist in declaring that they will yet win the right. Hugh O'Donnell, the handsome and misguided leader of the strike, is in the Allegheny County Jail, with two charges of murder and two of riot hanging over his head. John Clinard and Thomas Critchlow are with him.

Up to a few days ago the general organization of the Amalgamated Association had contributed nothing to the support of the strikers. Its first assistance came in the shape of $10,000. Hitherto what money and supplies were distributed among the Homestead men were the contributions of sympathetic labor organizations the world over, the aggregate reaching over $100,000.

With this, their savings, and their credit the men have been able to get along without the $600,000 in wages they would have had had there been no lockout and strike. A considerable number of the strikers, too, have secured work elsewhere, many going to the smaller mills of Allegheny County and the Shenango and Mahoning valleys. The Advisory Board has the addresses of all these men, and makes the claim that it can call them all into Homestead, ready for work or any other emergency, in twenty-four hours.

The actual desertions from the ranks of the strikers have been very few in number. This is the most remarkable feature of the affair, when it is noted that it is over two months since the Carnegie Company took in its first batch of new hands. The only theory upon which to account for this is that the Amalgamated people have made up their minds that defeat at Homestead means the death of the organization, and they are not ready to die.

Business in Pittsburg has only recently begun to recover from the setback given it by the Homestead riots. Just how much that struggle lost this town in dollars and cents will never be known. The cost was little short of paralyzing. For seven weeks all the iron and steel works in the county, which produces more iron than any state in the Union save Ohio, were at a complete standstill.

During the height of the Homestead difficulty some of the foremost merchants in the city declared that they were conducting their business at a positive loss. Other communities were similarly affected, Mr. Frick, for instance, having received a plea from an insignificant town in Maine, signed by the Burgess, clergy, and merchants, begging him to arbitrate, as the continuation of the fight was injuring business in the aforesaid town.

Penned in Factories and No Fire Escapes

State's Investigators Find Things as Bad as Before Triangle Factory Fire.

One Place Locks Girls In

Box Factories Found Heaped with Rubbish and Fire Exits Blocked— Unsanitary

Candymaking Shops.

Complete negligence of sanitary arrangements in factories and measures of prevention or escape in case of fire, despite the warning of the Triangle Shirtwaist Factory fire, were disclosed by the investigators who have been quietly at work for the State Factory Investigating Commission in the last two weeks, and who testified at the second hearing of the commission at the City Hall yesterday. Some of the conditions complained of were admitted by manufacturers directly concerned.

Police Commissioner Rhinelander Waldo, testifying concerning conditions while he was Fire Commissioner, declared that even now the area of newer loft building east and west of Fifth Avenue, and between Eighth and Twenty-third Streets, constitutes a constant menace in case of fire. He urged the establishment of a single Department of Inspection, with a Commissioner in this city, and one for the rest of the State, to take charge and responsibility for the rigid inspection of factories which is now divided ineffectually among the Building, Health, and Tenement Departments, and the State Labor Department.

Samuel Gompers, President of the American Federation of Labor, presided at the session yesterday, but the hearing was conducted chiefly by Abram I. Elkus, counsel, for the commission.

Henry L. Schnur, Assistant State Factory Inspector, like Commissioner Waldo, declared that the present system of divided responsibility for factory inspection among many departments should be replaced by one centralizing the authority in a single department, and giving that department full power to enforce its orders. At present, he said, the State Labor Department has no authority over factories in New York City, except in ordering that passageways to fire escapes be kept clear.

Powerless to Stop Abuses.

"It is powerless to enforce orders for the widening or removal of even a narrow two-foot wooden stairway," he said. "Likewise, though we have found children under the legal age of employment concealed in engine rooms of factories, we have been unable to punish the factory owner because the present law does not make the mere presence of children in factories during working hours prima facie evidence of their employment. Nor can the department interfere in cases where employees handle dangerous material or poisonous chemicals without proper safeguards: and it can do no more than attach condemnation tags to food products which are found to be scandalously unclean. Merchants can, however, buy such products with the tags."

Actual conditions found in factories here in the last week were described by Miss Rose Schneidermann of 60 Second Avenue, an organizer of the Women's Trades Union League, appointed by Mr. Elkus to carry on such an investigation. She told of one paper box factory in West Broadway from which there was no egress save by wooden stairs with doors opening inward, or one fire escape leading to a narrow eight-foot blind alley. The alley itself, she said, was choked up with paper and rubbish, and would imprison employees hopelessly, while "the alley itself would burn out." In this factory, she said, the machinery was so located that it barred the fire escape windows, and the floors were littered with inflammable paper and trimmings. There were no fire appliances in it. She found six or seven factories in one block on Wooster Street, she said, where the same conditions obtained, and where the narrow and flimsy fire escapes were littered with old clothing, paper, and refuse.

Another Fire Trap.

Miss Schneidermann told of three other box factories in one building in the Bowery where all the doors except one opened inward, and the windows to the fire escapes were barred by iron shutters that also jutted out over the fire escape. In these factories girls under 16 years of age, she said, worked for from $4 to $9 a week.

Dr. Henry Moskowitz, secretary of the Joint Board of Sanitary Control recently established by the employers and employees in the cloak and suit trade, reported that of 1,738 factories 63 had been found to lack fire escapes altogether, 101 to have fire escape ladders defectively placed, 158 to have openings to fire escapes obstructed, 378 to lack even fire buckets, and 25, even since the Triangle fire, have kept their employees locked in.

Commissioner Waldo, testifying at the afternoon session of the commission, declared that he believed the fire drill to be of only secondary importance to fire prevention. Panic, he said, often upsets fire drill in case of real fire. He recommended that it be made mandatory upon factory owners to equip their factories with automatic sprinkling devices, which, he said, in the great majority of cases, would check the fire almost at its start. The Fire Department, which, heretofore, he said, had no control whatever over fire escapes, should have such power in order to provide ample and safe means of egress in case of fire.

"The fire escape in the Triangle factory," he said "was of such poor construction and location that even if it could have been used it would have taken hours instead of minutes to empty the building. As it was the victims, finding the fire escape blocked by open shutters, could only jump."

Fireproof Stairs Necessary.

"Outside fire escapes are inadequate," continued the Commissioner. "The ideal escape is the inclosed fireproof stairs in one corner of the building without any connection with the rest of the house and shut off by fireproof, self-closing doors. Where the building is large, this system should be replaced by one in which fireproof walls divide one part of the building from another, allowing the occupants to take refuge behind one of these 'fire bulkheads' while the fire is confined to the compartment on the other side."

Commissioner Waldo declared that smoking among employees can scarcely be prevented. The next best precaution, he said, is to see to it that all factories be kept clear of refuse and litter.

"Moreover," he said, "the building plans for new structures ought to be submitted to the Fire Department before they are approved by the Building Department. Even the newer loft buildings east and west of Fifth Avenue and between Eighth and Twenty-third Streets, are to-day a menace. They should be provided with fire bulkheads, shutting off one part of each building completely from the other in case of fire."

A driven, charismatic man, Samuel Gompers organized disparate craft and trade unions into a cohesive whole as the American Federation of Labor in the late nineteenth century. (World Wide Photos)

Henry Ford Expounds Mass Production

Calls It the Focussing of the Principles of Power, Economy, Continuity and Speed—Tells Why Accurate Machines Produce the Highest Standard of Quality—Says System Develops the Worker

BY HENRY FORD

Mass production in industry and its effect on modern life are discussed in the following article by Henry Ford, which was prepared for the thirteenth edition of the Encyclopaedia Britannica, and will be published in that edition, which will appear in the Fall. The article is printed here with the permission of the editors of the Encyclopaedia.

The term mass production is used to describe the modern method by with great quantities of a single standardized commodity are manufactured. As commonly employed it is made to refer to the quantity produced, but its primary reference is to method.

In several particulars the term is unsatisfactory. Mass production is not merely quantity production, for this may be had with none of the requisites of mass production. Nor is it merely machine production, which also may exist without any resemblance to mass production.

The interpretation of these principles, through studies of operation and machine development and their coordination, is the conspicuous task of management. And the normal result is a productive organization that delivers in quantities a useful commodity of standard material, workmanship and design at minimum cost. The necessary, precedent condition of mass production is a capacity, latent or developed, of mass consumption, the ability to absorb large production. The two go together, and in the latter may be traced the reasons for the former.

I. The Origins of Mass Production.

In origin, mass production is American and recent; its earliest notable appearance falls within the first decade of the twentieth century.

With the coming of power machines the seat of industry was removed from the homes of the people and a new work centre, the factory, was established. Much harsh criticism has been uttered against "the factory system," but it is perhaps fair to say that its first effect was to emancipate the home from being a mere adjunct to the loom or bench, and its later effect was to provide the home with means to develop the dignified status which it has now attained.

The early factory system was uneconomical in all its aspects. Its beginning brought greater risk and loss of capital than had been known before, lower wages and [a] more precarious outlook for the workers, and a decrease in quality with no compensating increase in the general supply of goods. More hours, more workers, more machines did not improve conditions; every increase did but enlarge the scale of fallacies built into business. Mere massing of men and tools was not enough; the profit motive, which dominated enterprise, was not enough. There remained the scientific motive, which grew eventually into what is called mass production.

The new method came after the failure of the mercantile and financial emphasis in manufacture. The advent and progress of financial control of industry were marked by two developments, the corporation and the labor revolt. Artificial combination of industrial plans into vast corporations for financial purposes was the first movement toward mass in industry. It proceeded on the theory that complete financial control would automatically bring complete profit advantage. The theory ignored many vital principles of business and its fallacy became apparent, but not before serious social hostility had been incurred.

Old Problems Abolished.

However, it was out of the social strife thus engendered that the idea began to emerge that possibly the difficulty lay in the neglect of scientific manufacturing principles. Industry was conceded to be necessary and useful; the service it rendered was regarded as of sufficient value to afford fair compensation for all engaged in it: it was therefore urged that the attention of management should be more directly focused on the actual labor processes that were employed. This led to what was known early in the twentieth century as the "efficiency movement" with its accompaniments of time study and similar methods, although its roots were laid in the experiences of sound industrial observers as early as 1878.

To the motor industry is given the credit of bringing mass production to experimental success, and by general consent the Ford Motor Company is regarded as having pioneered in the largest development of the method under a single management and for a single purpose. It may, therefore, simplify the history of mass production and the description of its principles if the experience of this company is taken as a basis.

Vision of Public Need.

It has been already suggested that mass production is possible only through the ability of the public to absorb large quantities of the commodity thus produced. These commodities are necessarily limited to necessities and conveniences. The greatest development of mass production methods has occurred in the production of conveniences. The automobile represents a basic and continuous convenience—transportation.

The commodities that conduce to civilized living are thus far enjoyed by only a small fraction of the world's inhabitants. The experience of the Ford Motor Company has been that mass production precedes mass consumption, and makes it possible by reducing costs and thus permitting both greater use-convenience and price-convenience. If the production is increased, costs can be reduced.

If production is increased 500 per cent, costs may be cut 50 per cent, and this decrease in cost, with its accompanying decrease in selling price, will probably multiply by ten the number of people who can conveniently buy the product. This is a conservative illustration of production serving as the cause of demand instead of the effect.

II. The Principles of Mass Production.

As to shop detail, the keyword to mass production is simplicity. Three plain principles underlie it: (a) The planned orderly progression of the commodity through the shop; (b) the delivery of work instead of leaving it to the workman's initiative to find it; (c) an analysis of operations into their constituent parts.

These are distinct but not separate steps: all are involved in the first one. To plan the progress of material from the initial manufacturing operation until its emergence as a finished product involves shop planning on a large scale and the manufacture and delivery of material, tools and parts at various points along the line. To do this successfully with a progressing piece of work means a careful breaking up of the work into its "operations" in sequence. All three fundamentals are involved in the original act or planning a moving line of production.

This system is practiced, not only on the final assembly line, but throughout the various arts and trades involved in the completed product. The automobile assembly line offers an impressive spectacle of hundreds of parts being quickly put together into a going vehicle, but flowing into that are other assembly lines on which each of the hundreds of parts have been fashioned.

It may be far down the final assembly line that the springs, for example, appear, and they may seem to be a negligible part of the whole operation. Formerly one artisan would cut, harden, bend and build a spring. To-day the making of one leaf of a spring is an operation of apparent complexity yet is really the ultimate reduction to simplicity of operation.

Typical Operation Described.

For its illustrative value let us trace the course of a spring leaf after it has progressed from iron ore through ingot, bloom and billet stages, and is rolled into strips.

1. Beginning as a strip of steel prepared by the steel mill, it is placed in a punch press for cutting and piercing. The workman puts the strip into press until it hits a stop, then trips the press. The cut-off and pierced place falls on the belt conveyor which runs along the loading end of a series of heat-treating ovens.

2. A second workman takes the pieces from belt conveyor and places them on conveyor which passes through the furnace (in which temperature is automatically controlled); thence they are deposited at a certain temperature by this conveyor at the unloading end of the furnace.

3. The heated piece is lifted with tongs by a third operator and placed in a bending machine which gives the leaf its proper curve and plunges it in oil the temperature of which is maintained at a definite degree by apparatus beyond the operator's control.

4. As the bending machine emerges from the oil bath the same operator takes out the leaf and sets it aside to air-cool.

5. The leaf is then drawn by a fourth operator through molten nitrate kept at a regulated temperature.

6. A fifth workman inspects it.

As a set of springs on the Ford automobile requires on an average of seventeen leaves, and

25,000 springs are an average day's output, this operation must be visualized as employing a great battery of lines similar to the one briefly described. As all the leaves in a spring are of different length and curve, from the bottom or master leaf to the top leaf, this operation must be visualized as one of many carried on simultaneously by different batteries of machines, each battery working on its own special size. All of these lines, with their various machines and operations, are converging on the point where the leaves are assembled into springs. The leaf whose progress we are describing is the simplest one.

We now continue the operation.

7. A sixth workman removes the leaf from the conveyor which carries it from the molten nitrate, and inserts a bolt through this and the other leaves required in the spring.

8. A seventh workman puts the nut on the bolt and tightens it.

9. An eighth workman puts on the right and left hand clips and grinds off the burrs.

10. A ninth workman inspects it.

11. He bangs the spring on a conveyor.

12. The spring passes the tenth workman, who sprays it with paint, and the conveyor carries the spring above the ovens where it was originally heated, and the radiated heat "force dries" the paint.

13. The conveyor continues to the loading dock, where the eleventh workman removes it.

One workman under the old system could attend the leaf through all these phases, or even make a complete spring, but his production would be limited. Where large quantities of the same article are to be made, the simplest operation may involve the whole time of one man. A one-minute operation will require one man

a full day of eight hours to accomplish it on 480 pieces. Now this simple part, a spring leaf, must be identical in strength, finish and curve with millions of others designed to fulfill the same purpose, and this becomes a complicated and delicate procedure requiring automatic machinery, the most accurate of measuring devices, pyrometer controls, "go" and "no go" gauges—in fact, the best facilities that can be provided by modern management.

The story of this minor part illustrates what is meant by orderly progression of the article through the shop. It goes to meet other parts of the motor car which have come from other parts of the plant by similar processes. The story illustrates also what is meant by delivering the work to the workman; every workman's task is prepared for him by some other workman, and delivered to his hand. The third principle also is illustrated—the analysis of a single job into its constituent operations.

The economies arising from this method are obvious. The machinery is constantly in use. It would be economically impossible to maintain all this equipment for the service of men occupied in the entire operation of making springs. Presses, furnaces, bending machines, oil baths would be idle while the workman progressed from operation to operation. Under mass production it is the work that progresses from operation to operation. Use-convenience in this commodity would be lessened, while price-convenience would be destroyed. Economy in machine hours is, however, only one element; there is also economy in time and material and labor. Mass production justifies itself only by an economy whose benefits may be transmitted to the purchaser.

Gives $10,000,000 to 26,000 Employees

Ford to Run Automobile Plant 24 Hours Daily on Profit-Sharing Plan.

No Employee to be Discharged Except for Unfaithfulness or Hopeless Inefficiency.

DETROIT, MICH., JAN. 5.—Henry Ford, head of the Ford Motor Company, announced to-day one of the most remarkable business moves of his entire remarkable career. In brief it is:

To give to the employees of the company $10,000,000 of the profits of the 1914 business, the payments to be made semi-monthly and added to the pay checks.

To run the factory continuously instead of only eighteen hours a day, giving employment to several thousand more men by employing three shifts of eight hours each, instead of only two nine-hour shifts, as at present.

To establish a minimum wage scale of $5 per day. Even the boy who sweeps up the floors will get that much.

Before any man in any department of the company who does not seem to be doing good work shall be discharged, an opportunity will be given to him to try to make good in every other department. No man shall be discharged except for proved unfaithfulness or irremediable inefficiency.

The Ford Company's financial statement of Sept. 20, 1912, showed assets of $20,815,785.63, and surplus of $14,745,095.57. One year later it showed assets of $35,033,919.86 and surplus of $28,124,173.68. Dividends paid out during the year, it is understood, aggregated $10,000,000. The indicated profits for the year, therefore, were about $37,597,312. The company's capital stock, authorized and outstanding, is $2,000,000. There is no bond issue.

Personal statements were made by Henry Ford and James Couzens, Treasurer of the company, regarding the move.

"It is our belief," said Mr. Couzens, "that social justice begins at home. We want those who have helped us to produce this great institution and are helping to maintain it to share our prosperity. We want them to have present profits and future prospects.

We think that one concern can make a start and create an example for other employers. That is our chief object."

Sees Great Danger in New Efficiency

Expert Tells of Harm to Worker in Scientific Management if Wrongly Applied.

That scientific management is like a keenly cutting knife, whose value depends upon how it is used, was the contention of Miner Chipman when controverting the idea that modern efficiency methods were harmful to the worker, at a recent meeting of the Efficiency Society. Mr. Chipman was commissioned about a year ago by over 300 of the workmen engaged in the United States Arsenal at Watertown, Mass., where the Taylor system had been introduced for a number of years, to investigate the operation of scientific management in that establishment.

His investigation proved to him that the great discontent with the new system of the workers in the arsenal was due not to inherent defects in the system, but to what Mr. Chipman considered the autocratic manner in which it had been applied. Mr. Chipman believes that unless the workers themselves understand the principles involved and the reasons for the methods of its application it is worse than useless to try to introduce the system.

In speaking of the attitude of organized labor toward the new idea he said: "Organized labor is waging a relentless war against scientific management in all of its varied forms. On the face of it, it would appear that organized labor is opposed to any program looking toward national efficiency. Superficially it is apparent that organized labor has taken a stand for restriction of output, and reversion to medieval industrial conditions. A careful examination of the underlying causes of this opposition will reveal that such is not necessarily the case. The fundamental difference between the view points of the worker and the employer lies in the definition of efficiency, and the methods and devices used in achieving it.

"The problem of national efficiency far transcends in importance the problems of shop management. We cannot hope to find a solution to these problems by attacking the more or less superficial expedients of the contending parties.

"The fundamental objection of organized labor to scientific management is that it lacks the spirit of democracy. Organized labor is a social ideal, not an industrial ideal, and defines efficiency in terms which are not confined to the shop or to the amount of work which a laborer can turn out. To organized labor efficiency means the efficiency of a man as a citizen, and not as a working unit. If a worker is used so that at the end of the day he is exhausted, does not eat his meal with relish, cannot read his newspaper in ease, pushes the baby away from him with annoyance, he is not an efficient citizen.

"Organized labor as a social force measures the efficiency of men in terms of life. Eight hours of labor represents but 33⅓ per cent. of the day's task. Labor insists upon the measurement of efficiency in terms of twenty-four hours a day. Labor desires a voice in the management of the shop, not because of an inherent interest in the shop itself, but because of a desire to regulate that portion of the day over which it is supposed to have no control.

"Industrial democracy, however, under the capitalistic system, can only come through a realization upon the part of employer and employee that their mutual interests are represented in the attainment of the highest possible social efficiency. The employer will not give up his autocratic methods of management and give way to any system of democracy wherein majorities, rather than intelligent suggestion, form the basis of operation.

"Industrial democracy will be obtained through an adequate system of industrial education. I do not mean by industrial education a mere class-room exercise. Industrial education as a part of the efficiency system must undertake the intelligent development of the worker as a constituent part of the management. Industrial education must tend toward the development of a sense of management responsibility, not merely a greater productive efficiency.

"The worker must be taught the intricate relationship between operation and operation, between cost and values, between efficiency and profits. Industrial education must teach the worker the principles of efficient management. The worker must realize and appreciate what the expert is trying to do."

June 15, 1930

Shift from Farm to City, Goes Steadily On

New Census Reveals the Unabated Movement of People From the Country to Urban Centres, Presenting a Striking Social and Economic Problem

BY LOUIS I. DUBLIN

When the results of the recent census are finally published, two facts will prove more interesting to students of population than any other in the maze of figures. The first is the count of the total population of the United States as of April 2, 1930; the second is the proportion of that population which lives in cities.

In an earlier article which appeared in THE NEW YORK TIMES of Sunday, May 4, I estimated the population at 121,500,000, and discussed some of the implications in the recent trend of population increase. In this paper I propose to consider the second question, namely, the growth of our cities.

In the last analysis, nothing is happening of greater consequence to the nation than the gradual urbanization of our country. As time goes on our sociologists, our business men and the general public all will have to take more notice of this tendency in our lives and prepare to meet it. While the situation may have the greatest possibilities for the general good, it has also, if not properly directed, very grave possibilities for national deteriorations.

Beginning of Immigration.

In a real sense, the history of the United States is the story of the gradual conversion of a rural population into a nation of city dwellers. During the Colonial period and up to the time of the first census in 1790, the country was almost altogether agricultural. The people lived on the farms. Industry was virtually unknown. The few towns served to meet the needs of the farmers in trade and in other ways. Only six cities had 8,000 or more people, and the largest of these, Philadelphia (including suburbs), had only 42,000 people.

But this condition could not long continue. The gates of the country were wide open and beckoned to the overcrowded, impoverished and adventurous people of Europe. There was a continent to be conquered, rich in the things that men wanted. Immigration which developed on an ever-increasing scale found its way, for the most part, to the cities.

It was in this way that the great number of large cities on the eastern seaboard arose and grew. Later, the same movement took hold in the Middle West; the Southwest and, finally, in the Pacific Coast States. But even as late as 1880, the great mass of our people still lived on the farms or in the smaller communities of less than 2,500. At that time only a third lived in the cities and towns of more than 2,500, and only 12.4 per cent in the twenty cities with 100,000 or more people.

How completely the situation has changed in the brief interval of fifty years! Impetus to the new movement was given by the development of industry for which the immigrant served as the principal labor supply. Some day a gifted historian will tell the story of this stimulated immigration—how literally millions of vigorous workers and their families from the peasantry of Southern and Eastern Europe were encouraged to find new homes and their fortunes in the steel mills and other industrial plants of Pittsburgh, Buffalo, Cleveland and a host of smaller towns in the Middle West. That was how our cities grew apace. The movement of enormous industrial and urban expansion was definitely on.

By 1920 the urban population had already taken the ascendancy, constituting 51.4 per cent of the 105,000,000 people. The urban population had increased 28.8 per cent in the previous ten years, while the rural population increased only 8.2 per cent. Cities with 100,000 or more people had increased in number to sixty-eight and included more than one-quarter of the total population of the country. If the suburban area lying within ten miles of the boundaries of these cities were included, the population embraced virtually 35 per cent of the whole country. Twenty-five cities had each more than 250,000 people. The population movement was definitely in the direction of the largest cities to meet the increasing demands of industry and trade which had located in them.

The increase in the cities in the decade between 1910 and 1920 was primarily at the expense of the countryside. The unprecedented development of American industry to meet the needs of the nations engaged in the great war and the decline of foreign immigration brought about an immense migration from the farms to the cities. The natural increase, that is, the excess of births over deaths, among the 50,000,000 people who lived in the rural area in 1910 would alone have amounted to well over 6,000,000 lives in ten years.

Losses on the Farms.

Nothing is more indicative of this situation than the reports of Dr. C. J. Galpin, the expert of the Bureau of Agriculture, showing that the last ten years have in all probability seen a loss of 4,000,000 people on the farms of the United States. His estimate is that the farm population is now only about 27,000,000. At the time of the 1920 census the number was more than 31,000,000. If Dr. Galpin's figures prove to be true, then a very interesting situation has developed. It means that only a little more than a fifth of our people now live on the farms. The other four-fifths make their living from commerce or from pursuits other than agriculture.

It is still too soon to discuss with safety the 1930 figures for the ten leading cities of the country and their relative ranking. New York, Chicago and Philadelphia will certainly head the list. Los Angeles has enjoyed an enormous growth of 114 per cent. But even its 1,250,000 will probably not exceed the count for Detroit. It will, in any case, pass from tenth place in 1920, to fifth place in the new list. Cleveland will occupy sixth place and St. Louis, Baltimore, Boston and Pittsburgh will follow in the order named. The first ten cities are, accordingly, the same as in 1920, but the order has been somewhat changed, because of the extraordinary increase in the population of Los Angeles and the slowing up of the growth of Boston.

Future Problems.

Nevertheless, when the urbanization we have been describing has gone as far as it can, there will be much to give concern. What sort of a people will we then be? Obviously, we shall be more alert, more energetic—even dynamic. But shall we also take on the other qualities of the machine age, of which the city is the outward symbol? What will happen to serious thinking? The contemplative life does not go well with the tempo of the modern city.

And how about the family? What will happen to this bulwark of civilization? We know only that in the era just passed the family has grown smaller and smaller and the ties which bind the members together thinner and thinner. These are the real dangers—that in our adaptation to life in the city, we may become a nation given over to restless work and to the enjoyment of superficial pleasures which our wealth will make possible. Shall we thus lose our souls?

Flint Strikes End in G.M.C. Plants

15,000 Will Return to Work Tomorrow After Agreement Providing Wage Increases

FLINT, MICH., APRIL 3.—Peace returned to the industrial scene here tonight with the announcement that more than 15,000 workers in General Motors plants would return to their jobs Monday morning, ending a strike which has paralyzed all operations of the Chevrolet Motor Company since Thursday night.

Indications that the peace might be of more permanence than has been the case since the United Automobile Workers of America and the General Motors Corporation signed an agreement on March 12 were apparent in the statement of Homer Martin, union president, that "our members are beginning to realize that this kind of procedure (unauthorized strikes) is not only harmful to the corporation, but also is detrimental to their own organization."

Settlement of the Chevrolet strike came this afternoon after a four-hour conference of union representatives and the management. Terms of the agreement included a general wage adjustment to go into effect Monday. It will provide increases, but the amount of the advance was not divulged.

Robert C. Travis, organization director for the union here, stated that the management also had agreed to discuss a union complaint that certain sections of the assembly line have been under-manned.

Slowing of Production Will End

It was learned that the agreement to provide a wage adjustment called for resumption of normal production schedules Monday, with union workers ending their "slow-down" strike, which has cut motor production from more than 400 to less than 250 units an hour.

Both Mr. Travis and Arnold Lenz, in charge of all manufacturing operations in Flint, Saginaw and Bay City, said that today's conference was very satisfactory. Sitting in at the conference with them were Harry B. Cohen, newly-appointed general plant manager for Chevrolet here, and a union committee of nine, including shop stewards from each of the company's nine departments.

Difficulties which have arisen in connection with the institution of the shop steward system have been blamed for the latest series of strikes in the Flint units of General Motors. From the conduct of today's discussions, it was apparent that union leaders were apprehensive over the recent strikes which they have termed "unauthorized and unfortunate."

After conferring with union organizers here today, Mr. Martin declared:

"We look forward toward the future with hope and confidence for an amicable relationship with the corporation, based upon real collective bargaining."

Foundry Is Unable to Open

Returning to work Monday will be 14,750 Chevrolet employees and 1,200 workers at Fisher Body Plant No. 2. The latter group was not on strike, having been forced into idleness when the Chevrolet plants were closed. It was announced this afternoon that the Chevrolet gray iron foundry and the Chevrolet parts manufacturing plant at Saginaw would necessarily remain closed for several days. This affects 7,400 workers.

James F. Miller, manager of the iron foundry, and Harold F. Spears, head of the parts manufacturing plant, said that their units had caught up with supplies from Flint and would remain closed for several days.

Mr. Martin, who took part in the Chrysler conference in Lansing to-day, will return to Flint tomorrow morning for a conference with shop stewards from all the General Motors plants here. It is understood that he will urge the men to live up to the terms of the agreement which the union signed with General Motors, and to have all grievances handled through the shop committees set up under that agreement.

Mr. Martin was asked about reports that he planned to purge against Communists and radicals within the ranks of the United Automobile Workers. He replied that "there are only a few Communists within our organization," and added that "the labor situation always has been in the hands of the union itself."

Denies Union Is Communistic

"I don't believe there are 25 active members of the Communist party among our 300,000 members," he said in his statement. "We are not Communists and we never will be, and we shall not become severely exercised by the fact that 25 of our members are Communists. The union is an economic organization and not political."

Of the recent strikes in Flint and Pontiac, Mr. Martin said the outbreak which took place Thursday "was the first major disturbance since the beginning of the truce on Feb. 11."

"The one in Pontiac resulted directly from the discriminatory policy of the local plant managers who took it into their own hands to fire men without just cause and then refused to put them back on the job or bargain seriously about it," he said.

"In Flint, the disturbances occurred when workers became suspicious about not having proper representation through the shop steward system and the lack of a proper understanding and consideration on the part of the plant managers.

"It has been quite obvious from the beginning that certain plant managers and even high officials of General Motors accepted the agreement with their fingers crossed, so to speak, with an idea of evading real collective bargaining if they could do so.

Sloan Statements Criticized

"Practically all of Mr. Alfred P. Sloan's statements to employees of General Motors have smacked of a desire to minimize the contract and leave the impression that the corporation has not made an agreement of any consequence with the union.

"However, these uprisings were spontaneous and not sponsored or backed by the international union. Upon request of the international officers, the plants were evacuated and it seems absolutely certain that all plants will be back in operation Monday morning.

"After the bitter strike through which the men have gone, and after years of oppression and discrimination, it is not surprising that such outbreaks occur. The surprising and gratifying thing about it is that the men accept the leadership of the international union with such discipline and cooperation," Mr. Martin concluded.

Nation's Industry Goes on 40-Hour Work Week

Gains in Two Years Under Wage-Hour Law Cited by Administrator

in Announcing New Standard

BY LOUIS STARK

WASHINGTON, OCT. 19—The standard work week for industries in interstate commerce, with some exceptions, will bc forty hours beginning Thursday as the operation of [the] Fair Labor Standards Act begins its third year.

This does not mean that an employer in a covered industry cannot conduct his establishment longer than forty hours a week, but if his employees work longer hours than the forty prescribed under the law, they must be paid at overtime rates of time and a half the usual scale.

When the law was passed, after two years of study, the objective of Congress was to fix a ceiling of forty hours for the standard work week and a floor of 40 cents an hour under wages and to abolish child labor.

After two years of the law's operations Colonel Philip B. Fleming, administrator of the Wage and Hour Division of the Labor Department, feels that it has been effective in building as a permanent principle a floor under wages in the economic structure of the nation.

Dire prophecies were uttered when the law went into effect but threats that wholesale displacements of employees would result because of employers' inability to pay the minimum wages have not been borne out by the experience under the law. Perhaps this has been due to the gradual approach toward full fruition of the act. For the first year overtime rates were required only of employers working their establishments above forty-four hours a week, and the second year the standard work week was dropped to forty-two and now it is to be forty hours.

By Easy Stages to Goal

The method of attaining the act's goal of a universal 40 cents an hour for industries in interstate commerce, or in the production of goods for interstate commerce, is automatic. The first year the minimum wage was 25 cents an hour, for the following six years the minimum was set at 30 cents and thereafter 40 cents would be the final rate.

By penalizing overtime Congress hoped to encourage the employment of additional labor and it is felt that substantial gains have been made in this direction. The minimum-wage provisions were also designed to discourage cutthroat competition and to raise the consuming power of those at the bottom of the economic ladder.

Outside the University of Miami Coral Gables campus in 2006, a representative from the SEIU translates from Spanish to English a message of support from U.M. janitor Leonor Ramierez. Janitors had been on strike for eight weeks when an agreement was finally reached. (Barbara P. Fernandez for the *New York Times*)

A. F. L. and C. I. O. To Unite Today; Discords Arising

Meany and Reuther to Wield Single Gavel—Eisenhower Will Speak by Phone

Complaints Are Voiced

Teamsters' Pact With Leftist Metal Miners Frowned On—Racial Issues Loom

BY A. H. RASKIN

The biggest labor federation in the free world will be born in the Seventy-first Regiment Armory here today.

The organization of 15,000,000 unionists will start functioning when George Meany and Walter P. Reuther jointly bring down a single gavel at 9:30 A.M.

Even before the historic fusion of the American Federation of Labor and Congress of Industrial Organizations became official, however, internal strife began asserting itself.

Leaders of the old C. I. O. denounced a mutual aid pact between the International Brotherhood of Teamsters and the Mine, Mill and Smelter Workers Union, which the C. I. O. had kicked out five years ago on charges of Communist domination. The fight will be carried to the twenty-nine-member executive council of the new federation.

The C. I. O. also balked at full-scale admission of the teamsters to the new industrial union department. That union's 1,250,000 members made them the largest group in the A. F. L. Mr. Reuther, former president of the C. I. O., said he favored letting part of the truck union into the industrial department. Other high C. I. O. officials said they would vote to keep it out altogether.

Race Bias Issue Looms

The founding convention of the merged federation also seemed headed for behind-the-scenes trouble on the explosive issue of racial discrimination. The all-Negro Brotherhood of Sleeping Car Porters expressed disquiet at the prospective entrance into the amalgamation of two independent railroad unions. It charged that both still barred Negroes from membership.

There were strong signs last night that AFL-CIO officials already had made it clear to the two rail unions, the Brotherhood of Railroad Trainmen and the Brotherhood of Locomotive Firemen and Enginemen, that the new group would expect them to end discriminatory practices if they came in. It was understood that the heads of the two unions had indicated their readiness to recommend corrective action by their organizations, thus reducing the danger of discord.

Despite these birth pangs, aides of Mr. Meany, the organization's president-designate, expressed certainty that the convention would be harmonious and that all the fighting would be done in private. They minimized the danger that any permanent scars would be left by the intramural battles.

President Eisenhower will salute the combined organization in a telephone talk at 2:30 P.M. from his headquarters in Gettysburg, Pa. He is expected to indicate the tone he hopes the Republican Party will take in its approach to unions in the 1956 campaign.

He will talk against a backdrop of intense controversy within his party on whether to be friendly or cold to the leaders of organized labor. Yesterday two Republican Senators expressed widely divergent views on this point.

Senator Barry Goldwater of Arizona, chairman of the Republican senatorial campaign committee, called for a crackdown on misuse of union funds by "power-hungry labor bosses." He made his demand in a nationally televised interview.

Senator Clifford P. Case of New Jersey, on the other hand, told labor editors here that unions had "a clear right to encourage members to exercise their franchise at the ballot box." He described as "hysterical" such statements as those by Senator Goldwater that labor leaders were building up huge "slush funds" to capture control of the Democratic party and the Government.

The President is expected to take a cordial tone in his greeting to the convention. His decision to talk directly to the 1,450 union delegates instead of sending a written message was made after consultation with Secretary of Labor James P. Mitchell. The latter has made no secret of his disagreement with the Goldwater position.

Mr. Meany refused to comment on any of the incipient squabbles. It was indicated that action on most of the early problems would be put off until the midwinter meeting of the executive council in February. Until then "the Geneva spirit" will prevail, one high unionist said.

The New Boss

BY MATT BAI

Purple is the color of Andrew Stern's life. He wears, almost exclusively, purple shirts, purple jackets and purple caps. He carries a purple duffel bag and drinks bottled water with a purple label, emblazoned with the purple logo of the Service Employees International Union, of which Stern is president. There are union halls in America where a man could get himself hurt wearing a lilac shirt, but the S.E.I.U. is a different kind of union, rooted in the new service economy. Its members aren't truck drivers or assembly-line workers but janitors and nurses and home health care aides, roughly a third of whom are black, Asian or Latino. While the old-line industrial unions have been shrinking every year, Stern's union has been organizing low-wage workers, many of whom have never belonged to a union, at a torrid pace, to the point where the S.E.I.U. is [one of] the largest and fastest-growing trade union[s] in North America. Once a movement of rust brown and steel gray, Big Labor is increasingly represented, at rallies and political conventions, by a rising sea of purple.

All of this makes Andy Stern—a charismatic 54-year-old former social-service worker—a very powerful man in labor, and also in Democratic politics. The job of running a union in America, even the biggest union around, isn't what it once was. The age of automation and globalization, with its "race to the bottom" among companies searching for lower wages overseas, has savaged organized labor. Fifty years ago, a third of workers in the United States carried union cards in their wallets; now it's barely one in 10. An estimated 21 million service-industry workers have never belonged to a union, and between most employers' antipathy to unions and federal laws that discourage workers from demanding one, chances are that the vast majority of them never will.

Over the years, union bosses have grown comfortable blaming everyone else—timid politicians, corrupt C.E.O.'s, greedy shareholders—for their inexorable decline. But last year, Andy Stern did something heretical: he started pointing the finger back at his fellow union leaders. Of course workers had been punished by forces outside their control, Stern said. But what had big labor done to adapt? Union bosses, Stern scolded, had been too busy flying around with senators and riding around in chauffeur-driven cars to figure out how to counter the effects of globalization, which have cost millions of Americans their jobs and their pensions. Faced with declining union rolls, the bosses made things worse by raiding one another's industries, which only diluted the power of their workers. The nation's flight attendants, for instance, are now divided among several different unions, making it difficult, if not impossible, for them to wield any leverage over an entire industry.

Stern put the union movement's eroding stature in business terms: if any other $6.5 billion corporation had insisted on clinging to the same decades-old business plan despite losing customers every year, its executives would have been fired long ago.

"Our movement is going out of existence, and yet too many labor leaders go and shake their heads and say they'll do something, and then they go back and do the same thing the next day," Stern told me recently. A week after the election in November, Stern delivered a proposal to the A.F.L.-C.I.O. that sounded more like an ultimatum. He demanded that the federation, the umbrella organization of the labor movement, embrace a top-to-bottom reform, beginning with a plan to merge its 58 unions into 20, for the purpose of consolidating power. If the other bosses wouldn't budge, Stern threatened to take his 1.8 million members [including retirees] and bolt the federation—effectively blowing up the A.F.L.-C.I.O. on the eve of its 50th anniversary. Stern's critics say all of this is simply an excuse to grab power. "What Andy's doing now with his compadres is what Vladimir Putin is trying to do to the former Communist bloc countries," says Tom Buffenbarger, president of the union that represents machinists and aerospace workers. "He's trying to implement dictatorial rule."

The implications of Stern's crusade stretch well beyond the narrow world of organized labor and into the heart of the nation's politics. The stale and paralyzed political dialogue in Washington right now is a direct result of the deterioration of industrial America, followed by the rise of the Wal-Mart economy. Lacking any real solutions to the growing anxiety of working-class families, the two parties have instead become entrenched in a cynical battle over who or what is at fault. Republicans have made an art form of blaming the declining fortunes of the middle class on taxes and social programs; if government would simply get out of the way, they suggest, businesses would magically provide all the well-paying jobs we need. Democrats, meanwhile, cling to the mythology of the factory age, blaming Republican greed and "Benedict Arnold C.E.O.'s"—to use John Kerry's phrase—for the historical shift toward globalization; if only Washington would close a few tax loopholes, they seem to be saying, the American worker could again live happily in 1950.

About the last place you might expect to find a more thoughtful and compelling vision for the global age is in the fossilized, dogmatic leadership of organized labor. But Andy Stern is a different kind of labor chief. He intends to create a new, more dynamic kind of movement around the workers of the 21st century. And if some old friends in labor and the Democratic Party get their feelings hurt in the process, that's all right with him.

Re-engineering the Union

Stern . . . is about as far from a tool-and-dye man as you can get. His father built a profitable legal practice in northern New Jersey by catering to small Jewish businesses, helping their owners make the jump from corner store to full-service retailer. After college, where, by his own account, he mostly avoided thinking about classes or the future, an aimless Stern took a job with the Pennsylvania welfare department, compiling case histories for aid recipients. The department's social-service workers had just won the right to collective bargaining, and a group of young idealists, Stern included, seized control of the local union.

Unlike most union bosses, who rise up through the administrative ranks, ploddingly building alliances and dispatching their enemies, Stern spent most of his career as an organizer in the field, taking on recalcitrant employers and bargaining contracts. In 1984, John Sweeney, then the president of the S.E.I.U., summoned Stern to Washington to coordinate a national organizing drive. When Sweeney ran for president of the entire A.F.L.-C.I.O. in 1995, Stern helped run his campaign; after Sweeney won, the brash and ambitious Stern maneuvered to replace him as head of the S.E.I.U. The ensuing drama was a classic of labor politics. Before an election could be held, Sweeney left the union in the hands of a top lieutenant, who wasted no time in firing Stern and having him escorted from the building. As Stern tells the story, he vowed that he wouldn't set foot back in the L Street headquarters unless he was moving into the president's fifth-floor office. Six weeks later, his reform-minded allies in the locals helped get him elected, and he became, at 45, the youngest president in the union's history.

Having grown up around his father's small-business clients, and having spent much of his adult life at bargaining tables, Stern had learned a few things about the way business works. He came to embrace a philosophy that ran counter to the most basic assumptions of the besieged labor movement: the popular image of greedy corporations that want to treat their workers like slaves, Stern believed, was in most cases just wrong. The truth was that companies in the global age, under intense pressure to lower costs, were simply doing what they thought they had to do to survive, and if you wanted them to behave better, you had to make good behavior viable for them.

Stern talks about giving "added value" to employers, some of whom have come to view him, warily, as a partner. At about the time Stern took over the union, his locals in several states were at war with Beverly Health and Rehabilitation Services, an Arkansas-based nursing-home chain. The company complained that cuts in state aid were making it all but impossible to pay workers more while operating their facilities at a profit. Stern and his team proposed an unusual alliance: if Beverly would allow its workers to organize, the S.E.I.U.'s members would use their political clout in state legislatures to deliver more money. It worked. "I do believe Andy's a stand-up guy," says Beverly Health's C.O.O., Dave Devereaux.

At the same time Stern was employing inventive labor tactics to work with business, he was also using new-age business theory to remake the culture of his union. When Stern came into power, the S.E.I.U. represented a disparate coalition of local unions that identified themselves by different names and maintained separate identities. This was the way it had always been, which was fine in an era when employers and unions were confined to individual markets. To Stern, however, this was now a problem. If his members were going to go up against national and global companies, they were going to have to convey the size and stature of a national union. "You know your employer is powerful, so you want to believe you're part of something powerful as well" is the way he explained it to me.

Stern hired a corporate consulting firm versed in the jargon of the new economy and undertook a campaign to "rebrand" the union. He used financial incentives to get all the local branches of the union to begin using the S.E.I.U. name, its new logo and, of course, its new color. In some respects, the S.E.I.U. now feels very much like a Fortune 500 company. In the lobby of its headquarters, a flat-screen TV plays an endless video of smiling members along with inspirational quotes from Stern, as if he were Jack Welch or Bill Gates. The union sold more than $1 million worth of purple merchandise through its gift catalog last year, including watches, sports bras, temporary tattoos and its very own line of jeans. (The catalog itself features poetry from members and their children paying tribute to the union, along with recipes like Andy Stern's Chocolate Cake With Peanut-Butter Frosting.)

In all of this, Stern's critics in other unions see a strange little cult of personality. Another way to look at it, though, is that Stern understands the psychology of a movement; workers in the union want to feel as if someone is looking out for them.

As the S.E.I.U. was soaring in membership and strength during the late 90's, much of big labor was seeing its influence further erode. And there were those who thought the S.E.I.U. wasn't doing enough for the movement as a whole. Cecil Roberts, president of the mineworkers, personally challenged Stern to follow the example of the mineworkers' legendary leader John L. Lewis, who helped build up the entire labor movement in the 1930's. But Stern

demurred. Just running the union was taking all of his time, and what was left he wanted to spend with his son, Matt, and his daughter, Cassie. There would be time later, when his children were older, to think about reshaping the future of American labor.

Then, all at once, Stern's personal world collapsed. A little more than two years ago, Cassie, 14, who was born unusually small and with poor muscle tone, became ill after returning home from a routine operation, stopped breathing in her father's arms and died. In the aftermath, Stern's 23-year marriage to Jane Perkins, a liberal advocate, unraveled. He rented an apartment in northwest Washington and shed most of his furniture, hurling himself into his work at the union. He is very close to his 18-year-old son, but his son splits his time between his parents' homes. On weeks when Stern is alone, he told me, he looks forward to stopping by the Dancing Crab, a local bar, to eat dinner alone and read the paper. "I'm in a very transitional moment of life," he says.

"When Cassie died," Stern said, "it was like: 'I'm 52 years old. How many more years am I really going to do this? Why am I so scared to say what I really think?'" If he were a religious man, Stern told me, he might think that it was not a coincidence that he was given, through his loss, so much free time and clarity at the very moment when organized labor was in crisis. He says it would be comforting to believe he has been chosen for a mission. It is clear, from the way he says this, that part of him believes it anyway.

Big Labor's Big Brawl

Stern's plan to rescue the American worker begins with restructuring the A.F.L.-C.I.O. Since the 1960's, a lot of struggling unions have chosen to merge rather than perish, to the point where there are half as many unions in the federation today as there were at its height. Stern argues that this Darwinian process, so lamented by labor leaders, is in fact healthy, and hasn't gone far enough. Unions, he says, work best when they're large enough to organize new workers at the same time as they fight battles on behalf of old ones, and when they represent a large concentration of the workers in any one industry.

Stern's 10-point plan would essentially tear down the industrial-age framework of the House of Labor and rebuild it. The A.F.L.-C.I.O., he says, would consist of 20 large unions, and each union would be devoted to a single sector of the 21st-century economy, like health care or airlines. Ever the apostle of field organizing, Stern wants these restructured unions to put more time and resources into recruiting new members in fast-growing exurban areas—in the South and the West especially—where a new generation of workers has never belonged to a union. His plan would slash the amount that each union pays in dues to the A.F.L.-C.I.O. by half, provided that those unions put some of the money back into local organizing. This is not a small idea; it would, essentially, take resources away from the federation's headquarters, which uses it for policy studies and training programs, and give it back to the guys who set up picket lines and rallies.

Even Stern's allies admit that his ultimatum to big labor is a little high-handed. John Wilhelm, co-president of the union that represents hotel, restaurant and garment workers, is supportive of Stern, and Wilhelm is said to be considering a challenge to Sweeney when he runs for another term as A.F.L.-C.I.O. president this year. But he said he disagrees with Stern's idea of merging unions against their will. Because Stern's union is so powerful, Wilhelm told me, Stern doesn't always feel the need to tread as softly as he might. "Frankly, he doesn't have to be as diplomatic as others do," Wilhelm said. "There's a thin and perhaps indiscernible line between a person who comes across as arrogant and a person who tries to tell the truth even when it's unpleasant. And the truth about our labor movement is unpleasant."

Workers of the World, Globalize?

Even if big labor eventually does come to be made up of bigger unions, Stern sees a larger challenge: can you build a multinational labor movement to counter the leverage of multinational giants whose tentacles reach across oceans and continents? The emblem of this new kind of behemoth, of course, is Wal-Mart, the nation's largest employer. Wal-Mart has, in a sense, turned the American retail model inside out. It used to be that a manufacturer made, say, a clock radio, determined its price and the wages of the employees who made it and then sold the radio to a retail outlet at a profit. Wal-Mart's power is such that the process now works in reverse: in practice, Wal-Mart sets the price for that clock radio, and the manufacturer, very likely located overseas, figures out how low wages will have to be in order to make it profitable to produce it. In this way, Wal-Mart not only resists unions in its stores with unwavering ferocity but also drives down the wages of its manufacturers—all in the service of bringing consumers the lowest possible price.

"What was good for G.M. ended up being good for the country," Stern says. "What's good for Wal-Mart ends up being good for five families"—the heirs to the Walton fortune. Stern's reform plan for the A.F.L.-C.I.O. includes a $25 million fund to organize Wal-Mart's workers. But as a retail outlet, Wal-Mart doesn't really fall within the S.E.I.U.'s purview. What Stern says he is deeply worried about is what he sees as the next generation of Wal-Marts, which *are* on his turf: French, British and Scandinavian companies whose entry into the American market threatens to drive down wages in service industries, which are often less visible than retail. "While we were invading Iraq, the Europeans invaded us," Stern says. Most of these companies have no objection to unionizing in Europe, where organized labor is the norm. But when they come to the United States, they immediately follow the Wal-Mart model, undercutting their competitors by shutting out unions and squeezing paychecks.

Stern's big idea for coping with this new kind of multinational nemesis is to build a federation of unions, similar to the A.F.L.-C.I.O. except that its member unions would come from all over the world. As Stern explained it, a French company might not be so brazen about bullying American workers if it had to worry about a French union protesting back home.

At first, this global vision sounded a little dreamy to me, as if Stern might have been watching too many "Superfriends" reruns. Then he invited me, just before Christmas, on a one-day trip to Birmingham, England. The occasion was a meeting of Britain's reform-minded transportation union. Tony Woodley, the union's general secretary, flashed a broad smile and threw his arm around Stern when

Stern arrived, after flying all night, to give the keynote address. Two S.E.I.U. employees were already on hand; it turned out that Stern had dispatched them to London temporarily to help Woodley set up an organizing program.

As we drank coffee backstage, Stern and Woodley told me about the case of First Student, a company that in the last few years had become the largest, most aggressive private school-bus company in the United States. The company had become a target of S.E.I.U. locals in several cities because it wouldn't let its drivers unionize. "We keep seeing these things about them in the union newsletter," Stern said. "And it starts nibbling at your brain. I said: 'Who are these people, First Student? What's going on here?' And then we do a little research, and we find out what idiots we are. This is a major multinational company. They're 80 percent unionized in the United Kingdom. So we write a letter to the union there, and we say, 'Can you help us?'"

Woodley sent British bus drivers to Chicago to meet with their American counterparts. Then the American bus drivers went to London, and lobbyists for the British union took them to see members of Parliament. They also held a joint demonstration outside the company's annual meeting. Woodley told me that First Student—known as First Group in Britain—was now making a bid for rail contracts there, and his union intended to lobby against it unless the company sat down with its American counterparts in Florida and Illinois.

Stern [also] invited the top executives of about a dozen unions from Europe and Australia to a meeting in London this April, which will be the maiden gathering of what he says he hopes will become a formalized global federation.

There are, however, painful questions inherent in globalizing the labor movement. At a recent meeting with his executive board, Stern mused out loud about the possibility of conducting a fact-finding mission to India, along with executives from one of the companies outsourcing its jobs there. Perhaps that could be a first step, he thought, toward raising the pay of Indian workers who have inherited American jobs.

Then Stern stopped himself and considered a problem. Sure, there was an obvious logic to unionizing foreign phone operators or machinists: American workers won't be able to compete fairly for jobs until companies have to pay higher wages in countries like China and India. But how would it look to workers in America? How would you avoid the appearance that you were more worried about the guy answering the phone in Bangalore than you were about the guy he replaced in Iowa? John Kerry and other Democrats had been railing against the C.E.O.'s who outsourced American jobs—and here was Andy Stern, considering joining forces with those very same C.E.O.'s to make sure their Indian workers were making enough money.

"The truth is that as the living standard in China goes up, the living standard in Ohio goes down," Stern said. "What do you do about that? Are we a global union or an American union? This is a hard question for me to answer. Because I'm not comfortable with the living standard here going down. This is a question I think we need to think about going forward, but I don't think that means we should be scared."

Re-engineering the Party

The more Andy Stern looks at organized labor and the Democratic Party, the more he sees the parallels between them. Like big labor, the modern Democratic Party was brought into being by imaginative liberal thinkers in the 1930's and reached its apex during the prosperity of the postwar industrial boom. Like the union bosses, Democratic leaders grew complacent in their success; they failed to keep pace with changing circumstances in American life and didn't notice that their numbers were steadily eroding. Now, Stern says, Democrats and the unions both find themselves mired in the mind-set of a bygone moment, lacking the will or perhaps the capacity to innovate or adapt. What you see in both cases, Stern told me, borrowing from the new-age language of business theory, is "the change pattern of a dying institution."

The big conversation going on in Democratic Washington at the moment, at dinner parties and luncheons and think-tank symposia, revolves around how to save the party. The participants generally fall into two camps of unequal size. On one side, there is the majority of Democrats, who believe that the party's failure has primarily been one of communication and tactics. By this thinking, the Democratic agenda itself (no to tax cuts and school vouchers and Social Security privatization; yes to national health care and affirmative action) remains as relevant as ever to modern workers. The real problem, goes this line of thinking, is that the party has allowed ruthless Republicans to control the debate and has failed to sufficiently mobilize its voters. A much smaller group of prominent Democrats argues that the party's problems run deeper—that it suffers, in fact, from a lack of imagination, and that its core ideas are more an echo of government as it was than government as it ought to be.

Virtually everyone in the upper echelons of organized labor belongs solidly to the first camp. Stern has his feet firmly planted in the second. The economic policy of the Democratic Party, he says, "is basically being opposed to Republicans and protecting the New Deal. It makes me realize how vibrant the Republicans are in creating 21st-century ideas, and how sad it is that we're defending 60-year-old ideas." Like big labor, Stern says, the party needs to challenge its orthodoxy—and its interest groups—if it wants to put forward a program that makes sense for new-economy workers. Could it be that the Social Security system devised in the 1930's isn't, in fact, the only good national retirement program for today's wage earner? Is it possible that competition is the best way to rescue an imperiled public-school system?

"I'm not convinced that you can do this from the inside," Stern told me at one point. Just as he is willing to strike out from the A.F.L.-C.I.O., he doesn't rule out a split from the Democratic Party. "I feel like we have to do everything we can within our power to get both the labor movement and the parties in this country to represent workers the way they should," he said. "And if we can't, then we have to decide what our strategy is. Do we spend all our money running ballot initiatives and forget about candidates? Do we look for people to create an independent worker party? I don't know."

Stern told me he had been partly inspired, oddly enough, by the example of Stephen Moore, the arch-conservative ideologue who, until recently, ran the Club for Growth. The club, which is anathema to both Democrats and moderate Republicans in Washington, raises millions from corporate anti-tax crusaders, then spends it not only against Democrats (Tom Daschle was a prime target) but also against Republican incumbents who aren't deemed sufficiently conservative. Moore has infuriated some Republican leaders, who say he divides the party, but the Club for Growth has helped push the party to the right, putting moderates on the defensive and making Republicans think twice before they cast a vote against a tax cut.

Stern invited Moore to speak at an S.E.I.U. meeting in Chicago a few years ago—which is roughly the equivalent of Michael Moore being asked over to the National Rifle Association for lunch. Now Stern has begun to emulate the club's model; last year, the S.E.I.U. ran its own candidate, a union ally, against the Democratic House speaker [Representative Helen Sommers] of Washington State, because the speaker voted against a health-benefits package for home health care workers. The union's challenger lost—but only by about 500 votes. "I think we need to spend more time running candidates against Democrats," Stern says matter-of-factly.

This approach holds some risk for a union boss. Most of Stern's members, after all, are lifelong Democrats. Will they be O.K. with a leader who's willing to entertain an overhaul of Social Security? Would they support Stern if he crossed the teachers' unions and came out for school vouchers? Stern seems convinced that his members want new solutions to these problems, not dogmatic answers, and he is betting that they're more loyal to him and the union than they are to the party. He seems poised to fill a space—between the world of organized labor and the world of social and economic policy—that hasn't been filled since Walter Reuther, the head of the United Auto Workers, advised the Kennedys and Lyndon Johnson on civil rights. "There's been no analog to Andy in the last 30 or 40 years in America," says Simon Rosenberg, who heads the New Democrat Network and is running for Democratic Party chairman. "There's been no labor leader who has emerged as a thought leader as well."

The Big Questions

The question that Stern's detractors ask is this: What is Andy Stern really after? Does he long to be the Reuther of his day, phoning presidents and holding forth to rooms full of reporters?

"I don't like politics," Stern said more than once. "After the last election, a lot of people called me and said everything from 'You should run for president' to 'You should be chairman of the D.N.C.' And neither of them had the slightest bit of reality or held any interest for me." That Stern can mention this casually—that someone suggested he not merely phone a president, but run for president—would indicate that he is as susceptible to self-glorification as the next guy, and maybe more so. But if what Stern really wanted was to run the world, he could surely spend his nights in more powerful company than that of the bartender at the Dancing Crab. When I asked what he envisioned himself doing in his 60's, Stern said, "I hope I find someone to fall in love with and travel with and watch my son have grandkids."

His adversaries will say this is disingenuous, but, as so often happens in public life, they may be misunderstanding the human factor that compels Andy Stern. Everyone who knows him well will tell you that he is driven by an authentic passion for workers. And yet, at the same time, it doesn't take a psychology degree to see that he lives these days in a state of suspended agony. Stern gives the impression of having been shaken loose from conformity by the death of his daughter and the end of his marriage; nothing can hurt him more than he has already been hurt, which breeds in him the kind of abandon that can be dangerous to the status quo.

This is how history often changes; it's the people who are running from something worse who are willing to hurl themselves into walls that others won't scale. The facts of our time are clear enough: a ruthless kind of globalized economy is upon us, and it is not going away. Many American industries are bound to be surpassed by leaner competitors, and the workers left behind by this tectonic shift have little power to influence the decisions of corporate barons whose interests know no national boundaries. More Americans now hold stock—often in a 401k—than are members of a union. And the institutions that have, for the last century, protected the ideal of the American worker—organized labor and the Democratic Party—are clinging mightily to structures and programs born in the era of coal and steel, perhaps out of fear that innovation would somehow discredit the things they have worked for all these years, or perhaps for the simple reason that no one knows what to do next.

The visionary men who built big labor and the modern Democratic Party met the challenges specific to their moment. What Andy Stern is doing, in his own way, is provoking an argument more relevant to our moment. Can American workers ever be secure in a global market? Can a service economy sustain the nation's middle class? And are we brave enough to have the conversation?

April 12, 1998

Working, The Habit of a Lifetime

BY JACK CAVANAUGH

When Lionel Dusseault went to work for the John M. Dean Company in Putnam [Connecticut], America was at war—World War I, that is. It was the summer of 1918 and Mr. Dusseault, at 17, was too young to be drafted into the Army but old enough to work at the factory, which had opened in 1898.

Eighty years later, Mr. Dusseault is still working at Dean in its centennial year; indeed, he is still doing the same job at the same work bench—sorting, weighing and packaging a variety of pins and other wire metal products made by the company.

Mr. Dusseault—whose 67-year-old son, Joseph, retired a decade ago from the University of Connecticut in Storrs—no longer works a full 40-hour week. But he still drives to work, Monday through Friday, and puts in four hours a day, from 11:30 A.M. until 3:30 P.M. "He can't wait to get to work every day," said his son, in whose house the elder Mr. Dusseault occupies an apartment. "We usually have breakfast together every morning at a local restaurant before my Dad goes to work."

In 1918, as Mr. Dusseault went to work for Dean, Harry Kupperblatt was a 14-year-old student at Morris High School in the Bronx who was working as a part-time delivery boy for a New York City drugstore. Now, just short of his 94th birthday, Mr. Kupperblatt is also still going strong, as a luggage salesman for Macy's in the Stamford Town Center.

Mr. Dusseault and Mr. Kupperblatt—who, coincidentally, share the same birthday, May 27—are two of the oldest workers in Connecticut in an era when more and more people are continuing to work into their 80's and even their 90's.

Some put in fewer hours than Mr. Dusseault and Mr. Kupperblatt. One of them is Tony Valorie of Hartford, 95 years old, who works Mondays only at the Professional Barber Shop on Trumbull Street in downtown Hartford.

But then some of the older workers put in much longer hours. For example, Joe Del-Monico, who will turn 88 in August, puts in at least 40 hours a week as a salesman at Del-Monico Hatters in downtown New Haven, which may be the only men's hat store left in the state and where he has worked since his father opened the store in 1925. "Why do I keep at it?," he asked rhetorically. "Because I enjoy doing it."

Mr. DelMonico is enjoying it even more these days since, as he puts it, "Hat wearing is coming back." He remembers when the store would sell as many as 200 straw hats before Yale crew races on the Housatonic in the 1920's and 30's. Nowadays, he said, "We're selling more casual hats than ever, including the 'crushers' that you can pack in a briefcase or suitcase. And more men are concerned about skin cancer and wearing big-brim hats."

Ed Benoit of West Hartford, at the age of 91, is a full-time salesman for the Duratest light bulb company. Five days a week, he makes his rounds of industrial accounts and prospective customers in central Connecticut.

A musician (violin, bass violin and viola), Mr. Benoit once played for the Hartford and the New Britain symphony orchestras "until I realized that I wasn't going to make my mark in music." After spending 20 years as an accountant, he went to work for New Jersey-based Duratest in 1955.

How much longer will he continue working? "As long as I feel good," said Mr. Benoit.

Then there are 80-year-old Carmella Unker and 73-year-old Anthony Perrotta, both of whom work for the United States Postal Service in Stamford. Ms. Unker—a corrections officer at the Bedford Hills, N.Y. women's prison from 1943 until 1956—is a distribution clerk at the West Avenue center in Stamford. Mr. Perrotta makes his daily rounds delivering mail on Atlantic Street in the city's business district, walking, by his estimate, "between three and four miles a day."

Both put in 40 hours a week—and sometimes more—but they are not complaining. "Sometimes they ask me to work overtime and I do," said Ms. Unker, a postal worker for 31 years. "A lot of people ask me when I'm going to retire, and I tell them, 'I don't think I ever will.'"

Mr. Perrotta, who has been a letter carrier for 40 years, said, "As long as my legs hold out, I'll keep working."

So, too, apparently, will another postal worker, Pete Aceto, who will turn 75 on July 4. In his 51st year as a mail carrier in Manchester, Mr. Aceto has had the same route for more than 40 years and, according to the Manchester Postmaster Ron Boyne, has no intention of retiring.

"He's an exemplary carrier, a gentleman's gentleman, and his customers love him," Mr. Boyne said. "In many cases he's now delivering mail to people whose parents he used to deliver to."

Mr. Aceto has a route that entails both curbside delivery from the small mail truck that he drives and foot delivery to mail boxes on customers' porches.

At the age of 77—she will turn 78 on June 19—Marion Riley's legs are as good as ever as she demonstrates dance steps for her students at the Riley School of Dance in Enfield. A dancer since the age of 6, Ms. Riley took over the school in 1938, when she was 17 and her dance instructor, who ran the school, had to step down because she was pregnant.

"I love it," said Ms. Riley who is now in partnership with one of her seven children, K. T. Riley DeSilva. "And I don't know what I'd do if I didn't have the dance school to go to." Her hours can be long. On a recent Tuesday, for example, Ms. Riley started her day with a class at 10 A.M. and did not finish until 10:45 that night. "Tap is my favorite, but I also teach ballet," she said.

Ms. Riley's most memorable dance number was short, but unforgettable. "It was in 1940 in New York and Gene Kelly, who was appearing in 'Pal Joey,' was conducting a class at a dance convention that I was attending when he picked me out to do a tap routine with him," she recalled. "He was so nice, a real sweetheart. Someone took a picture, and they ran it in The New Britain Herald. I'll never forget that."

Mr. Kupperblatt differs from the other older workers in that he did not start working at his current job, as a luggage salesman at Macy's in Stamford, until he was 92 years old. That is, he was 92 in calendar years but 66 on that employment application he filled out for Macy's.

"I didn't think they were going to hire a 92-year-old guy, so I put down my stepdaughter's date of birth," Mr. Kupperblatt said. "They asked for my Social Security card and my driver's license, which has my actual age, and then made copies of both of them, but I don't think they checked."

The management at Macy's did not find out about Mr. Kupperblatt's true age for four or five months. "After I proved I could do the job, I told a sales associate how old I actually was," said Mr. Kupperblatt, who cuts a dapper figure and could easily pass for a man in his 70's.

By then, Macy's was not about to fire Mr. Kupperblatt for fibbing on his application. No wonder. He was selling as much as $2,500 in merchandise on some days while only working four hours a day. "The average would be about $200 an hour," said Karen Mackay, the manager of the Macy's store, "so on some days Harry was selling three times as much as that."

A self-described workaholic, Mr. Kupperblatt lived in Miami Beach for 19 years until 1996 when his second wife died.

"I was retired but I was always slipping out to get temporary jobs," said Mr. Kupperblatt, who has been working since he was 7 when he would call up to people in tenement houses telling them that they had phone calls in the neighborhood drug store, for which service they would give him a nickel or a dime.

Shortly after his wife died, at the suggestion of one of his two stepdaughters, Marcia Selden, who lives in Stamford, he moved into an apartment house across the street from the Stamford Town Center.

"I would go out for walks and sometimes I would walk inside the mall," recalled Mr. Kupperblatt, who owned a garment factory in the Bronx from 1945 until 1975. "Then one day I said to myself, 'Why don't I try for a job at Macy's?' I told Marcia and she thought it was a great idea."

So does Macy's. "Harry could sell anything to anybody," said Ms. Mackay. "And he treats everybody so special. He takes so much pride in what he's doing. Harry's a delight to see at work and he's an inspiration to all of us."

Mr. Kupperblatt revels in recounting how, at times, other salespeople in the Macy's store inform people that the salesman is waiting on them is 93 years old. "'He's 93?' they'll say," Mr. Kupperblatt said, beaming. "Then when my sales associate tells them it's true, they'll say, 'Impossible.'"

In general, though, Mr. Kupperblatt's age is lost on his customers, few of whom ever ask how old he is. "I don't think anybody really cares as long as I'm doing my job," he said.

Mr. Kupperblatt, who often drives to Long Island on weekends to visit relatives and the cemetery where his first wife is buried, proudly recalled how, on a recent Saturday, he sold $2,600 worth of merchandise and followed up that accomplishment by selling another $1,500 worth on Sunday. "A lot of it is repeat business—people who I've sold to before," he said.

Some of his new customers come looking for Mr. Kupperblatt after having seen him on either the "Today" or "Rosie O'Donnell" television shows this past winter. "Some of them tell me I look much better in person," he said.

Lionel Dusseault, meanwhile, will turn 97 on May 27—a Wednesday that he expects to spend at his work bench. The president of John M. Dean, Robert A. Main, said of Mr. Dusseault— who is known to everyone as Toots: "He enjoys his work and he does a good job. And he sets an example for everybody else. And Toots's job is not a 'make-work' position. When he retires, I will have to replace him."

And when might that be? "If I pass away, I want to do it at work," Mr. Dusseault said.

His job at Dean is only the second full-time position he has ever had, one found at the recommendation of his father, a night watchman at the factory, who lived until he was 92. Mr. Dusseault's first job had been as part of a work crew with the New York, New Haven & Hartford Railroad. For 40 years he also was a volunteer fireman in Putnam, retiring in 1978.

"He had a pacemaker put in about six years ago and he has arthritis in one leg," said his son, Joseph, who was an assistant director of publications at the University of Connecticut until he retired in 1989. "He doesn't have any hobbies, but he reads several newspapers every day and likes to go out to restaurants."

The elder Mr. Dusseault also likes to go to bed early—at 7:30 P.M. "after he watches 'Wheel of Fortune' on television," his son said.

Longevity apparently is not uncommon at the Dean company. Until he retired last June at the age of 86 because of illness, Norman (Buck) Berthiaume had spent 69 years operating a production machine at the plant. "And he worked full time, 40 hours a week," Mr. Main, the company president, said.

Unlike Mr. Dusseault and Mr. Kupperblatt, Tony Valorie, the 95-year-old barber from Hartford, does want to retire. And in 1980 it looked like he would have to after cataracts left him nearly blind. "But I had them removed and now I have 20-20 vision," said Mr. Valorie who returned to work the following year at the Professional Barber Shop in Hartford.

Mr. Valorie began cutting hair in 1914 at the age of 11 in an uncle's barber shop in Donora, Pa. "But now I want to quit, but they won't let me" he said. "They say, 'Tony, we need you.'"

Donald Rome, a Hartford lawyer whose hair he has been cutting for 55 years, "used to come in twice a month, but then I told him once a month was enough," said Mr. Valorie.

Mr. Valorie laments the fact that no one asks for a shave anymore. "When I started, a lot of men got shaves," he said. "But then a haircut only cost 20 cents and a shave was 15 cents. Or you get both for a quarter. Now a haircut costs $12 and a shave is $8. But, as I said, no one asks for a shave anymore."

CHAPTER 6

THE FRUITS OF OUR LABOR

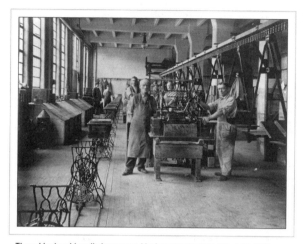

The cabinet and treadle base assembly department of the Elizabeth, NJ, Singer
sewing machine plant before the turn of the twentieth century. By 1890, the
sewing machine was [fast becoming] commonplace in many American homes.
(*New York Times*)

CONSUMPTION IS ONE OF THE MOST IMPORTANT DRIVERS OF American business today. What women, men, and children buy, how much they spend, and how willing they are to keep buying as the economy trends up or down all exert powerful influence on the scale and scope of business activity. Low consumer spending stalls business growth; freer spending spurs it. Small wonder, then, that consumer confidence, along with other measures such as the unemployment rate or business investment, is considered a key indicator of the economy's health. If we think about the entire

1873
Levi Strauss patents process for creating riveted work pants.

1879
First demonstration of incandescent electric light bulb.

1902
First permanent movie theatre opens.

1914
Max Factor creates makeup line.

1915
Alfred Mellowes invents an electric refrigerator.

output of the U.S. economy as represented by gross domestic product (GDP), more than two-thirds of that output or national income is used for consumption. This means that in 2005, for example, Americans spent $8.7 trillion—of a total GDP of $12.4 trillion—buying Big Macs, iPods, new cars, acupuncture treatments, baby strollers, cell phone service, and many, many more goods and services.

Today, thanks in part to a proliferation of various kinds of credit, we have the ability to spend more than we actually earn. Millions of Americans do just this. In 2007, the average household carried about $24,000 in debt, exclusive of mortgage liabilities.[1] Credit cards, car loans, mortgages, and other kinds of IOUs helped us purchase necessities—food, clothing, shelter—and countless goods and services less essential to survival.

Whether we have earned the money or borrowed it, we have generally put our consumption dollars where we felt our most pressing needs. We bought goods, such as a pair of Air Jordan sneakers or a Chanel lipstick, that fed our aspirations and those, such as a BlackBerry, that bought us time or a feeling of control in our life. We purchased certain car models and after-school lessons for our kids that helped us express our position in a particular place on the social landscape. And we bought home security systems and blood pressure medicines because we worried about our safety and our health. Taken together, the choices Americans made in getting, spending, and borrowing serve as a powerful lens on our needs, wants, hopes, and fears.

It wasn't always this way. In the early years of our country, when a majority of Americans lived and worked on farms, the fruits of their labor were, literally, the food and other necessities that they produced themselves. Few settlers made enough in goods or money to buy much more than what they needed to survive. Yet even in the late 1700s, consumers were keenly aware of the power

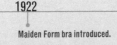

1922	1919	1934	1954	1958
Maiden Form bra introduced.	RCA established following end of World War I.	Television demonstrated.	Swanson creates "t.v. dinner."	American Express offers its first credit card.

they wielded when they chose to spend or withhold their earnings. The American Revolution was precipitated in part by colonists' anger against British taxes on imported goods and the subsequent mass boycotts of these items.[2]

One hundred years later, the Second Industrial Revolution enabled the mass production and consumption of thousands of goods. Some of these, such as guns and corsets, had existed for centuries, but the revolution in production and distribution made them cheaper and much more accessible. Others, such as processed foods, ready-to-wear clothing, the radio, and automobiles, were brand new. Consumers responded to this explosion in choice in different ways. Women bought bottled mustard, for example, because it was more convenient than making it themselves. But a family purchased an upright piano for different reasons—because it was a symbol of the affluence that many Americans aspired to as well as an outlet for their leisure time.[3]

Young businesses succeeded or failed depending on their ability to convince consumers that their goods were worth a portion of a household's hard-earned wages: that their products would make daily tasks easier or consumers' lives more pleasurable, or that these offerings would express and signify to others something about an individual or family's identity. Isaac Singer, for example, employed female demonstrators and trained salesmen to show women how simple and efficient his sewing machines were to use. Other entrepreneurs, such as Alfred Sloan at General Motors, marketed their products as symbols of quality and distinction. A 1925 company ad extolled the "beauty and grace and high quality appointments" of the Oldsmobile DeLuxe Roadster with its "capacity for unusual passenger comfort and convenience."[4]

With the increasing availability of so many goods, such messages became ever more ubiquitous. In the late 1800s, department stores

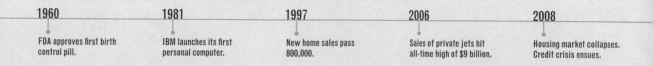

1960
FDA approves first birth control pill.

1981
IBM launches its first personal computer.

1997
New home sales pass 800,000.

2006
Sales of private jets hit all-time high of $9 billion.

2008
Housing market collapses. Credit crisis ensues.

such as Marshall, Field & Company in downtown Chicago displayed previously unimaginable stocks of the latest, most stylish goods to all who entered.[5] Aspiring entrepreneurs, such as Field and Gustavus Swift, whose "disassembly line" for slaughtering cattle and pigs helped revolutionize the meatpacking business, quickly learned to distinguish their offerings by using brands as signifiers of quality and other values.[6] They also created institutions—that is, companies—that could deliver on the promises of their respective brands over and over again. So successful were many of these initiatives that many of the brands and organizations created in the midst of the Second Industrial Revolution—Coca-Cola, IBM, Quaker Oats, Campbell Soup, and General Electric, to name a few—remain market leaders today.

To help build their reputations and attract customers, firms turned to mass advertising, which itself quickly became a by-product of the rapid-fire mass production and consumption that did so much to define America in the decades after the Civil War. With the help of young, growing advertising companies such as J. Walter Thompson (founded in 1878) or on their own, businesses touted their products in daily papers, on the sides of delivery trucks, and in displays at public fairs and other galas.[7] In 1893, for example, Henry Heinz mounted a huge exhibition at the World's Columbian Exposition held in Chicago. At the company pavilion, as many as ten employees dispensed samples of pickles, ketchup, relish, celery sauce, and more to the hungry and curious. By 1900, U.S. companies were funneling $450 million per year (about $10 billion today) into various forms of advertisements.[8]

These messages helped feed demand for new and existing goods. So, too, did rising incomes. Between 1869 and 1929, per capita income, adjusted for inflation, rose more than 300 percent, climbing to $847 in the latter year (or about $10,300 today).[9] With greater means, more people could afford the products they saw in advertisements, or at least mass-produced imitations of them. At the same time, the anonymity of city life made physical appearance more important as an indicator of place and wealth for the growing number of Americans living in urban areas. Advertisers encouraged consumers to seek access to the world of privilege and power by mimicking the spending habits of the rich—for instance, by buying a well-tailored suit for work or a refrigerator or electric washing machine for their homes.[10] The development of installment credit greased the wheels of such commerce by bringing many big-ticket items, such as cars and appliances, within financial reach of working-class families.[11] By the end of the 1920s, installment plans had become so popular that consumers relied on credit to purchase most of their durable possessions, such as sewing machines and radios, as well as many other products, such as china and books.[12]

The deluge of goods and the eagerness with which most Americans greeted their new options prompted a variety of responses. Some wealthier consumers began to shun as "common" goods that mass production had made less scarce and more affordable.[13] (Almost a century later, in 2007, many rich households would react similarly to the widespread availability of products once considered luxury goods).[14] Public moralists—including magazine editors, authors, and ministers—denounced emulative spending, especially by middle-class women, as tantamount to deception.[15] Other critics opposed the increasing emphasis on consumption on the grounds that it was used to heighten, rather than obscure, class distinction. In his book *The Theory of the Leisure Class*, sociologist Thorstein Veblen argued that material possessions with few, if any, useful functions had become the markers of wealth and, therefore, of status in society. "The basis on which good repute in any highly organized industrial community ultimately rests is pecuniary strength," he wrote, "and the means of showing pecuniary strength, and so of gaining or retaining a good name, are leisure and a conspicuous consumption of goods."[16]

If consumption itself had become a marker of social repute, it did so partly by giving women a new, more public role. Since colonial times, women had been responsible for making, gathering, and assembling the basic household necessities. At times, this included shopping at local markets or small stores for goods they could not provide at home. Prior to the end of the nineteenth century, however, shopping—as we think of it today—was not part of most women's ongoing experience. For one thing, it was generally not considered acceptable for women to move about public places, particularly city streets, unaccompanied. For another, men often controlled a family's purse strings. Finally, many stores, especially general stores in rural areas, were gathering places for men to meet, talk, and, often, drink. They were not organized, practically or socially, for women buyers.

The coming of mass production and distribution changed all this, expanding and formalizing women's roles in household consumption. One of the first places this occurred was in urban department stores, which catered to women in their merchandise, environment, and service.[17] It quickly became acceptable for women to shop alone—or with a female friend—at stores such as Macy's in New York or Wanamaker's in Philadelphia.[18] The rise of chain stores such as F.W. Woolworth and A&P also created environments where women were encouraged to shop by themselves. In purchasing products for her family, a woman had to make decisions, allocate financial resources, and otherwise exercise her agency in the public sphere.

At about the same time that women were becoming more visible as consumers, a significant number were also entering the paid workforce, some of them as salesclerks in the same department stores where other women shopped. The fact that many women now earned independent incomes only reinforced their growing influence on household spending decisions. As women's public roles increased, so did their interest in their own appearance, stimulating the young markets for ready-to-wear clothing and cosmetics.[19] These trends did not escape advertisers, who began to market more specifically to them. During the 1930s, for instance, Procter & Gamble invested heavily in sponsorship of radio dramas geared toward adult women, a genre forever after known as the "soap opera."[20]

In the end, Victorian-era anxieties about changing gender norms and consumer habits did little to hinder the widespread enthusiasm for new products, services, and forms of leisure.[21] Buying a radio or a vacuum cleaner, for example, let families participate in the technological advances of the age. Going to the cinema did the same thing; at the same time, it provided a medium in which working-class Americans could view, by way of stage sets, the modern accoutrements of the rich.[22] Between 1909 and 1929, spending on recreational goods and services—including magazines, toys, cameras, amusement park tickets, and vaudeville shows—rose from $860 million to $4.4 billion (about $53 billion today).[23] Even the Great Depression could not dampen the lure of some popular entertainments. Although most recreational expenditures declined in the wake of the 1929 stock market crash, consumer spending at movie theaters remained strong and, after a dip in the early 1930s, increased markedly, more than doubling between 1933 and 1943.[24] (The number of movie tickets sold per person in the 1930s was seven times *higher* than it was at the end of the 1990s.)[25]

World War II effectively ended the Great Depression in the United States. When peace came in 1945, it ushered in a period of increased national productivity and prosperity, with corresponding growth in Americans' spending power. Between 1946 and 1970, real gross national product increased 230 percent. Per capita income rose more slowly, climbing 60 percent in real terms during this period.[26] As in the past, millions of men and women used their higher incomes to buy new things. Some of these goods, such as big cars, phonographs, and imported perfumes, had been available for decades but had been beyond the reach of most families. But others, such as television, frozen foods, and birth control pills, were relatively novel.

The choices available to consumers in the postwar boom transformed societal norms and expectations. With the advent of fast food, for example, millions of men, women, and children began to break bread—or hamburgers, chicken wings, and pizza slices—at chains such as McDonald's or Dairy Queen. At the same time, American families flocked to locations such as Walt Disney's Disneyland to experience new forms of leisure.[27] Shopping itself became another form of entertainment, as the number of shopping malls skyrocketed: in 1945, there were 8 malls in the United States; in 1960, there were 3,840.[28] For many households, the most important symbol of their place and economic possibilities was where they lived. Before World War II, about 40 percent of families owned their own home. In 1970, a firm majority—62 percent—did.[29]

By the late 1990s, getting and spending played ever more visible roles in American life. New technologies, such as the cell phone and BlackBerry, came to be viewed as necessities. Firms selling small luxuries—such as Starbucks, which created an enormous market for specialty coffee—grew to rival the size of more standard fast-food chains. Most Americans enjoyed a range of goods and services—from a second or third vehicle to health clubs to text messaging—that their great-grandparents could hardly have dreamed of. At the same time, the underlying sources for all this consumption—wealth and income—shifted significantly. In the late twentieth and early twenty-first century, the distribution of both wealth and income became increasingly unequal. The top 5 percent of the income distribution saw their fortunes rise as both their livelihoods and assets grew. At the same time, real wages for middle- and lower-income households stagnated and, in some cases, declined.

As the twenty-first century unfolded, many families found themselves caught between the rock of expanded consumption and the hard place of seemingly static incomes. To make matters thornier, the costs of some of the most important goods that American families bought—goods such as health care, higher education, and housing—climbed steeply.[30] To finance what they needed and wanted, growing numbers of households turned to various forms of credit. By 2001, almost three-quarters of all American families owned at least one credit card, and 41 percent owned three or more.[31] By 2006, the average cardholder owned 4.6 credit cards.[32] On some of these cards, interest rates were as high as 30 percent.[33] The use of consumer credit, while by no means new, reached unprecedented levels in the early twenty-first century.

The nation's transformation to a consumer society, which began in the late nineteenth century, had been a boon to American business and, in many respects, to households. But the consequences of this shift stretched far beyond consumers and companies, encompassing politics, family, and the environment. Contemporary critics cited the wastefulness of so much buying and selling and the futility of trying to infuse life with meaning through things. Educators and others lambasted businesses for marketing to young children. Meanwhile, millions of Americans turned their attention to the environmental effects of so much abundance.

In the sweep of U.S. history, consumption had been a force for great change. Much of this change played out in the standard of living enjoyed by countless men, women, and children. But part of the transition, which continues into our own time, has been political and social. From the Boston Tea Party to the Civil Rights boycotts, consumers have used their buying power to express dissatisfaction with the status quo.[34] In the late nineteenth century, the workers who manufactured consumer goods first used the union label as a way to show solidarity through their purchases.[35] One hundred years later, men and women, and even teenagers, organized to protest sweatshop production in various countries around the world and to demand environmentally friendly goods.

Entire industries, such as organic agriculture, grew up to serve these and other demands. And individual business leaders, experimenting with forms of social entrepreneurship, developed product offerings and built firms that were intended to both create value and spur social change through the things people bought and how they spent their money.

Earth-friendly cloth lunch bags are just one of the products on sale at an ecologically conscious store in Park Slope, Brooklyn, in the early 1990s. The twentieth century's waves of mass production were slowly being replaced by concern for resources and scarcity by the turn of the millenium. (Marilynn K. Yee/*New York Times*)

The Wonders of Electricity

Edison Company Shows Them in Its Pearl Street Plant.

Cooking by Heat with Invisible Source—Electric Elevators

and Machinery—Many Visitors.

Electricity has for ages been of absorbing interest to mankind. Since it has become subjugated in multitudinous forms to the uses of mankind, it has become even more attractive. So, when the Edison Electric Lighting Company issued invitations to the public to inspect its magnificent establishment in Pearl Street last night, and, as an inducement, invited its guests to hear the piano played by electricity, eat tempting viands, cooked by electricity, witness ice made by electricity, and view other wonders controlled and operated by the unseen power, there was an overwhelming response.

For three hours a constant stream of people, numbering nearly 6,000, passed through the building and went away enchanted with that which they beheld.

In addition to the new and improved machinery which the company has recently installed, there were on exhibition numerous devices, showing the application of electricity for different purposes. The visitor, upon entering last night the building, illuminated by myriads of multi-colored electric lamps, was ushered into an electric elevator, which took him swiftly to the third floor. Here were to be seen on an exhibition platform electric motors, incandescent lamps of different candle power, and colors, and various kinds of electric cooking utensils. One of the most interesting objects exhibited here was the Quimby hydraulic electric elevator pump. By this new combination it is possible to operate the present hydraulic elevators by electricity far more economically than by the old-fashioned steam pump, which requires so much attention.

In the lecture room was shown a large number of novel exhibits. The Λ. B. See Manufacturing Company had in full operation one of its new direct-connected elevator outfits, illustrating the simplicity and economy of its apparatus.

Electric cooking, a novelty some six months ago, and which has been gradually finding its way into public favor, was practically illustrated under the direction of Mrs. Lamphe. The women were delighted as they saw the meat roasted and the cakes baked within a few feet of them without finding any visible source for the heat.

The greatest source of attraction, however, was the electric piano. The attachment can be fitted to any ordinary piano as made by the Automaton Piano Company, and renders it possible for the ordinary piano to produce the most difficult music without human aid.

Among the interesting things shown were sewing machines operated by electricity, an exhibition of low-tension arc lamps of ornamental design for inside lighting, a sample electric switchboard, displaying skilled machine work and ornamental design, and "Boosters," the invention of W. S. Barstow, Superintendent of the company. These machines are for the purpose of restoring the power of the current that has failed in transmission over a long distance.

Automobile Topics of Interest

Increasing Demand for Machines for Business and Pleasure Purposes—

Vehicles of Immense Power on the City Streets—

Cost of Running Some Motor Carriages.

Five or six years ago, when the automobile first appeared as a practical vehicle the doom of the horse as a motive power in the city streets was generally predicted, and fanciful pictures of the public highways as it was imagined they would appear under the new order of things became a feature of the illustrated publications of the day. Various estimates of time ranging from ten to twenty years in which the change was to be brought about were made by enthusiasts, but were generally considered visionary.

At that time there were less than fifty motor vehicles of various patterns in the whole of what is now Greater New York, and all were pleasure vehicles. Motor cars for business purposes had been planned, but were not in operation. Prices moreover were so high as to be almost prohibitive, except for those of large means.

During the past two years, however, such rapid progress has been made in the production of motor vehicles for almost every condition of usage, and their ease and economy of operation has been so unquestionably demonstrated that it is now believed by careful and competent observers that the disappearance of the horse from our city streets is much nearer at hand than has been generally expected, and that for business purposes at least this useful animal will become practically extinct in much less than four or five more years.

For pleasure driving the automobile is not likely, on account of sentimental reasons, to displace the horse to as great an extent as it will for business purposes. The riders and drivers of fast horses as a class are not likely to be easily converted, and the converts to the new vehicle are more likely to be drawn from the great army of non-drivers, or those who drive horses only occasionally and usually hire their rigs.

For business purposes, however, the use of the horse is governed by business principles pure and simple, and as soon as business men find that they can conduct their business more economically by using motor vehicles the horse will be displaced.

This condition of affairs has actually arrived, and the substitution of motor trucks, delivery wagons, and other self-propelled business vehicles for those drawn by horses is in active operation and is only limited by the ability or inability of the makers of the motor vehicles to keep up with their orders. As a matter of fact all the makers of motor vehicles for business purposes are several months behind with their orders, and confess their inability to keep up with the sudden demand.

Intending purchasers of automobiles will find that, although a wonderful variety of machines is now on the market, prices have not been appreciably reduced in the past two years, but, on the contrary, in some cases there has been a considerable advance.

Most of the manufacturers of motor vehicles have confined their efforts to the production of pleasure vehicles exclusively. It is estimated that there are over 200,000 horses in New York City, of which less than 50,000 are used for pleasure driving, the remainder being employed for business traffic. It is apparent, therefore, the field for motor vehicles for business purposes is several times larger, and in consequence of heavier and more powerful vehicles being required much more profitable than that for vehicles for pleasure use.

Already the motor vehicles for business purposes in use in this city include eight ambulances in use by various hospitals, a truck used by a safe manufacturing company, which has a hoisting attachment under the seat; a large furniture van, a brewery truck which carries fifty half barrels of beer, and over a hundred delivery wagons of various sorts. One express company uses motor wagons exclusively for its delivery service.

Most of these are electric vehicles, but some are propelled by steam or gasoline. At present electricity is the favorite motive power for use in city streets, but a recently perfected steam truck for very heavy work will soon be marketed in large numbers, and is expected to prove more economical than the electric vehicles.

One of the most important results of the endurance run of the Automobile Club of America on Memorial Day was the demonstration of the remarkably low cost of fuel for the trip. According to the official figures of the Automobile Club, the average cost per passenger per mile was only about a quarter of a cent for the gasoline vehicles and about half a cent for the steam carriages, the exact figures in fractions of a cent being as follows: Gasoline carriages, .27833; steam carriages, .6502. This shows that the fuel cost of the gasoline propelled vehicles was about half that of the steam motors when the two classes are grouped, but several of the steam vehicles made the trip at a less cost than some of the gasoline carriages.

The best showing was made by a twelve-horse power Mors gasoline carriage, which consumed on the trip of 100 miles but seven gallons of gasoline, costing, at 12 cents a gallon, 84 cents. As this vehicle carried five passengers the cost per passengers per mile was .168 of a cent. Next was a twelve-horse power Packard, with four passengers, which consumed 61/8 gallons of gasoline at a cost of 73½ cents. There were only four passengers in this carriage, which made the cost for each mile traveled by each passenger .18375 of a cent. An eight-horse power Searchmont machine with four passengers used seven gallons of gasoline at a cost of 84 cents, an average cost per passenger per mile of .21 of a cent.

In connection with the proposed revision of the local speed ordinance, the regulations in effect in Cleveland, Ohio, are interesting, as they were passed after having been approved at a conference between Director Charles P. Salem of the Department of Public Works and the Cleveland Automobile Club, and are considered fair to all concerned.

The provisions of the ordinance cover all the city streets, boulevards, and park drives. In the downtown districts the speed is limited to seven miles an hour, but elsewhere a rate up to fifteen miles an hour is allowed. All cars are licensed and the license number in large figures is mounted on the back of the car for the purpose of identification. For violations of the law a fine not exceeding $50 may be imposed.

The electric street cars in Cleveland frequently attain a speed of thirty miles an hour in the outlying districts, though the legal limit is twelve miles, and Mayor "Tom" Johnson, speaking of this in connection with the automobile speed regulations, said: "We do not expect the street cars to keep within the twelve miles an hour limit at all times, nor shall we hope to keep the automobiles at all times within the fifteen miles an hour limit, but we do expect the automobile drivers to use good judgment and common sense at all times, and above all to refrain from speeding when there is the slightest chance of doing injury to either horse or foot traffic."

Patterns and the Ready-to-Wear

Why There Should Be No Antagonism Between the Two Branches of Business.

Ready-to-wear apparel has made such tremendous strides during the last few years that it would be natural to suppose a corresponding loss in the sale of patterns, dress materials and accessories. This, however, has not proved the case, according to an authority in the pattern business. If the demand had remained stationary over a period of years it is quite probable that trade would have been diverted to the ready-to-wear distributors from the sources supplying materials for home dressmaking. The increase in population, rapid style changes and other conditions have greatly increased the demand and made possible the wonderful development of the ready-to-wear business without at the same time holding back in any way the steady progress of pattern companies. Sooner or later, the production of ready-to-wear apparel will find its level, and when it does, home dressmaking is expected to show a more rapid growth.

Several factors in the retail situation are taken by close students of conditions to mean that dressmaking in the home may come to the fore again sooner than expected. The most important has to do with the rising cost of doing business in the retail trade. The statement has been made that the average merchant cannot afford to offer real values at the prices he asks. This, it is said, is especially true of ready-to-wear, in which an up-to-the-minute style may bring an exorbitant price. The mark-up on ready-to-wear in many cases is higher than that used in any other department, chiefly because the policy of "putting on all the traffic will stand," [charging what the market will bear] is necessary to overcome large expenses.

This distortion of values has not passed unnoticed by the women, and a reaction must come.

"In some stores," said the pattern man, "the mark-up on ready-to-wear may be over 100 per cent. The cost of doing business has gone up so high that values have become distorted. The ready-made garment is deteriorating in both the quality of the materials and the workmanship employed. To suit the passing fad of the moment in dress, cheap materials are simply thrown together and need immediate repair when the purchaser receives them at her home. This cannot go on forever without the women raising serious objection that will mean loss of trade to the ready-made garment manufacturers.

The ready-to-wear department is often the 'goat' for other departments. It frequently is made to pay not only the cost of running it and a profit, but the expenses of other branches of the business which are run at a loss.

"There are signs to indicate," he continued, "that the reaction has already set in, and that the opportunity to develop dress goods and dress accessories departments is at hand.

"It is a feature peculiar to the pattern business alone, I think, that it has prospered despite all handicaps, many raised by the pattern manufacturers themselves. Ironclad contracts that prevented anything like fair competition, poor service, and distribution, and many other obstacles have not stepped in the way of progress. The companies that were originally in the business are larger, and there have been many new companies started. But there will have to be a general house-cleaning before the pattern manufacturers are prepared to take advantage of the opportunity afforded them. The readjustment will come; and then, when the business has been placed on an equitable basis, there is no reason in the world why there cannot be a wonderful increase in both the retailer's business and in that of the pattern companies as well.

"Styles change much more rapidly than in the past, and it is logical to suppose that all women would like to be dressed up to the minute all the time. Twice the amount of clothing can be obtained if the materials are bought and the dress made up than if it is bought ready to wear. The more clothes a woman has the happier she is, and the only thing that prevents her having twice the amount she does now is the poor service rendered by many of the pattern companies.

"If pattern designs were universally improved and a prompter service given there is no reason why the pattern, dress goods, and dress materials department of the stores should not do a greatly increased business. There has been almost an absolute lack of co-operation between the retailers and the pattern companies. The idea seems to rest in the minds of most retailers that the pattern is designed to take away business from them rather than help their sales. But such an opinion is far removed from the actual circumstances.

"Opposed as they are in the general belief of retailers, the ready-to-wear department and the pattern department should not work in opposite directions. They can be made to be of mutual help to one another, to the merchant's benefit. Properly conducted, the two departments should be operated along parallel lines. In the pattern department there should be displayed illustrations of garments sold in the ready-to-wear branch, and in the ready-to-wear department it should be brought to the notice of customers that patterns for garments in the stock, might also be obtained in the store. A sale lost in the ready-to-wear department might be saved in the pattern department. Co-operation of this sort should greatly increase the sale of dress materials and at the same time, in an ably conducted store, lead to better results in the ready-to-wear business."

How We Spend Our Time

If we worked only four hours a day—enough in a properly organized world according to some efficiency engineers—how would we spend our leisure? The problem has bothered social scientists, statesmen, ministers, newspaper editors and reformers, even though we are not yet even in sight of Utopia. It is supposed, at least by moralists, that if we had much leisure we would devote it to reading, listening to uplifting music, contemplating beauty, doing good works, enjoying healthful recreation. Alas! for this innocence. Professor Edward L. Thorndike, one of our leading experimental psychologists, brings us face to face with reality in The Scientific Monthly—or is it the joy of life? If his analysis of our low-mindedness is right—and right it seems to be in the light of such statistics as he can muster—our craving for entertainment is so insatiable that most of us give ourselves up wholeheartedly to joy-riding, dancing, games, sports, listening to the radio, going to the movies and other forms of amusement and recreation, no matter how much leisure we may have.

After men and women have spent respectively an estimated five and eight hours a week on the care of the body and personal appearance, after routine eating which consumes about ten hours of a man's time and eight of a woman's, some forty hours a week are left for self-improvement. Try as he will to put the best face on our leisure activities, Professor Thorndike finds that twenty-five of these forty hours are spent for entertainment, and other large fractions of time in gratifying a desire for companionship (another form of entertainment) and in games and sports. EDISON'S electric lamp, brighter and better than gas, oil or candles, which was supposed to lead men and women to the library, merely lures human moths to Main Street.

This study of our giddiness is introduced by a table which was compiled by Professor Nissen, authority on anthropoid apes, and which indicates in a general way how chimpanzees spend the day in French Guiana. Accepting it as it stands, the young chimpanzee bouncing with life makes a good showing, even though there is no evidence that he improves his mind or consciously basks in beauty or thinks high moral thoughts or does many good works. It is hard to conclude just what he does after he has slept eleven hours at night, climbed after food and prepared it for consumption, groomed himself or some companion, built nests, looked for water, and fought off rivals in courtship. But there is no denying that all his leisure is spent in getting all the fun possible out of life. DARWIN would have found no difficulty in explaining why we like the movies, radio, Coney Island and dancing.

July 9, 1955

Disneyland Gets Its Last Touches

Fantastic Amusement Park, at Cost of $16,500,000, to Open July 18

Juvenile World's Fair

BY GLADWIN HILL

ANAHEIM, CALIF., JULY 8—The final fantastic touches are being put on Disneyland.

The $16,500,000 amusement park created by Walt Disney, the film producer, is scheduled to open July 18.

It covers sixty acres, and is calculated to draw about 5,000,000 visitors a year.

Disneyland is situated in this citrus-ranching suburb twenty-two miles from Los Angeles. For it the appellation "amusement park" is inadequate, for it has no such banalities as roller-coasters, Ferris wheels and dodge-'ems in a milieu of honky-tonk.

In concept, it is an integrated juvenile world's fair of fantasy.

The entrance gate takes you into "Main Street—U.S.A."—a re-creation of the typical American town of 1890. Like everything else in the park, down to railroad trains and park benches, "Main Street" is built on a five-eighths scale.

Real Horse-Cars Used

Along a gas-lighted street of old-time business establishments, real horse-cars carry you into the park's central plaza.

Radiating from it are four theme-"lands"—Adventureland, Frontierland, Fantasyland and Tomorrowland.

Within is a remarkable array of mechanized adventures—an aerial monorail that duplicates Peter Pan's flight from the Darling mansion to Never-Never-Land; a Mad Hatter's Tea Party [carousel] and expeditions to Alice-in-Wonderland's rabbit hole and Snow White's gold mine.

Throughout the park are a thousand typical Disney touches—scaled-down operating railroads both passenger and freight; a blacksmith shoeing horses, and bending nails into rings; a remarkable collection of nickelodeons—one a fantastic German antique that simulates a twenty-piece band—to lend the old-time flavor.

Park Carefully Planned

In designing the park, Mr Disney retained the Stanford Research Institute to make an exhaustive study of just what a park of the sort should comprise, how it should be arranged, and where it should be located.

A year ago, he bought a 200-acre orange grove just off the Santa Ana Freeway, a high-speed thoroughfare running from downtown Los Angeles.

One hundred acres was allocated to parking space for 12,000 cars. The park was designed to accommodate up to 60,000 people a day, with an average of 15,000 expected.

There are restaurants and refreshment establishments in the park, in décors ranging from gay-Nineties to Tahitian. No alcoholic beverages will be served in the park.

On a thirty-acre track adjacent to the park, a $10,000,000, 650-room hotel-motel with a capacity of 1,250 guests is being completed.

Bank Cards Thrive as Some Stores Say No

BY ISADORE BARMASH

In your mail box or even under your door, often unwanted and unwelcomed, they keep coming—a maze of bright new, plastic credit cards to be heaped on top of all the others you already have.

Your favorite bank and banks you may never have heard of are on the prowl, both for your money and for the charge and installment business heretofore claimed as their own by the big, local stores.

In New York Interbank, the clearing house for the Master Charges bank card [later renamed MasterCard], said yesterday that some 3 million cardholders are now listed in the metropolitan New York area. And BankAmericard [later renamed Visa], the credit card franchised by the Bank of America of San Francisco to the Bankers Trust Company here, is said to have 600,000 card holders in the metropolitan area.

Big Stores Say No

But the big New York stores, such as Macy's, Gimbels, Abraham & Straus, Bloomingdale's, B. Altman and others, say they have no intention of honoring these cards. "They're not for us," said one credit man yesterday.

However, thousands of smaller stores, as well as the discount or promotional stores that have either not been in the credit field very long or haven't reached anything like the credit customer saturation they want have signed on with either Master Charge or Bank Americard or both.

And the situation is true in almost every major city in America.

The traditional department stores do not like bank cards because they say it is new competition, rather than an aid to them.

Robert Thiel, vice president of the National Retail Merchants Association and manager of its credit management division, said yesterday, "I don't think the bank cards have hurt the department stores, although it is probably too early to tell. At the same time, it is providing new competition because many small stores and specialty shops now subscribe to the bank cards and are offering credit for the first time."

Other merchants fear that honoring the bank cards would mean giving up control of the credit policy that they maintain as a competitive measure.

"Setting the terms, deciding on maturity dates, how and when to get tough on slow payers—these have been considerations that we have made for years," a retail credit manager said. "Now we are asked to give up what we consider to be a competitive edge over the other stores. Why?"

The bank-credit-card community, however, sees this as only a short-term view. On a long-term basis, several prominent bank-card officials feel, they will triumph—and it will be to the great advantage of the retailer.

The end of 1969 will probably see 50 million card holders signed up between the two big bank credit cards, said Garrison A. Southard, president of the Interbank Card Association, the clearing house for Master Charge and other cards in other cities.

"The great market we can provide for stores, plus the strong possibility that we can develop an important direct-mail program for selling merchandise are elements that stores can only use to their great benefit," he said. Because of the "great volume" of bank cards, he added, "we can handle the big stores' credit system and mail-order selling more efficiently and economically."

Asked how the bank cards were affecting the standard credit cards, Richard Howland, General Manager of American Express's credit-card division, replied, "Our business remains 33 per cent higher this year on a base of $1.3-billion, which makes us about the biggest credit card in the country."

In this typical example of early-2000s "McMansion growth" in Delray Beach, Florida, an original "bash and build" house was replaced by a much bigger one. Such expansion was suddenly halted by the housing crisis of 2008, when many homes were abandoned—some half-finished. (Len Kaufman for the *New York Times*)

The American Diet, Then and Now

We eat seven times more pickles than they did in 1910.

BY PATRICIA WELLS

We Americans love to eat. And we love nothing better than eating lots of the foods we love best. In 1976, for instance, the "average American" satisfied his ever-growing sweet tooth by downing 493 eight-ounce soft drinks, treated himself to more than 18 pounds of ice cream and between 1950 and 1976 increased consumption of beef by 90 percent. Not surprisingly, we are eating less and less of the foods we believe, for a variety of reasons, we should avoid. And so over the years we [have] cut back on candy bars (seen as "empty calories"), drastically reduced consumption of foods considered "fattening," such as bread and fresh potatoes, and cast a dietary frown upon foods we are told contribute to a high cholesterol level: eggs, butter, whole milk, heavy cream.

We Americans are also quite inconsistent. Does giving up candy bars for soft drinks, baked potatoes for french fries or eggs for ice cream make much sense? No. But then no one ever asked us to change our eating habits with perfect logic.

Anyone interested in comparing the diet of our grandparents with the foods of the 1970's will want to examine "The Changing American Diet," a new publication written by Letitia Brewster and Michel Jacobson of Washington's Center for Science in the Public Interest, a non-profit consumer organization. What the book does, quite simply, is to compare the diet of 1910 with the diet of today, and comes up with some fascinating figures.

The modern American, for example, consumes nearly the same number of calories—about 3,400—as Americans did in 1910, but since we get less exercise, our weight has increased substantially during the last 15 years. The report notes that the most alarming dietary change is the drastic rise in the amount of fat consumed between 1910 and 1976. Fat provides 42 percent of our calories each day, or 27 percent more dietary fat than our grandparents got in 1910, an increase many health professionals link to increased cardiovascular disease and possibly certain cancers.

The book is not without statistics that some readers will find a bit amusing. We don't love watermelon the way they did in 1920. We consume a mere 12.2 pounds annually per capita, while back then each American slurped up some 20 pounds of that sweet red melon each year. We also eat three times more fresh carrots and fresh corn than they did in 1910, and seven times the amount of pickles.

The report, based on figures compiled by the United States Department of Agriculture, suggests that the fast food restaurants have had the greatest impact on the contemporary diet, and account for our rapidly increased consumption of ice milk, frozen french fries, fish, chicken, beef, hard cheese, soft drinks and, of course, pickles.

Tomorrow—'A Video Supermarket'

BY PETER FUNT

For most of its life, cable television has been a medium without a message, an industry whose chief concerns were technology and marketing, not programming. But now, as cable nears 30 percent saturation of all homes in the United States—the point at which it can command national advertising, which industry experts expect cable to achieve sometime in 1981—there is frenzied interest in the medium among those who hope to provide it with original program material. If current claims can be believed, cable viewers will soon be offered an entire network designed for persons over age 50; a 24-hour news network featuring a two-hour newscast in prime time; an all-sports network; an all-Spanish language network; a network providing electronic material for those equipped to play video-computer games, and a cornucopia of other special-interest programs.

So great is cable's potential that its suppliers do not speak in terms of individual programs or series but rather of whole "networks." And, although the talk at this stage seems to center on quantity more than quality, cable television is clearly on the verge of a programming explosion. As explained by Jim Heyworth, a vice president with the Home Box Office pay-cable network, "Cable television is a video supermarket, now faced with the challenge of determining how best to fill its vacant shelf space."

For many years, cable's primary utility was to provide clear reception in areas where over-the-air broadcast signals were weak or obstructed by tall buildings or the terrain. Accordingly, it was popular in remote and sparsely populated areas of upstate New York, Kansas and other isolated places, but was little known elsewhere. At that stage of the evolution of cable, occasional promoters would offer to send programs on video-cassettes by mail to the existing cable stations, but this arrangement did not prove economically feasible. The situation changed dramatically in the early 1970's when improved satellite communications made it possible to beam dozens of television signals simultaneously to any cable company equipped with an earth-receiving station. In 1977, there were fewer than 100 of these earth stations; today, there are nearly 1,500.

This satellite technology, coupled with cable's increased circulation, has provided both the means and the motive for increased programming, which in turn has created a boon for program producers and suppliers. Some are rushing in with what is referred to within the industry as "basic cable" programming: programs with commercials, offered as part of the regular monthly improved-reception service. Other production companies are developing new "pay-cable" material: programs presented without commercials on special channels for which subscribers pay an extra fee. In many areas of the country where the public has access to perhaps only two or three local channels, the prospects of multichannelled cable is an option viewers seem willing to pay for almost regardless of the content or quality of the programming offered. But as cable proliferates in major markets, the challenge to producers is: Can innovative programs be created to gain a following and thus take advantage of the new technology?

One entrepreneur who is eagerly taking up the challenge is R.E. (Ted) Turner, the flamboyant owner of WTCG-TV (Channel 17) in Atlanta, Ga. Since 1977, Mr. Turner has used a satellite to distribute WTCG's signal to cable companies nationwide, giving birth to the term "superstation" and expanding Channel 17's potential audience to a level that today exceeds 5 million homes.

Now, Turner Communications is at the forefront of original cable programming with its 24-hour Cable News Network, the nation's first all-news television network, which is scheduled to begin operations in June 1980.

Mr. Turner has hired Daniel Schorr, the former CBS News correspondent, to head the new network's Washington bureau. Several other nationally known contributors have also been signed, and construction is underway on a new studio in Atlanta from which most of the programming will originate.

But Mr. Turner, among other things an America's Cup winner, knows that with this project he is sailing in uncharted waters. Even with a pre-launch budget that could run as high as $35 million, it is doubtful the Cable News Network can mount a news service that approaches the scope of those at CBS, NBC and ABC.

An equally ambitious cable operation, due to begin in September, is the Entertainment and Sports Programming Network (ESPN), based in Bristol, Conn. With the Getty Oil Company as its major backer, ESPN plans to become the nation's first all-sports network, offering not only play-by-play coverage but also sports-related news and feature programs.

Both ESPN and Turner Communications' Cable News Network will include commercials and are intended to be offered as part of "basic-cable" service. Until advertising revenues, however, are able to support the network, cable companies will have to help offset the production costs.

[Thus far, many cable companies, like ESPN, have relied on familiar programming formats.] Such mimicking of the established networks, however, can only make cable networks more vulnerable to criticism and less the programming "alternative" they hope to be.

The same can be said about pay-cable networks, which emerged in the early 1970's, primarily as an outlet for recently released motion pictures. However, while theatrically released films remain their major product, the larger pay networks, such as Time, Inc's Home Box Office (HBO), are now expanding their schedules to include more original material.

"We made a decision a few years ago to try producing our own shows," says HBO vice president Michael Fuchs. "Our first effort was 'On Location,' which featured performers in nightclub and concert settings. But that form burns up quickly, so we have started acting more like a network, looking for new forms to try."

One new form, according to Mr. Fuchs, is "Docutainment"—a mix of documentary and entertainment forms. HBO's first effort in this field is a mini-series titled "Time Was," which is scheduled to begin in November. The series of six, 90-minute programs will have Dick Cavett as host and will explore American history, decade by decade, from 1920 to the present.

Elsewhere on the pay-cable scene, HBO's major competitor, Showtime—owned jointly by Teleprompter and Viacom International—will soon turn its attention to Broadway and Off-Broadway productions. The first four presentations are being taped this summer and will be included on Showtime's fall schedule.

Beginning Sept. 1, there will also be a Spanish-language pay-cable network called Galavision. Initially, Galavision will operate seven hours per day, presenting first-run Spanish-language films, sports and variety specials, most of which will be imported from Mexico.

How much expansion of this type will the television market bear? And what impact will new cable programming have on public television and the established commercial networks? Some officials in public broadcasting have expressed the fear that as viewers pay more for cable, they will be less inclined to make contributions to public-television stations. As for the major networks, they are keeping a close watch on cable's growth. Studying the matter for NBC—and its parent company RCA, the leader in satellite operations—is Richard Sonnenfeldt, executive vice president of Operations and Technical Services.

"Despite cable's high growth rate," he says, "we don't see it having any significant impact on the three networks over the next 10 years. Some cable programmers are going to be very successful, certainly. But when you add up the numbers, it's not a threat to any network. In fact, it's like comparing a sailboat to a freight train."

Mr. Sonnenfeldt estimates that the number of homes with cable, now put at about 15 million, could climb in the next 10 years to anywhere from 28 to 50 million—out of a total of nearly 75 million U.S. households.

"We expect overall use of television by the public to increase during the next decade," says Mr. Sonnenfeldt, "but since we do not foresee much change in the networks' total viewing audience, most of the growth will be by other television media."

In Nile Huts, TV and Old Values

BY RICHARD CRITCHFIELD

Will the stampede toward the consumer society cause unbearable strains on Islam? Everybody in Egypt keeps watching for signs.

Suddenly, there is a television set in every mud hut along the Nile. Sometimes there is a washing machine or refrigerator. Migrant workers, mainly going to the Arab Gulf states, have been sending home $3 to $4 billion a year. These remittances go to buy land, new houses, pumps, tractors, livestock and farm machinery in villages where cultivation methods had survived since the pharaohs. Peasants who still believe the earth is flat and surrounded by the mountains of Kaf, where the djinn [genies] live, watch "I Love Lucy" reruns.

Mosque attendance at Friday prayers is way up. The sermons are a bit more provocative, the amplifiers a little louder. Liquor is no longer served in Cairo's clubs. Sects of sufi mystics, dervishes and Moslem saints are getting bigger. Holier-than-thou piety is not unknown. In May, 14 members of the long-illegal Moslem Brotherhood were elected to the 448 seat Parliament, sending a chill down many spines. They would create an Islamic state.

Cairo asks itself: Can it happen here? Besides being the cultural center of the Moslem world, Cairo is also the world's most densely populated city. Despite elbow-to-elbow crowding, Cairenes are a remarkably cheerful, tolerant lot (if fiery-tempered and raucous voiced: it takes a while to realize that a riot is not imminent). Nobody goes hungry, for one thing. The average Egyptian gets half his daily calorie intake from three loaves of heavily subsidized Arab bread costing the equivalent of one American penny each. Cairo is probably the last place left where you can get a tasty, filling, nourishing meal of bread, beans and salad for six cents.

Even so, everybody's tolerance has its limits. ("Beans!" one man erupted, when told his meal was cheap. "You want us always to eat beans?") And unlike the newly rich peasants, virtual serfs until the 1952 revolution, Egypt's post-1976 economic boom has passed by low-paid, government-salaried civil servants, junior army officers and public-sector factory workers, who may swell the Moslem militants' ranks. In contrast, unskilled workers among the village peasants have seen an annual 9 percent rise in income in real terms the past eight years.

Workers, remittances are now more than Egypt will get this year from oil exports ($2.6 billion), foreign economic aid ($2 billion, half of it from the United States and worthily spent on getting food production up and the birth rate down), Suez Canal revenues ($1 billion) or tourism ($600 million).

The villagers seem torn between wanting all the new consumer goods while sticking to their older values. They want the TV set but they want to watch good Moslems praying on it. Or, as the writer V. S. Naipaul once put it, they like the West's tools but not its ideas. The snag, as every anthropologist knows, is that the tools shape the ideas. You can't have one without the other; all culture has an economic basis. The late President Anwar el-Sadat saw this trouble coming. In a 1976 interview, he told me he warned those who tried to Westernize and modernize too fast to "look to our community, our people and our Moslem heritage."

Thoughtful Moslems—and, despite their reputation for terrorism and conspiracy, this includes a good many Moslem Brotherhood members—would like to reconcile Islam as far as possible with modern science and technology. They recognize that Islam has never had its version of the Protestant Reformation, which transformed Christianity by offering salvation through hard work and a more scientific control of matter and energy. They also see that Confucianism, by subordinating individual interest to group interest, has played much the same role in the fast economic growth of East Asia.

But where is Islam to find its Calvin or Confucius? Until it does, it may be fated—doomed, one might say—to keep giving battle to the process of modernization. And what happens in the villages when all those new appliances wear out?

Reprinted by permission of S11/Sterling Lord Litaristic, Inc. Copyright by Estate of Richard Critchfield.

November 8, 2001

U.N. Says Four Billion Will Be Living in Hunger by 2050

UNITED NATIONS NOV, 7—The world population stands at 6.1 billion, double what it was in 1960, and is projected to reach 9.3 billion by 2050, the United Nations Population Fund reported today in its annual report. All the growth will be in developing countries; industrialized countries will remain stable in population.

The report said two billion people already lacked sufficient food, and water use had increased six times over the past 70 years. By 2050, it said, 4.2 billion people would be living in countries where their basic needs cannot be met. "The report shows that poverty and rapid population growth are a deadly combination," the executive director of the fund, Thoraya Obaid, said at a briefing. "Poor people depend more directly on natural resources such as available land, wood and water, and yet they suffer the most from environmental degradation." The increasing impact on the environment, Ms. Obaid said, resulted not only from growing population but also from "rising affluence and unsustainable consumption patterns."

"The world's wealth is some $30 trillion, but half the world lives on $2 a day or less," she said. "The message here is clear: while some of us practice wasteful consumption, others cannot consume enough to survive."

The report called for universal education, basic health care and specific actions to empower women to have only the number of children they want.

Where Silence Was Golden, Pocket Phones Now Shriek

BY MOLLY O'NEILL

The hushed conversations and gentle clicks of cutlery against china at Campton Place, an elegant San Francisco restaurant, were shattered recently by a high-pitched squeal that seemed to emanate from one diner. A pacemaker gone awry? A stray white-collar criminal with an electronic handcuff? No, it was another sort of tie that binds: Brad Kendal's new portable telephone, a $1,200 Pocket Commander.

"I forgot to turn it off," he said to his companion. "Yeah!" he answered into the phone.

The Sound broke The Silence. It's happening in theaters, on golf courses, at tennis matches and other bastions of silence, and it's bound to happen more. Last month the Motorola Company introduced "Microtac Lite," a miniature portable telephone that weighs less than eight ounces, and other manufacturers have followed with pocket-size telephones that could become as ubiquitous as Walkmans.

"Personal portable telephones are the fastest growing segment of the cellular industry," said Norman Black, a spokesman for the Cellular Telecommunications Industry Association in Washington. He said that there were 5.3 million cellular telephones in the United States today, and that he expected 33 million cellular phones to join the chorus within the next 10 years, which means bleating garments, briefcases and handbags can only proliferate.

So far, no clear-cut etiquette has quelled the interlopers, especially where they are least expected. "I heard one in church last week," said Letitia Baldrige, author of "Letitia Baldrige's Complete Guide to the New Manners for the '90's," (Rawson, 1990). She was speaking on a desktop telephone from her home in Washington. "Can you imagine if it had been a wedding? A call-in objection?"

Etiquette always trails revolutions. Since this product of the technological revolution only made its debut in 1983, a code of cellular telephone courtesy is still evolving.

Some greet the electronic bleating with a cosmic shrug. "My father rode this train and read the papers in peace; so did my grandfather," said Thaddeus Whitmore, an investment banker who takes the train daily from New Canaan, Conn., to his office on Wall Street. "The code has been shattered, absolutely shattered. There is nothing I can do."

Mr. Whitmore is resigned to the half-life of conversations that drift through his train. "I've heard the future," he said. "I hear the future every morning."

Others are more militant. "I've been threatened," Arthur Crayton, a political consultant who lives in Cambridge, Mass., said in a telephone interview as he walked across Harvard Yard. Mr. Crayton uses a portable phone when he is commuting between Boston and Washington. "You would not believe how hostile people get over a little hand phone," he said, sounding baffled.

The arrival of electronic bleats and brays [has] drawn both resigned and militant responses in other traditionally phone-free areas.

In theaters, the demographics of the clientele seem to shape management's policies. Lincoln Center hasn't taken an active role in restricting cellular activity in any of its concert halls or theaters. "People come here to listen to the symphony or the ballet, not to talk on the telephone," said Joe McKaughan, vice president of public affairs at the vast mid-Manhattan complex. "Patrons are self-policing in this area."

On the other hand, the Wometco Theaters, a string of 17 movie theaters in southern Florida, banned personal phones last summer. "We had a number of complaints and skirmishes and finally a fist fight in one of our most upscale theaters," said John Ray, president of Wometco. Signs suggesting that moviegoers turn their telephones off were not heeded.

"The more important people think they are, the louder they insist on their quote unquote rights," Mr. Ray said. Customers no longer have a right to carry personal telephones into Wometco's movie houses.

Restaurateurs are divided along similar lines. The Teahouse Restaurant in Vancouver, British Columbia, posted a no-phoning notice on the Teahouse's menu last year.

But at Le Cirque in Manhattan, "Our customers prefer to check their personal telephones with their coats," said the owner, Sirio Maccioni. Speaking on the wall phone near the restaurant's front door, he added, "If they get a call, the coat-check person alerts the guest who can then leave the table to take the call."

Mrs. Baldrige, still speaking from her desk phone, called that "an elegant solution. People like physicians and construction foremen who need to be in touch can be, and they can attend to their business without inflicting its particulars on the people at the next table who might be trying to have a romantic meal."

The problem of intrusion has been addressed within the portable telephone industry. Under the guise of "Ms. Mobile Manners," Cantel Industries, one of two companies that offer cellular service in Canada, advised port-a-phoners to use a low voice in social settings.

When Fujitsu America introduced its Pocket Commander portable phone, it also issued 10 commandments for the phone's polite deployment. They ranged from "Don't interrupt formal business meetings," and "No calls after the movie starts," to "In restaurants let ambiance be your guide," and "Remember to excuse yourself from the person you are talking to if you accept an incoming call."

These common courtesies help neutralize the intrusiveness of cellular telephone conversations. But they don't address the exhibitionist element of some porto-phoning. In "Miss Manners' Guide for the Turn-of-The-Millennium," (Pharos Books, 1989) Judith Martin also advises porto-phone users not to annoy other people with noise or to ignore "those with you in favor of the disembodied voice." Like most manners mavens, she suggests that even the most discreet should be prepared to be the center of attention.

"Oh, they love that," Mrs. Baldrige said of cellular-phone swaggerers she has seen. "Some people have their secretaries call them at restaurants or the theater in a pathetic attempt to show how important they are. Men drive the roads of this country with a phone pressed to their ear and nobody on the other end. People talk to their answering machines in the theater. All to say, 'I'm important and you are not.'"

Exhibitionists among the cellular-phone set could be giving all users a bad name. White knights with wireless phones are not unknown. Last month, when the 8 A.M. train from Princeton Junction to Manhattan was delayed for several hours, E. Jay Williams Jr., president of Sheridan Broadcasting in Manhattan, was besieged by fellow passengers who offered to pay him for the use of his 1989 Oki700. He related his "first brush with cellular good will" from his office phone, explaining, "I got your message on my wireless and I came in here for some privacy."

Then he turned his attention to cellular good Samaritanism: "To accept payment didn't seem humane. These were people desperate to call family, to call the office. I let them use the wireless for free until I started to feel like a phone booth. Then I put it back in my briefcase."

Such moments of modern heroism are, unfortunately, drowned by exhibitions of one-upmanship. As Jim Courier, the tennis player, was serving in the quarterfinals at the United States Open in Queens several weeks ago, he said he heard "this funky kind of ring, right by the court." The bleating shattered the moment that fans and players have always shared, the silence and concentration before the swish and heave of a serve.

"I thought, 'Could anybody be *that* important?'" Mr. Courier said, speaking on one of the phones in his Kansas City hotel room last week.

Sometimes humor is the best paste for a crack in a time-honored code. At the Open, he paused at the electronic ring, loosened the grip on his racquet, put the ball in his pocket, and yelled, "I'll get it!"

That's Not a Skim Latte.
It's a Way of Life.

BY JENNIFER STEINHAUER

The last time you pulled a shirt out of a drawer, it is possible you were not simply getting dressed. You were actually living out a small moment of a life style, one shared with thousands of others, and one you probably didn't know you were leading.

More and more, retailers and makers of products from T-shirts to watering cans are broadening their pitch, selling their wares by marketing an entire way of living.

Calvin Klein isn't content to have its customers wear its underwear; the company longs to have them serve food on its dishes and towel off with its bath sheets. Starbucks executives don't want people to just drink their coffee in the morning; they want them to eat their ice cream and listen to their music CD's in bed. That way, Starbucks becomes more than a network of caffeine-delivery outlets—it elbows its way into consumers' lives and becomes an essential part of their day.

"Coffee is a very emotional and romantic beverage," said Howard Schultz, Starbuck's chief executive and life-style marketing evangelist. "It is an extension of people's front porch. Our stores are a place where people are very comfortable, because people trust us. Starbucks is more than a coffee. It is a feeling, it is an experience."

Perhaps this sounds like hokum. But tell that to Levi Strauss & Company, one of the most famous brands in America, which announced recently that declining sales and tough competition would result in the dismissal of 5,900 workers and the closing of 11 plants. Maybe one of Levi's problems is that it has no cola. It has no denim-toned house paint. Levi makes what is essentially a commodity: blue jeans. Its ads may evoke rugged outdoorsmanship, but Levi hasn't promoted any particular life style to sell other products.

Once people get to know a brand's most famous product, the thinking goes, they will trust that brand to deliver any number of items, even if the original product has no relationship to the subsequent stuff the company hawks. To wit: Brooks Brothers now has its own line of wines, and Jack Daniel's sells clothes.

"Great marketers say the brand can be the thing that holds their group of consumers together," said Sam I. Hill, a principal partner at Helios Consulting in New York. "The life-style label is an intelligent reaction by marketers who want a deeper relationship with consumers."

The retail industry generates $2.7 trillion in annual sales, so those deeper relationships are worth a great deal. There are two basic steps in life-style branding. The first is to plaster the brand's name or logo on every imaginable product. Ralph Lauren is not just a polo pony stitched to the front of shirts and dresses; it's a name that appears on linens, towels, eye-glasses, bras and house paint. Gucci sells home decor items that resemble their belt buckles, and nearly every clothing designer has at least one perfume.

Retailers must also spend a lot of money to create advertisements that depict their products among people and in situations that embody what their marketing whizzes call a "state of mind"—preferably one that appeals to con-sumers of all ages. This will insure that young girls will want to wear your inappropriately low-cut shirts, because they are older at heart, and those a bit long-in-the-tooth will buy your wedge-cut sandals, reasoning that they share a youthful outlook.

The best way for retailers to get lots of people living a life style is to reach them through a variety of media. Martha Stewart—who may actually be the first human to embody a life style—has this down pat. She has a weekly television program, a magazine and several lines of products—pricey ones sold through her catalogue and magazine, and a set of household items at much lower prices sold through Kmart stores. The genius of Ms. Stew-art's strategy is that her life style is decidedly upscale, even as she makes it accessible to middle-class consumers, the nation's biggest group of purchasers.

To promote a life style, a company must ob-sessively market its products through ad cam-paigns in which the product is not nearly as central as the people using it. Who cares what jeans the models are wearing in a Ralph Lauren ad? All that matters is that everyone looks wholesome, athletic and delighted to be frol-icking or lounging on the grounds of an expen-sive beach-front property.

In most Nine West ads, it is hard to make out the shoes or bag for sale. But the women are young and sexy and never far from a great-looking guy and a romantic setting. A shopper is meant to believe that if she buys the whole package—clothes, tables, sheets and bras—she will join the elite club of those living out the brand's life style in its ads.

"What people feel about themselves is a much greater predictor of buying behavior" than who they actually are, Mr. Hill said. "And that is really what you care about."

Stacy Lastrina, a spokeswoman for Nine West, which has expanded from footwear to handbags, sunglasses and belts, said: "We posi-tion Nine West as aspirational yet attainable. The one carry-through is that the wearer has a contemporary, modern, upbeat attitude."

Every marketer fantasizes that it knows its customers intimately. But they are often not quite on the mark. Jill Virkus, 31, a production manager for a publishing company in Chicago, owns several pairs of Nine West shoes and a purse. Her motivation for buying Nine West seems fairly straightforward. "I think that their stuff is wearable and cool looking without being too out there," she said. "Am I contempo-rary? Yes. Am I upbeat? Sure. Am I modern? I'm not sure. That to me is black leather and chrome."

Ralph Lauren is among the most experienced and relentless retailers pursuing life-style marketing. The company's clothing ranges from the very high end to T-shirts and jeans, and it sells sunglasses, house paint, home furnishings, shoes and many other products.

Mr. Lauren says he knows who he's designing his wares for. "I know where they live, where they want to go," he said. "I know how they dress and the kind of restaurants they go to."

His vision, he acknowledges, is somewhat flexible: "A guy who works on Wall Street may go to the Cape as opposed to the Hamptons, but the Hollywood guys go to the Hamptons. The photographers go to Martha's Vineyard."

By and large, the Ralph Lauren shopper is "sophisticated and has his choice of things to buy," said Mr. Lauren. "My brand is about consistency of style and taste, not formula."

Camille Walker, 27, a nursing assistant in Philadelphia, said half of her clothes have a Polo label. She also owns sheet sets and bath mats.

Here is her take on Mr. Lauren's vision: "He advertises to the rich because he is rich. But mostly poor people wear the sportswear. All my friends wear the T-shirts and the pants; I am the only one who wears the designer clothes. Rich people wear his higher-end line, but Polo is for kids from the ghetto. I don't think he knows that, but I know that."

"I wouldn't say I live his life style," she added. "I would say I just thank God for my health."

November 29, 1999

Jeremiah Speaks

BY WILLIAM SAFIRE

In changing around the clothes in my closet to get ready for winter, I made a dismaying discovery: I have 38 shirts.

What kind of person needs 38 shirts? I am not a clothes horse, much less a shirt freak. Even after subtracting the purple polyester corduroy given to me that I would not be caught dead in, that leaves more shirts than a man can wear in a month.

My first reaction is defensive. What's wrong with having a vast assortment of shirts? I make a good living; the good times are rolling. So what if there's no more room on my shelves? That means only that it's time to build more shelving.

What's more, my shirt acquisition program makes me an economy-driving consumer. This adds to the profits of Van Heusen or Brooks Brothers, thereby raising the stock value of America's pension funds and putting rice in the mouths of impoverished Malaysians who sew on the sleeves. Spending can thus be justified as a virtue, even when it buys the unneeded.

Muttering the millennial mantra, "spendthriftiness is next to godliness," I went to the factory-outlet mall in Hagerstown, Md. There, on Thanks-for-your-patronage Weekend, consumer consummation was rife. Hordes of buyers lined up to snatch items reduced from "list prices" that only fools in department stores pay.

Accompanied by my value-savvy family, I experienced the thrill of the bargain hunt. Nine West and Timberland shoes went for a pittance; Ralph Lauren suits from only last season were swept off a clearance rack; Donna Karan cashmere sweaters that hung down to the ankles were offered in all their dark-gray glory for a measly 99 bucks.

Every plastic-carded purchase seemed to be vengeance against the evil forces of "list." To get an early-bird reduction from the sale price—with 50 percent off for the second pair of unneeded whatever—was a buyer's bliss.

And yet, and yet. Standing here in the epicenter of pre-Christmasism, laden with shopping bags of merchandise that proved my worth both as a provider and conspicuous consumer, a nagging thought rooted in the dim past intrudes: is this the way I want to spend my leisure time? What kind of cheap triumph is a cheap sweater? Who needs all this stuff anyway?

Never say "piffle"[nonsense] to an epiphany. Today's rush to buy is not yesterday's addiction to acquisition. We have gone past that lust for possessions that motivated the hoarders of yesteryear. Greed is no longer the game; in our time, shopping has become the primary form of entertainment.

So here we are in the Age of Shoppertainment. What we buy and wear merges with what we see and hear; this great blob of self-absorption and inter-amusement takes up our time and occupies our minds. The moving finger writes the message on the T-shirt: To fill the shopping cart is to fulfill oneself.

The philosophy of the shoppertainers holds that the act of spending and not the object acquired is the source of fun. In the past, the poet worried that "getting and spending, we lay waste our powers," but as the getting gets easier, it's the spending that gives us the kick.

You can shop the world, but I want to get off. Mall mania may be the marketing majority's way of living, but it's no way of life. Doing the outlet center does not stimulate the mind or recreate the body or satisfy the soul.

The modern Jeremiah asks: as you snatch the merchandise off the shelf, are you learning something, or—just as important—are you teaching anything? The money you spend today you might re-make tomorrow, but the time you spend spending can never be bought back.

Worry not, the sensual sybarites of suburbia assure us, the malls and the factory-outlet centers are transitory. Coming generations will turn to the virtual virtues of Internet intellect, and knowledge and art will be the intercourse most desired.

But do you know what our offspring are already doing on that brave new medium? They say they are "engaged in e-commerce," but what they are doing is amusing themselves shopping.

This Jeremiah sees that future and it works all too well. Picked up a couple of nice shirts, though.

38 Shirts

Probing the Consumer Culture

To the Editor:

Since I rarely agree with William Safire, allow me to commend him for his realization that our consumer society has indeed turned in on itself (column, Nov. 29). As a 30-something veteran of the suburban mall culture, I too feel the emptiness around me and recoil from the glazed countenances of my neighbors as they pursue ever more elusive "bargains" at the expense of an inner life.

Parents generally lament the difficulties of raising children in this hyped environment as well as the lack of time available for family life. Would that we all spent fewer hours shopping and watching television and devoted more time to our family and friends. Consumers, heal thyselves!

John Bennett
Scituate, Mass., Nov. 29, 1999

Caught in the Credit Card Vise

BY BOB HERBERT

"I'm still paying for groceries I bought for my family years ago," said Julie Pickett.

She meant it literally. Mrs. Pickett and her husband, Jerry, of Middletown, Ohio, are trapped in the iron grasp of credit card debt. Except for the fact that no one is threatening to damage their kneecaps, they're in the same dismal position as the classic victim of loan-sharking.

People used to get thrown in jail for the very things credit card companies can now do legally. While banks and money markets are paying pittances in interest, it's common for the annual percentage rate on your friendly Visa or Mastercard to approach 30 percent.

This used to be called usury.

Julie Pickett stopped working full time when she had the twins. Jerry Pickett's business hit a downturn at about the same time. The family's credit cards, said Mrs. Pickett, suddenly loomed as "lifelines" to the daily necessities—food, gas, auto repairs, clothing for the children.

Another child was born and the credit card debt eventually reached $40,000—an amount (with its perpetually increasing interest) that the Picketts are unable to pay off.

"We had one card that had about an $8,000 balance," Ms. Pickett said in an interview. "With interest and late fees it's now $18,000. The interest when we started out was like 18 percent. But after a year of not paying, it jumped to 28 percent."

Families like the Picketts are indeed responsible for the payment of their debts. But the credit card companies are engaged in one of the many big-time legalized rackets that are flourishing in this age of deregulation. The Picketts are profiled in a new report, titled "Borrowing to Make Ends Meet," by a nonpartisan public policy group called Demos: A Network for Ideas and Action.

The economy may have boomed in the last half of the 90's. But over the course of that decade, millions of American families sank deeper and deeper into debt, in large part because of the overuse of credit cards.

"Between 1989 and 2001," the report said, "credit card debt in America almost tripled, from $238 billion to $692 billion. The savings rate steadily declined, and the number of people filing for bankruptcy jumped 125 percent."

Few things are easier than flashing the plastic and saying, "Charge it." And few heads of households, when broke, can resist the urge to use a credit card to buy food for the family or gas up the car to go to work.

In the period studied, the credit card debt of the average family increased by 53 percent. For middle-class families, the increase was 75 percent. For senior citizens, 149 percent. And for very low-income families, with annual incomes below $10,000, the increase was a staggering 184 percent.

The theme of the report is that while credit card use is frequently associated with frivolous consumption, the evidence seems to show that more and more Americans are using credit cards to bridge the difficult gap between household earnings and the cost of essential goods and services. Men and women struggling with such structural problems as job displacement, declining real wages and rising housing and health care costs have been relying on their credit cards as a way of warding off complete disaster.

At the same time the credit card companies have leapt gleefully into an orgy of exploitation.

"Late fees," the report said, "have become the fastest growing source of revenue for the industry, jumping from $1.7 billion in 1996 to $7.3 billion in 2002. Late fees now average $29, and most cards have reduced the late payment grace period from 14 days to zero days. In addition to charging late fees, the major credit card companies use the first late payment as an excuse to cancel low, introductory rates—often making a zero percent card jump to between 22 and 29 percent."

How high can interest rates go? According to Tamara Draut, one of the authors of the study, all of the major credit card issuers are located in states that have no limits on the rate of interest they can charge. (The state where the credit-card holder resides is irrelevant.)

And how crazy has the situation become? The Pickett family, which is absolutely unable to pay off the debt it has now, gets offers in the mail to open new credit card accounts every day.

CHAPTER 7

THE CHANGING WORKPLACE

A call center in a Delhi suburb. Outsourcing of tasks such as customer service to contract workers in different countries offered late-twentieth-century companies a way to control labor costs. (Zack Canepari for the *New York Times*)

N THE LATE TWENTIETH CENTURY, LONG AFTER THE RISE OF BIG BUSINESS and all that it wrought for working Americans—including scientific management, organized labor, and the urbanization and suburbanization of the workforce—men and women began to experience a series of new upheavals. In many ways, the shifts were deceptively subtle. There was no mass migration from the family

1844	1870	1906	1920	1942
Lowell Female Labor Reform Association (LFLRA) formed.	15th Amendment gives African Americans right to vote.	Upton Sinclair's *The Jungle* published.	19th Amendment grants women the vote.	United States enters World War II.

farm to the urban factory, no catastrophic happening such as Black Tuesday or the bombing of Pearl Harbor to unite the country in the face of an astounding, disastrous event. But for millions of families, the transformation of the workplace that unfolded in the late twentieth and early twenty-first centuries was no less acute than these earlier shocks. The reversal of long-standing labor trends, the disintegration of the social contract, the widespread adoption of new technologies, and the emergence of new opportunities changed our experience of work, leisure, and family.

One of the most significant trends of the late twentieth century was the decline of job stability, which had first become part of the socioeconomic landscape in the late 1800s. During these years, the railroads, hungry for skilled, experienced managers, had been the first corporations to use job security as a means to retain and develop workers.[1] Other industries soon followed suit, advertising year-round employment and advancement opportunities for both white- and blue-collar workers.[2] As its influence expanded early in the twentieth century, organized labor encouraged this development.

The onset of the Great Depression threw Americans and the working patterns they had come to know into chaos as millions lost their livelihoods. To lessen the trauma of widespread, seemingly chronic unemployment and financial insecurity, the federal government funded thousands of public works projects. Through the Public Works Administration (PWA), about half a million people were employed every year in projects that ranged from the completion of the Hoover Dam to the construction of public schools, post offices, and roads in communities across the United States.[3] For men and women from all walks of life, such work was a critical source of income, stability, and validation in an uncertain moment.

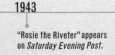

1943

"Rosie the Riveter" appears on *Saturday Evening Post.*

1944

Union membership rises to 14,146,000.

1946

Employment Act promotes "maximum employment, production, and purchasing power."

1973

HMO Act provides $375 million for the development of managed health care.

1975

Stagflation sets in with 12 percent inflation and 8 percent unemployment.

The shock of the Great Depression did not derail the longer-term trend toward steadier, more secure employment, which resumed in the 1940s. The onset of World War II mobilized the American workforce on a massive scale, enlisting more than ten million men in military occupations and creating jobs for three million women, many of whom went into factories that manufactured aircraft, munitions, and other wartime goods.[4] As the U.S. economy boomed in the postwar years, corporations—from General Motors to General Foods—saw their sales climb rapidly. Many, including manufacturers of women's hosiery, household furniture, kitchen appliances, cameras, and soap, struggled to keep pace with demand for their products.[5] New industries, such as jet aircraft manufacturing, mainframe computing, and television production, also enjoyed rapid growth. Like the railroads eighty years earlier, these emerging sectors sought thousands of white- and blue-collar workers. The growing significance of the Cold War stimulated research and yet more job growth, especially in the sciences. To attract workers in such an environment, established and newer companies promised stable work and, in many cases, career opportunities.[6] A range of businesses also offered health care and retirement benefits, effectively taking on some of the social responsibilities that, in other countries, postwar governments assumed. By the mid–1970s, job security with its attendant benefits had become part of an implicit, widespread social contract that millions of men and women—executives as well as workers—bought into as part and parcel of the "American Way of Life."

In the late 1970s and early 1980s, several factors caused this far-reaching model of job security to start breaking down.[7] One was the collapse of American corporate hegemony. Not only did overseas markets begin to rely less on U.S. products, but also foreign

2001	2004	2006	2007	2009
Ratio of pay between CEOs and an average production worker is 525:1.	Wal-Mart employees number 1.2 million in the United States.	Temporary and contract workers comprise 10 percent of the workforce.	Nearly 29 percent of Americans over twenty-five have college degrees.	Unemployment at 9.5 percent as recession takes hold.

manufacturers—especially the Japanese—began to compete more actively with American firms on their own turf.[8] At about the same time, the U.S. government began deregulating formerly protected industries such as airlines and banking. These sectors quickly became more competitive, which put a new premium on cost control in virtually all aspects of these businesses, including labor. On Wall Street, the growing frequency of hostile takeovers and debt-financed buyouts encouraged management in a wide range of industries to view employees as an expendable asset.[9] Undercut by foreign competition and assailed by the financial markets, American manufacturers began to slash payrolls. Thousands of workers, mainly blue-collar, lost their jobs. Many firms moved their operations from the North, where unions were powerful, to the South, where they were much less so. Others began to transfer manufacturing to even cheaper labor markets overseas.

Within years, the term *layoff*—in the sense of a permanent, rather than temporary or cyclical, end to work—entered into common parlance.[10] For millions of men and women, it also became a common experience. A 1996 *New York Times* survey found that 72 percent of Americans had been affected by a layoff themselves or were close to someone, such as a relative or neighbor, who had.[11] Families that had sent several generations of workers into the steel mills, the auto plants, or appliance and machinery factories lost a way of life and, in many cases, a standard of living. Displaced workers who found new full-time jobs often did so at lower salaries. A significant portion found only part-time or temporary work, often without benefits such as health insurance. (By 2006, temporary and contract workers made up 10 percent of the workforce, compared with 2 percent to 3 percent in the 1970s.)[12] Some displaced workers left the labor force for good.

The drop in manufacturing was, in some respects, an inevitable step in America's larger evolution toward a service-centered economy. However, the jobs created by the influx of information processing, consulting, legal, and other forms of knowledge work in the late twentieth century were hardly more protected from corporate downsizing than those in manufacturing. Between 1981 and 1982, the displacement rate of long-tenured blue-collar workers was nearly three times the rate for white-collar workers.[13] But by the mid-1990s, the gap had narrowed significantly.[14] More Americans than ever were earning college degrees, traditionally a ticket to the middle class and the relative economic stability it had historically offered. Yet even college-educated workers were being laid off, and many of these men and women were forced to accept significant drops in pay at their next job.[15] Like blue-collar workers, increasing numbers of white-collar Americans—from information technology technicians to data processors to management consultants—found that workers outside the United States could perform similar jobs more cheaply.

In all, between 1984 and 2004, at least thirty million full-time U.S. workers lost their jobs. Many searching for new jobs did so in an economy that increasingly produced a large number of low-wage, high-turnover positions. By 2004, almost 30 percent of the labor force was working for $10 an hour or less in businesses such as retail stores, restaurants, nursing homes, and call centers.[16] Without the incentives of high wages, profit sharing, and other benefits to attract and retain workers, annual turnover in these jobs was often more than 100 percent.[17] (In the fast-food industry, for instance, annual turnover was 300 percent to 400 percent.)[18] At the same time, thousands of companies reduced training, career development programs, and other investments in workers, making them seem even more expendable. For many in the low-wage sector of the labor force—especially displaced skilled laborers, former union members, and college-educated workers—the new terms of work marked out a path of downward mobility.

By many measures, the 1990s were a productive and profitable decade for American business. Between 1990 and 1998, gross domestic product (GDP), adjusted for inflation, rose 27 percent, and productivity in the nonfarm business sector climbed 16 percent.[19]

The S&P 500 increased by 224 percent.[20] Corporate profits grew by more than 100 percent, and CEO pay by more than 400 percent.[21] But all this growth (and consequent prosperity) was not distributed equally. During the same period, average weekly earnings, adjusted for inflation, climbed only 5 percent.[22] This was a departure from much of the country's postwar history, in which productivity, wages, and standards of living had all grown at relatively similar rates—at times, in near lockstep.[23] It was also a departure from the relatively low levels of income inequality that had characterized American society at midcentury. By the early 2000s, a tiny fraction of families were reaping extraordinary rewards. In 2005, for example, the top 1 percent of Americans made 17.4 percent of gross personal income, up from a share of 8.2 percent in 1980.[24] (The inequality in wealth distribution was even more glaring. In 2004, the top 1 percent of households held roughly 34 percent of the nation's wealth.)[25] While a relatively small number of Americans became much richer, the wage gains that the typical worker had come to know—and that helped shape so many Americans' sense of the nation's promise—had slowed to a near halt.

In the early twenty-first century, a worker was more likely to be college educated, more likely to work in the service or knowledge sector, and more likely to experience a layoff. She was also more likely to be a woman. The entry of women into the paid workforce—steady but gradual for much of the twentieth century—sped up considerably in the 1970s and 1980s. Between 1970 and 2004, women's participation in the labor force rose from 43 percent to 59 percent.[26] Especially noticeable was women's entry into higher-status, higher-pay positions from which they had historically been excluded. By 2004, half of all the nation's professional and managerial positions were filled by women.[27] At the same time, their wages as a percentage of men's increased from 62 percent to 80 percent.[28]

At the very top of the corporate hierarchy, important gaps persisted. Male workers still claimed more than 90 percent of the highest titles in *Fortune* 500 companies and made up nearly 95 percent of the top earners in these same firms.[29] In specific high-skilled industries, women made up a disproportionately low number of workers even outside the managerial ranks. In computer science, for instance, the percentage of jobs held by women actually decreased between 1983 and 2002, falling from 30 percent to 27 percent.[30] In engineering, women claimed only 10 percent to 15 percent of jobs.[31] As the twenty-first century took hold, key discrepancies in pay and power remained between women and men in the workplace, but there was no doubt that the differences were smaller—by some measure—than ever before and that they continued to narrow.

Women's new, expanded roles changed the dynamics and structure of both work and home. By the 1990s, 69 percent of married mothers with children under age seventeen worked for pay, up from only 12.6 percent in 1950. By choice and by necessity, dual-income families, rather than single-income, became the norm. According to Elizabeth Warren and Amelia Warren Tyagi, authors of *The Two-Income Trap*, fixed costs such as a mortgage, child care, and health care rose so quickly and so much during the last quarter of the twentieth century that a dual-income family in the early 2000s actually had *less* discretionary income, adjusted for inflation, than a single-income family of the early 1970s.[32] Thus, many families depended on the woman's income to survive. With women working many more hours outside the home, domestic life changed as well. Tasks that had traditionally fallen to women for no pay—caring for children and the elderly, preparing food, and managing a household—were frequently "outsourced" to others, at a price. Whether they purchased child care, house cleaning, and other services or not, families often found that domestic life—including who did and did not do what, when and how child care and other household responsibilities were completed, and what "home" was and how it felt—had become a source of emotional and practical tension.

The crunch on family time and energy created a powerful demand for flexible hours, job sharing, telecommuting, on-site daycare, and other family-friendly policies that would have been all but unrecognizable in earlier moments. (Even the term *family-friendly* was a product of the late twentieth century and the enormous social shifts that accompanied women's enlarged roles in the economy.) In 2004, nearly 28 percent of workers had some form of flexible schedule—allowing them to choose different times to start and end work—up from 12.4 percent in 1985.[33] This loosening of the rigid "nine-to-five" schedule made it possible for some workers to better accommodate family responsibilities, particularly caring for children.

During the same period, however, the full-time workday was getting longer. For much of the late nineteenth and early twentieth centuries, workers had campaigned for—and won—a shorter day. But in the late 1940s, the steady, gradual trend toward a shorter day began to reverse.[34] Sociologist Juliet Schor has estimated that, from 1969 to 1987, the time the average worker spent on the job each year increased by about a month.[35] While workers were spending more time in the factory or office or restaurant, the demands of the home remained pretty much the same. Meals still had to be made. Children had to be cared for. Laundry had to be done, bills paid, and much more. Historically, these tasks had all been women's work. They remained largely so, even as women took up paid positions outside the home. In the mid-1980s, women spent about twenty-seven hours weekly on housework and family care, nearly ten hours less than they and their counterparts had two decades earlier.[36] Men, on the other hand, spent about thirteen hours a week on the same tasks—about four hours more than they had in the 1960s, but still far less than their female counterparts.[37] By the early 2000s, women were still doing about twenty-five hours of housework and child care a week; men, about thirteen hours.[38]

For many Americans, home had become less a stable refuge from the rhythms and uncertainties of their jobs and more another place of work with its own sources of stress and reward. Not only were families spending time discussing and doing household chores, but also more and more employees—especially those in the white-collar world—were staying longer at the workplace or bringing work home, adding new ingredients, including tension, into the household mix. Part of the reason that work time had seeped into family time was that workers were increasingly accessible. With a personal computer and a cell phone, workers could read e-mails, check voice mails, and download documents at any hour of the day or night. They could communicate with colleagues and clients from their kitchen, car, or even the beach. Technology blurred boundaries between work and leisure time just as it blurred the boundaries between countries, allowing firms to outsource work thousands of miles away from their core operation, and creating a new climate of "24/7" work in which men and women at many levels of organizations felt tied in to their jobs regardless of where they were and—often—of what they were doing.

Another related reason that work had spilled into home and family was the growing emphasis that many companies placed on measuring employee performance and then paying individual workers on this basis. In the 1990s, about 40 percent of jobs had a performance-pay component, up from 30 percent in the 1970s.[39] With layoffs a permanent threat, many workers felt a new pressure to perform (and compete) for raises, promotions, and a steady job. Staying later at the office, responding to e-mails late at night, and working weekends were all ways for men and women to demonstrate their commitment and contribution to their employer. Finally, as sociologist Arlie Russell Hochschild noted in her book *The Time Bind*, many corporate employees reported finding in the workplace some of the emotional benefits usually associated with the home. One reason for this, she argued, was that they felt "more appreciated and more competent" at work.[40] The same employees said that home "very often" or "fairly often" felt like a workplace.[41]

The social, economic, and technological changes of the last quarter of the twentieth century dramatically altered the American work experience. Jobs were different. Hours were longer. But for many workers, their pay, adjusted for inflation, was not substantially greater. At the same time, work—in white-collar as well as blue-collar positions—was less secure, and the rewards distributed less equally. At all but the very top rungs of the income ladder, families could no longer survive on one income. All this seemed to paint a disappointing opening to the twenty-first century.

Other aspects of the changing workplace were more hopeful, however. Professional opportunities for women had expanded significantly. And for the very highest-paid workers—hedge-fund managers, venture capitalists, CEOs, and others—the potential payoffs were enormous, greater than they had been since the Gilded Age of the late nineteenth century. Distances were smaller, thanks to huge advances in communications technology and an increasingly mobile global village. Like all major developments in the history of U.S. business and the broader economy, these left Americans with many questions: In the future, which jobs would be safe? In the absence of employers, who would pay for health care and retirement? How would families with two income-earning parents raise their children, care for older members, and keep a home in a satisfying and worthy way? Did technology improve or intrude on our lives? As the workplace became more fluid and less secure, what constituted the American dream?

September 14, 1930

Women Who Work Increase in Numbers and Influence

BY R. L. DUFFUS

JUST HOW MUCH AND how little woman's place is in the home in the year of grace 1930 comes out clearly in the occupational statistics made public recently by William M. Steuart, Director of the Census. Almost exactly 73 out of every 100 American females between the ages of 16 and 64 consider their places to be in the home. They wash dishes, cook and clean house, or direct others in these necessary chores, to a sufficient extent to justify listing them as housewives.

Woman has escaped little by little from her ancient shackles until now she is a partner rather than a possession. On election day she goes to the polls—at least she is about as likely to do so as her husband is—and takes a hand in the once exclusively manly art of governing. She is decreasingly inclined to put up with any nonsense from the erstwhile head of the household, even if she has to go to the lamentable extreme of divorcing him.

But the home fires burn on. In seven cases out of ten the woman spends enough of her time in the modern adaptation of the cave to see that they keep on burning.

But the three women out of every ten—or, to be more precise, the twenty-seven out of every 100—who are taking part with men in the modern equivalent of hunting the bear and the deer cannot be ignored simply because they are a minority. They are important out of proportion to their numbers because their numbers are increasing rapidly, because they are branching out into fields not long ago reserved exclusively for males, and because what they do and think has an influence on the acts and thoughts of the women who stay at home.

Gain in Women Workers

Apparently the number of "gainfully employed" women has been increasing in late years a trifle more rapidly than general population. One has to say apparently because the Bureau of the Census, by changing its methods of classification between 1910 and 1920, disturbed the equilibrium of the statistical apple cart. In 1920 the number was a little more than 8,500,000. If it is now 10,000,000 its percentage of increase has beaten general population by a neck.

But the accumulating decades tell a more spectacular story. In 1870, for example, about one female in twelve of the total population of all ages was working for wages or salary. Now the proportion is nearer one in six. The change cannot mean that women work harder now than they did two generations ago. It means that more of them are paid, in cash, for what they do. The one additional woman worker in every dozen perhaps represents principally the energy released by labor-saving devices in the home. She may to some extent represent the more compact home and the smaller allotment of children to the average family.

It is the pay envelope rather than the work itself that is symbolic. Women can hardly be said to be new in industry, since most industries began in tasks carried on within the household. Nor has she, in any country, east or west, been spared at some time in her career the heaviest of toil. Women still work in the fields in many parts of Europe. As late as 1842 women were working in the English coal mines, dragging heavy cars along underground passages. They were absorbed into the factory system, in this and other countries, as soon as it developed.

Opposition from Professions

But while this was taking place our grandparents and great-grandparents were going from one spasm into another at the thought of women doctors, women lawyers, and—direst of all—women politicians. Women could drag cars of coal and bring up families of a dozen or more children, but they were altogether too delicate to sit with their feet on a desk and read Blackstone or drive from sick bed to sick bed with a little case of pills or vials.

In 1920 the most important occupation for women, quantitatively speaking, was "domestic and personal service," which took the time of about one in every four of those who worked for wages. Mechanical industries came next, with 22.6 per cent; clerical work third, with 16.7 per cent; professional service fourth with 11.9 per cent, and trade fifth, with 7.8 per cent.

Probably it is the item of "professional service" which bulks largest in the minds of those who reflect upon the liberation of women, with trade next. Doris E. Fleischman, in a symposium published a year or two ago, listed some forty-five "careers" for women. At that time some sixty women had qualified as certified public accountants in the United States. In advertising—following the list alphabetically—the feminine touch was in demand. Architecture had a few feminine practitioners, though not all schools were broad-minded enough to admit them as students. In the fine arts, judging by "one-man shows" held in a typical season in New York City, men were four times as numerous or considered four times as important as women.

Women as Bankers

In banking, as long as two years ago, about 2,000 women held executive positions. In the fields of child welfare, costume designing, dietetics, drama, education, home economics, interior decorating, librarianship, motion pictures, music, nursing, secretarial work, social service and merchandise styling, women were easily successful. Yet there were significant gaps. Although no motion picture producer could get along for a day without his women stars, there have been only about half a dozen recognized motion picture directors who were women. In the legitimate theatre women stage managers or assistant stage managers are rare. Three women, in 1928, had managed to get and hold official places in the American Consular service.

That is history—and rather dusty history at that. But its moral is that we shall learn more by considering "gainfully occupied" women in terms of what they do than in terms of absolute numbers. The detailed data on feminine occupations in 1930 has still to be compiled, but there is evidence from the preceding census and from other sources to indicate the expansive quality of woman's "sphere." The World War naturally had much to do with this expansion.

Miss Mary Van Fleeck, writing several years ago, noted that "five and a half pages of close, small type of a government report were required for a mere listing, in paragraph form, of the processes in which women were actually substitutes for men" during that war. Miss Van Fleeck added that these processes "ranged in their main divisions from blast furnaces and steel works to logging camps and saw mills."

Women were found to be very good in the manufacture of light parts in machine shops, in woodworking, in the making of optical and other fine instruments, and in handling some kinds of sheet metal. This may not have been a victory for feminism: after all, a "female" might ask, who wants to handle sheet metal? But every piece of work that women did that women had never or rarely done before helped establish her as a fifty-fifty partner—sometimes competitor—of her husband, brother or father.

Other Fields Opened

In the field of industrial relations woman, with her long experience in soothing the hungry male and settling the squabbles of childhood, is at home. If she is as sympathetic as a woman ought to be she can sell insurance. Nearly 6,000 women were engaged in journalism as editors and reporters at the time of the last census. Not by any means all of them were "sob sisters" either. Women lawyers have long ceased to be regarded as freaks of nature, and so have women physicians. Women are making their way into railroading. One feminine railway president is on record, and one railroad is said to have had in its employment at one time five women passenger representatives, one woman lawyer, seventeen crossing watchwomen, five women shopworkers and one woman "engineer of service" who kept a housewifely eye on the railroad's relations with its patrons. There were successful women stock-breeders.

In short, it is now difficult to find an occupation of any consequence in which women are not represented, in large numbers or small. The interest in the detailed occupation statistics of the 1930 census will lie in their picture of increasing armies of women in fields which have been sparsely peopled with them.

August 9, 1959

New Southerner: The Middle-Class Negro

Paradoxically, the change may mean both a short step back and leap forward in race relations.

BY WILMA DYKEMAN AND JAMES STOKELY

A YOUNG NEGRO FATHER in one of the South's larger cities said recently, "I can't understand why they [certain white politicians in his city] keep shouting that when we try to send our children to the best schools we can, it means we want them to marry whites. What it means is that we want our children to have a chance at owning a station wagon and a ranch-style house and carrying a briefcase instead of a shovel."

If many white Southerners could understand the implications of this man's statement, then the equality which they envision largely as nightmare might be reappraised as closer to the fulfillment of a dream—the American dream. For one of the major forces shaping and energizing the Negro's drive toward full integration into our national life today is a strengthened belief in every man's right to earn his living, own his home and better his place in society, the traditional goals of the white middle class.

And one of the major forces hindering the Negro in this drive, especially in the South, is the white man's persistent image of the Negro as the eternal hewer of wood and drawer of water. One of the matters to which professional segregationist orators have given closest attention is reviving the picture of the "African savage" whom slavery "rescued" from the jungles and brought into beneficent contact with white civilization. Even thus, a century ago, slavery was made to seem the appropriately inferior role of an inferior race.

Although slavery was abolished, the agriculture rooted in it was not, and so generation after generation of white Southerners have grown up seeing the black man behind the mule, wearing the patched overalls, performing the menial tasks, living on the margin. His poverty and limited opportunity served to strengthen the convenient image of Negro shiftlessness which, in turn, could be made to attest to a natural inferiority. "To keep the Negroes in their place" still means, to most people who use the phrase, keeping them behind sledge hammers and mattocks, brooms and axes and plows, in the jobs requiring the most muscle for the least money.

Against this popular image, compounded of dirt and debt and irrepressible gaiety, the Negro, however, has launched a successful assault in the South. He is creating a middle class—with picture-window homes, shiny new cars, hardworking P. T. A.'s and all the other gadgets and accomplishments of similar groups anywhere in the United States. And the rise of this Negro middle class, while its most immediate impact may be in the South, has great meaning for the whole nation.

There are two points of departure from which to examine the importance of the emerging Southern Negro middle class. It may be compared with its white counterpart and the total American economy—in which case it appears small and severely handicapped. For instance, individual Negro incomes are still only 52 per cent as large as white incomes, and two out of every five Negro families still earn less than $2,000 per year.

Or, this middle class may be studied in the light of its own background and recent history—in which case it appears highly significant. For instance, the pre-war percentage difference between Negro and white incomes has been cut by better than 20 per cent and today the total annual cash purchasing power of the Negro population equals the market of the whole of Canada.

Contributing to the growth of this middle class are two basic movements. They can be summarized in two colloquialisms: "going to town" and "heading North."

Both the Negro and white South are "going to town" in a drama of change gripping the entire region. The South is in the process of shifting from a rural, predominantly single-crop economy to urban industrialization. In the brief period between 1940 and 1944, a million Negroes left farming in the South. From 1950 to 1954, the number of Negro farmers in the South declined 17.1 per cent.

Many of these "headed North." Their exodus has meant not only that the South is getting whiter all the time but also that new ways, new standards, new ambitions filter down the family grapevine (as well as the TV aerial which sprouts on every roof), replacing the familiar old acceptance of subservience.

[T]he true center of the Negro's Southern middle class is Atlanta. One of the so-called "walled cities" in the presently turbulent South, it was recently described as "a twentieth-century capital of a feudal province." While rural votes rule the Georgia counties and "keep the Negroes in their place," there is considerably more latitude in the metropolis, where the colored man has assumed a new place.

Atlanta boasts that Auburn Avenue is the richest Negro street in the world. Here is the largest Negro stock company in the United States, the Atlanta Life Insurance Company; one of the nation's two Negro daily papers (the other is in Chicago); the Mutual Federal Savings and Loan Association of Atlanta, with assets of $11 million. Such institutions have played a role beyond their obvious business one: they have helped break down the myth, crippling to an emerging middle class, that the Negro is a bad credit risk.

Atlanta has provided its Negro middle class with reasons for dignity, too—a need sometimes as real as that for bread, though more frequently overlooked. A Negro has been elected to the city school board, has served as a policy maker for the Community Chest, and Negro exhibitors and spectators have participated in the Atlanta Art Festival. Municipal golf courses were desegregated without incident.

"Life's not perfect for Atlanta's ambitious Negroes," one liberal white resident has remarked, "but it is possible."

More slowly than the Negro wishes, more swiftly than the white admits, the influence of this middle class expands throughout the South. Instances of occupational progress during the past five years include: in the Gulf Coast area Negro employees were upgraded to formerly white-only positions in the major oil refining companies; Negro saleswomen were hired in Dallas; Negro airline clerks were hired for the first time in Tulsa, as were insurance agents in Jacksonville and textile retail salesmen in North Carolina.

As the Southern Negro comes closer to entering the total pattern of American life, he also becomes more aware of those educational and economic opportunities essential to securing and maintaining position in the middle class. His status is still low—but it is changing for the better: it is the combination of these two facts that provides part of the dynamic behind the Negro protest. Because this dynamic is also such a firm part of the American ideal of self-betterment and progress, the protest will neither diminish nor disappear, as so many impatient white leaders, both North and South, who have not yet understood its full meaning, seem to hope.

The question is frequently asked, and not only in the South, why Negro leadership did not wage to a successful conclusion the fight for full equality in civil rights or the field of health or housing before tackling the emotion-laden realm of schools. The reasons are obvious. Education is one of the master keys unlocking the door of opportunity—economic, political, social—into the middle class world, and Southern Negroes, no less than other Americans who want to "get ahead," seek ways to improve educational opportunities. As one young white college graduate put it, "It's funny that a white professional man in the South will send his son to one of the Ivy League schools because he thinks his boy can make 'contacts' there that will help him later on, and yet that same man will say he can't understand why a Negro father would rather send his son to a first-rate white high school than a second-rate segregated one."

Here, as elsewhere, the image is distorted. If the Southern white father could stop seeing the Southern Negro father as a *Negro* and could see him, even for a moment, as another *father*, he might comprehend more clearly some of the determination behind the drive for desegregation.

As these trends accelerate, perhaps the South will begin to realize how much all of its people have lost by keeping one segment of its people from developing a strong middle class long before this. All of the South stands to gain today by improving the productive capacity and increasing the purchasing power of those Negroes who are potentially part of a middle-class bulwark.

Finally, the emergence of the Negro middle class in the South confronts the white South with a quiet, responsible, solid group of fellow citizens who are determined in their demand to be no less than full participants in democracy. Their spokesmen are leaders like Dr. Martin Luther King Jr., who speaks of working for a better city of Montgomery, rather than for a better *Negro Montgomery*.

"WHAT does the Negro want in this new Southland?" Dr. Harry V. Richardson, speaking to a Negro club in Atlanta, asked this question and answered it a while back.

"He wants that every Southern child shall be able to live and grow and learn in the South, without having the stigma of inferiority stamped on his skin or burned into his soul.

"He wants the right to secure any kind of work of which he is capable, without being denied because of his skin.

"He wants access to every public privilege or service to which a citizen is entitled, without having to crawl in through back doors or to stand behind screens like an outcast or a dog.

"He wants an American's participation in the processes of his Government, receiving all rights and protections, and bearing all responsibilities.

"This is what he wants, this is all that he wants, and he believes that under God this is fair."

The South's emerging Negro middle class, the leaders who guide it and the bulk who follow it, will hardly be content with less.

March 12, 1981

Rising Trend of Computer Age: Employees Who Work at Home

BY ANDREW POLLACK

Louise Priester used to key-punch insurance claims into a computer in the office of Blue Cross–Blue Shield of South Carolina. Now she does the same thing from a bedroom in her house in Columbia, S.C., using a terminal connected to the office's computer by telephone.

Like Mrs. Priester, a small but growing number of workers are doing office work at home on small computers or terminals with typewriter keyboards. Corporations encourage the practice, to save commuting time for their employees and to recruit some workers, such as mothers of small children, who might not be able to hold conventional jobs.

Working at home gives employees more flexibility in scheduling other activities. "I can get up when I want to and work when I want to," said Mrs. Priester, adding that she can now take better care of her elderly mother.

Companies and workers say the new system can transform relationships between co-workers, between employees and employers and between workers and their families.

"What we're really talking about is returning production to the home, which is where it was before the Industrial Revolution," said Alvin Toffler, author of the book "The Third Wave," in an interview. Although Mr. Toffler is dismissed by many as an unrealistic visionary, he has drawn attention to working at home with a phrase, "the electronic cottage."

People have always worked at home, of course. Nearly 2.6 million people, or 3.2 percent of the United States labor force, worked at home in 1975, according to the latest figures available from the Census Bureau. More than one-third of them were farmers, and many of the rest were in business for themselves. What electronics can do is extend that option to more people in a diversity of occupations, including employees of large corporations.

Some see working at home as part of a trend in which telecommunications, growing more sophisticated, replaces transportation, growing more expensive because of rising energy costs.

In an experiment in Knoxville, Tenn., people bank electronically without leaving home. Others elsewhere in the nation shop electronically from home. In Columbus, Ohio, people can use two-way cable television to vote at home. And business people, instead of traveling to other cities, can now hold meetings in which they see as well as hear colleagues across the nation.

These new activities are called teleshopping and teleconferencing. Working at home has been dubbed telecommuting. So far, the number of full-time telecommuters is small. There are probably hundreds of them nationwide. They are confined to jobs that lend themselves to solitary effort: writers, typists and computer programmers. Thousands of others in various jobs, including corporate executives, do extra work at home on personal computers or terminals.

Employees have mixed feelings about working at home. Although it gives them more freedom, it removes them from the social life of the office. Some think their fellow workers or supervisors mistrust those who work at home.

"I still think there's a mentality around here that people who work at home are not working," said the vice president of a New York-based management consulting firm who works out of his home in Florida. His house contains a small computer, a word processor and a printer, allowing him to prepare reports.

"I like to have uninterrupted periods to work alone," he said. "If I have to stop and go to a meeting for two hours, I lose more than two hours."

He concedes that he was able to work out such an arrangement only because of his stature in the firm, and he asked that his name not be used because the management did not want other employees to know about the setup.

John Pistacchi of Control Data, who last year worked at his home in San Jose, Calif., found that his business associates hesitated to call him because they did not want to disturb him at home, even though they knew he was working there.

Some people could not work at all except at home. "I have a small child and don't have to get a baby-sitter," said Terry Medlin of Columbia, S.C., one of Blue Cross-Blue Shield's four "cottage keyers."

Mrs. Medlin said, however, that working at home "gets kind of lonesome some of the time." The hardest part, she said, is "putting yourself on a schedule."

Being with one's family can be an advantage, but it can also be a distraction. David A. Pimley, a Control Data employee in Sunnyvale, Calif, who worked at home last year, said his daughter continued to go to a neighbor's house after school, even if her father was at home. "I was there to work, not to baby-sit," Mr. Pimley said.

Vincent E. Giuliano, who works for Arthur D. Little Inc., the Cambridge, Mass., consulting concern, uses a portable terminal that allows him to work not only from his home but also from a cottage in New Hampshire or from a motel while on business trips.

Working at home can give handicapped people a chance at employment they would not otherwise have. Lift Inc., a nonprofit organization based in Northbrook, Ill., has trained about 30 handicapped workers who now write computer programs from their homes for companies such as the Standard Oil Company (Indiana), the First National Bank of Chicago and Montgomery Ward & Company.

Some of the handicapped workers operate the keyboard with sticks strapped to their hands. In a compromise between saving commuting time and retaining workers' contact with others, some companies have opened neighborhood offices and allowed employees to work at the one closest to home. Control Data will soon open such a center for 55 workers.

The Southern New England Telephone Company tested a remote business center in 1978. The center, in Meriden, Conn., 15 miles from company headquarters in New Haven, was equipped with phones, facsimile machines and message-handling terminals.

Feeling of Isolation

Yet the four workers at the remote center felt isolated. Among other things, they had trouble obtaining files from the central office.

"Being away from the home area was almost like the old cliche 'out of sight, out of mind,'" said Anthony J. Francalangia, a planner who worked at the remote office.

Work-at-home programs can save corporations the cost of expanding office space in expensive downtown areas and can allow them to recruit workers who otherwise would not be available. This is especially important for jobs where qualified workers are in short supply— secretaries and computer programmers, for instance.

"The industry is starving for computer talent, so we make available a resource that is hidden from the market," said Leah L. Tracy, branch manager of Heights Information Technology Service Inc. This data processing consulting company, with offices in Tarrytown, N.Y., and Oakland, Calif., employs 180 persons who write programs, mainly at home.

Yet many companies balk at the idea because having employees work at home raises problems. It requires new ways of making sure that an employee puts in a full day's work.

"A lot of companies are really conservative about this," said Margrethe Olson, an assistant professor at the New York University Graduate School of Business Administration, who is studying work-at-home programs. "They want those employees in sight."

Output Quotas Set

Blue Cross-Blue Shield of South Carolina and Continental Illinois both require a certain minimum daily output from their clerical workers who stay at home. Other companies restrict work at home to salaried employees who are judged by output, not hours worked.

Companies must also decide if they save money by having employees stay home. Blue Cross-Blue Shield has found that its cottage keyers process claims less expensively than its office keyers. But that is because the cottage keyers get no fringe benefits and must pay for their own terminals, paper and phone bills—at a cost of $2,640 a year.

Technological problems can arise. At Continental Illinois, occasional computer breakdowns prevent home typists from sending in their finished text. The taped dictation has to be sent back over the phone and transcribed in the bank.

If working at home catches on, the long-term effects could be widespread, according to Mr. Toffler and Charles C. McClintock, a psychologist in the College of Human Ecology at Cornell University, who is studying the phenomenon.

When work is done at home, they said, family members can share a job and can work for more than one company.

Distance Unimportant

Data can be transmitted long distance as well as locally, so there is little need for workers to be in the same city as their employer.

When a person gets a new job, instead of moving, he or she may merely "plug into a different line," Mr. Toffler said. No one expects the office or factory to disappear. Too many jobs require face-to-face meetings. This may bar full work-at-home programs.

"There are not that many types of white-collar or blue-collar jobs that can be done on a lonely basis," said Kenneth G. Bosomworth, president of International Resource and Development Inc., a consulting concern that studies office automation. "What you end up with is a scenario in which only 1 or 2 percent of the work force can commute in this way."

Jack M. Nilles, director of interdisciplinary programs at the University of Southern California, is more optimistic. He estimates that 15 percent of the urban work force may work at home by 1990.

But Dr. Nilles, a proponent of telecommuting, finds it hard to practice what he preaches because meetings require him to come to campus at least four times a week.

"If I could schedule the rest of the university better, I wouldn't have to," he said.

'Big Mac' Supplants Big Steel As Manufacturing Jobs Lag

BY WILLIAM SERRIN

Karen Brieck and Phyllis Wilburn sat in a booth and smoked one cigarette after another, six, eight, perhaps 10 in all, and talked of why they had gone to work selling hamburgers at McDonald's. It was, they said, a matter of necessity.

Unlike many of their co-workers, they are not teen-agers; Mrs. Brieck is 37 years old and Mrs. Wilburn is 41. Their husbands, both steelworkers, have been laid off.

The fact that the women are working and the men are not reflects an important change in the American economy over the last decade: a dramatic growth of jobs in service industries and a decline in manufacturing positions as a share of the total labor force.

It is a change that concerns many business and labor experts, including Lane Kirkland, president of the American Federation of Labor and Congress of Industrial Organizations, and Felix G. Rohatyn, the New York investment banker. They ask whether America is becoming a nation of short-order cooks and say the nation needs a strong manufacturing capability to retain its strength.

Service jobs, many of which are not unionized, usually pay less than jobs in manufacturing, particularly in such basic manufacturing industries as steel, automobiles, glass and rubber. Because of this differential, work experts say, service jobs generally make a smaller contribution to the overall economy than do manufacturing jobs.

Nor do service jobs have as great a ripple effect in the economy as do manufacturing jobs. When steel is made, for example, jobs are provided not only in the steel mills, but ultimately in the production of items made from steel, such as cars, farm equipment and home appliances, and in the sale and repair of those items. But when a hamburger is sold, it is merely consumed; no further jobs are created.

Before being laid off a number of months ago, Mrs. Brieck's husband, Daniel, 43, had worked at U.S. Steel's Irvin works for 19 years, and Mrs. Wilburn's husband, David, 44, had been employed at U.S. Steel's Homestead works [located near Pittsburgh, Pennsylvania] for 20 years. They were loaders, preparing steel for shipment, and earned $9 or $10 an hour in good times.

Now Mrs. Brieck and Mrs. Wilburn sell Coca-Cola and four kinds of shakes and Big Macs and Quarter Pounders and Chicken Mc-Nuggets and Filet-O-Fish sandwiches; they also clean up papers, used cups and polystyrene containers from tables. They earn the minimum wage, $3.35 an hour.

They are among the 72 percent of all Americans employed as service workers. A service worker is a worker, such as a sales person, a nurse or a fast-food worker, whose output does not consist of a tangible item, such as the production of a toaster or an automobile, but of a transaction or similarly intangible act.

Service industries are an area in which the number of jobs increased 36 percent from 1971 to 1981. Jobs specifically in eating and drinking establishments increased by 2.1 million in the same decade. Meanwhile, manufacturing employment nationwide rose a total of 2.7 million jobs, or 12 percent. But jobs in the steel industry decreased 14 percent, and today the industry has 30 percent unemployment.

Steel Mills Called Antiquated

McDonald's Corporation outlets are highly sophisticated; the company installed its first computer in 1965, the first fast-food company to do so. Such advanced technology is not the norm at U.S. Steel. Many of the mills along the Monongahela [River near Pittsburgh] are antiquated, union officials and steel industry critics say.

U.S. Steel blames cheaper imported steel and the economic recession for the decline in the American steel industry. Critics say that steel companies in the United States have not invested in new methods and machines and that some companies, like U.S. Steel, appear interested in leaving steel production for more profitable activities.

Officials of U.S. Steel, whose 1981 steel shipments were 16.6 million tons, the lowest since 1946, say the company must attempt to acquire profitable assets, in or out of steel, but that it remains committed to steel production. They say they believe the Monongahela Valley will return to prosperity.

At McDonald's, 1981 revenues were $2.5 billion, with net income of $264.8 million, with a return on average equity of 21.1 percent. That compares to sales of $13.9 billion for U.S. Steel, with $1.07 billion in net income, and a return on common stock equity of 17.2 percent.

Composition of Work Forces

One major difference between the businesses is the composition of their work forces. At McDonald's many are teen-agers and many work part time. U.S. Steel workers are mostly adult, full-time workers. Typical pay at McDonald's, at the minimum wage or less, is about one-third [of] what workers earn in the steel industry.

Moreover, McDonald's has a non-unionized work force.

Robert Cadwell, organizing director of the United Food and Commercial Workers, says the union has found it almost impossible to organize McDonald's and other fast-food chains, with their immense numbers of separate facilities, young workers interested only in wages and high employee turnover.

Mrs. Brieck and Mrs. Wilburn's husbands are union men, as were their fathers—Mrs. Wilburn's father helped organize the union at

Homestead—but neither woman displays interest in having a union at McDonald's.

Commenting on the economic conditions in the valley, Mrs. Wilburn said, "It scares the death out of me." She added that she told her sons, both in the Air Force: "Stay in and make a career out of it. There's nothing here."

"All the men around here want is their jobs back," she said. "Thank God for McDonald's."

September 2, 1985

For the Worker: Changing Times, New Challenges

BY ROBIN TONER

He was a radio operator during World War II, and afterward Raymond Liebgott decided there was a future in all those tubes and wires. By the late 1940's, he was working on black-and-white televisions. By the 1980's, he was peering at circuitry so tiny he sometimes needed a microscope.

When Quentin Headen graduated from high school in 1981, he went to work as a trucker's helper, delivering freight in New York City. But he decided secretarial work was the wave of the future, and signed up for a course in word processing. Today, he said with a laugh, he considers himself "light-blue collar."

Mary Coradin became a directory assistance operator in 1963. She remembers hearing about the technology of the future, but said she could not comprehend it at the time. Today, she has grown accustomed to computerized directories and automated voices.

To many Americans, the archetype of the working-class laborer was the steelworker or the autoworker—blue-collar men in mills and factories, direct economic descendants of the workers who marched through New York City on the first Labor Day, 103 years ago.

A Changing Work Force

But American workers today present a tableau of striking diversity and constant flux. They include people like Mr. Liebgott, foot soldier in the electronics revolution; Mr. Headen, adaptable member of the service sector, and Mrs. Coradin, veteran of technological change that has transformed a traditional job.

Today, the old lines between blue and white collar are often blurred, some experts say. The workingman is often a woman. The sounds of work can be the soft hum and plunk of advanced automation. And, increasingly, the end product of labor is not goods, but services.

According to the Federal Bureau of Labor Statistics, New York City's economy has undergone sweeping structural change in recent years. Since 1977, the city has lost more than 100,000 jobs in manufacturing, while it has gained more than 150,000 jobs in finance and business services, said Samuel M. Ehrenhalt, regional commissioner for the bureau.

Word processors, health technicians and millions of other workers in service industries are increasingly dominant in the ranks of labor—in the city, the state and the nation.

"During the 1970's, about 90 percent of all new jobs were added in service organizations," said a recent report by the A.F.L.-C.I.O. "By 1990, service industries will employ almost three-quarters of the labor force."

To that fundamental shift add the impact of technology.

"The computerization of the work place is fundamentally different than previous forms of automation," said Harley Shaiken, a research associate at M.I.T. [Massachusetts Institute of Technology].

"It's a far more powerful technology, it's a far more pervasive technology, and it reorganizes not just specific jobs, but how factories and entire corporations are run," Mr. Shaiken said. Behind such trends are the lives of individual workers. In their attitudes toward their jobs, in their perceptions of the future, are glimpses of the American worker, circa 1985.

A 'Word Oriented' Environment

When Mr. Headen, son of a maintenance foreman, was searching for a vocation while a Brooklyn high school student, his advisers suggested cosmetology. So he pursued that training, although he heard throughout his high school years that secretarial work—of the computerized variety—was a growing field.

He took a detour after high school, working on trucks and in warehouses, but finally decided to enroll in an eight-month course in word processing at the Katharine Gibbs School. At the end of the course, the school asked him to stay on as an instructor.

Mr. Ehrenhalt suggested that workers like Mr. Headen were well-equipped for the future.

"More than ever, today's workers need to be able to function successfully in a word-oriented, information-intensive work environment," Mr. Ehrenhalt said in a recent report.

But Mr. Headen, polished and confident at the age of 21, indicated that change was the only constant he was counting on. "It's hard to say that anyone is in 'the right field,'" he said. "You can be an expert with one machine today, and then tomorrow that machine is outdated."

'You Really Never Know'

He has taught himself basic computer programming, he said, and prides himself on his adaptability. Where will he end up in the economy?

"I have no idea," he said with a laugh. "That's the fun part about it. You really never know where you will land."

As Mr. Headen embarks on his career, Mr. Liebgott, at age 64, stands just a year from retirement. In Federal labor statistics, Mr. Liebgott would be classified as a manufacturing worker. But the quiet intensity of the Loral Electronic Systems plant in the Bronx, where Mr. Liebgott works, is a world away from traditional factories.

He works in the testing department of the plant, which produces electronic systems for the military, such as radar warning devices. "Everything is getting smaller and smaller all the time," said Mr. Liebgott, who works with the concentration of a jeweler.

When he first began working on radios "it was all tubes," Mr. Liebgott recalled. "I figured it was a good steady job, because of new improvements and new technology and everything."

'Pride in Their Work'

Mr. Liebgott's career took him from radio to the telephone to television, and then on to the intricate circuitry of military electronics. But while production has changed, Mr. Liebgott suggests that the American work ethic has not.

"There are so many people who are still conscientious in their work," he said. "They take pride in their work. There are some goof-offs, but I believe most of the people are still earning their pay for what they do."

And the satisfaction of a production job is still the same, one of Mr. Liebgott's co-workers said. "I love it, I really do," said Lucille Lebel, who was weaving multicolored wires into a complicated pattern that would eventually go into a radar system. "You start out with nothing—they give you connectors and wires—and when you finish, it looks like something."

New technologies have moved quickly throughout the economy. Experts debate the long-term effects of automation and computerization on the economy, on worker satisfaction, on labor-management relations. Meanwhile, workers like Mrs. Coradin quietly learn to live with change.

Adjusting to Technology

Mrs. Coradin joined the New York Telephone Company 22 years ago as a directory assistance operator. It was called "information" then, she said. She sat amid long rows of operators, all wearing heavy headsets, all armed with telephone and street directories. She used a rubber finger cover to leaf quickly through the pages of the Manhattan and the Bronx phone books. "You learned to do it fast," she said.

As the years passed, the books were replaced by video display terminals. The headsets grew lighter, the pace of work quicker. A year ago, New York Telephone put an automated response system in the New York City area. Operators like Mrs. Coradin can now push a button and a voice will convey the number to the caller.

Mrs. Coradin said that when she first saw some of the new equipment, "I thought, 'Oh, my goodness, will I ever learn it?'"

But she adjusted. "It's just like anything else," she said. "You learn it and you get used to it."

Children at work in a men's clothing factory, circa 1910. The beginning of the twentieth century
saw the fight for the protection of the rights of child workers, and as the century drew to a
close changes in the workplace continued to unfold. (Brown Brothers)

More Women Gaining Entry to Boardrooms

BY JOAN M. LANG

A seat on the board of directors has always been one of the ultimate signs of achievement. Increasingly, the doors to the boardrooms of major corporations and foundations have been swinging open to admit women.

Moreover, the role of women on boards has been changing. In the 1970's, the small number of women who were invited to sit on a board was often asked to do so for the sake of appearance. Well-known and highly visible, these women were active in nonprofit organizations or in government, or they were major shareholders. But over the last decade, as women have entered the corporate world in larger numbers, they have had the opportunity to wield influence on the boards of major corporations.

"It's really the logical progression as a woman moves into top management," said Beth Bronner, a senior vice president and general manager of the shop division of the Häagen-Dazs Company in Teaneck [New Jersey] and the highest-ranking woman at the ice cream manufacturer and retailer. In addition, for the last two years she has served on the board of MasterMedia Limited, a New York-based publishing company. "As we progress as individuals," she said, "we need to find new ways of affecting policy, and being on the board is an excellent way to do that."

Today, women are being selected to fill board seats in much the same way as men: on the basis of expertise. As more organizations begin to expand the strategic role of their boards, more women are being sought for their specific skills and contributions. Yet because women as a whole have not achieved equal representation among the ranks of executives, female board members tend to be younger and at earlier stages in their careers than their male counterparts.

And while an increasing number of companies and foundations are actively seeking women to fill board positions, many people involved in women's issues believe that it will be years before women are fully represented on boards.

"Women have made tremendous professional strides, but it's going to take another 10 to 20 years before they truly attain equality in the workplace," said Patricia Harrison, president of the National Women's Economic Alliance, a nonprofit organization formed in 1983 to help women develop more career and economic opportunities.

Women will constitute about two-thirds of new entrants to the work force from 1985 to the year 2000, according to the United States Department of Labor's Bureau of Labor Statistics. Currently they account for about half of the work force, or about 57 million, and as the workplace becomes more integrated, it is expected that the proportion of women in management will begin to increase at a faster rate.

In 1989, 59 percent of Fortune 1,000 companies had women on their boards, compared with 36 percent in 1979 and just 11 percent in 1973, according to the 1990 Board of Directors study, which is conducted annually by Korn/Ferry International, a New York City-based executive recruitment concern.

According to Directorship, a consulting organization based in Westport, Conn., there are 30 Fortune 1,000 companies with headquarters in New Jersey, and 28 women holding seats on their boards. Several companies, including Merck & Company, the American Telephone and Telegraph Company and C.P.C. International, have more than one female director.

Nationwide, Directorship says, women hold 693 board positions or nearly 7 percent of the 10,199 seats on the 818 public companies on the Fortune 1,000 list.

"There is no doubt that gaining a position on the board is a more efficient route to establishing a power base," said Arlene Johnson, the director of work force programs for the Conference Board, a New York City-based global resource organization for corporations. "It's easier for a company to bring a woman onto its board than it is to integrate its senior management staff. Advancing through the ranks takes a long time, and the cooperation and commitment of all the people involved are essential."

Actively Seeking Women

Today, many companies are actively seeking female board members. Dr. Carolyne K. Davis serves on the boards of four companies, including the Prudential Insurance Company of America and Merck, and says she believes that in every instance their chief executives were making deliberate attempts to bring a woman onto the board.

"They had made up their minds to have a woman director and were vigorously seeking women candidates," Dr. Davis said, "That gave me an added advantage."

Which is not to say that sex was the only criterion. As head of the Health Care Financing Administration until 1985, Dr. Davis ran the nation's Medicare and Medicaid programs, and today she is national and international health care adviser to Ernst & Young, a Washington-based accounting company with more than 700 clients in the health care field.

Barbara Roberts, the chairwoman of the directors' resource committee of the Financial Women's Association of New York, an organization dedicated to the professional development of women, said there was a natural progression at work regarding board membership.

"Younger women, women in their 20's and early 30's, can learn how boards function and establish valuable contacts on nonprofit boards," she said. "Later, they can move on to local government boards and then into the boardrooms of public companies."

Yvonne Shepard, division manager for new business development in consumer communications services at A.T.&T., was recently named to the board of the $30 million A.T.&T. Foundation, the philanthropic arm of the communications company. She said she was appointed to the board because she is both Puerto Rican and a woman—which makes her a "twofer" in executive search parlance.

"The company had made a conscious effort to add representation of both Hispanics and women, and I am the only Hispanic women on the foundation's board," Ms. Shepard said. "I have taken it upon myself to help effect change for minorities and women through to activities of the foundation, and I suspect that that is one of the reasons the foundation asked me to sit on its board. And it is a wonderful place to influence policy—even though it's not the board of A.T.&T. itself."

Special Role as Mentors

Many women who are board directors do indeed see a special role for themselves as mentors and advocates for younger women within the organization and the community at large. Irene Kramer, a practitioner of naturopathic medicine, has served on the board of the First National Bank of Toms River since 1976—one of the first women in New Jersey to sit on the board of a for-profit organization. During that time, she has worked with a number of women within the bank to help them advance.

"I see that as a very important role for women like me," she said. "Several of my male colleagues have commented to me that they expected it to be strange to sit across the board table from a woman, and then found that not to be the case at all. And I'm delighted by that."

In addition to providing their management and functional expertise, many women say they feel that they add something "different" to the mix simply because they are women.

"C.E.O.'s and board chairmen are realizing that women offer a tremendous pool of untapped talent, one that can make different but highly valuable contributions to an organization," Ms. Harrison said. "Women can bring as much to the board as men can from the point of view of the experience, along with their own unique perspective.

"The real issue over the next decade is going to be how rapidly and how successfully women can move into the ranks of top management. Until that happens, organizations will continue to have to make a conscious attempt to place women on their boards, rather than simply finding the best candidate for the position, male or female."

Many Will Become Contract Workers

Most workers, some experts predict, will have tailored employment contracts, and portable pension funds, roving from company to company to suit the needs of businesses and their own preferences. "We'll have extraordinarily sophisticated employer-worker relationships, so that almost everyone will be a contract worker," said William Davidson, a professor at the University of Southern California business school.

The process, they say, will move well beyond big companies, and to some degree it already has. Today's service subcontractors often pay outsiders to do chores for the same reasons that big companies do: to curb costs and keep their in-house experts focused on their specialties.

Wendy Liebmann, a former Revlon marketing executive, founded a New York marketing research consulting firm in 1986. Since then, the client list has grown to include Revlon, Colgate Palmolive, Condé Nast and others, but the firm still operates with a core of three professionals. Tasks like field research are farmed out to others. "We believe in hiring outside specialists just as our clients hire us as specialists," Ms. Liebmann said.

Analysts predict that temporary help companies are poised for strong growth, once the economy recovers, because companies will hire crews of outsiders instead of adding permanent people.

And Manpower Inc., the nation's largest temporary-help company, expects to see further growth in its business of supplying clients with teams of people to handle entire service functions. Today, about 20 percent of its $1.5 billion-a-year business comes from managed services, meaning Manpower comes into a company with people and runs services like mailrooms, copy centers or telephone-marketing operations. Two years ago, contract services accounted for only 8 percent of the business, estimates Mitchell Fromstein, the company's president. John Poland, vice president for managed services, said his customers "are pushing us in this direction as fast as we can go."

In Cary, N.C., the Knowledge Systems Corporation is a high-tech subcontractor. The 35-person company is a specialist in an advanced computer software method known as object-oriented technology, which allows programs to be written in modules that can be linked together in different combinations. Its clients include Hewlett-Packard, Texas Instruments and I.B.M., and its employees are typically rented out as consultants or team leaders to product development groups in the big companies.

"Ours is a niche business with highly talented people in a specific domain," explained Reed Phillips, chief executive of Knowledge Systems.

John Mason, a 36-year-old computer scientist for Knowledge Systems, has just finished a two-year assignment as a player-coach working with a development team at a nearby I.B.M. programming lab. "Because I know the technology, I can speed up their work by pointing out shortcuts and how to avoid problems," he said.

Yet I.B.M. is a supplier of contract services as well as a buyer. A services subsidiary, Integrated Systems Solutions Corporation, runs much of the data processing under contract for companies like Eastman Kodak, United Technologies, Continental Bank and Supermarkets General.

In the first half of this year, I.B.M.'s revenue from services, including Integrated Systems, jumped 42 percent. "This kind of outsourcing is a real growth business," said Lane Jorgensen, manager for market support and planning.

March 3, 1996

On the Battlefields of Business, Millions of Casualties

BY LOUIS UCHITELLE AND N. R. KLEINFIELD

More than 43 million jobs have been erased in the United States since 1979, according to a New York Times analysis of Labor Department numbers. Many of the losses come from the normal churning as stores fail and factories move. And far more jobs have been created than lost over that period. But increasingly the jobs that are disappearing are those of higher-paid, white-collar workers, many at large corporations, women as well as men, many at the peak of their careers. Like a clicking odometer on a speeding car, the number twirls higher nearly each day.

Peek into the living rooms of America and see how many are touched:

- Nearly three-quarters of all households have had a close encounter with layoffs since 1980, according to a new poll by The New York Times. In one-third of all households, a family member has lost a job, and nearly 40 percent more know a relative, friend or neighbor who was laid off.

- One in 10 adults—or about 19 million people, a number matching the adult population of New York and New Jersey combined—acknowledged that a lost job in their household had precipitated a major crisis in their lives, according to the Times poll.

- While permanent layoffs have been symptomatic of most recessions, now they are occurring in the same large numbers even during an economic recovery that has lasted five years and even at companies that are doing well.

- In a reversal from the early 80's, workers with at least some college education make up the majority of people whose jobs were eliminated, outnumbering those with no more than high school educations. And better-paid workers—those earning at least $50,000—account for twice the share of the lost jobs than they did in the 1980's.

- Roughly 50 percent more people, about 3 million, are affected by layoffs each year than the 2 million victims of violent crimes. But while crime bromides get easily served up—more police, stiffer jail sentences—no one has come up with any broadly agreed upon antidotes to this problem. And until Patrick J. Buchanan made the issue part of the Presidential campaign, it seldom surfaced in political debate.

Yet this is not a saga about rampant unemployment, like the Great Depression, but one about an emerging redefinition of employment. There has been a net increase of 27 million jobs in America since 1979, enough to easily absorb all the laid-off workers plus the new people beginning careers, and the national unemployment rate is low.

The sting is in the nature of the replacement work. Whereas 25 years ago the vast majority of the people who were laid off found jobs that paid as well as their old ones, Labor Department numbers show that now only about 35 percent of laid-off full-time workers end up in equally remunerative or better-paid jobs. Compounding this frustration are stagnant wages and an increasingly unequal distribution of wealth. Adjusted for inflation, the median wage is nearly 3 percent below what it was in 1979. Average household income climbed 10 percent between 1979 and 1994, but 97 percent of the gain went to the richest 20 percent.

The result is the most acute job insecurity since the Depression. And this in turn has produced an unrelenting angst that is shattering people's notions of work and self and the very promise of tomorrow, even as the President proclaims in his State of the Union Message that the economy is "the healthiest it has been in three decades" and even as the stock market has rocketed to 81 new highs in the last year.

Driving much of the job loss are several familiar and intensifying stresses bearing down upon companies: stunning technological progress that lets machines replace hands and minds; efficient and wily competitors here and abroad; the ease of contracting out work, and the stern insistence of Wall Street on elevating profits even if it means casting off people. Cutting the payroll has appeal for gasping companies that resort to it as triage and to soundly profitable companies that try it as preventative medicine against a complicated future.

The conundrum is that what companies do to make themselves secure is precisely what makes their workers feel insecure. And because workers are heavily represented among the 38 million Americans who own mutual funds, they unwittingly contribute to the very pressure from Wall Street that could take away their salaries even as it improves their investment income.

Many Americans have reacted [to such insecurity] by downsizing their expectations of material comforts and the sweetness of the future. In a nation where it used to be a given that children would do better than their parents, half of those polled by The Times thought it unlikely that today's youth would attain a higher standard of living than they have. What is striking is that this gloom may be even more emphatic among prosperous and well-educated Americans. A Times survey of the 1970 graduating class at Bucknell University, a college known as an educator of successful engineers and middle managers, found that nearly two-thirds doubted that today's children would live better. White-collar, middle-class Americans in mass numbers are coming to understand first hand the chronic insecurity on which the working class and the poor are experts.

Those who have not lost their jobs and their identities, and do not expect to, are also being traumatized. The witnesses, the people who stay employed but sit next to empty desks and wilting ferns, are grappling with the guilt that psychologists label survivor's syndrome. At Chemical Bank, a department of 15 was downsized to just one woman. She sobbed for two days over her vanished colleagues. Why them? Why not me?

The intact workers are scrambling to adjust. They are calculating the best angles to job security, including working harder and shrewder, and discounting the notion that a paycheck is an entitlement. The majority of people polled by The Times said they would work more hours, take fewer vacation days or accept lesser benefits to keep their jobs.

One factor making this period so traumatic is that since World War II people have expected that their lives and those of their children would steadily improve. "It's important to recall that throughout American history, discontent has always had less to do with material well-being than with expectations and anxiety," David Herbert Donald, a social historian at Harvard, said. "You read that 40,000 people are laid off at AT&T and a shiver goes down your back that says, 'That could be me,' even if the fear is exaggerated. What we are reacting against is the end of a predictable kind of life, just as the people who left the predictable rhythms of the farm in the 1880's felt such a loss of control once they were in the cities."

Only 28 percent, versus 44 percent of the entire population, say they are as well off as they imagined at this juncture of their lives. The vast majority feels the country is going in the wrong direction, and they are more pessimistic about the economy. They are more likely than the overall population to be divorced or separated. They are better educated. Politically, they are more apt to label themselves liberal. They are more likely to favor national health insurance, and to say that curbing government programs like Medicare, Medicaid and welfare is a misguided idea. And more than 63 percent, compared with 47 percent in the whole population, want the Government to do something about job losses.

A Portrait of the Victims

Imagine the downsized posed shoulder to shoulder for an annual portrait, some sort of dysfunctional graduation picture. Mostly young, male, blue-collar workers dominated the glossies of the 1980's. Now, white-collar people stare out from every row. Many more of them are women and those whose hair flashes with gray. Instead of factory clothes, far more wear adornment appropriate for carpeted offices.

At his office in the Labor Department's Bureau of Labor Statistics, Thomas Nardone, an associate commissioner, keeps a chart that tracks the correlation between income and layoffs. In the 1980's, the chart shows, the higher the income, the less frequent the layoffs. Now the two lines rise in tandem.

The job insecurity reaches beyond corporations. Government is also scaling back, although not as drastically as corporations, erasing many of the jobs that historically elevated the poor. Between 1979 and 1993, 454,000 public service jobs vanished.

Academia is contributing to the dislocation by paring its rolls and increasingly leaving college teachers in jeopardy by denying them tenure. Doctors, once leading the way along the smug path to American bounty, are succumbing to the cost-containment convulsions in health care.

What so many middle-class workers are experiencing for the first time is achingly familiar to poorer people. Job security never seemed to apply to them. Indeed, those at the lower end of the economic ladder are slipping even further. Rene Brown is a thrice-downsized woman who is still in her 40's. Since the start of the 1980's she has been downsized out of an $8.50-an-hour job at a meatpacking plant, a $7.25-an-hour job in a bank mailroom and a $4.75-an-hour job loading newspapers. Presently she earns $4.25 cleaning office buildings in Baltimore.

Ms. Brown has done this menial work for three years, without a raise. She is annoyed that, despite a high school diploma and a year of community college, she cannot find a way back up the income ladder.

The poor are losing out in another way. The newly pinched middle class has grown increasingly intolerant of having its tax dollars applied to social programs benefiting the disadvantaged.

What Changed

People, of course, always lost their jobs. In the 19th and early 20th centuries, it didn't take much; job security was not yet an American concept.

World War II, however, ushered in an unprecedented era of economic growth. Demand for workers soared. The post-war years led many people to the succoring belief that they had an almost divine right to a very particular American dream entailing a home, a secure job and a raise every year. An unwritten social contract, codified in part by strong labor unions, came into being, under which managers and workers pledged their loyalty to one another.

The booming economic growth that made this possible slackened in the 1970's, and the economy has remained stuck at a lower volume.

The steady and pronounced progress of technology has kept taking tasks from human beings and giving them to machines, undermining the bedrock notion of mass employment. Whereas the General Motors Corporation employed 500,000 people at its peak in the 1970's, today it can make just as many cars with 315,000 workers. Computer programs rather than lawyers prepare divorce papers. If 1,000 movie extras are needed, the studio hires 100 and a computer spits out clones for the rest. Behind every A.T.M. flutter the ghosts of three human tellers.

Labor Department statistics show that more than 36 million jobs were eliminated between 1979 and 1993, and an analysis by The New York Times puts the number at 43 million through 1995. Many of the jobs would disappear in any age, when a store closes or an old product like the typewriter yields to a new one like the computer. What distinguishes this age are three phenomena: white-collar workers are big victims; large corporations now account for many of the layoffs, and a large percentage of the jobs are lost to "outsourcing"—contracting out work to another company, usually within the United States. Far more jobs are being added than lost. But many of the new jobs are in small companies that offer scant benefits and less pay, and many are part-time positions with no benefits at all. Often, the laid off get only temporary work, tackling tasks once performed by full-timers. The country's largest employer, renting out 767,000 substitute workers each year, is Manpower Inc., the temporary-help agency.

At the same time, some layoffs seem rooted in economic fashion. An unforgiving Wall Street has given its signals of approval—rising stock prices—to companies that take the meat-ax to their costs. The day Sears announced it was discarding 50,000 jobs, its stock climbed nearly 4 percent. The day Xerox said it would prune 10,000 jobs, its stock surged 7 percent. And thus business has been thrust into a cycle where it is keener about pleasing investors than workers.

The Hardest Hit

In a society in which identity is so directly quantified by work, the psychological fall involved in losing a job is leading many to stress-induced illnesses. "What makes it so hard for people is very often these situations come about very suddenly," said Dr. Gerd Fenchel, the head of the Washington Square Institute for Psychotherapy and Mental Health in New York, who has seen his caseload swell with down-sized workers. "We have a diagnosis called post-traumatic stress syndrome that applies to this."

The impact of job loss on marriages varies. The divorce rate, according to several studies, is as much as 50 percent higher than the national average in families where one earner, usually the man, has lost a job and cannot quickly find an equivalent one. On the other hand, many families where both husband and wife are employed seem to be drawing closer to muster their energies against the common enemy of job insecurity.

The effect on community unity seems more straightforward. In city after city, downsized people are withdrawing from the civic activities that held communities together. Sociologists report that involvement has tumbled at P.T.A.'s, Rotary clubs, Kiwanis clubs, town meetings and church suppers. Bowling leagues are unraveling, even though more people are bowling than ever. The reason is they are visiting alleys not as part of corporate or community leagues, but singly or with a friend. "The 'we' has become a 'me,' or at least a narrower 'we,'" Robert D. Putnam, a Harvard professor who has documented this contracting participation, said. He fingers downsizing as a culprit, although not as insidious as television.

The country's feeling of American mastery, of a nation that stands astride the world, is unquestionably being bruised. The job insecurity is unleashing a "floating anger that is attaching itself to all sorts of targets as a form of scapegoating," Daniel Yankelovich, president of DYG Inc., a polling firm, said. Polls have shown this anger directed at targets as diverse as immigrants, blacks, women, government, corporations, welfare recipients, computers, the very rich and capitalism itself. Some experts say that part of the growth in membership of so-called hate groups is traceable to disaffected downsized workers.

The floating anger is also influencing people's attitude toward politics. Pollsters say it is making centrist politics harder to practice and making people less faithful to any one party, less likely to vote and more willing to entertain the idea of a third party.

Adapting to New Times

The downsizing has set off unmistakable currents of adjustment. Increasing numbers of families are scaling back their lifestyles. Two-thirds of those in The Times poll said that in recent years queasiness about their economic future had compelled them to curtail their day-to-day spending. One-fifth said the cuts had been "severe."

Many of the dispossessed are stepping up their involvement in new networks rooted in job pursuit. There are assemblages like "Xerox-ex" for laid-off Xerox workers. There are groups like the 40 Plus Club in New York for people over 40 who have lost jobs. And there are arrangements like the job-seekers club at the Trinity Episcopal Church in Princeton, N.J.

Some are fulfilling dreams by initiating their own businesses and otherwise tapping into some new inner serenity.

After twice losing jobs at computer companies in six years, Marilyn Collins, a 52-year-old computer systems expert, got fed up feeling she was "dispensable" and joined her husband in the small New York direct-mail consultancy he had founded. Since her arrival, the once marginal business has flourished.

Many workers are returning to school. High school graduates in their mid-20s, for example, are flocking to community colleges in unprecedented numbers.

Behavior in the office is taking on bizarre twists. Leslie Perlow, a University of Michigan business school professor who studied a team of 12 software engineers at a Xerox office near Rochester, N.Y., found that the engineers, gripped by job insecurity, felt driven to show off their prowess before their peers and bosses. They spent the bulk of their workday in meetings and crisis sessions, some that were little more than stages where they could advertise their abilities. Not until after 5 P.M. did they get around to what they were paid for: inventing software. "They felt they were rewarded for individual heroics, and their crisis meetings gave them an outlet for heroics," Ms. Perlow said.

"The layoff atmosphere exacerbated this need to 'show' performance."

A lot of workers no longer think of their jobs as entitlements. Robby Smith is a 34-year-old engineer at Maitland & Hoge Enterprises, a Houston oil and gas consulting firm that did some downsizing. While he sees no likelihood that his job is at risk, he hastens to point out, "I don't take employment for granted. It is not a right, so to speak, granted by education and experience. That is an attitude I have developed over the past few years."

Like the downsized themselves, Mr. Smith keeps his eye trained on his personal balance sheet. He is part of a two-earner family; his wife is an assistant school principal. They have a 2-year-old daughter. They have stopped using all but one credit card. When they buy a car, they finance it through his wife's father instead of the bank. All debt is considered suspect.

The View of the Firing Squads

It was time, no question. On a cool, pale afternoon, Charles Allen stepped across Fifth Avenue and entered St. Patrick's Cathedral to attend noon Mass. He knows the rite by heart. He goes every day.

Daily Mass is an old habit with new meaning for him. Things are on his mind. One signpost of this era is the multitude of executives who decided who would go. As a $90,000-a-year banking executive, Mr. Allen had to fire his share. Many, to his mind, were not competent and got their just outcomes. One, however, will not vacate his mind.

As an officer in charge of operations of the Standard Chartered Bank, Mr. Allen had to dispose of one of the three currency traders in the

Toronto branch. The consensus choice happened to be a woman who was indisputably the top performer, but had the weakest political bonds. "I knew that she was the best in the department," he said. "But she had not networked. And I had to inform her that she was terminated. And she looked at me with tears in her eyes and said, 'But Charlie, you know better.' I will never forget what she said and how she looked that day."

Each afternoon at Mass, he looks to put the past and the present in perspective. "It is a mark on my character," he said. "I feel a lesser person."

There is a sullen irony to Mr. Allen's story. He lost his own job last May and now wanders with the dispossessed.

The Children

There is one final cast of characters in this unspooling drama, and they are the characters of tomorrow.

When workers come home with frayed nerves and punctured expectations, what are the children to make of it? The layoffs and the rejiggered lives have caused parents to search themselves for some new song of hope to sing to their children. What is the path to security anymore? What are the safe jobs? What, in short, is an American dream worth dreaming?

In the unlovely apartment of John Castner in North Arlington, N.J., all conversations seem to lead to work and its meaning. For much of his accounting career, Mr. Castner traced the predictable path of better work and pay. Starting in 1989, he was swept into the downsizing grinder.

Last April, he lost his third job in six years. Now, at 47, he makes do with intermittent work.

A widower, he lives with his two children, Julie, 14, and Stephen, 11. "I say to my kids, not only will you have to look for jobs anywhere in the United States, but in Singapore and Hong Kong," he said. "You are competing against kids from other countries." He tells them it is no longer enough to be very good, it is imperative to be a star. He feels it vital that they attend a "brand-name college," certainly not the Trenton State stenciled on his own diploma.

His children said they have not been embarrassed by their father's lost jobs any more than they are by neglected ink stains on their hands. After all, many of their friends have downsized parents.

Julie, in particular, seems to have been forced into a response common to a lot of middle-class children—growing up earlier in a way reminiscent of what happens to poor children on shoestring budgets and deprived of intact families. She did not try out for the basketball team so she can hold an after-school job as a day-care counselor. "I don't mind work," she said. "It's fun."

Despite her adolescence, she demonstrates an adult's knowingness and fortitude. "I wish my father had a job, but since he doesn't you kind of get a little smarter and think about what you have to do more," she said. "How you have to go about, like, choosing a profession. And school is more important, a lot more important. In my school, it is kind of like the in thing to be really smart."

Chairman and CEO of the Fiduciary Trust Company International Anne M. Tatlock (in center), along with some of the firm's female executive and senior vice presidents. In 2001, 51 percent of the 700 employees at Fiduciary Trust were women, and 30 percent of the senior management positions were held by women. (*New York Times*)

Honey, I Am Not Home

BY NICHOLAS LEMANN

THE TIME BIND: WHEN WORK BECOMES HOME AND HOME BECOMES WORK. *By Arlie Russell Hochschild. Illustrated. 316 pp. New York: Metropolitan Books/Henry Holt & Company. $22.50.*

The photograph accompanying the 1953 Fortune article that William H. Whyte expanded into "The Organization Man" showed a tide of humanity (to the extent that guys in fedoras qualify as a tide of humanity) flowing across a train platform in Park Forest, Ill., over this caption: "5:57, back from the Loop."

The unmistakable message was that ominous big corporations were turning us into a race of work-automatons. Today, however, looking at the picture, you can't help thinking that they would have had to leave the office not much past 5 to make that train, and that their wives had probably been home all day attending to home, community and children. What a leisurely life!

Arlie Russell Hochschild's book "The Time Bind" is based on the same kind of intensive firsthand research into Midwestern corporate life that Whyte did, except that she is a sociologist rather than a journalist, and so doesn't tell us the real name of the town or the company. She spent three summers at the headquarters of "Amerco," an enlightened multinational in the low-key town of "Spotted Deer," and found that in most families both spouses put in much longer hours than just the husbands had back in the 1950's. Ten- to eleven-hour workdays are common (that's 8 A.M. to 6 or 7 P.M.), and family life is brutally squeezed.

Ms. Hochschild writes in a calm, understanding tone that tends to disguise how truly subversive and depressing her message is. Subversive, because although we've already heard, in Juliet Schor's book "The Overworked American" and elsewhere, that our hours are too long, the blame is usually laid at the feet of a demanding new economy. It isn't our fault. Ms. Hochschild says we work too much because we want to—because we like it better at work than at home. Depressing, because in her account home has changed from a refuge into an arena of stress, and children are the victims.

At Amerco an elaborate series of family-friendly personnel schemes with hilariously earnest names (like the Work-Life Balance program) go mostly unused. Only 53 of 21,000 employees, none of them men, have chosen to work part time in response to the arrival of a new baby. Fewer than 1 percent share a job. And 1 percent of Amerco employees work from home, though the company permits it. Most employees don't even use all their vacation days.

A minor reason for all this office time is that Amerco is "a pretty workaholic place" where employees are judged more on input (that is, hours worked) than on output. "What matters is how much time you put into the job, the volume of work," one of Ms. Hochschild's interviewees is told by her boss. The major reason is volition. No dark satanic mills in Spotted Deer! Over and over Ms. Hochschild conveys Amerco's employees' attitude toward their work by using such sun-dappled terms as "sweet joy," "fun," "carefree," "emotionally supportive" and "more interesting than life at home." One interviewee tells her, "I come to work to relax." Ms. Hochschild has exposed something that feels like an unacknowledged home truth, America's clean little secret: work, not even the substance of it but the buzzy surface feeling of office life, is for many of us a source of intense pleasure.

Amerco has become somewhat homelike—even, Ms. Hochschild insists, for the hourly workers in its "well-lit, fairly quiet, relatively pleasant" factories. At work people have buddies, they carry on flirtations, their birthdays are celebrated, they even have staged "commitment ceremonies" (to the company, that is). Home, on the other hand, has become "another workplace." The increased presence of women has led to a mild feminization of work, with more emphasis placed on cooperation and support, but also to a pronounced masculinization of home, where efficiency is now the overriding concern.

Parenthood, too, is judged by outputs, not inputs: one mother measures her performance "by how well her children were doing, not how much time she spent with them." Children are subjected to factory-style "speedups," hurried from one place to another all day and made to squeeze all their emotional needs into the hour or less that their parents have to spare in the evening. Home has developed its version of corporate "outsourcing" and "downsizing," with many traditional maternal functions off-loaded to baby sitters and therapists. In one of Ms. Hochschild's most horrifying anecdotes, two parents dash off to give presentations at work on a day when they know their son has to be taken to the hospital because of a medical emergency. Ms. Hochschild notes that Hallmark has introduced a new line of cards "for parents who are too busy to see their children," which say things like "Sorry I can't be there to tuck you in."

A cycle develops. Home, because it is continually shorted, keeps getting messier. Sullen children, resentful spouses, inconvenient stepchildren, elderly parents and manipulative exes lurk there. Relationships at work, which get the nourishment of time, become deeper and richer. One executive, typically of Ms. Hochschild's subjects, finds dealings with his "office children"—subordinates, that is—more rewarding than those with his flesh-and-blood children. The reversing of home and work has got to the point that Amerco employees who can't handle their family lives can now turn to the company to teach them how, through free workshops on such subjects as "Dealing With Anger."

Ms. Hochschild's previous book, "The Second Shift," found that in two-career couples, women still do the lion's share of the child care and housework. In "The Time Bind" she identifies a "third shift," consisting of emotional work at home, which nobody does. Many of her subjects have invented a "potential self" who would do all the things they are not doing at home; their garages fill up with recreational equipment, bought for the potential self to use, ignored by the real one. Although Ms. Hochschild's ideal plainly is that men and women would work side by side on all three shifts, she is also unsparing in pointing out that it was women's changing their priorities that produced the net reduction in emotional effort at home. Everybody knows men have never carried their share of the load of family life, she writes: "This isn't news. The news of this book is that growing numbers of working women are leery of spending more time at home, as well."

Several years ago Daniel Yankelovich, the psychologist and management consultant, observed that one of the main changes in American culture since the Second World War has been the emergence of a tendency "to view work as a source of personal satisfaction." When mothers entered the work force en masse, it was partly out of economic necessity and partly a manifestation of this alteration of the culture of work. Reread "The Feminine Mystique" and you'll see that Betty Friedan made her case for women working with a rhetoric not of justice or power, but self-fulfillment. (Ms. Friedan had the temerity to attack Sigmund Freud back when that took real courage, but she was completely under the sway of Abraham Maslow and his glorification of people who can ascend to the satisfaction of "higher-order needs.") Men, less noticeably because they were already working, made roughly the same change at the same time— that's why "The Organization Man," with its dutiful drones, has become a period piece.

Ms. Hochschild ends "The Time Bind" by calling for a "time movement" whose members would organize to reduce work hours. This used to be a sturdy liberal-labor cause, but it has fallen into disuse since the Depression. Recently writers like Juliet Schor and Jeremy Rifkin (in "The End of Work") have also suggested reviving it. The trouble, judging by Ms. Hochschild's evidence, is that nobody would want to join.

PART III

DEFINING MOMENTS IN TECHNOLOGY

CHAPTER 8

THE TRANSPORTATION REVOLUTION

Stewardesses in a full-scale model interior of the newly released Boeing 707 jet pose for a press photo for "the first-class airliner of the future" in 1956. Early commercial jet travel was luxurious, but as airlines grew larger it became more accessible and commonplace. (*New York Times*)

I N THE EARLY YEARS OF THE UNITED STATES, BUSINESS DEPENDED ON many of the same aspects—reliable capital markets, a competent workforce, effective leadership, and a consuming public—that concern large firms today. But one of the biggest challenges to business growth in the late eighteenth and early nineteenth centuries is harder for us to appreciate. In our own time, most of the things we buy, including some services, travel thousands of miles from where they were produced to our homes or workplaces. Our blue jeans are cut and sewn by workers in Mexico or the

---

1817
Erie Canal plans approved.

1862
Pacific Railway Act authorizes building transcontinental railroad.

1869
Transcontinental railroad completed.

1881
Jay Gould controls largest network of railroads in nation.

1887
Congress passes Interstate Commerce Act.

Philippines; our computers contain parts manufactured in China, Taiwan, and Japan and are serviced by technical support staff in India; even the local supermarket boasts a cornucopia of jet-setting fruits and vegetables. Distance matters little when a product can be made cheaply and efficiently across the globe and then easily transported to relevant markets. For most of our country's history, however, distance was both time and money, and it mattered a lot.

One of the biggest obstacles to trade and other forms of westward expansion in the young United States was the difficulty of overland transport. Before the railroads, people or goods traveling on solid ground could move no faster than a human being or a pack animal could walk. By modern standards, this was very, very slow. A loaded wagon pulled by a team of oxen, for example, traveled about twenty miles in a day. A stage coach powered by four horses that were changed at stations along the way could cover twice this distance in the same period. In winter, speeds slackened considerably, as men and animals slogged through water, ice, and snow. Regardless of the season, overland travel in the early days of the republic was subject to the vagaries of a crude and limited road system. Where roads existed at all, they were often muddy, deeply rutted, and punctuated by obstacles such as tree stumps and rocks; in seasons of heavy rain, they could be nearly impassable.[1] In the 1790s, inland transport was so cumbersome that a merchant could ship a ton of goods to England for about the same price as it would cost to ship them overland a distance of forty miles, or about the width of Rhode Island.[2]

In the early 1800s, a spate of construction produced a number of new, improved toll roads paved with stones or wooden boards and known as turnpikes.[3] Many of these roads, such as the National Road built between 1811 and 1839 and stretching from

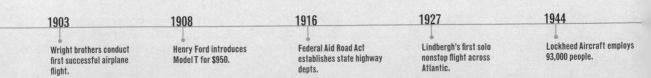

1903
Wright brothers conduct first successful airplane flight.

1908
Henry Ford introduces Model T for $950.

1916
Federal Aid Road Act establishes state highway depts.

1927
Lindbergh's first solo nonstop flight across Atlantic.

1944
Lockheed Aircraft employs 93,000 people.

Cumberland, Maryland, to Wheeling, Virginia, and eventually to Vandalia, Illinois, stimulated the westward movement of people and goods. Others promoted the commercialization of agriculture along their routes.[4] Creating this infrastructure required large amounts of capital, most of which was privately raised, and turnpike companies were often structured as corporations.[5] Some early roads—such as Pennsylvania's Lancaster Pike, completed in 1793—turned out to be profitable enterprises.[6] For other ventures, however, government regulation of toll rates, the high costs of turnpike maintenance, and the number of travelers who were willing to pay rather than take their chances on the free roads limited financial returns.[7] Many turnpike companies went bankrupt, and their roads were abandoned. In New York, for instance, more than half of the 4,000 miles of turnpike operating in 1822 had fallen into disuse by the mid-1830s. A similar ratio obtained in Massachusetts during this time.[8] Until the mid-nineteenth century, travel by water was infinitely faster (and much more efficient) than any form of overland transportation.

The superiority of water travel led to a brief, intense period of investment in canals designed to connect cities not linked by natural bodies of water. By 1830, more than 1,500 miles of canals snaked their way throughout the Northeast, many funded by state governments as a means of promoting settlement and commerce.[9] In 1817, the New York State Legislature approved plans to finance a canal that would run from the Hudson River to Lake Erie. The Erie Canal began operation in 1825 and quickly proved an enormous success, promoting economic growth along its 340-mile course and helping fuel New York City's rise as the nation's most vital urban port.[10] Other states followed suit with their own canals, often constructed through much more difficult terrain.[11] By the

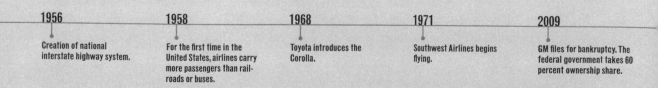

1956
Creation of national interstate highway system.

1958
For the first time in the United States, airlines carry more passengers than railroads or buses.

1968
Toyota introduces the Corolla.

1971
Southwest Airlines begins flying.

2009
GM files for bankruptcy. The federal government takes 60 percent ownership share.

onset of the Civil War, more than 4,000 miles of canals had been created, at a cost of almost $200 million.[12]

Not surprisingly, nearly all major centers of commerce in this period, from New York to St. Louis, grew up beside rivers, lakes, and ocean ports. In the early 1800s, the advent of steam power made inland water travel quicker and cheaper than current, wind, or human brawn (pulling a canal barge) had allowed. The steam engine, developed in England in the 1760s by James Watt, who refined an earlier invention by Thomas Newcomen, was first used to run machinery in British textile factories.[13] In 1807, the American engineer Robert Fulton adapted the technology to drive the first successful commercial steamboat, the *Clermont*, up the Hudson River.[14] Within four years, steamboats traveling up and downstream were common sights on major rivers such as the Ohio and the Mississippi.[15] By 1855, a steamboat traveling downstream reached an average speed of 10.8 miles per hour, more than six times the average speed of a flatboat.[16] Voyages that had once taken months could be completed in a matter of days for a fraction of the former price.[17]

These were big improvements. But by midcentury, a new form of transportation arose that soon eclipsed all previous modes. Railroads were developed using the same technology that made the Mississippi steamboats run. In 1804, the first high-pressure steam locomotive made an experimental run in Wales. About twenty years later, the British began to build commercial railroad lines. The first railroad in the United States opened in Baltimore in 1830 and was followed soon after by a line in Charleston.[18] By 1840, the number of operating railroad miles was roughly equal to that of the canals; by 1860, railroads crossed more than twenty states and outdistanced canal miles by more than seven to one.[19] But it was after the Civil War that railroad construction really took off, fed in part by private European investment capital and by millions of acres of free land granted to railroad companies by the federal and state governments.[20] All told, railroads received 180 million acres of land, which made an important contribution toward funding this huge investment in overland transport.[21] The web of steel tracks, which soon spanned the continent, affected everyone from the farmers in the Great Plains to the bankers on the eastern seaboard. American society, the historian Henry Adams noted, "dropped every thought of dealing with anything more than the single faction called a railroad system . . . The generation between 1865 and 1895 was already mortgaged to the railways, and no one knew it better than the generation itself."[22]

For nineteenth-century passengers, riding the rails was a heady experience marked by the thrill of high speed and, at times, real danger.[23] Falls from bridges, collisions with other trains, loose rails, and fires in wooden cars occurred with some frequency in the first decades of the railroads.[24] The industry soon grew more organized, however, and invested in extensive track and bridge construction. Road managers pressured the government to adopt standard time zones so that traffic could be run more safely and efficiently.[25] The first rudimentary boxcars and (open-air) wooden passenger benches were also transformed. By the 1870s, prosperous travelers slept and dined in Pullman Palace Cars surrounded by luxurious, plush furnishings and elaborate décor. For the less well-to-do, there were enclosed cars with large, glass windows and upholstered seats. Regardless of means, early train passengers were struck by the speed at which they moved. Laura Ingalls Wilder, author of the *Little House* books, was twelve when in 1879 she took her first train ride, traveling west to Dakota Territory. She remembered trying to count the telegraph poles outside her window. But the poles and farmhouses and fields "went so fast that [she] could not really look at them before they were gone. In one hour that train would go twenty miles—as far as the horses traveled in a whole day."[26] The speed, reliability, and sheer novelty of the rails called Americans from all walks of life to climb aboard. And they did. In 1890, nearly 500 million people embarked on train journeys, each for an average trip of twenty-four miles.[27] Small wonder then that by the late

1800s, railroads had become what Walt Whitman termed "the pulse of the continent."[28]

As the century drew to a close, railroads dominated both freight and passenger traffic over long distances. But in densely populated cities, horse-drawn streetcars were still the most common form of carriage as late as the 1880s.[29] The advent of the steam-powered cable car in San Francisco in the 1870s inaugurated the era of street railways in urban areas (it also spared horses the burden of pulling heavy loads up and down the city's steep roads). Within a decade, cable cars were pulling millions of passengers through the California city and other urban centers.[30] Then in 1888, Julian Sprague, a young inventor who had worked with Thomas Edison, convinced the West End Street Railway Company of Boston to equip its city with streetcars powered by electricity. Electric trolleys quickly became a common feature of the changing city landscape, along with tall buildings and department stores. By 1902, electric trolleys were transporting five *billion* passengers a year.[31] Investors in the new technology began to build longer electric lines, called interurbans, to serve traffic between cities and compete directly with the mighty railroads.[32]

Outside the cities, the state of the dirt roads had scarcely changed. But as the new century dawned, pressure for improvement began to mount from several sources. The bicycle had been an immediate hit with the American public since its introduction at the 1867 Paris Exposition, and bicyclists needed smooth paths on which to pedal.[33] In 1893, the roads became a cause of concern for the federal government as the U.S. Post Office Department instituted a system of rural free delivery (RFD).[34] Members of the National Grange of the Patrons of Husbandry—an association of farmers known as the Grange—organized a grassroots campaign to curtail the power of the railroads and usher in a system of free roads.[35] Perhaps most important, the automobile and its makers began to take the stage as a force big enough to rival the rails.

In 1900, motor vehicles were still the plaything of the elite, who donned goggles as they drove—without speed limit or license—wherever the dusty, rugged roads would allow.[36] Within ten years, however, the ranks of automobile owners had increased to the hundreds of thousands, and scores of (mostly small) manufacturers had emerged to serve this nascent but growing demand.[37] Road improvements lagged well behind automobile production, stalled by conflicts over where they should be built, who should control them, and how they should be funded.[38] Finally, in 1916, responding to the petitions of car-owning citizens and the young auto industry, Congress passed the Federal Aid Road Act, appropriating $25 million annually to the states for the construction of better roads.[39] In 1921, the U.S. government set aside some of these funds for the creation of a nationwide highway system.[40] Road construction continued apace during the Depression. As employment in the private sector plummeted, both Herbert Hoover and Franklin Roosevelt authorized public road projects on a massive scale.[41]

The cooperation between the government and the budding automobile industry helped make motor transport the dominant mode of the twentieth century. Trucks, at first used to shuttle goods from remote areas to railway stations, became a viable form of cross-country conveyance in their own right. Many truckers were independent, but some operated as a group. The American Messenger Company—later known as the United Parcel Service (UPS)—was founded in 1907, purchasing its first delivery car in 1913.[42] By 1939, motor vehicles were responsible for about 10 percent of intercity freight traffic; by the 1960s, they accounted for more than 20 percent.[43] In the last decades of the twentieth century, the ranks of trucks and truckers continued to increase. By 1996, more people were employed by trucking and warehousing businesses than by the railroad, air, and water transport industries combined.[44]

Across the country, many cities also turned to motorized systems of public transit. Forced by the Wheeler-Rayburn Act of 1935 to divest themselves of their streetcar subsidiaries, electric companies needed to find buyers quickly.[45] National City Lines (NCL), a holding company backed by General Motors, Standard Oil, and Firestone Tire and Rubber Company, was happy to comply.[46] The trolley lines purchased by NCL were quickly shut down or sold to the public and replaced by motorized buses, which depended on the production capacity of GM, Standard Oil, and Firestone.[47] By 1949, when the companies involved in NCL were prosecuted for the scheme, the conversion in dozens of cities across the country was already complete.[48] Only in some of the largest cities, such as Boston and Chicago, did large-scale streetcar systems survive.

At the same time, the American automobile industry was entering a golden age. The cars of the 1950s boasted big bodies, grand (and often whimsical) details such as tailfins, and iconic names like the Bel Air, the Fairlane, and the Super 88.[49] Between 1948 and 1968, the share of families owning at least one automobile increased from 54 percent to 79 percent (and 26 percent owned two or more).[50] The price of gasoline at the end of the 1960s was less than $0.35 a gallon (about $2.00 in today's dollars, adjusted for inflation).[51] Support for the auto industry continued in the nation's capital, where billions of dollars were allocated to the construction of public roads. The most important legislation in this respect was the Federal-Aid Highway Act, signed into law by Dwight D. Eisenhower in 1956, which authorized the expansion of the interstate highway system by more than forty thousand miles.[52]

During this time, Ford, Chrysler, and General Motors—the "Big Three" American auto manufacturers—dominated car sales at home and abroad.[53] The outsized cars they produced underwent aesthetic changes from year to year and offered optional features such as air conditioning, whitewall tires, and leather upholstery.[54] But few real technical improvements were made to American cars in the three decades after World War II.[55] Eventually, this failing, in combination with the perceived security afforded U.S. auto executives by years of market dominance, allowed European and Japanese manufacturers to move in on the Big Three's home territory. In the 1950s, the Volkswagen Beetle had emerged as an alternative to hefty American models and became a best seller among imports.[56] But it was the oil crisis of the 1970s that greatly compounded the need for small cars, creating huge inroads for Japanese automakers in the American market.[57] In 1960, for example, Japanese imports, including Nissan and Toyota, had virtually no market share in the United States. By 1980, they had captured more than 20 percent.[58] That same year, the Japanese motor vehicle industry took its place as the world leader.[59] Over the next decades, Japan and the United States remained close competitors, with Japan claiming the top spot in the global car market and nearly 30 percent of the U.S. market in the early twenty-first century.[60]

Air travel was the second enormous innovation in twentieth-century transportation. In 1903, brothers Wilbur and Orville Wright flew their airplane successfully and briefly—the flight lasted twelve seconds—down a stretch of beach in Kitty Hawk, North Carolina. Less than thirty years later, in 1927, Charles Lindbergh completed the first solo nonstop flight over the Atlantic Ocean.[61] Airplane manufacture, already on the rise in the early century, grew exponentially during the World Wars. Annual aircraft production increased from less than two thousand in 1935 to nearly fifty thousand in 1945.[62] During World War II, the United States followed England and Germany in developing jet engines for military planes.[63] Additional refinements to the technology made it a faster, more economical way to fly, paving the way for commercial jets and the rise of international tourism in years to come.[64] The onset of the Cold War in the 1950s further stimulated public investment in air and space travel. Eleven years after the creation of the National Aeronautics and Space Administration (NASA) in 1959, millions watched a televised broadcast as astronaut Neil Armstrong took "one small step for a man, one giant leap for mankind" on the moon.[65]

As the first generation of human beings to view the earth from thousands of feet above, commercial jet passengers in the postwar years enjoyed an experience that combined something of the excitement of the first railroads with the elitism of the early automobiles. Jet airline travel in these years was an expensive, special occasion, and passengers dressed accordingly in suits, hats, and pearls. Like previous forms of transportation, however, airlines lost some of their luster as they became much bigger and air travel more accessible. The frequency of air travel accelerated with the Airline Deregulation Act of 1978, which eliminated rate controls and opened the market to new competitors and new travel routes.[66] In the decade leading up to deregulation, the number of aircraft in operation had barely budged; in the ten years following the act, it more than doubled, from 2,545 to 5,660.[67] In 1998, there were more than 8,000 air carriers in service.[68] At the same time, more affordable tickets and additional airport locations helped increase the number of U.S. passenger-miles traveled from 147 billion in 1975 to upward of 500 billion by the end of the 1990s.[69] Airport terminals, the gateway to countless family vacations, also became the familiar haunt of business travelers. By the twenty-first century, flying the friendly skies was a crowded, high-security, and more often than not, tedious ordeal.

In our own time, goods and people continue to move around the United States and the larger world by water, rail, roads, and air. The innovations of the past century, along with the more recent rise of Internet communication, have made us a much more mobile society with high (and rising) expectations for the speed, efficiency, and cost of business conducted over long distances. We have also become increasingly dependent on the energy sources that fuel this commerce, a fact that now poses important economic and environmental problems. In the years to come, public pressure on government and the private sector may inspire new advances in transportation—and perhaps some reinventions. For example, now, decades after the death of the electric trolley, many automobile firms are beginning to research and produce hybrid and electric cars.

By the end of the nineteenth century, electric trolleys had replaced cable cars and horse-drawn streetcars as the primary mode of urban transportation. Here passengers board a BRT 4573 and Connecticut Company Open Air "Breezer" (c. 1911) in East Haven, Connecticut.
(*New York Times*)

June 16, 1895

Horses in the Streets

The progress made in applying mechanical modes of traction and propulsion gives hope of a time when horses may be excluded from the streets of cities, at least those occupied for purposes of residence. How much this will conduce to cleanliness, comfort, and health can easily be imagined.

The stage horse and the car horse still linger, but it is an almost superfluous lagging. It is evident that the cable and electric motor will soon render this variety of the noble and useful animal extinct. The bicycle, tricycle, and quadricycle, propelled by human muscle or by mechanical devices, are surely encroaching upon the field of the saddle and carriage horse and threatening that of the cart horse and the truck horse. There was in France last week an exhibition of horseless carriages, and runs were made from Paris to Bordeaux, at better speed than horses can make with a variety of vehicles. The bicycle is not used merely for pleasure or healthful exercise, but for practical forms of light transportation as well, and the vehicles to which petroleum or electrical motors have been applied are capable of development and extension in useful directions indefinitely.

Why may we not look forward to the time when all transportation through the city streets shall be effected by mechanical devices for propulsion, and even indulge the belief that it is not "far distant"? Pavements will have to be adapted to the change, but that will be in itself an improvement, for they can be made smoother, less noisy, and less retentive of dirt.

But consider the advantage in the way of cleanliness and health. What makes it so difficult and costly to keep streets decently clean? What is the chief substance of the dust that is blown about the streets and in at windows, permeating the air we breathe and irritating throat and lungs with the seeds of disease? To ask the question is to suggest the answer, which is itself a provocative of nausea.

The horse has earned the gratitude of mankind and has received it in abundant measure, but in the streets of cities he has become a terrible nuisance, which nothing but necessity made tolerable. When, like pigs and cows, he is relegated to his place outside the purlieus of urban residence by the ceasing of that necessity, there may be comfort and health as well as pleasure and zest in dwelling in cities. The horse should go.

November 15, 1903

Twenty Years of Standard Time

Revolution Wrought by Its Adoption by the Railroads.

There is to be no ceremonial on Wednesday of the twentieth anniversary of the adoption by the railroads of "standard time" in this country, a change from the old system, where in every locality the people had been accustomed to live their lives by the solar schedule, with the result that there was endless confusion in timetables.

William F. Allen, Secretary and Treasurer of the American Railway Association, who is credited with having secured the adoption of standard time, when seen yesterday afternoon at his office, 24 Park Place, said:

> People of this generation can hardly understand the revolution delivering them from difficulties of travel and the shipment of goods effected by the adoption of standard time. Old readers of THE NEW YORK TIMES, which fought for the movement, will remember. At noon on Nov. 18, 1883, fifty different standards of time resolved themselves into four, the minute hands of clocks and watches being reset at all points to the same minute mark of the dial. Only a few of the railroads did not make the change at once, but they fell in line within a few weeks.

Some of the cities and hamlets were slower, it being something over two years before Cincinnatians adopted the standard. There they had the solar, Columbus, and Louisville times, with the result that there was a good deal of confusion, and it was easy for those who were late to insist that they were early according to the time they fancied, and for the others to insist that they were late. The question as to changing to a standard time was bitter in certain places, and among them Charleston, where a local prophet insisted that the fooling with the reckoning of time would lead to some manifestation of divine displeasure. Three years later there was the earthquake.

The movement by which the reform in time reckoning was brought about in 1883 has many interesting features. It is told in the history of the proceedings of the American Railway Association, which covers the doings of its predecessors from 1875 to 1893, the General Time Convention and the Southern Railway Time Convention, which united and formed the present association.

In October, 1881, Dr. F. A. P. Barnard, with Prof. Cleveland Abbe and Prof. Ormonde Stone, presented the subject of the desirability of a reform in time keeping to the meeting of the railway managers then known as the General Time Convention. The papers were referred to me as the Secretary and editor of The Official Railway Guide.

On April 11, 1883, I presented my plan, which was adopted. Briefly it provided for an elastic instead of a right boundary line between the four sections. It designated every point on the boundary lines where the change from one hour section to the other was to be made. It arranged a method of passing from the use of one hour standard to another without danger of interference or mistake. It suggested a common sense adjustment between local and standard time by the statement that in fact local time would be practically abolished.

I was able to report that I had secured agreements from the managers of 78,000 miles of roads to put the plan in actual use, and that the co-operation of the Naval Observatory at Washington and the Cambridge Observatory and certain city governments was assured. Among those who helped me most in the accomplishment of securing the adoption of standard time were many prominent railroad officials and men of scientific attainments, notably Prof. J. K. Rees of Columbia University and J. Raynor Edmunds of the Cambridge Observatory.

Since the adoption of the system in the United States its use has been extended to many parts of the earth. In every country in Europe, with the exception of France and Russia, railway and local clocks are regulated by the time of either the Greenwich meridian or by that of meridians differing exactly one hour or two hours therefrom. South Africa, Australia, Japan, the Philippine Islands and [Puerto Rico] also base their time reckonings upon meridians differing by even hours from that of Greenwich. In Russia the time differs from the even hour by one minute only. In nearly all parts of the civilized world, therefore, the clocks and the watches, if precisely regulated, beat seconds exactly together, their minute hands point to the same part of the dial—only the hours differ according to the governing meridian.

The Gasoline Age

On Wednesday at Detroit there was given to the world the ten-millionth specimen of Henry Ford's model "T" car, in which so many serious-minded people discern the fullest embodiment of contemporary American civilization. The face that launched these ten million automobiles is as familiar to the American public as that of any living man or woman. Mr. Ford's name will remain imbedded in the language when that of Mary Pickford is forgotten. The conjunction of these two names is not arbitrary. They stand for the two most spectacular triumphs of American industry of the last quarter of a century.

Between the motor industry and the moving-picture industry there is this difference, however, that the former was not created out of a void. Before the movie there was nothing. Before the motor car there was the horse and wagon. The movie has created the need which it satisfies. The automobile has done so only in part. The automobile is, in large measure, only doing better the work which was, after all, done before. A few figures are illuminative. Twenty years ago the capital invested in the automobile industry was $23,000,000. In 1919 it amounted to $1,780,000,000. The number of workers in the industry rose from 13,333 to 161,000. But in the same fifteen years the capital invested in the carriage and wagon industry declined from $152,000,000 to $97,000,000 and the workers from 91,000 to 30,700. Suppose that in the year 1904 the automobile had—well, flivvered—and that the horseless vehicle had followed its normal course of development along with the rest of American industry. There would be today employed in the manufacture of "carriages and wagons" nearly 150,000 men, instead of the 190,000-odd actually employed in the manufacture of vehicles horse-drawn and horseless. That gap of 40,000 men fairly represents what we may call the new use of the automobile. It largely substantiates the motor men's denial that the motor car is a "luxury" product.

New uses for the automobile there are in plenty. The carriage and wagon never would have become the gigantic gasoline freight carrier which now competes with the railroads. Both for business and pleasure the gasoline engine has created radius. People still "drive" a car as they used to drive in buggies and shays, but the area of the circle of which the motor owner is now the proud surveyor if not the master, in a single day, has been multiplied fifteen-fold. The change has been greatest for the city dweller. To the farmer the Ford is a magnified buggy, but essentially that. But the New York of today, even with its present wealth, would not have shown one horse-drawn pleasure vehicle for every twenty-five of its present automobiles. There the record of the movie has been paralleled. A new need has been created and satisfied simultaneously. HENRY FORD'S name is associated with "quantity production." Much less emphasis has been laid on its correlative quantity consumption.

It has been a development laden with vast moral and social implications. The dizzying speed of modern life over which people are concerned has here its concrete illustration. Educators have regarded with mixed feelings the influence of the automobile on the temperament and world outlook of the young. Business men in other fields of merchandising have deplored the expenditure upon automobile "luxury" of money that should be going into more homely necessities. Battles have been won with motor trucks and taxicabs. Revolutions have been made with a couple of armored cars. But the record is not all on the side of social instability. England defeated at least one serious railroad strike by the use or the threat of the automobile. And it might be argued that social stability has gained by the rise of what may be described almost as a new middle class composed of automobile owners, with a stronger sense for the rights of property.

When the first Ford Model T was completed on September 27, 1908 in Detroit, Michigan, Henry Ford called it "a car for the great multitude." The automobile's success led to the widespread establishment of motorized systems of transit. (From the collections of the Henry Ford. Copy and reuse restrictions apply.)

Automobile As Maker of Better Americans

BY DAVID BEECROFT

Former President Society of Automotive Engineers.

America has the international reputation of developing and building the most utilitarian automobile the world has produced. This is the opinion of European engineers who are familiar with the industry in America.

France, the mother of the motor car, builds some of the finest cars produced, representing the highest engineering attainments and perhaps finest workmanship, but the French car has not made a conquest of the nations of the world as has the American car. The reason may be found in the environment that surrounded the American car in its swaddling clothes day, contemporaneous with the birth of the century.

Charles E. Duryea, with his pioneer car of 1892, aimed at producing a machine of transportation that would fill a place lower than that of the horse that was then at its zenith. To Duryea the car was for the man who could not afford a horse. There was no thought that the mechanical buggy, or horseless vehicle, as it was then designated, would displace the horse in the affection of the American man or woman, or even supplant it to any extent, but there seemed a possible place for the horseless vehicle in a lower scale of transportation.

A few years later the development of Duryea, together with that of Haynes, Stanley, Olds, Winton, King and others gave a suggestion of what the future would reveal, but it was not until Henry Ford in 1906 electrified the nation—by the announcement of his $500 car—that even a few saw a faint glimmering of what the morrow would produce. Ford on that memorable occasion uttered some prophetic words, not appreciated to the full by himself or by those he addressed himself to, to wit: "My aim is to build a car good enough for any American to ride in and cheap enough so that any man can afford to have one."

That year marked the birth of what might be designated the conception of the great utility car, the car not for the classes alone, but primarily for the masses, the inception of the car that was to be the servant of his Majesty the American citizen.

No better cradle of democracy as a birthplace for this new transportation servant of man could have been selected than the zone of the Great Lakes, which has in the last ten years developed into the great production centre of the industry. This area, in which were to develop such manufacturing centres as Detroit, Flint, Toledo, Cleveland and many smaller places, possessed an ideal environment and contained a set of conditions that played a determining part in the development of the industry during the last ten years.

This environment to a large extent is the answer to our utilitarian type of car. Motor car manufacturers in France, England, Italy, Belgium or Germany had no such setting, no such stimulating environment, no such commanding atmosphere, no such alluring market.

The unconquered Mississippi Valley, with its myriad farms, demanded the car. The social fabric of this agricultural domain craved that agent that would reduce miles to furlongs, and that would bring the backwoods farmer closer to the city and so remove one great obstacle of rural life.

The business texture of this area waited for some factor of transportation that would not only fill in the gaps between railroad and trolley lines, but that would give individual transportation which was impossible with either steam or electricity. The telephone, the telegraph and the Rural Free Delivery had done their part in weaving the net of humanity over these gardens of the desert, and it remained for the motor vehicle not only to fill in the finer meshes of the network, but to bring into greater completeness life in these areas which are now the granaries of a continent.

But the call for the utility car came also from the then far-off Pacific Coast, where 150,000 miles of highway gave evidence of what the needs of that area were to be, and the conditions of the timber area of the Puget Sound whispered the demands of industry for a more flexible form of transportation than then existed.

The 2,800,000 miles of roadway lying as a loosely knit, patternless network over the 3,000,000 square miles of the United States of America was a challenge to the manufacturer to build for the millions whose farms lined these highways, and the 4,000,000 cars in the ownership of farmers today bears indisputable testimony to the role the motor vehicle has played in our agricultural development in the last decade.

The car has not only added from 25 to 40 per cent to the value of the land, but additional increased land valuation has followed as a result of nearly 400,000 miles of improved highway built since the advent of the car. No estimate can be placed on the ethical progress resulting from hard-surfaced roads in any area, yet this is one of the immeasurable national assets that followed the conquest of the virgin highway by the car and today this is approaching 50 per cent nation-wide, because when our projected Federal and State highway system is completed 90 per cent of the population of the country will be within ten miles of some part of this gigantic system and every centre of 5,000 population or over will be on this network of hard-surfaced roadway system.

With nearly 15,000,000 vehicles in use, or five for every mile of highway, the perpetual discussion as to when the saturation point will be reached continues and has more years to run. The saturation point of the motor vehicle will be reached when the saturation point of transportation is reached. The two are coincident. Man has not yet correctly set his slide rule to determine this period of transportation, for he has not yet completely comprehended the necessity for individual transportation in its fullness of usefulness.

Enhanced American Knowledge.

What part the motor car has played in forging the homogeneity of a nation future historians will record, but nothing breeds national patriotism so much as familiarity. The motor car has introduced millions to their own land. The farmer no longer ekes out an existence without being more than twenty miles from home. His conception of living has broadened. His familiarity with the face of the country has increased.

Transportation still ranks as the great humanizer of mass population, and the fact that America has produced a utility type of vehicle at a phenomenally low price has been a great contributing factor in stamping out destructive movements such as have gained headway in other lands. The American citizen with a few hundred dollars can purchase motor transportation that gives as many miles per day as the millionaire, and both can exceed the speed permitted by law, so that neither envies the other. The fact that the motor car is no longer a criterion of social status in a community has been one of the great leveling influences between classes in the last few years. It is a 100 per cent remedy against communism and other cults that tend to split people into hostile groups.

The rapid growth of our cities and the failure of fixed-route systems of transportation to keep pace with population increase have resulted in city concerns using the motor vehicle in large numbers. The largest wholesalers in Chicago have taken advantage of such a system for many years. Our public service corporations have hundreds of vehicles for all departments of their business, and departments of municipal government have had to adopt the motor car and the motor truck in order to cope with the growth of population and the enlargement of the city.

Spanning the gap between business centres and pleasure grounds of the country by the motor car can be illustrated by the way our fifteen national parks have been so linked together, and while it is only a few years since motor cars were admitted to such places as the Yellowstone National Park, yet last year more than 750,000 tourists visited the national parks by motor, nearly 60 per cent of all visitors touring to these national monuments in their cars. Statistics show that families travel more in their motor cars than by any other agent of transportation, and these national shrines for nature worship are destined to entertain increasing pilgrimages of motorists as our improved highway systems are hooked up.

We stand today on the threshold of a new form of motor transportation, the motor coach, which is giving a collective form of motor transport that promises to spread far and wide as our highways are built up and extended. Today the traveler can go from San Diego, Cal. to Seattle by a series of motor coach lines, averaging for distances of hundreds of miles the speed of the railroad lines, and traveling with a luxury that our most imaginative grandparents of stage-coach days did not even dream of. These coach lines on the Pacific Coast average 40 miles per hour, and have all traveling conveniences.

Appeal to the Inventive Mind.

The unprecedented growth of circles of suburbs surrounding our great cities has only been made possible by the motor car, the motor coach and the motor truck. In the environs of Greater New York in horse days the limit of a Sunday excursion by horse was a drive to Bronxville for luncheon and home in the afternoon. Today Bronxville is scarcely forty minutes from Columbus Circle, and Long Island and Jersey are within closer reach than Mount Vernon was before the motor made its debut.

The myriad lakes of Wisconsin, Minnesota and Michigan have been drawn closer together and brought within the pale of summer residence colonies for the business man by virtue of the car. Golf courses have sprung up where deserted farms once existed, and the earning capacity of man has been multiplied by his introduction to the outside world. The business strains of the past decade would have exacted a much higher toll of life had it not been for the clarion call of outdoor life sounded by the motor.

We are too much in the midst of this great transportation revolution today to measure its Atlas-like proportions: we are groping in the dark for new measures to organize and systematize this movement; we are, as the light permits, laying plans for tomorrow, but the movement is still too close to be appreciated. Too often we fail to see the forest for the trees.

The day is at hand when we will build anew our highways—build them to meet the needs of motor travel. New highways for commercial vehicles will be built in many thickly settled areas. Roads paralleling present ones will be constructed, transport surveys will be made so these roads will prove adequate for fifty, perhaps a hundred years, and just as Napoleon remade the great avenues of Paris one hundred years ago so that they are adequate for the needs of today, so must cities and States of the nation remake their highway systems so that the motor vehicle may deliver that measure of usefulness which it is capable of giving and so free it from the manacles that are so hampering it today.

Railroads Seeking More Passengers

Officials Believe Automobile Is Losing Attractiveness for Travelers.

One of the principal problems of the railways continues to be that of making passenger service more attractive. Passenger traffic officials agree that the novelty of cross-country trips in automobiles, which for a time seriously detracted from railroad patronage, is wearing off and that if the railroads will add comforts and conveniences not obtainable in the automobile they will do a larger passenger business.

It is conceded generally also that the railroads should cooperate with the "Save to Travel" movement. Thirty-six railroads are now members of the "Save to Travel Association" and others are willing to cooperate with banks in a movement to popularize the slogan "Open a vacation travel account in your bank."

Reduction in fares has been suggested as a means to stimulate short-haul traffic, but a difference of opinion due to officials' different experience with week-end excursions has prevented its general adoption. Some officials report that these excursions are not profitable. The statement has been made that reduction in the fare of round trip tickets causes a decrease in one-way sales, while at the same time there is a decrease in revenue.

"Compared with the whole," says L. A. Blatterman, general passenger agent of the Wabash, "it is seldom that the Wabash finds justification for the operation of special trains, and as the most attractive centres on the road for excursions are places like Chicago, Detroit and St. Louis, we avail ourselves of regular service with additional equipment. Of course, this sometimes necessitates additional sections. From experience extending over a period of years, a constant scrutiny is necessary in connection with these excursions.

"The Wabash operated 349 excursions in 1926, which is an increase of 38.5 per cent over 1925. The road's revenue increased 8.6 per cent, while our total passenger revenue shows an increase of only 0.11 per cent, or approximately the same as last year. In 1926 we operated a total special train mileage of 13,009 miles, which is 7.8 per cent of the total mileage used in handling special excursion business."

There is doubt as to whether the use of the rail motor cars will regain the lost traffic which now uses buses and private automobiles. It is agreed, however, that these cars justify their use by cutting down the cost of operation per mile.

Experience of some roads shows that innovations in equipment attract attention. Both the Baltimore & Ohio and the Louisville & Nashville report satisfactory results from the use of cars of other than standard design. Advertising to induce rail travel has been discussed and it has been shown that $13,644,355, or 1.3 per cent, of the total passenger revenue of all railroads was spent in 1925 for that purpose. Joint advertising by two or more roads of the same rate to the same point has been advocated.

Says Flight Proves Age of Air Is Here

Assistant Secretary Jahncke, After 12,000-Mile Navy Tour,

Declares Plane Travel Safe.

WASHINGTON, AUG. 24.—The airplane as a means of long and short distance transportation is now completely dependable, Assistant Secretary of the Navy Ernest Lee Jahncke said tonight over the radio. Mr. Jahncke has just concluded a tour of inspection by air of all the naval stations in the Continental United States as well as in the Hawaiian Islands, although the journey to and from San Francisco to Honolulu was made by boat. Within ten years he predicted the airways will be as dotted with airplanes as the highways today are with automobiles.

The peace-time activities of the navy, reflecting increased comfort, efficiency and progress in civil life, form one of the outstanding impressions of my tour of inspection of the American fleet and the naval activities in the Pacific [he said]. I made the entire trip by air and in 120 hours crossed the North American Continent twice, once by the northern rim and once by the southern rim. We had flown every inch of the Pacific Coast from Mexico to British Columbia. We had traveled more than 12,000 miles by air and I had learned the lesson of the complete dependability of modern air travel.

Airplane No Longer Novelty.

By grace of the airplane I have been able to imprint upon my mind such pictures of the yards at Pensacola, New Orleans, San Diego, San Francisco, Seattle and Honolulu as I never could obtain by any other means. By grace of the airplane I have spanned a continent twice, as easily and comfortably as when a business man I had stepped into my automobile and spanned the distance between my home and my office, and as safely and dependably.

As a civilian I see things through the eyes of business, as do millions of other Americans, and I today see America through the eyes of the airmen who are bringing to this nation as great a transportation revolution as the railroad men once brought, as the automobile men brought, within the memory of millions living today.

America has taken to the air, the airplane is no longer a novelty; it is hardly an adventure. It is nothing mysterious any more.

The airplane is, with us, as much routine as the automobile, if not as numerous, and is as dependable as the railroad train, and the next ten years will see our skyways charted and filled as our highways are charted and filled today.

American cities which recognize the facts of the airplane and its future and are building airports are, Mr. Jahncke declared, tapping new sources of wealth so great that the most optimistic are more likely to underestimate it than to overestimate it.

American cities, he said, which fail to envision the future of air transportation will in the not distant future find themselves in the same position as the cities of two or three generations ago which ignored the possibilities of rail transportation.

Small Cities Have Airports.

The lack of community foresight in cities and towns [Mr. Jahncke continued] that fail to provide airports today can only be compared to the lack of foresight in a community that today would build a road for three or four buggies when from 150 to 500 automobiles a day would use a modern highway were it built.

On this 12,000-mile flight it gave me a thrill to see the little cities, keen and alert to the future, that have built modern airports. In my memory stands such names as

these: Medford, Ore., a little city that saw sky traffic over the crests of the Klamath [Mountain] range and built a great airport to meet it when it came. We refueled there.

Cheyenne, Wyo., a clean, keen city set in the midst of endless plains, where today the airplane can find all it needs on a great landing field just as once that city stood ready to equip a cowboy.

North Platte, Neb., where, in the midst of the Nebraska prairie once the home of the buffalo, the transcontinental air fleets today can come to anchor and do.

Patterson, La., where the enterprise of one Louisianan has provided an airport in which one can refuel between New Orleans and Houston.

Moline, Ill., just across the river from Davenport, Iowa.

These are the little cities that have won their places on the air maps of America. They have tapped this new source of wealth; money is coming into their coffers already from that investment.

"Swift, Dependable, Safe."

Just as American communities had to awaken a generation ago to the great new movement of the people brought by the automobile, so America's cities, small as well as large, must awaken to the great new movement by air.

The era of air has come. The airplane, properly inspected, competently piloted, is swift, dependable and safe. The plane in which I flew 12,000 miles started the flight after 1,700 air hours without a major overhauling.

In the 12,000 miles it carried me across the great American Desert, over the Rocky Mountains, over the Alleghany Mountains and over the Mojave Desert, from border to border and coast to coast. One spark plug wore out and one rocker arm was renewed, and that was all. The airplane has come not merely to stay, but to grow.

It is up to the States and cities of America to build airports to handle this traffic that is here. When an American can breakfast in El Paso and dine in Los Angeles, as I have done, can take off in San Francisco in the morning and reach Salt Lake City before sunset; can awaken in Dayton, Ohio, and lunch in Washington. D. C., it is time for America's cities to provide the airports that will put these cities on the map and reap the harvest that is waiting to be gathered.

In California I found the gasoline tax that, collected from automobiles, goes to build that State's superb roads is remitted to aviators. I took the liberty of suggesting there that it be collected from them and spent for airports.

The suggestion was welcomed and approved, and now I take the liberty of suggesting to every State and city of America that, by whatever local means are deemed best, a definite program be adopted looking to the immediate financing and construction of modern, adequate airports that meet the requirements of the United States Government to put them in the classification of the best, for the time is coming soon when the city without an airport will be in the same plight as the city without an automobile highway or without a railroad station.

Mr. Jahncke told of the peace time aviation activities of the navy, the work of the naval aviators in surveying and discovery in Alaska, its varied activities in the continental United States, as well as in the insular possessions.

Alfred P. Sloan Jr. Dead at 90; G.M. Leader and Philanthropist

Alfred P. Sloan Jr., who shaped the General Motors Corporation into one of the world's largest manufacturing enterprises, died of a heart attack yesterday afternoon at Memorial Sloan–Kettering Center here. He was 90 years old.

Mr. Sloan was acclaimed last night as one of the great captains of industry of his age, not alone for his managerial skills but also for the pioneering automotive advances that he oversaw. These included four-wheel brakes, ethyl gasoline, crankcase ventilation and knee-action front springs.

Mr. Sloan made his mark, his associates said, "as a planner, organizer and administrator."

Roy Abernathy, president of the American Motors Corporation, called Mr. Sloan "the most advanced practitioner of modern management of our time."

In Detroit, Henry Ford 2d, chairman of the Ford Motor Company, extolled Mr. Sloan as "one of the small handful of men who actually made automotive history."

"Under his leadership," Mr. Ford said, "General Motors developed from a loosely organized group of companies into the present highly efficient giant corporation."

At his death Mr. Sloan was honorary chairman of General Motors, and in this capacity he had attended a board of directors meeting here last month. Associates who talked with him then said yesterday that he participated in the session with his usual acuity.

His Work, His Hobby, His Love

When Mr. Sloan became vice president of operations of General Motors in 1920 the company accounted for less than 12 per cent of motor vehicle sales in the nation; when he stepped down as chairman in 1956 its share was 52 per cent. Moreover, General Motors had expanded into one of the world's largest companies. It was also among the most profitable and, operationally, one of the smoothest.

These accomplishments were credited to Mr. Sloan's management policies. He centralized administration and decentralized operations, grouping together those that had a common relationship. He also realigned the company's products so that one brand of automobiles did not conflict with another. Each product—cars, electric iceboxes or whatever—was set apart in its own division. It was part of Mr. Sloan's genius that he was familiar with every detail of each division.

Along Staff Lines

In his 14 years as president of General Motors (1923–37) and in almost 20 years as chairman of the board (1937–56) Mr. Sloan ran the company on the staff principle, with himself as chief. But despite the eminence of his position he did not comport himself like an autocrat, nor did he hoot and holler. (He was known throughout the organization as "Silent Sloan.") He also refrained from ordering underlings about.

"I never give orders," Mr. Sloan once said. "I sell my ideas to my associates if I can. I accept their judgment if they convince me, as they frequently do, that I am wrong. I prefer to appeal to the intelligence of a man rather than attempt to exercise authority over him."

An associate likened him to a roller bearing— "self-lubricating, smooth, eliminates friction and carries the load."

Father Was Well-to-Do

Summarizing his recipe for success, Mr. Sloan said:

"Get the facts. Recognize the equities of all concerned. Realize the necessity of doing a better job every day. Keep an open mind and work hard. The last is most important of all. There is no short cut."

He was born in New Haven on May 23, 1875. His father was a well-to-do coffee and tea importer, and later a wholesale grocer. The Sloans moved to 240 Garfield Place, Brooklyn, when Alfred Jr., was 10. He attended public school until he was 11, when he entered Brooklyn Polytechnic Institute where he established a reputation as a prodigy in mechanics and engineering. At 17 he enrolled in the Massachusetts Institute of Technology in Cambridge, and by grinding away every possible minute he graduated in three years.

With his father's help Alfred got a draftsman's job in the Hyatt Roller Bearing Company at Harrison, N.J. The company was not doing very well, but Alfred had confidence that it could be made to show a profit. He persuaded his father and another man to put up $5,000 and place him in control. In the first six months the business yielded $12,000 in profits.

It was the automotive industry, however, that made the company's fortune. Automakers had been using a heavily greased wagon axle until Mr. Sloan persuaded the Olds Motors Company to try his bearings. Henry Ford and the other manufacturers soon followed suit, and Hyatt Bearing started making money hand over fist.

By 1916 the company was doing a gross business of $10-million a year and making profits as high as $4-million. Of equal importance, Mr. Sloan had made a name for himself in Detroit as a knowledgeable and reliable business man with keen insights into the auto industry.

His First $5-Million

By that year General Motors, replacing Ford, had become Mr. Sloan's largest customer, and there was some hint that it might make its own bearings. Instead, General Motors, which had been stitched together from several independent auto concerns by the mercurial William Crapo Durant, bought Hyatt for $13.5-million.

[It was promptly] merged with some other parts and accessory companies into the United Motors Corporation and installed Mr. Sloan as president. In the process Mr. Sloan pocketed his first $5-million, a start on a fortune that was to rise to $250-million.

Late in 1918, through the initiative of John J. Raskob, General Motors took over United Motors as its own parts division, and Mr. Sloan went along as its executive head.

Successively, he was named a member of the G.M. board of directors and a vice president.

A Sloan visit was not soon forgotten for Mr. Sloan was 6 feet tall and weighed 130 pounds. He arrived [at car dealerships] dressed in what was then the height of fashion—a dark, double-breasted suit, a high starched collar, conservative tie fixed with a pearl stickpin, a handkerchief cascading out of his breast pocket and spats. It was enough to awe any dealer.

When Franklin D. Roosevelt took office in 1933 Mr. Sloan at first cooperated with the new Administration, becoming a member of the Industrial Advisory Board of the National Recovery Administration. When the dollar was devalued, however, the New Deal lost a friend and gained a persistent critic.

Early in 1937 Mr. Sloan encountered one of the major crises of his business life when newly organized workers in General Motors plants staged a 44-day sit-down strike to obtain union recognition.

Mr. Sloan did not carry on the negotiations personally. He remained in New York, delegating the distasteful job to William S. Knudsen, then vice president in charge of operations, and other executives. A few months later he turned over the company presidency to Mr. Knudsen and became chairman of the board.

Mr. Sloan also took time to reply to critics of General Motors and its success. "General Motors has become what it is because of its people and the way they work together, because of the opportunity afforded these people to participate in an enterprise which combined their activities efficiently."

In World War II General Motors, under Mr. Sloan's direction, converted its automotive plants to the manufacture of armaments. A total of 102 plants was involved, and from February, 1942, to September, 1945, no automobiles were produced. [By the end of 1945], virtually all G.M. lines were back in civilian production.

In 1946, Mr. Sloan stepped down as the company's chief executive officer after 25 years in that post. He remained as chairman of the board until 1956, when he was elected honorary chairman, a position he held until his death.

It's Different in a Jet Airplane

BY RONALD WALKER

LONDON—It may sound crazy in 1952, when the world's airlines travel some 19,000,000 miles each week and carry 800,000 passengers, to come back from a trip in a commercial transport and pronounce it a unique and exhilarating experience. But after thirty-four years of vigorous growth air travel is entering a new age—the jet age. And a flight on the first jet passenger transport to go into commercial service, the British de Havilland Comet, is rather a thrill.

It is an experience still rare for American travelers, for Comets are now in service only from London to Johannesburg and to Singapore. But Pan American World Airways has announced the purchase of three Comet jets, for delivery in 1956. They will be Mark III models, larger and more powerful versions of the present Mark I.

The present Comet seems powerful enough. At one jump it has increased the maximum cruising speed of commercial flights by some 200 miles an hour, to 490, bringing the 600-m. p. h. jetliner within sight and the supersonic airliner to just around the corner. Its four kerosene-burning jet engines develop so much power that piston engines with equivalent output would have to weigh as much as the complete Comet.

But the customer who buys a seat is not concerned with the technicalities—fuel consumption or pressurization and heating at the high altitudes used by the Comet.

Just what is it like to fly in one of these jetliners?

A Feeling of Remoteness Grips Even Experienced Traveler Once Aloft

After years of traveling to most parts of the world on the major international airlines, on practically every type of plane and flying-boat, flying in the Comet was definitely an experience for this passenger. Even the seasoned air traveler is surprised to discover that what appears at first sight to be a quite orthodox airliner, if one overlooks the absence of propellers, can provide travel so different.

From the accommodation point of view the Comet I, having only thirty-six seats against the many more of the Constellation, Stratocruiser and the Douglas DC-6, seems small. But jolly comfortable seats they are. Up to this moment there has been no difference. There is the old and familiar routine of passengers filing out to the waiting airliner, being directed to their seats, hand luggage and coats being stowed, and the passengers belted down.

Engines On

But from the moment the door bangs shut, the new experience begins. The pilot switches on the jet turbines. There is noise; about equivalent to that of a well-behaved Stratocruiser. You cannot have four great pieces of whirling machinery close in to the fuselage with no noise. It is a low hum, accompanied, as the engines are accelerated, by the just audible high-pitched whine of the turbines. Right at the start there is a notable lack of the vibration common to the modern piston-engined airliner, in which, efficiently sound-proofed as they are, the vibration rumbles through the feet through the soles of one's shoes often making a window vibrate loudly.

There is no warm-up at the head of the runway. Jet engines do not require it. With special clearance the Comet taxis directly from the apron to the runway for an immediate take-off to avoid wasting fuel. As the pilot opens the throttles for the take-off the passenger realizes the enormous power of the engines. The Comet surges forward with such rapid acceleration that the passenger is pushed back into the seat cushions. Only one piston airliner produces a take-off approaching this surge of power—the Convair.

The nose of the Comet lifts and it climbs away from the airfield at an initial rate of 2,000 feet a minute—which was the rate of climb of crack fighter aircraft when World War II began. It is exhilarating—something like going up in one of the Empire State Building elevators. The climb is firm and steady, the pressurization effective, and the passenger gains a real impression of the rate

of ascent only as the Comet bursts through the cloud layers.

A Comet flight is normally broken into three phases. There is about half an hour of climbing, at a slowly diminishing rate of ascent, to around 40,000 feet; cruising; and a descent beginning some 200 miles before the destination.

The Comet cruises at eight miles a minute, eight miles above the earth. (The first British air service to Africa flew at ninety miles per hour, 800 feet up.) Today's jet travel is real over-weather flying in an upper region far above the winds and rain that affect the earthbound. This is a new world of clear, infinite space, belonging to the jetliner.

Map of the Earth

Usually, over Europe anyway, the distant earth is hidden by the upper cloud layer. But if the passenger is lucky he looks down to see not a small section of the world's surface but a map of part of it. Leaving England, there is the Channel with the North Foreland sticking out to mark the Thames Estuary, the waggle line of the south coast with the Isle of Wight as a pendant blob, and bounding it to the south the French coast and the estuary of the Seine, all clearly visible.

When the spreading cloud layer covers the earth there is no sense of speed, in fact little or no sense of movement. Below is the vast plain of cotton wool cloud. Above and all around is limitless space which somehow oddly is not bright blue, but a darker, dull gun-metal blue. The Comet might be suspended on a string. There is none of the motion that obliges passengers in conventional planes to clutch at seats for support.

There is a pleasant feeling of utter remoteness, and the passenger suddenly remembers when the wartime fighter pilots used to tell how they felt alone and exhilarated in this upper world of endless space. A rim of frost outlines the edges of the windows. Inside the fuselage it is warm and comfortable. The noise from the jet engineers is but a low hum. The utter lack of vibration is shown by the glass of scotch on the table. There is not a ripple on the surface. Conversation, reading and writing are all easier than in a train.

Curiously there is a tremendous sense of peace, followed by a feeling of slight resentment when the Comet begins its let down to land.

Ocean Air Travel Seen at New High

Trans-Atlantic Fares May Exceed Ship Traffic in '58,

Transport Experts Say

BY EDWARD HUDSON

Trans-Atlantic travel may undergo a transportation revolution this year, transport experts believe. For the first time more travelers may go by airplane between Europe and North America than go by ship.

This is a conclusion drawn by industry experts from a comparison of air and sea passenger traffic across the Atlantic in 1957.

Scheduled trans-Atlantic air travel passed the million-passenger mark in 1957 for the first time. E. S. Pefanis, secretary of the North Atlantic Traffic Conference of the International Air Transport Association, says that about 1,023,000 passengers were carried during the year by the sixteen scheduled airlines on the route.

The New York office of the Trans-Atlantic Steamship Passenger Conference reports that twenty-seven ships on the North Atlantic transported about 1,030,000 passengers last year. The difference between the number of air passengers and sea passengers on the route last year was set at 7,000.

The difference in totals for 1956 was much larger—173,458. That year the steamships carried a total of 1,008,248 passengers while the airlines carried 834,790.

Airlines Catch Up

The airlines are speedily catching up. Their passenger traffic increased by 20 per cent in 1957 while that of the steamship lines rose by about 2 per cent. Unless there is some drastic change in these traffic growth rates, the airlines will move ahead by a decided margin, it is held.

Several factors could influence the rates this year. For one, the steamship lines do not plan to add to the total number of ships in service. Last year they did add to the number of ships. This contributed substantially to the modest traffic increase that was registered.

Shipping officials, however, hope that the stabilization of ship numbers will be offset by a better travel market in the first months of the current year. In the same period of 1957, passenger traffic declined following the Suez crisis.

The airlines, on the other hand, are continuing to add new and larger planes. They plan to increase their capacity across the ocean during the peak travel period this year by 20 per cent. The ability to meet heavy traffic demands in the peak spring and summer months greatly determines how many more passengers will be carried, shipping and airline experts agree.

At least two other factors enter the air picture. One is improved equipment. New planes such as the long-range Bristol Britannia, introduced in North Atlantic service last month, may attract new business. The other factor is the new third-class air fare that will go into effect April 1. This new fare must still be approved by the carriers' governments, but the expectation is that it will be approved.

New Fares Listed

The third class, or "economy" service, will peg fares at $252 one-way between New York and London against a tourist fare that will rise on April 1 by $25 to $315 and a first-class fare that will rise by $35 to $435.

Whether this new service, featuring denser seating arrangements and sandwiches, will attract new business is an open question. Some airlines believe it may only serve to draw traffic from tourist flights. Some officials have hopes that it may tap new travel markets.

If air traffic exceeds ship traffic between the United States and Canada and Europe in 1958,

does this portend a decline in ocean passenger trade? Not at all, say transport officials. Ships have carried more passengers each year since 1947. Last year's passenger figure was a twenty-seven-year high. The demands for ship accommodations still exceed available space in the heavy travel season.

Ship fares are set differently from air rates, and comparisons are difficult. The steamship conference agrees on certain minimums that may be exceeded by individual lines. Tourist rates in the summer season for a one-way passage from New York to British ports may be as low as $180.

A blue-ribbon ship such as the Cunard Line's Queen Elizabeth will cost at least $197 for tourist and a minimum of $395 for first-class, according to current published rates.

The gains that the airlines have made since they began extensive long-range overseas flying just after World War II have apparently not been greatly injurious to the steamships. Both forms of transport have prospered. Air transport has developed a separate travel market among passengers with only limited time. Though the airlines do siphon off traffic that cannot book steamship passage during the heavy seasons, they apparently do not look solely to the wooing of ocean travelers for the large gains they expect to make in the future.

Southwest Manages to Keep Its Balance

BY RICHARD A. OPPEL, JR.

A decade ago, the airline industry was in its worst recession to that point, brought on by the Persian Gulf war, a broad economic slowdown and brutal fare cuts. But Southwest Airlines, then a regional carrier in the process of going national, managed to make money even as the rest of the industry lost more than $6 billion over two years.

To analysts, Southwest, now much larger, is once again the only airline with a chance to post a profit this year after the terrorist attacks. "It's a worthy goal, at this point, to be profitable for the year," says Gary C. Kelly, Southwest's chief financial officer. "But that's not a prediction." Unlike other major airlines, Southwest has not announced layoffs or schedule cutbacks, though flights will be eliminated if business does not pick up.

In an effort to put travelers back in the sky, Southwest could begin a national broadcasting ad campaign as soon as this week. It will include new fare sales on some flights, according to industry officials. Many in the industry are watching to see whether Southwest can smoothly negotiate the changes in how airlines operate in the aftermath of the attacks.

Investors clearly think it can, and they believe the Southwest franchise to be as valuable as the rest of the industry combined. Though the seventh-largest airline by such measures as total miles its passengers travel and revenue, Southwest's total stock market value, $10.5 billion, is roughly the same as that of the nation's other major carriers added together. Since the attacks, Southwest's stock has fallen 20 percent, far less than other airlines'.

What remains to be seen is how much heightened security may impede Southwest's vaunted efficiencies, especially its quick "turn times," or its ability to get planes back into the air after only about 20 minutes on the ground, compared with 45 minutes for most other airlines. Also in question is whether Southwest's many short-distance flights will be most hurt as travelers opt to take a train or drive. So far, Mr. Kelly said in an interview on Friday, the airline's return to the skies shows that such apprehensions appear to be "totally false."

In fact, the industry's current crisis points up Southwest's strength compared with that of other airlines that now appear dependent on the federal bailout for survival. Part of that resilience is because the company focuses on less-congested airports where it can be one of the largest carriers and yet avoid costly delays.

But most investors' current relative loyalty comes from the airline's strong finances and low costs. Between cash on hand and its available credit line, Southwest has more than $1.4 billion. At the same time, flying a full schedule last week with, at most, perhaps half its normal load of passengers, its daily cash burn was no more than $5 million, according to Mr. Kelly, a fraction of the industry's losses.

What's more, should the federal bailout not provide enough cushion, Southwest has 200 planes—about $5 billion worth, in theory—that could be mortgaged.

It is also the most efficient airline, although it may take a while to see whether that distinction will be affected by the new security measures after customers return.

Before a recent Southwest flight from Dallas, a ticket agent called over an inspector who searched one traveler's roller bag being checked as luggage. The inspector put on gloves, opened the bag and removed everything. She opened the toilet kit, carefully examining a disposable razor cartridge. After asking another inspector whether it was all right to keep it in the luggage—it was—she then repacked the bag.

All told a three- or four-minute procedure—repeated for several passengers—that could slow check-in times on Southwest's normally busy schedule, which includes flights to some destinations every half-hour.

Industry-wide, analysts say load factors—the percentage of seats occupied by paying customers—have dropped to about 30 percent to 40 percent. Some say Southwest's loads may be at the low end of that range, partly because the airline has yet to cut its flight schedule. Mr. Kelly said loads are "down consistent with the rest of the industry," but he declined to be more specific.

Betsy R. Snyder, an analyst at Standard & Poor's, said that customers' shying away from short flights "could have an impact," but that since Southwest has been lengthening its average flight, "the impact won't be as dramatic as it would have been several years ago."

Mr. Kelly said that based on last week's performance, "I would totally discard this notion that short-haul flights will be impacted more than long-haul flights."

While shorter flights have lost more passengers than have long-haul flights, he said, it is "not a remarkable difference."

Southwest has asked Boeing to defer deliveries on five 737's due this month, and the airline will almost certainly seek more delays. "To be blunt, we don't have a plan right now for 2002," Mr. Kelly said. "I don't see how we could."

But he said that layoffs were unlikely; before the attacks the airline was actually short of employees and had been paying a lot of overtime.

Though Southwest is not cutting back its schedules right now, it will if passenger loads do not improve, Mr. Kelly said. This will not mean ending service to any markets, but, instead, reducing the number of flights. Perhaps instead of every half-hour, he said, they would be every hour.

"We don't want to do things in the short term that hurt in the long term," he said. "But at the same time, if we can't get through the short term, we won't have a long term."

December 6, 2002

No Clear Way Forward for Airlines

BY MICHAEL E. LEVINE

Now that the Air Transportation Stabilization Board has rejected United Airlines' application for a $1.8 billion loan guarantee, perhaps the airline industry can finally begin the painful process of restructuring. Most airlines have a business model created in a time of high traffic and high fares. Those days aren't coming back—and the sooner the airlines realize that, the better.

The board's actions, and its reasons for them, signal that we are now at a turning point in the 25-year saga that has been airline deregulation. In an unusually detailed letter, the board said that United's problems were not temporary but structural, and that United's recovery plan "does not position the company to meet the challenges of the current airline industry environment and to achieve long-term financial stability."

United's plight is not unique. To a greater or lesser degree, its situation is shared by all of the large hub-and-spoke airlines that survived deregulation—American, Continental, Delta, Northwest and US Airways (which is already in bankruptcy). Put simply, these airlines are competing for customers with a greatly expanded discount airline sector, and they all have contractual commitments—labor, fleet and infrastructure—that they can no longer meet.

These discount airlines—Southwest, Jet-Blue, Frontier and others—are one artifact of deregulation. They were meant to provide the competitive spur that would ensure that deregulation benefited the public by offering customers more choice and forcing the established airlines to become more nimble. The early flowering of the discount sector required the old-line carriers to adapt with hub-and-spoke systems, discounted fares, frequent-flyer programs and the like.

It worked. Given more convenient service at competitive fares, customers stuck to the airlines they knew. By the mid-1980's, the first wave of discount carriers had subsided, with discounters reduced to a slowly growing single-digit percentage of the domestic industry.

The industry then endured its usual boom-and-bust cycles. Some airlines (Pan Am, Eastern, TWA) simply disappeared; the ones that survived expanded or were forced to contract along with the economy. In good times they bought more planes, upgraded their facilities and agreed to ever more generous labor contracts. During bad times employees accepted "givebacks" or wage freezes, but they bargained hard to preserve the underlying contract structure. During the late 1990's, when the economy was vibrant and growing, the airlines expanded rapidly. Unions took advantage of the growth to negotiate favorable contracts that raised labor costs to unprecedented levels.

In part to pay for these higher costs, airlines attempted to raise fares. But leisure travelers do not buy expensive tickets. So the airlines looked to business travelers booking tickets on short notice, who valued the convenience of frequent service at nearby airports. Business fares rose almost 50 percent between 1999 and 2001; walkup business fares often were 10 times more than leisure fares booked in advance.

This strategy backfired. First business travelers looked to travel on leisure fares even if it meant advance purchases and Saturday night stays. Then they started to look for airlines with cheaper fares. In this environment, the discount sector flourished again. Southwest Airlines grew rapidly and is now the most profitable airline in the industry. Soon other discount airlines appeared, and today one of every four tickets sold in America is on a discount airline, compared to fewer than one in 10 four years ago.

Then came Sept. 11. In the aftermath of the terrorist attacks, many business travelers stayed home. When they finally did start to fly again, they found that they had more alternatives than ever before—they didn't have to pay the exorbitant prices of the late 1990's. They could fly on a discount airline or find a cheap Internet fare on one of the traditional airlines.

Thus we arrive at the present day. What the Air Transportation Stability Board recog-

nized—but United did not—is that even when business improves, the old fare structure isn't coming back. Business customers will no longer pay $600 or $900 each way to go from Sioux Falls, S.D., or Newark to New Orleans. They'll find another airline to take them for much less, even if they have to drive to Omaha or Kennedy Airport. The hub-and-spoke airlines will have to offer more competitive fares to all customers.

The very same hub-and-spoke system that the airlines created in response to deregulation is now being exploited by the discount airlines, which operate on its fringes. Yet the established airlines need not abandon the hub-and-spoke system, which has served both airlines and passengers well. They simply need to operate it more efficiently.

Airlines now have to do the restructuring that they have been putting off for the better part of a decade. This restructuring can be done under the protection of bankruptcy or outside it. But it will succeed only if bankruptcy is a threat, which means no more federal loan guarantees. An aircraft lessor, for example, will insist on its monthly payments even if the airplane is sitting in the desert—but only as long as it is confident that its customers can't go to bankruptcy court and send the keys back. A pilot will insist on the right to make $200,000 a year or more flying 50 hours a month—unless he or she faces the prospect of a job at another airline involving more flying and less pay.

If they can reduce labor, equipment and other costs to more reasonable levels, these airlines will find that the hub-and-spoke system will allow them to prosper. By concentrating their flights at a hub, they can offer more frequent service to more destinations than the discount airlines. And they can offer reasonable fares on many seats by using the Internet or other technology. Only this kind of restructuring will enable airlines like United, American, Delta and Northwest to run their businesses profitably. Only actions like the Airline Transportation Stabilization Board's will force these airlines, and their workers, to face this reality.

CHAPTER 9

COMMUNICATIONS

A forerunner of today's mainframes, this tabulating machine—shown here in 1985—contained 25,000 vacuum tubes and had the capacity to add 83,000 numbers per second. (Photo for the *New York Times* by Joe Wrinn)

THE HISTORY OF COMMUNICATIONS IN AMERICA IS ONE OF TECHNOLOGICAL innovations that enabled a quickening and tightening of the social fabric. In today's hyperconnected world, the Internet, cellular phones, and other wireless devices such as BlackBerrys move information among individuals all over the world at the touch of a button or the click of a mouse. Other, older media, such as radio and television, have given large audiences access to programs that entertain and—less frequently—instruct while offering advertisers access to millions of potential customers. These and other advances have been critical for the development of American

1844	1876	1896	1922	1934
First electric telegraph message: "WHAT HATH GOD WROUGHT?"	Bell files patent for the telephone.	First commercial motion picture exhibited in United States.	RCA advertises first personal radios.	FCC created.

business; in fact, many have formed the basis for entirely new industries themselves. As communication technologies have broken down the barriers of time and distance, they have also transformed our notions of community, in and outside the market.

The exchange of knowledge has always been particularly important for business. Before the mid–1800s, however, the pace and reliability of exchange—be it goods or information—depended on the existing transportation infrastructure, with its limitations and vagaries. Businesspeople in rural areas or other remote locales experienced significant, and often costly, delays in corresponding with their trading partners and rivals. In the early nineteenth century, for example, it could take as long as four weeks for information, merchandise, or individuals from the East Coast to reach the town of Peoria, located in Illinois Territory, on what was then considered the western frontier of the country. In bad weather, even residents and firms in established cities found themselves isolated from the events and activities in the rest of the world. "In winter, or in wet and frosty seasons of the year," reported the Cincinnati *Daily Gazette* in 1836, "the city is cut off from communication from every side."[1] During such periods, letters sometimes took weeks—or months—to reach their intended destinations.

Early on, the federal government sought to alleviate some of these delays by strengthening the system of domestic communication. In 1792, acting on the authority granted by the Constitution to "establish Post Offices and Post Roads," Congress passed the Post Office Act.[2] Between 1791 and 1801, the number of post offices increased from less than 100 to more than 1,000; by the 1830s, it had grown to more than 10,000.[3] As Americans moved west, thousands of miles of postal route were added.[4] Sorting, shipping, and delivering the written communications of a growing population called for

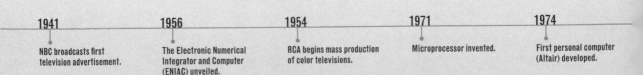

1941	1956	1954	1971	1974
NBC broadcasts first television advertisement.	The Electronic Numerical Integrator and Computer (ENIAC) unveiled.	RCA begins mass production of color televisions.	Microprocessor invented.	First personal computer (Altair) developed.

the development of a human organization that would grow in tandem with the physical infrastructure of buildings and roads. And grow it did. In 1831, the nationwide postal system employed almost 9,000 people, some 2,400 more than the U.S. Army.[5]

Mail delivery became faster and much more reliable with the advent of the railroad in the mid-nineteenth century. But in the 1830s, there was no means of exchanging information over long distances in anything like real time. In 1836, the U.S. Congress considered improving the speed of correspondence by building a network of optical telegraphs—contraptions that would signal messages in visual code from the tops of high towers—from New York to New Orleans (such a system had been in place in France for more than forty years).[6] But in 1838, a painter named Samuel Morse approached the legislature with a competing idea for an electric telegraph.[7] Messages sent in code by an electric telegraph traveled even faster than a steam engine and, unlike optical signals, were not limited by weather conditions, nightfall, and the visual reach of a telescope. It was such a remarkable, seemingly impossible, technology that at first the federal government turned Morse down. Five years later, in 1843, the determined inventor finally convinced a slim majority of lawmakers to fund the nation's first electric telegraph line.[8]

In 1844, Morse sent the first message by telegraph from Washington, D.C., to Baltimore: "WHAT HATH GOD WROUGHT."[9] By 1852, the 40-mile demonstration telegraph line originally funded by Congress had turned into a network of more than 23,000 miles.[10] Over the following years, the telegraph grew in lockstep with the railroads in a dynamic relationship that yielded important advantages for both players as well as the larger nation. Railroad corporations expanded the telegraph network by donating thousands of

1977	1981	1992	2005	2007
Apple II introduced.	IBM launches its first PC.	World Wide Web introduced.	Facebook is incorporated.	An estimated 80 percent of adults report using the Internet.

acres of land for new lines. At the same time, communication by telegraph helped road managers run their trains on tighter schedules with greater efficiency and safety. By 1865, thanks in no small part to this symbiotic relationship, more than 200,000 miles of telegraph wire stretched across the American landscape.[11] The resulting system revolutionized communication (not to mention transportation) by allowing individuals and organizations to exchange information much faster and more accurately than previously possible. A variety of businesses quickly made the new technology their own. Investors, for example, followed the financial markets from a distance via stock tickers, and newspapers across the country began receiving frontline reports from an organization called the Harbor News Association, later renamed the Associated Press.[12]

In the years following the introduction of the telegraph, several inventors began to experiment with ways to transmit not only signals, but also sounds, using electricity. In 1876, Alexander Graham Bell became the first to file a patent for such a device, beating competitor Elisha Gray's caveat filing by mere hours.[13] A few weeks later, Bell used his telephone to successfully call his assistant in the next room, saying, "Mr. Watson, come here, I want you."[14] The telephone initially met with skepticism.[15] But the convenience of instantaneous verbal communication soon won the invention a place in businesses—especially doctors' offices and hospitals—and to a lesser extent in individual homes. Unlike the telegraph, the telephone proved useful for local as well as long-distance communication and did away with the need for interpreters and code.[16] Just ten years after Bell filed his patent, there were about 170,000 telephones connected by as many miles of wire.[17] During the next fifty years, American Telephone & Telegraph (AT&T), the long-distance company created out of Bell's firm in 1885, grew to become to become the biggest corporation in the world.[18]

As telegraph and telephone wires snaked across the continent, another technology was eliminating the need for wires altogether.

Italian inventor Guglielmo Marconi was one of many scientists to study radio waves, but he was the first to develop a practical system that could send and receive signals over this spectrum.[19] His firm, the British Marconi Company, founded in 1897, originally marketed the wireless system to ships to help them communicate with stations on land.[20] During World War I, the United States assumed control of radio communication within its borders, and when the war ended, Congress considered a bill that would extend government control of the industry into peacetime.[21] The bill's sponsors hoped to eliminate the possibility that the British Marconi Company, through its American branch, would come to dominate radio in the United States.[22] In 1919, when it became apparent that this legislative effort would fail, the U.S. Navy gave the radio patents it had acquired to General Electric in an effort to establish a new radio company independent of foreign ownership.[23]

The company created by the Navy's move was dubbed the Radio Corporation of America, otherwise known as RCA. Under the leadership of David Sarnoff, a Russian immigrant who had worked his way through the ranks of American Marconi before it was bought out by RCA, the new firm's electronics division flourished.[24] In 1921, Sarnoff also helped build the first network of radio stations, later known as the National Broadcasting Company (NBC).[25] Early radio programming on this network and other stations included broadcasts of weather reports, market prices, sports contests, religious services, political speeches, and music. Fast-growing demand for access to these programs drove U.S. radio production from 100,000 sets in 1922 to more than 4 million in 1929.[26] Like many forms of technology then and now, the radio also became a marker of social cachet. An early advertisement declared the radio a "real ornament to the cultured home."[27]

RCA gained independence from its parent companies—General Electric, Westinghouse, AT&T, and General Motors—in 1932.[28] With Sarnoff's energy and purpose guiding the rapidly expanding company, RCA became famous for its emphasis on research.[29] Even during the Depression, Sarnoff increased spending on new technology, including a system that would transmit visual images as well as sounds.[30] RCA did not invent the television—that honor belonged to Philo T. Farnsworth, a Utah-born inventor, who conceived some of his best ideas harvesting hay on the family ranch.[31] But the company did a great deal to further the existing technology and, eventually, bring it into the homes of millions of people. Television production, which had been halted as the nation entered World War II, took off almost as soon as the troops returned home in 1945.[32] Between 1949 and 1959, the number of households with television sets grew from less than 1 million to nearly 44 million, about 85 percent of the total.[33] By the 1960s, more than nine in ten households were able to tune in every night.[34]

Both radio and television manufacturers depended on regular network programming to attract consumers to their products. To fund this programming, the three major networks—NBC, ABC, and CBS—turned to advertisements. Different types of advertising, from Procter & Gamble's early "soap operas" in radio to visual product placement in television programs to regular commercials breaks, helped to broaden the market for countless consumer products introduced during these years. The more popular the show, the more money consumer-products companies were willing to pay for a time slot during its run. This arrangement helped keep network television free for the viewing public. But it also gave some people pause. In the late 1950s and early 1960s, a lively debate developed about the broader significance and consequences of the young, powerful medium of television. Did the constant stream of advertising information feed materialism? Was wholesome entertainment being replaced by sensationalist fare that drew a better price? Were we becoming more connected as a society, or more isolated, planted in front of the boob tube?

On some fronts, at least, there could be no doubt that broadcast programming on both the radio and television played a role in building and maintaining connections. During the Great Depression and World War II, for example, millions of Americans listened to President Franklin Delano Roosevelt's "fireside chats," broadcast by radio every few months across the country. Along with helping Americans to nurture a national identity, radio and the television allowed smaller communities to connect within and between U.S. borders. African Americans who moved North in the Great Migration of the early twentieth century listened to southern radio stations to keep abreast of the news and music scene in their hometowns. Seventy years later, cable and satellite television channels allowed a variety of immigrant groups, large and small, to follow shows that were broadcast in their native languages and even produced in their mother countries.

The next major communications breakthrough would extend the range and reach of information even further by putting content creation directly into the hands of individuals. In the late 1940s and early 1950s, however, the computer was a long way from realizing this potential. Most computers were large, heavy, and extremely expensive machines marketed mainly to businesses and other institutions for data processing.[35] The Electronic Numerical Integrator and Computer (ENIAC), completed in 1945 at the University of Pennsylvania, one of the first digital computers, weighed thirty tons and took up 1,800 square feet of space.[36] In 1971, Marcian E. "Ted" Hoff, an engineer at Intel, helped to blast open the possibilities for smaller, cheaper computers with the invention of a microprocessor. Also in 1969, a phone-based communication system—the forerunner of today's Internet—was set up between three computers at universities in California and a fourth at the University of Utah.[37]

The personal computer, first developed in the mid-1970s, attracted thousands of computer hobbyists and gave rise to an array of start-up companies.[38] One of these start-ups, Apple Computer, struck gold with its consumer-friendly Apple II.[39] By the end of 1980, more than 120,000 Apple IIs had been sold to computer enthusiasts, engineers, and businesses.[40] The next year, business-equipment giant IBM—which already dominated the market for industrial mainframes—entered the market with its own PC.[41] Shipments of PCs in the United States rose from 760,000 in 1981 to 2.5 million in 1982 and to over 6 million four years later.[42]

Although a majority of these were purchased by corporate customers, a market for the devices in individual households was steadily developing as well.[43] The fraction of U.S. households with a computer grew from less than 10 percent in 1984 to 23 percent in 1993; it continued climbing in the twenty-first century: to nearly 62 percent in 2003 and 81 percent four years later.[44] A significant factor in this growth was the transformation of the PC from a device that could process numbers and run games to one that helped individuals communicate through written messages, pictures, and video. In the early 1990s, researcher Tim Berners-Lee designed several important standards that would allow people around the world to use their computers to exchange information over telephone lines.[45] With a set of rules for the way Internet pages were addressed and the way information was formatted and shared, computer-based communication could be brought to a vast, global audience.[46] Berners-Lee and his colleagues at the CERN laboratory in Europe also created the first browser and decided to call it the World Wide Web.[47] In the following years, several companies began to introduce competing browsers, and Web use became widespread. The proportion of U.S. households with Internet access, which had been virtually zero throughout the 1980s and early 1990s, reached 18 percent in 1997, 55 percent in 2003, and 62 percent in 2007.[48]

By the end of the 1990s, individuals were using the Internet to communicate in a vast array of new ways. E-mail enabled correspondence between two people or between an individual and a group. Instant messaging allowed for typed conversation in real time. Chat rooms, social networking sites, and blogs helped people connect with family, friends, colleagues, and, more and more frequently, with strangers.

In less than a decade, the Internet transformed the communication capabilities of businesses and individuals. It made sharing a document with a client, introducing a new song, or sending a message to a loved one half a world away much easier, cheaper, and faster than ever before. As the Internet altered our sense of time, distance, and connection, it both contracted and widened the world in which we live. The swift, powerful effects of the Internet—quicker and more far-reaching than those of television— also raised social and political concerns. As Web use increased, formerly solid barriers between public and private information, friends and strangers, and the workplace and the home began to shift and perhaps weaken. Privacy advocates warned that the Internet created permanent electronic records of e-mail, digital photographs, and other personal documents. Parents lamented the pressure to check work-related e-mail not just at the office but around the clock and worried about their children's exposure to online pornography and other undesirable information or unscrupulous users. Many workers worried that the Internet would make their jobs obsolete or transferable to a country with cheaper labor costs.

In fact, by the early twenty-first century, online exchange was so common that the Internet had disrupted, and threatened to replace, long-standing forms of business and communication. Americans could look for an apartment, order a pizza, read the daily newspaper, and complete work for college credit all on the Web. They could search for goods, such as airline tickets and library books, or people, such as long-lost high school friends or potential dates. Movies and music could be downloaded—both legally and illegally. In the wake of these new applications, newspapers lost advertising money, publishers and record labels lost revenues, and even network and cable television lost viewers. At the same time, the Internet allowed thousands of small businesses and start-ups to reach national and global markets. And, like many new technologies that had altered connections among Americans, for a few enterprising individuals it had created enormous wealth.

February 7, 1881

A Rival of Telegraphy

The History and Possibilities of the Telephone.

WASHINGTON, FEB. 6.—The formation of a gigantic monopoly by the combination of the telegraph companies has directed the attention of some persons to the commercial condition of the other means of electric communication—the telephone. Although the invention was made practical only two or three years ago, it has very rapidly come into general use, and experiments seem to be gradually extending the distance over which messages can be carried by it. Bearing in mind the wonderful nature of recent discoveries in this direction, the extension of the message-bearing power of the telephone until it becomes equal to that of the telegraph system may certainly be regarded as within the bounds of possibility. At present the telephone has only a local use and is confined to cities and large towns, in which the circuits are short. It is applied to a district system of communication, subscribers relying upon a central office, in which, by switches, each subscriber can be placed in communication with every other. Already there are signs of the grasping power of monopoly in many of the cities where these systems have been established, and already the telephone is becoming, like the telegraph, a means of amassing wealth for great corporations. In conversation with a TIMES correspondent recently an expert electrician, who is acquainted with the history of the invention, set forth some of the prominent facts of that history.

"As early as 1667," said he, "Robert Hooke, of England, published an account of the transmission of articulate speech by means of what is now known as the mechanical telephone, and in this account the following statement was made: 'It is not impossible to hear a whisper distinctly at a furlong's distance, it having been done already. I can assure the reader that I have, by the help of a distended wire, propagated the sound of my voice to a very considerable distance with as quick a motion as light.'

"The wonderful work of the electric telegraph in the years following 1839 led to the application of electricity to the transmission of tones, and it may be said that many experiments made by scientific men were suggested by the successful operation of the mechanical telephone.

"Charles Boursal published in France, in 1854, a paper on the transmission of articulate speech by electricity, and it received the careful attention of European students. Boursal said: 'After the telegraphic marvels already achieved, it will not appear impossible to penetrate further into the region of the marvelous. We know that sounds are made by vibrations. If a man speaks near a movable disk adapted to produce electric disturbances, you may have at a distance another disk which will simultaneously execute the same vibrations, and in this way the articulations of the human voice may be transmitted. It need not be said that numerous applications of the highest importance will immediately follow the transmission of speech by electricity, as any one without apprenticeship may use this mode of transmission, the apparatus required being only the disks, the connecting wire, and its battery. At a more or less distant future speech will be transmitted by electricity. I have made some experiments; they are delicate and demand patience, but the approximations obtained promise favorable results.'

"In 1855," he continued, "L. Scott, of England, made experiments in the transmission of tones by electricity, which led to the production of a telephone by M. Reiss in 1860, which embodied the elementary features of the approved telephone.

"Coming down to a later day, it appears that in 1874 Elisha Gray, of Chicago, Ill., invented a system of harmonic telegraphy which embodied the principles of telephonic telegraphing,

and upon this he secured several patents. In 1875, Charles E. Buell, of New-Haven, Conn., filed at the Patent Office a preliminary description of a system adapted to the transmission of articulate speech. It was on Feb. 14, 1876, that Messrs. [Alexander Graham] Bell and [Elisha] Gray simultaneously filed specifications which described apparatus for transmitting articulate speech. Mr. Bell claims Jan. 15, 1876, as the date of the invention of his modification of the telephone. The device spoken of in his specification, in the few words which could refer to a telephone with articulate sounds, applied to an instrument which, by Mr. Bell's own admissions, had not produced any satisfactory results, and is not identical with the instrument placed before the public by the Bell Telephone Company. To Mr. Bell, however, belongs the chief credit of the introduction of this valuable means of communication. The introduction of this instrument has been followed by the organization of companies in the cities and towns of the country. These companies use instruments furnished by the Bell Company, which rents them at such prices as to make the use of the telephone a luxury."

Marconi Recounts Birth of Wireless

Silver Jubilee on Sunday of First Transatlantic Signals Recalls Humble Beginnings.

BY T. R. YBARRA

LONDON, DEC. 10.—Twenty-five years ago next Sunday Guglielmo Marconi, waiting with every nerve and sense taut in an old, dilapidated building on the coast of Newfoundland, received the first signal ever transmitted by wireless across the ocean. That signal proved that his dream of linking together the nations by a method of communication infinitely more mysterious and more uncanny than any hitherto discovered had at last been snatched once and for all from dreamland and ranked among the solid facts of existence.

Today the Italian wireless wizard, still modest and retiring despite the overwhelming fame which his discovery has brought him, gave for the first time his own personal account of those wonderful moments of a quarter of a century ago. It was the privilege of THE NEW YORK TIMES representative to obtain from Senator Marconi himself this personal narrative, describing the arduous preparations, trying hours of suspense and glorious thrill of achievement when the instrument devised by him—how primitive it would seem today—ticked off on that lonely Newfoundland shore a message from Cornwall, England, three thousand miles away, which told him and the whole world that his marvelous child of science, until then reckoned merely a "child prodigy," was a full-grown reality, with an illustrious future shining before it.

"On Dec. 12, 1901, in a room of a disused barracks on Signal Hill, St. John's, Newfoundland," he said, "on a table stood some instruments connected by a thin wire with a kite that was held up at a height of about 400 feet by an Atlantic gale. To the same instruments there was connected a telephone, in which shortly after noon were heard sounds constituting evidence that in far-distant Cornwall rhythmical signals that corresponded to the letter S in Morse code had been projected into the ether of space and had actually crossed the Atlantic.

"In 1895 and 1896 I had proved the possibility of transmitting signals to a considerable distance by means of raised antennae and an earth connection. In 1899 I had proved that the curvature of the earth did not interfere with a propagation of ether waves over short distances and in 1909 I felt that the time had come to venture further afield. Having regard to the many improvements I had lately introduced into the methods of tuning the transmitter and receiver, I was absolutely convinced that transatlantic wireless telegraphy, not merely as an experiment but as a sound commercial proposition, was possible. Naturally, I realized that my first endeavor must be directed to prove that an electric wave could be sent out across the Atlantic and detected on the other side.

The First Work in Newfoundland.

"On the 26th of November I sailed from Liverpool on the Allan liner Sardinian. As it was clearly impossible at that time of year, owing to inclement weather and especially in view of the shortness of the time at our disposal, to erect high masts to support an aerial, I had arranged to have the necessary aerial supported in the air by a small captive balloon, and so we took with us two balloons and six kites.

"We landed at St. John's on Friday, Dec, 6. On Monday, Dec. 9, I began work on Signal Hill overlooking the port. On Tuesday we flew a kite with 600 feet of aerial as a preliminary test, and on Wednesday we inflated one of the balloons, which made its first ascent during the morning. Its diameter was about fourteen feet, and it contained some 1,000 cubic feet of hydrogen gas, quite sufficient to hold up the aerial, which consisted of wire weighing about ten pounds. Owing, however, to a heavy wind, after a short while the balloon broke away and disappeared. I then came to the conclusion that perhaps the kites would answer better, and on Thursday morning, in spite of a gale, we managed to fly a kite to a height of about 400 feet.

The Critical Moment.

"The critical moment had come, for which the way had been prepared by six years of hard and unremitting work, despite the usual criticisms directed at anything new. I was about to test the truth of my belief.

"Suddenly, at about half-past twelve, unmistakably three scant little clicks in the telephone corresponding to three dots of the Morse code sounded several times in my ear as I listened intently, but I would not be satisfied without corroboration.

"'Can you hear anything, Mr. Kemp?' I said handing the telephone to my assistant.

"Kemp heard the same thing as I, and I knew then that I had been absolutely right in my anticipations. Electric waves which were being sent out from Poldhu [Cornwall] had traversed the Atlantic serenely ignoring the curvature of the earth which so many doubters considered would be a fatal obstacle, and they were now affecting my receiver in Newfoundland.

"I knew then that the day on which I should be able to send full messages without wires or cables across the Atlantic was not very far distant.

"As to the application of wireless in the future you know I am always averse from entering into the realm of prophecy, but perhaps I might suggest that, apart from the ordinary transmission and reception of wireless messages of which I have spoken, there is a possibility that the transmission of power over moderate distances may be developed, and that television will become an actuality.

"I must leave to your imagination the uses which can be made of these new powers. They will probably be as wonderful as anything of which we have had experience so far."

Telephones Across the Sea

In 1897 MARCONI predicted that the day would dawn when a telegram would be sent through the air a distance of twenty miles. Beginning tomorrow, we shall be able to raise an ordinary telephone receiver on an ordinary desk in New York, ask for any number listed in the London telephone directory and talk as readily as we would to a neighboring city.

Where is the Morse or Bell, the Edison or Field, to whom for this invention we shall pay our tribute of admiration? Whose was the ingenious brain that conceived the technical principles applied in this new means of international communication? We look in vain for one shining, heroic figure. We read no story of hardships endured, of misunderstanding, of ridicule by the unimaginative and ignorant.

This invention is anonymous—necessarily so, because it represents the culmination of twenty years of research conducted by physicists and engineers. No longer are new technical achievements the result of casual and haphazard experimenting. Industrial corporations do not wait for an inventor to turn up with a new process or a new machine. Research is as much a function of industry as is manufacturing. Organized research solves the problems of industry so systematically, so rapidly, that generations need not elapse before improvements are made. Thus are to be explained the extraordinary strides which

have been made in illumination, transportation and communication. Invention may lose some of its romance because it ceases to be identified with single, great personalities, but it is surer because it is more systematic.

Perhaps the beginning of transatlantic telephony is received with no such outburst of enthusiasm as that which marked the opening of the first telegraph, the first telephone or the first cable. We accept with unruffled complacency the social, political and economic consequences that must follow the introduction of a means of transatlantic communication so swift and so direct. Just what these consequences will be even the great company which has poured millions into research for twenty years would scarcely dare to predict. A new means of communication such as this is not devised because of a public demand. A new utility creates its own demand. BELL never dreamed that the largest private telephone switchboard in the world would be installed in a New York bank. CYRUS FIELD certainly never foresaw that the prices of wheat and cotton would be cabled back and forth across the ocean, or that arbitrage—the art of taking instant advantage of the fluctuating rates of exchange in New York, Berlin, Paris and London—would be developed for the benefit of shrewd traders in domestic and foreign money.

The side-by-side development of the tele-graph and telephone on land leads us to sup-pose that the radio telegraph and submarine cable companies need view the advent of transatlantic telephony with no great concern. Telegrams will still be flashed in code across the sea in less than two minutes. The transat-lantic telephone will create its own traffic.

David Sarnoff as a teenager in the experimental shop of wireless pioneer Guglielmo Marconi, where he learned the basics on which he built his radio and television career. Sarnoff later founded NBC and headed up RCA in a number of different capacities for most of his career. (*New York Times*)

February 23, 1930

David Sarnoff Grew Up in Radio's Vast Field

President of R. C. A. at the Age of 39, He Foresees a Great Development in Communications Service and Broadcasting—The Future of Television

BY CHARLES G. POORE

AT the age of 9 David Sarnoff could not speak a word of English. Now, at 39—his birthday is next Thursday—he is probably doing more than any man who ever lived to make English the language of the world. For, as president of the Radio Corporation of America, his time is devoted to saturating the earth's ether with sounds emanating from this country. And as director, president, or chairman of the boards of numerous subsidiary companies that make radio sets, phonographs and talking pictures, he is constantly finding new ways to broadcast the language that once was Saxon.

Some Dates in His Life.

1891—Born in Uzlian, Minsk, Russia, Feb. 27; 1900—Came to the United States of America in July, and became an American citizen on reaching required age; 1906—Employed as a messenger boy with the Commercial Cable Company. Entered the employ of the Marconi Wireless Telegraph Company of America as office boy (Sept. 30, 1906).

The biography makes a short leap to the time when he began to take an increasingly large part in the affairs of the Radio Corporation. The swiftness of his rise, paralleling—where it does not outstrip—the amazing expansion of the radio industry may be most graphically indicated by considering this foreground first.

When the Radio Corporation was formed at the end of [World War I] it absorbed the Marconi Company and with it the young man who had been commercial manager for the English firm, David Sarnoff. The corporation had been created as the result of a direct appeal from the government, which saw the need of an American owned, operated, and controlled radio communication company powerful enough to meet the competition of the radio interests of other nations.

The idea was that unless America acted quickly she would not have much of a place in the ether. So the great electrical companies were called upon, and presently the Radio Corporation of America took form.

Swift Changes That Ensued.

That form, however, was not, to quote a word much used in radio at that time, static. It began as a communications company. But amid a bewildering and unpredictable series of inventions and developments, the corporation had to assume the protean shape it was heir to. And the guiding hand of the young man who was named traffic manager of the corporation when it was founded, and who is now, ten years later, president, may be seen as each new enterprise is tied to the parental company's apron-strings.

Mr. Sarnoff began by witnessing the development of the great trans-oceanic wireless communication service which, through the Radio Corporation, carried the American service to every leading country in the world. He began mobilizing patents and industrial equipment early enough to make that possible.

Then came broadcasting. The first faint glimmering of that stupendous development caught his attention. The early programs were not wholly felicitous. They were imperfectly conceived and badly launched. The radio business was ranked by manufacturers with the novelties. But they were soon to realize its importance. In 1925 it was announced that after protracted negotiations conducted by David Sarnoff with the leading phonograph manufacturers, radio and the phonograph would be combined in the same cabinet.

The [radio] broadcasting remained on an erratic footing while the radio industry as a whole was buoyed up by figures showing that it was on a $500,000,000 basis. If it was to continue in prosperity it must have a permanent broadcasting service, improved broadcasting programs, more talent, and national coverage.

Mr. Sarnoff then turned his energies to the promotion of high-powered broadcasting stations for the leading cities.

Then the talkies appeared on the horizon. And with the development of synchronized sound and sight on the motion picture screen the Radio Corporation organized its own company—RCA Photophone—and entered the field. Mr. Sarnoff was in the midst of the new development, and in 1928 he became president of the subsidiary which supplies talking motion picture equipment to theatres.

The new move in the entertainment field made by the Radio Corporation was to obtain an interest in the amusement field itself, to supply among other things the necessary motion picture technique in the use of its patents and facilities.

Discussing some aspects of the future of radio Mr. Sarnoff recently said:

"In the field of communication, radio will develop, I believe, not only along the line of telegraph transmission at higher speeds but also facsimile transmission; by which I mean that it will be possible to reproduce the original message such as a typewritten page, a drawing, photograph, or even a complete page in a newspaper, instantaneously, through space.

Arrival of Television.

"In the field of sight transmission by radio, which is popularly called television, there is no longer any mystery, and I have no hesitancy in saying that in my judgment television will eventually arrive. I cannot say exactly when, but I am confident that in less than five years you will be able to receive images through space as well as you are able to receive sound through space at the present time.

"We shall then realize how patient we were back in 1930 in our willingness to listen to a speaker in the broadcasting studios without being able to see him or to hear a singer without being able to see her personally.

"The imagination is intrigued by the possibilities of sight transmission," Mr. Sarnoff said, "for, once it can be done over a reasonable distance, it can be done throughout the world. The difficulty is not with the transmitting apparatus or the receiving apparatus. The difficulty lies in space itself. Nature has not yet given up all of the secrets of space; she still challenges the imagination of the scientist and the engineer."

August 21, 1930

N.B.C. Seeks Television License

WASHINGTON, AUG. 20.—An application for renewal of its experimental television license for a 5,000-watt portable station at Bound Brook, N. J., was filed with the Federal Radio Commission today by the National Broadcasting Company. With the call letters W3XAK, the station operates on the short-wave television channel ranging from 2,000 to 2,100 kilocycles.

Television Effect on Families Shown

Survey in Washington Terms Video's Influence

on Habits Biggest Since the Auto

WASHINGTON, FEB. 7—Television is the most important influence on family habits since the automobile was introduced, a survey of 400 families in this city asserted.

In a report titled "Television—Its Effect on Family Habits in Washington, D. C.," published today, Charles Alldredge and a staff of researchers present statistics on what adults say television has done to their homes.

The report said television had cut into movie-going, reading, radio listening, card playing, knitting and ironing.

Those who made the survey contend that television "is having a considerably more significant influence than radio, as great as the influence of that medium has been."

The survey was made because three theatre executives sought to get data on television's effect.

The 400 families interviewed reported that before they bought their sets the adults went to the movies an average of 4.51 times a month. After buying the sets, they went 1.27 times, or a reduction of 72 per cent. For the children of the families, movie-going dropped from 5.13 times a month to 2.75 times, a 46 per cent reduction.

Among the adults who owned sets more than two years magazine reading was down 18.9 per cent; book reading was down 33.7 per cent, and newspapers, 4.7 per cent. Radio listening declined from 2 hours 30 minutes during the day and 3 hours 30 minutes at night to 1 hour 55 minutes during the day and only 15 minutes at night.

Football attendance was down 30 per cent; baseball, 30.9 per cent, and wrestling and boxing, 53.7 per cent.

Wives, husbands and children in the families that had owned sets more than two years reported that they stayed home more than did the members of families that had owned sets for less than two years.

The living room of the future will become more theater-like, the report predicted.

"For the first time since the disappearance of the pot-bellied stove, the living room has a central object around which the remainder of the objects must be arranged," the report said, continuing:

"At present, television is playing hob with the standard American living room, dragging many objects out of their accustomed places. There is little question but that architects and designers of the future must take television into their consideration."

The interviewers said they had great difficulty in finding sets among families in the lowest income brackets, but finally turned up one or two.

Ideas & Trends: the Networks and Advertisers Try to Recapture Our Attention

BY RICHARD W. STEVENSON

Watching television is not as simple as it used to be.

Gone are the days when the family would settle down in front of its one television set and automatically tune to one of the three major networks. Today, viewers have a bewildering array of choices. The technology available to them, particularly in the form of cable and the video cassette recorder, offers freedom from the confines of the old-style television schedule. The changes are causing problems for the networks, the companies that advertise on television and even the concerns that monitor viewing habits.

"Since the late 1970's and the early 1980's, we've seen a gradual change in the way people use television," said William S. Hamill, an executive vice president at the A. C. Nielsen Company, the television ratings concern.

Nielsen announced last week that it would begin experimenting with a new method of tracking television viewing that better takes into account the diverse options available to the public. The system, which Nielsen will begin using next March, is based on a device known as a "people meter." It is a hand-held box with buttons that allows family members to identify themselves and allows Nielsen to determine not only who is watching and what they are watching, but how often they switch channels and which commercials they choose to avoid.

Viewers, experts say, are gaining control over the medium. No longer are they just passive recipients of what a few networks have to offer. They are active participants with a wide variety of choices and the technology to jump easily from channel to channel, tape shows they would otherwise miss, watch movies not available on broadcast television and in general create their own, personalized programming schedules.

"Television was a baby sitter, not just for babies but for adults as well," said Laurence R. Stoddard Jr., a senior vice president in charge of media research at Young & Rubicam, the advertising agency. "The networks called the shots, and you had to accept what they offered. We're moving from that to a point where television will be used for a variety of purposes and where the viewer will have more control."

Researchers point to several developments in explaining the evolution.

More Choices

Most important is the growth of viewing options. In addition to the three major networks, viewers can choose from the soaring number of independent stations, the plethora of stations offered on cable and, for a few, by satellite, plus whatever fare is available on a video cassette recorder.

The cable box and the VCR are becoming staples in American homes. In addition to the added programs they provide, both cable and VCR's bring with them remote-control devices that make it easier to switch channels at the first twinge of boredom and to skip commercials.

Demographic shifts, such as the increase in the number of working women, are also affecting when and how some shows are watched. For example, the VCR enables many working women to tape the afternoon soap operas and watch them after work. When they replay the shows, they can fast-forward over the commercials.

Whatever other effects these changes are having, they are making television a more popular medium.

The average time a family spends watching the tube each week rose from 47 hours and 44 minutes in 1982 to 49 hours and 58 minutes last year—more than seven hours a day, seven days a week. Those figures include the time it takes to tape a show on a VCR, but not the time spent watching the results.

The big losers in all the changes have been the networks. In the 1977–78 television season, ABC, CBS and NBC were watched by 91 percent of the prime-time viewing audience, according to Young & Rubicam. By the 1984–85 seasons, it was 73 percent.

The causes of that shift are easy to find. The number of independent broadcast stations—those not associated with one of the major networks—has increased to almost 250 from 160 three years ago. In addition, the number of households with cable increased from 29 million in 1982 to a projected 41 million, or almost 50 percent of the total, by the end of this year.

The VCR Boom

Even more dramatic has been the growth of the VCR market. First available in the mid-1970's the machines are now in more than a quarter of the nation's homes and are selling at the rate of almost 1 million a month, according to the Electronic Industries Association.

So far, networks and advertisers have had little success in finding ways to recapture viewers' attention. For the networks, the obvious solution may also be the most difficult—developing programs that more people want to watch. For advertisers, similarly, the solution may be in commercials that are more entertaining and visually attractive, and so less likely to be turned off or skipped over. While ad agencies say they are developing such commercials, most admit that so far the results have been minimal.

But the networks are not surrendering to the trends. Programming designed to be more visually compelling—particularly to the younger, video-oriented viewers who are the secret to the success of MTV: Music Television—has made some inroads. Television executives point to NBC's "Miami Vice," a fast-paced police show with a rock music score, as the type of innovation the networks need more of.

But ABC, CBS and NBC are likely to find the competition getting tougher as alternative technology advances and the quality of non-network programming improves.

February 15, 1946

Electronic Computer Flashes Answers, May Speed Engineering

BY T. R. KENNEDY JR.

PHILADELPHIA, FEB. 14—One of the war's top secrets, an amazing machine which applies electronic speeds for the first time to mathematical tasks hitherto too difficult and cumbersome for solution, was announced here tonight by the War Department. Leaders who saw the device in action for the first time heralded it as a tool with which to begin to rebuild scientific affairs on new foundations.

Such instruments, it was said, could revolutionize modern engineering, bring on a new epoch of industrial design, and eventually eliminate much slow and costly trial-and-error development work now deemed necessary in the fashioning of intricate machines. Heretofore, sheer mathematical difficulties have often forced designers to accept inferior solutions of their problems, with higher costs and slower progress.

The "Eniac," as the new electronic speed marvel is known, virtually eliminates time in doing such jobs. Its inventors say it computes a mathematical problem 1,000 times faster than it has ever been done before.

The machine is being used on a problem in nuclear physics.

The Eniac, known more formally as "the electronic numerical integrator and computer," has not a single moving mechanical part. Nothing inside its 18,000 vacuum tubes and several miles of wiring moves except the tiniest elements of matter-electrons. There are, however, mechanical devices associated with it which translate or "interpret" the mathematical language of man to terms understood by the Eniac, and vice versa.

The Eniac was invented and perfected by two young scientists of [the Moore School of Electrical Engineering at the University of Pennsylvania], Dr. John William Mauchly, 38, a physicist and amateur meteorologist, and his associate, J. Presper Eckert Jr., 26, chief engineer of the project. Assistance also was given by many others at the school.

Army ordnance men had been on the lookout for a machine with which to prepare a large volume of ballistic data, which in turn was needed to break a threatened bottleneck in the production of firing and bombing tables for new offensive weapons going overseas. Without the tables the guns could not be used efficiently.

Project Took Thirty Months

Capt. H.H. Goldstine, Army ordnance mathematician, then at the school, heard of Dr. Mauchly's ideas, told Col. Paul N. Gillon of the Aberdeen (Md.) Proving Ground, enlisted his enthusiastic support and the project went forward with Government aid. Thirty months to the day later it was finished and operating, doing easily what had been done laboriously by many trained men. The Eniac soon will be permanently installed at Aberdeen.

"A very difficult wartime problem" was sent through its intricate circuits soon after it was completed. The Eniac completed the task in two hours. Had it not been available the job would have kept busy 100 trained men for a whole year. So clever is the device that its creators have given up trying to find problems so long that they cannot be solved.

This resolver of difficult problems is what computing experts call a "digital" counter. Basically, it does nothing more than add, subtract, multiply and divide. It does this by generating very accurately timed electrical impulses at a speed of 100,000 per second, and can do one operation every twentieth pulse, thereby adding, for instance, at the rate of 5,000 per second.

Since all mathematical tasks, no matter how abstruse or involved, can be resolved to basic arithmetic if enough time is available, the Eniac can reverse the process, eliminate time, and arrive at an answer to virtually any problem. So say its inventors.

Machine Has Memory, Too

The machine, however, can do much more. It has the human faculty of "memory," four kinds of it, to perform certain tasks in the proper sequence. It also has "control" elements, and can, up to a point, dictate its own action. It can, for instance, compare two numbers and, depending on which one is larger, choose one of two possible courses.

First, it gets its original numbers from a series of cards in which holes are punched to indicate the "initial and boundary conditions" of the problem. One of the Eniac "minds" performs this job.

When the problem is punched on the cards they are dropped into a slot in a "reader." The man who wants the answers may then sit down and await results. He seldom has to wait long; the Eniac does most of its tasks in seconds.

A unit called "a master programmer" oversees the whole computation and makes sure it is carried out.

The Eniac has some 40 panels nine feet high, which bristle with control and indicating material. Pink neon lights blink on several panels as buttons are pressed. Numbers are printed beside the lights.

Those who witnessed the demonstration entered a 30-by 60-foot room. The computer took up most of the space.

Machine Cost $400,000

More than 200,000 man-hours went into the building of the machine. It contains more than half a million soldered joints, and cost about $400,000. Three times as much electricity is required to operate it as for one of our largest broadcasters—150 kilowatts.

In the field of peacetime activities Mr. Mauchly foresees not only better weather-predicting—months ahead—but also better airplanes, gas turbines, micro-wave radio tubes, television, prime movers, projectiles operating at supersonic speeds carrying cargoes in peace and even more and better accuracies in studying the movements of the planets.

Tiny Computer on a Chip Ready for Soaring Sales

BY VICTOR K. MCELHENY

After years of electronic industry ballyhoo, the microprocessor—a microscopic computer laid out on a fingernail-size square of silicon—is on the threshold of mass markets.

This so-called computer on a chip, which has been declining sharply in price since its invention in 1971, has been pushing its way into more and more uses and is expected to become a billion-dollar industry in a few years. It has served the public in pocket calculators, video games and microwave ovens. It has helped businesses speed sales, control costs and watch inventories with sophisticated grocery scales, gasoline pumps and point-of-sale terminals, or "smart" cash registers.

Now the microprocessor is poised to enter markets where it will serve basic purposes of individual consumers—in automobiles, telephones and utility meters, for example. Following sales of nearly $200 million in microprocessor systems last year and as much as $400 million expected this year, the electronics industry expects sales to soar before long.

Critical steps in this direction were taken in the last few months by America's largest automobile manufacturers, the General Motors Corporation and the Ford Motor Company. A few days ago Ford announced selection of two major semiconductor manufacturers, Texas Instruments Inc. of Dallas and the Intel Corporation of Santa Clara, Calif., as its partners for installing millions of microprocessors in new cars of 1980 and beyond.

In the years ahead, such devices are planned for virtually all new cars, not only for timing the firing of spark plugs and regulating the flow of gas from carburetors (to help fuel economy) but also for controlling the recycling of exhaust gases in pollution-control systems, operating dashboard displays of information about the car's operations, running antiskid braking systems and, eventually, controlling the transmission.

The prices of these relatively complicated microprocessor systems are generally expected to fall well below $10, and the experience of manufacturing them is expected to help drive down the price of other microprocessors to be used in such things as telephone receivers and utilities' electric meters.

A microprocessor inside the telephone could remember frequently called numbers so that only one or two buttons would be pushed to place a call, forward calls automatically or automatically keep dialing a busy number.

The microprocessor industry essentially began with an invention in 1971 by an Intel engineer who was developing circuits intended for use in a pocket calculator planned by a now-defunct Japanese company, Busicom.

Big I.B.M.'s Little Computer

Its Desk-Top Model Brings a New Image

BY ANDREW POLLACK

The International Business Machines Corporation, once slow to recognize that computers were getting smaller, is apparently determined not to make the same mistake in the emerging personal computer market.

In the 1960's, I.B.M. was slow to enter the minicomputer field, allowing upstarts, particularly the Digital Equipment Corporation, to acquire a dominant share of the market and to grow into companies with billions in annual revenue.

Yesterday I.B.M. announced that it would sell a desk-top computer for use in homes, schools and businesses, thereby staging a relatively early entry, some analysts contend, into a market now dominated by Apple Computer Inc. and Tandy Corporation's Radio Shack division.

"I don't think they want to allow another Digital Equipment to rise through the ranks in personal computers," said Thomas J. Crotty, an analyst with the Gartner Group, an investment adviser specializing in the computer field.

Although I.B.M.'s entry into the personal computer business had been expected for months, it still sent reverberations through the industry.

Besides marking the company's entry into consumer electronics, the endorsement of personal machines by a company whose name is synonymous with computers is expected to stimulate the growth of an already fast-growing business.

But in helping the business in general, I.B.M. is expected to pose the stiffest challenge yet to Apple and to Tandy, which together have a 39 percent share of a personal computer market that posted total sales of $2.4 billion last year.

"People will now know that personal computers are not a fad or a flash in the pan," said Michael McConnell, executive vice president of Computerland, a chain of retail stores that will market the new I.B.M. products.

The price of the machines will range from $1,565, for a simple system that will require users to provide their own television-like display screens and cassette tapes, to more than $6,000, for the most elaborate versions.

American companies are increasingly buying desk-top computers to increase the efficiency of executives and other personnel.

Until yesterday's announcement, I.B.M.'s least expensive computer was a $10,000 desk-top model for small businesses, the sort of computer useful to a doctor or small company for billing, record-keeping and similar tasks. That model was announced only two weeks ago.

"It's not as aggressively priced as I expected," said Mr. Crotty, the analyst at Gartner. "It doesn't blow [Apple or Tandy] out of the water, that's for sure."

Chances are, there will be room for all the companies, many analysts believe. The personal computer market is growing explosively, although accurate figures are hard to get because there is no clear distinction between home computers, personal computers for other users and desk-top computers designed for business use.

International Data estimates that 327,000 desk-top computers, ranging in price from several hundred dollars to $20,000, were sold in the United States in 1980. It projects that this total will increase to 1.3 million by 1985. In dollar volume, the market is expected to grow from $2.4 billion last year to $9 billion in 1985.

According to estimates by International Data and others, there are approximately a million personal computers in use. Most are actually used in business and professional applications. The home and education markets are still small, but are expected to grow rapidly, though perhaps not for another few years.

For I.B.M., the entrance into personal computers is further evidence of a change that has been taking place over the past few years in the company's image and the way it does business.

To some users of personal computers, who have been known to say, "Never trust a computer you can't lift," the International Business Machines Corporation has sometimes been viewed as the enemy, according to a recent editorial in Byte [a microcomputer magazine].

After all, the magazine said, I.B.M. rode to its dominance of the computer industry on the strength of mainframe computers—large, forbidding machines with banks of blinking lights that stood in special rooms by themselves, attended to by technicians whom no one else could understand.

I.B.M. was so wedded to the big machines that in the 1960's it paid little attention to the emerging minicomputers. Although I.B.M. eventually became a major player in that market, that did not occur until after upstarts, particularly Digital, had captured a large part of the minicomputer market and had grown into major companies. Nevertheless, Digital, which still has a larger share of the minicomputer market than I.B.M., grossed only $2.4 billion in revenues last year, compared with I.B.M.'s $26.2 billion.

In the past few years, as the prices of its computers and office products have declined and their potential markets have widened, I.B.M. has been willing to alter the way it had done business when computers were high-priced items affordable only by large companies.

It has begun to rely more on mass marketing techniques, has opened a few retail stores and has been willing to buy more parts, or even complete products, from other vendors, like the low-priced copier it now sells made by Minolta. I.B.M.'s entry into the personal computer market, and the way in which it has done it, attest to that trend.

In particular, I.B.M. will allow non-I.B.M. vendors to sell its personal computers, something it has done only sparingly in the past. And, while I.B.M. has traditionally made its products and software incompatible with those of other vendors, this will not be the case with the personal computer.

I.B.M. is also allowing anyone else who wants to do so to write programs for the I.B.M. machine, which the company would evaluate. If the programs were accepted for marketing, the writer would be paid a royalty on sales of the program.

November 22, 1984

Apple's Mac Taking On I.B.M.

Seeking Sales to Business

BY ANDREW POLLACK

CUPERTINO, CALIF., NOV. 21—When Steven P. Jobs, the brash and free-wheeling 29-year-old chairman of Apple Computer Inc., appeared before the top data processing executives of some of the nation's largest corporations earlier this year, it seemed likely to be the ultimate clash of cultures.

"I was afraid to have him here, frankly," said Naomi Seligman, senior partner of the Research Board, a low-profile New York group composed of chief data processing executives of 50 of the nation's largest corporations. These customers are "the slickest, toughest, most critical large users," she said. "I've seen them eat even some I.B.M. corporate vice presidents for lunch."

But Mr. Jobs came through his ordeal with flying colors. "They have never been as impressed with any single individual," Mrs. Seligman said. Since then, she said, Apple has received a few orders, still not publicly announced, that are worth millions of dollars a piece.

Market Share in Office Computers

Mr. Job's appearance before the Research Board was one of the early battles in a major war Apple will be waging over the next few years. Already strong in the home and education markets and among independent professionals, Apple is mounting an assault to sell its easy-to-use Macintosh computers in the corporate market, the bastion of its larger, more powerful rival, the International Business Machines Corporation. Its success there will determine how big a computer company Apple will ultimately become. Sales to business account for two-thirds of the overall personal computer market in dollars. In addition, Apple must succeed in the corporate computer world to attract the independent software necessary for survival, said Michael Murphy, editor of the California Technology Stock Letter.

"This is the million-dollar question for 1985," said Michele Preston, microcomputer analyst with L.F. Rothschild, Unterberg, Towbin.

Mapping Out the Wireless–Phone Future

BY ANTHONY RAMIREZ

A multibillion-dollar telephone revolution that caught almost everyone by surprise is occurring in the United States, with a potential as great as that of the telegraph and transistor radio for changing communications.

Vigorous debate over how to apportion the benefits and costs appears likely to delay pending Government approval of the system and bring the issue before the Clinton Administration.

Millions of Americans are now buying cellular phones—about 7,000 a day, many more than had been anticipated—to carry around with them in cars, handbags and briefcases. And it appears almost certain that millions more Americans will flock to a new system being developed: shirt-pocket or even fountain-pen-size wireless phones smaller than cellular and not unlike the old Dick Tracy two-way wrist radio.

The Handheld Servant

The system, called personal communications services, or P.C.S. in industry argot, is designed to be more versatile than cellular communications and may—or may not, depending on the Government decisions ahead—be much cheaper for everyone to use. The handheld phones will also work as wireless computers to send data to other computers or relay it for fax transmission.

"One thing we know about P.C.S is that it will provide people the electronic equivalent of butlers and secretaries," said James E. Katz, a staff sociologist at Bellcorc, the research arm of the regional Bell companies. "It spreads to the middle class what only robber barons once enjoyed."

In less than a decade, the cellular business has grown larger than the McDonald's fast-food empire. And last week, A.T.&T., the world's largest telecommunications company, placed a $3.8 billion bet on its wireless future, saying it seeks to buy one-third of McCaw Cellular Communications, the nation's largest cellular carrier.

High Cellular Prices

Nevertheless, cellular-phone users are finding that the price of making wireless phone calls has remained very high—in some cases, as much as 80 times the price of a conventional call. And part of the excitement over the new P.C.S. system is its potential for changing that.

"Cellular calls are not cost based; they're insanity based," said Herschel Shostek, a telecommunications consultant in Silver Spring, Md. The history of the cellular industry should serve as a ready guide for what to avoid, others contend.

The cellular industry denies that prices are artificially high, arguing that the costs of constructing radio transmission stations and maintaining equipment have kept the business from being profitable.

The factors for the success of P.C.S.—consumer cost, industry profit, the speed of putting the system in place—all depend on how the Government views the cellular experience, on how the new markets will be organized, with how many companies, how many customers each and in what size geographic regions.

The Federal Communications Commission had planned to act as early as the end of the year. But with the change of Administrations and the likely replacement of at least two of the five commissioners, including the chairman, Alfred C. Sikes, the decision will no doubt be delayed.

The Prospect: A Portable Phone for Use Anywhere

The new devices, like cellular phones, will in essence be battery-operated radios. They will communicate via receiving and transmitting stations that feed the calls into the world's network of wired telephones.

Cellular phones work best in open spaces. P.C.S. phones, however, will operate from a great many more locations—from inside office buildings, elevators, trains and subway platforms, for instance.

Unlike a cellular phone, which can have a range of about 20 miles, a P.C.S. unit will be limited to perhaps a few thousand feet. But it will send signals to many more transmitter stations that themselves will be much smaller, cheaper and easier to install than cellular stations. Where a city might have a dozen cellular stations, a P.C.S system might have hundreds, permitting lower-power transmission and very small phones. It is because the user will never be far from a transmitter that the devices will work within buildings and tunnels.

The phones will be relatively cheap to manufacture because of advances in electronics miniaturization and computing power.

For the present, P.C.S. is not threatening to make cellular immediately obsolete, because P.C.S. has a short range. But in the future, as the technology moves forward, there may be a single wireless phone for each person that will work everywhere. People will carry their phones with them at all times, with one phone number that will reach them at home, office or golf course.

Lessons Learned: Cellular Theory Has Fallen Short

Critics of the cellular-phone industry say it has been given control of a public resource, scarce radio frequencies on the electromagnetic spectrum, in a way that is a bit like deeding it the Brooklyn Bridge and letting it collect tolls from all who cross. Cellular executives counter that their use of the airwaves requires significant investments, and they are still not making any money.

Back in 1982, when the F.C.C. set up rules for the cellular markets, the agency divided the country into 734 territories and permitted no more than two companies to operate in each region. The theory was that competition between two companies in each market would eventually bring prices down, and that so few people would be interested in toting a phone around that no more than two companies per area could thrive. Not so.

The Cellular Telecommunications Industry Association says 10 million people now subscribe to cellular services, a level once forecast for the turn of the century. Industry revenue this year may well exceed $7 billion. Within a few years, the personal communication systems are expected to add $30 billion more annually.

The boom defies the high prices.

Lee L. Selwyn of Economics and Technology Inc., sees "no intrinsic reason why a cellular call shouldn't be priced at 10 or 15 cents a minute." But the prices range from 25 cents to more than 90 cents a minute.

Within at least two-thirds of the regions, the prices charged by the two cellular carriers have been found to be almost the same or even identical. The General Accounting Office, the investigative arm of the Congress, made that finding in July but said it could not learn why, in part because the industry was not required to provide detailed revenue and cost data.

Critics and industry analysts say consumers are paying for much more than the service they get, like helping one cellular company pay billions to acquire another. The industry does not deny this, but re-emphasizes its own high costs as factors in the fees.

"We have a competitive market today," said Brian D. Kidney, a senior officer at Pacific Telesis. No company, he says, is getting rich from the high prices.

The Rule Makers Trying to Insure More Competition

If the wireless-phone field is competitive now, the F.C.C. seems eager to make the new personal communications services more so.

A former senior official of the F.C.C, Albert Halprin, the nation's top telephone regulator in the mid-1980's, said: "The amount of competition is not what I would have hoped for. 'Mistake' is far from the right word to describe our action, but it was not perfect. With hindsight, we should have authorized a third carrier."

John Cimko, a longtime F.C.C. official who is the current chief of the commission's mobile services division, agrees. "Two competitors is not an optimal number of players," he said, noting that the commission is determined to mandate at least three companies.

After the F.C.C. divided the country into 734 territories, the companies subdivided these markets into smaller service areas, or cells— hence "cellular." Each cell has a diameter of between one and 20 miles, depending on population and local obstructions like mountains and skyscrapers, and each cell contains one base station consisting of a transmitter and receiver.

The F.C.C. gave one of the two licenses in each market to the local phone company, in many cases a carrier owned by the GTE Corporation or a regional Bell company like the Nynex Corporation. By including the established communications company in each market, the agency thought the service would be established more quickly. It was.

In most markets, the second licensee was determined by lottery, and the plan led to a total of 120 different cellular companies—Lilliputians in an industry dominated by Brobdingnagians.

Ten carriers, seven of them Bell companies, served 95 percent of the population.

Because the country was cut into so many slices, national service has been difficult to establish, as if there were hundreds of little duchies, each with its own interests. To use a cellular phone while crossing from one market to another, a customer must enter into an expensive "roaming agreement" with the various companies.

December 12, 1993

A Growing Internet Is Trying to Take Care of Business

BY PETER H. LEWIS

The phenomenal growth of the Internet, a world-wide web of connected computer networks, was underscored earlier this year in a New Yorker magazine cartoon showing two dogs sitting at a computer. The bigger animal, paws on the keyboard, turns to the smaller and says, "On the Internet, nobody knows you're a dog."

Yet many executives may find themselves howling at the complexity of the Internet, which was not designed with business in mind. Originally intended to serve the academic and research communities, the Internet has until recently been the playground of computer enthusiasts, government researchers and educators who have been willing to learn the intricacies of the Unix operating system and who have been patient enough to dig through its labyrinthine depths to find, amid the millions of pages of electronic data, the bits of information they needed.

According to research supplied at the Internet World '93 conference in Manhattan last week, the Internet is attracting some 150,000 new users each month, who join a population now estimated at 15 million or more.

Many of these new users are businesses that sense the importance of being on the "Net" but may not understand why, beyond the obvious appeal of electronic mail.

"It's like magic, it's like an incantation," said Elizabeth Lane Lawley, director of Internet Training and Consulting Services of Tuscaloosa, Ala. "You don't have to know what it means. You just say 'Internet' and everyone smiles and nods their heads and says, 'Oh yeah, it's the wave of the future, yeah.'"

The Internet World conference drew some 3,500 people to the Jacob K. Javits Convention Center, and a random sampling revealed that many were from businesses rather than academia. One indicator of the Internet's allure for businesses was the small mob surrounding Mary J. Cronin, whose new book, "Doing Business on the Internet" ($29.95, Van Nostrand Reinhold), was one of the two most popular books at the show. The other was "The Internet for Dummies" ($19.95, IDG Books), which "sold out in about two minutes," one visitor said.

Scores of people stayed on after the conference to attend special workshops billed as "Internet Hands-On," which were supposed to give novices the chance to spend a day exploring the Internet with expert supervision. The workshops proved so popular, however, that most people had no more than a few minutes at the keyboard.

The business trend was clear in one small hands-on group as the novices introduced themselves to one another and told why they were there:

- "I'm in a worldwide strategic product development group for a pharmaceutical company in Philadelphia, and my job is to analyze future trends."
- "I'm with I.B.M., and we're looking at the Internet as a way to access supply information and distribute product information."
- "I'm director of information and technology for a company that distributes medical books and supplies to universities and libraries. We also own and operate bookstores and have a software package we sell. We're looking at the Internet to increase contact with our customer base and to connect our bookstores."
- "I work in systems at a brokerage firm in Jersey City that would like to offer brokerage services on the Internet."

Thinking cosmically was Nancy M. Powers, president of the Powers Research and Training Institute of Bayville, L.I. "I run Master Mind support groups for entrepreneurs to brainstorm ideas, and I look at the Internet as the ultimate Master Mind," she said. "I think it would be incredibly valuable to create these groups globally." Master Mind is a motivational and support seminar program for business people.

The source of the Internet's appeal is that anyone on the Net can post and retrieve information, but the practical result, which is often frustrating to businesses accustomed to logical hierarchy and order, is that there is no defined or enforced structure for posting that information.

As a result, even experienced Internet users often wind up chasing their tails when they try to fetch information.

For example, a company might want the text of the recent North American Free Trade Agreement and an analysis of its impact on, say, the automobile industry. Such information exists on the Internet, but one is likely to hear a giant sucking sound as the Internet user is drawn ever deeper into the network in search of it.

It is relatively simple and inexpensive to gain indirect access to the Internet's electronic mail services through popular on-line information services like Compuserve, America On-Line and MCI Mail, which are known as Internet "gateways." But woe to the individual executive or computer novice who wants to tap directly into the rich depths of the Internet.

It will almost certainly get easier as more commercial Internet service providers spring up to meet the growing demand from businesses, and as increasingly powerful computers and software make it possible to hide the Internet's Unix command system behind graphical, point-and-shoot interfaces like Mosaic (a free software program developed with Federal financing by the National Center for Supercomputing Applications) or even Microsoft Windows.

The graphical interfaces are still quite new and rare, and users should plan to learn some Unix commands and terms like TCP/IP, Gopher, Veronica and Archie. Even simple Internet addresses can seem as if they are written in Martian, for example, bigk9@avm1.hq.umars.edu.

Adding to the confusion is the historical aversion among some Internet veterans to conducting commerce on "their" system. This philosophy, born in the early years of the Internet when the Government subsidized the network, essentially holds that the Internet is a pure pool of information that should not be polluted by business opportunism.

Times have changed. In 1991, the first commercial Internet connection services appeared, and suddenly the system was opened to anyone, not just the community of academics and computer gurus. As millions of new users linked themselves to the Internet, they viewed the Internet as a service, not as a sort of electronic commune.

There is still a strong aversion to crass commercialism; anyone using the system for the electronic equivalent of junk-mail marketing can expect to be pilloried on the electronic commons and pelted with indignant e-mail responses, called "flames." But there appears to be a growing acceptance of noninvasive marketing and advertising, even as debates rage on the Internet as to how such advertising should be handled.

Plugged-In Nation Goes on Vacations In a New Territory

BY AMY HARMON

The children were belted in, the radio was tuned to alternative rock and Jake Ice's cellular telephone was trill-trill-trilling as the family headed from San Mateo to Palm Springs, Calif., for its annual summer vacation.

At the wheel, Mr. Ice, who took his beeper and phone over the objections of his wife, Valerie, made five calls and received four pages on the drive.

But Mrs. Ice, a salesclerk who moderates an on-line discussion group, had packed the portable computer. That night, she checked her E-mail from the hotel and played her favorite on-line game, Slingo

"I would prefer that we just enjoy our vacation and not worry about what's going on outside our own personal lives for a while," said Mr. Ice, 35, a technology manager, recalling the vacation last month. "But it seems impossible to do that."

Or at least extremely difficult these days. The summer vacation, once a near-sacred ritual of withdrawal from everyday life, is under electronic siege. Simply traveling hundreds of miles to get away from it all is no longer enough as business demands, personal compulsion and ever-cheaper technology are inducing many vacationing Americans to keep their hailing frequencies open.

Work has been oozing over phone lines into the home for a long time, and E-mail in the evenings has become an often welcome routine for the digitally inclined. But only recently have mobile communications and computing devices mounted such a full-scale assault on personal space that individuals, couples and families—even while on vacation—must make conscious decisions about whether and when to draw the boundaries between down time and on-line time.

The resulting negotiations are potentially more divisive among traveling companions than such old-style flash points as where to eat or who got the directions wrong. But from the fray, social critics say, may emerge a new set of assumptions about what it means to be away without necessarily getting away.

"With this technology there are no rules about when to stop," said Kelly Moore, a sociologist at Columbia University who studies the effect of technology on social relations. "And that may make the whole idea of vacation a misnomer."

And yet, the same gadgets that threaten to intrude on the wilderness fishing expedition can allow many job-stressed Americans to take time off without fear of falling hopelessly behind or to stay in touch with friends and family back home.

More than a quarter of American households own pagers, double the number of a year ago, and more than one-third use cellular phones, the Consumer Electronics Industry Association says. Seven million people regularly check their business E-mail from outside the office, reports the IDC Corporation, a research concern in Framingham, Mass.

And it is on summer vacation, when distances open up and the days unfold more slowly, that both the benefits and burdens of technologies that relentlessly compress time and space are most apparent.

Andrew Cohen, 28, and five friends sharing a rented weekend house in Amagansett, N.Y., this summer, have found it necessary to draw their line in the sand. "Our rule is not to take the cell phones to the actual beach," Mr. Cohen said, although one housemate has been known to take hers mountain biking.

An electronic etiquette for the traveling public remains in embryonic form, at best. Ray Umashankar, an administrator at the University of Arizona, plans to book his vacation flight early and insist on the aisle seat after sparring with an airplane laptop user earlier this year who had turned his tray table into an office.

"I went through an intense internal struggle since I had to disturb him for something as mundane as going to the toilet," said Mr. Umashankar.

Whatever high-technology civilities vacationers do or do not observe in the presence of others, though, the toughest conflicts are typically within themselves. On a recent trip to Montreal, Cheryl Moreau, 38, who lives in Portland, Me., and keeps in touch with several close friends by E-mail, found herself surreptitiously looking over her hosts' homes for Internet connections. She recalls, too, her joy last summer in Prague to find a cybercafe where she could send and retrieve messages.

But Ms. Moreau has misgivings about indulging her on-line craving. "In Prague," she said, "I began thinking to myself, 'I've been in this windowless basement place for an hour and there's a whole interesting city out there. What am I doing?'"

The urge to stay in touch is driven in part by changing expectations among employers and clients, whose respect for the sacrosanct vacation time seems to be fading with the growing ease of impinging on it.

"They are not putting it in policy and procedures manuals," said Marge Yanker, of the American Management Association. "But as companies provide more electronic means to be in touch, there is an unspoken expectation that people will be reachable, even on their own time."

Jon Stapleton, a New York lawyer who sometimes spends hours at his weekend home in Rhode Island on the phone and computer, said the technology had radically changed clients' demands of him on vacation. While he used to be available by phone, and documents could be faxed or delivered overnight, he can now receive them in minutes by E-mail.

"Clients anticipate you'll see it immediately, and I'm in a service business, and part of the service is to be available," said Mr. Stapleton, who sometimes wonders whether it would be better for his wife and 11-year-old son if he stayed in the office.

Many people may have simply acquired a wired habit that encompasses social ties and an insatiable appetite for information.

"There's a thrill to being connected that is much more than the feeling that you have to be working all the time," said David Shenk, author of "Data Smog: Surviving the Information Glut" (HarperCollins, 1997).

Sometimes even the hard-core high-tech feel a need to be incommunicado. Such was the case with Michelle and Mark Crump of Milford, Mass., who were camping near Acadia National Park in Maine last week. Ms. Crump develops World Wide Web sites and Mr. Crump, a computer systems administrator, is partial to Internet computer games.

"We left the laptop at home; we left the beeper at home," Ms. Crump said by telephone from Ellsworth, a few miles from the park.

The Crumps' resolve crumbled when they stumbled on the Cafe Cyberway in Ellsworth, which was jammed with people waiting for one of the cybercafe's seven computers. "We just didn't expect to see this here—we had to stop," Ms. Crump said. "Mark's thinking about playing Quake over the network. I'm drinking a cappuccino. But I might have to check my E-mail."

A TSA worker scans a Continental Airlines employee's BlackBerry at the security checkpoint during a demonstration of the airline's electronic boarding pass program in 2008. By the mid-2000s, mobile devices were widely used, and companies were creating new ways to interact with customers on their handheld phones, pagers, and computers. (Michael Stravato for the *New York Times*)

Email You Can't Outrun

BY AMY HARMON

You know they've gotten a BlackBerry when they stop calling.

No matter that the tiny keyboard on the Black-Berry, a wireless e-mail device, requires a kind of thumb-typing nobody learned in high school. Or that reading messages on a pager-size screen while driving is a health hazard. For a fast-growing group of BlackBerry fans, getting and sending text messages while away from home and office beats verbal contact any day, all day.

"It teaches you that most of the time on the phone is small talk," said Tom Scott, chairman of the Nantucket Nectars juice company, who like many recent BlackBerry converts said his phone bills had gone down. "I don't like dealing with the cell phone. It always goes in and out. I'm always worrying that I'm getting cancer. And honestly sometimes I would just rather talk to less people than more people."

Members of the BlackBerry cult won't ask how you are in their electronic communiques. Nor are they very likely to give you their full attention when you are in their physical presence, since the messages flashing on their pager-size screens demand a quick glance, and perhaps a response. But they will return your e-mail almost immediately, no matter where they are.

Which is more important?

The answer may not matter. The BlackBerry is the forerunner of a set of tools that offer constant contact without the need to actually talk to anyone. About a million Americans use a wireless e-mail service, with BlackBerry leading the pack, according to the Yankee Group, of Boston, a telecommunications consulting firm.

In recent months, the BlackBerry has become much coveted by America's business professionals, who are increasingly judged by how accessible they are to colleagues and clients. A key draw: unlike cellular phone calls, which require a clear distraction of attention, BlackBerrys allow users to do two things at once.

Internet executives rave about watching messages roll in while they conduct other business. Along with higher salaries and concierge service, BlackBerrys headed a list of demands submitted by junior analysts at Salomon Smith Barney to their superiors last spring. Even lawyers, notoriously slow to embrace e-mail in the office, have become enthralled by the BlackBerry.

"I've heard colleagues say that when they've had the poor taste to return e-mails from their bedrooms, it hasn't been a welcome gesture," said David Grais, a partner in the law firm of Gibson, Dunn & Crutcher in New York. "It definitely makes you more of an e-mail junkie."

Mr. Grais uses his BlackBerry to receive messages when he's out of the office and when he's not. "If I'm two floors away and I get a call, my secretary knows I can always be reached," he said. "It's completely indispensable."

It is harder to see why ordinary consumers would crave such continuous connection, or be willing to pay for it. Research in Motion, or RIM, the Canadian company that makes the original BlackBerry models ($349 and $399) and a slightly larger version ($499), has marketed its $40-per-month e-mail service to corporations, and about 5,000 companies now pay for employees to use it. Individuals can buy the BlackBerry online, and RIM said it would soon be available in retail stores like Staples. America Online has announced plans to make its e-mail and instant messaging service available through BlackBerry-like gadgets. And Earthlink, the nation's second-largest Internet service provider, is conducting a pilot test with BlackBerrys.

"I can't tell you what motivates people to want e-mail on their hip when they leave home," said Roland Wilcox, a senior product manager at Earthlink. "But they do, and we want to provide it to them."

The BlackBerry will soon face more competition, most notably from cellular phones, which allow users to talk and type messages with one device and are the mobile e-mail method of choice among Europeans and Japanese teenagers.

Because the cellular network in the United States is a patchwork of often incompatible standards, the BlackBerry, which uses a wireless data network built for two-way messaging, has so far been able to provide better coverage and lower prices here than most phone services. But even as this country's wireless providers find ways to weave their networks together, it is unclear whether Americans will take to typing

with the cell phone's number pad, which requires two presses of the 2 key to enter the letter B, for instance.

The BlackBerry's QWERTY keyboard and its calendar and address book features have also pitted it against the wireless models of the Palm and the Handspring Visor personal digital assistants. The Palm and the Visor require users to log on to collect e-mail, while the BlackBerry receives e-mail automatically whenever it is on. And since the smaller version uses a AA battery that lasts about two weeks with continuous use, users tend to keep it turned on.

The BlackBerry's biggest competition comes from Motorola, whose new T900 is a sort of stripped-down BlackBerry that is considerably less expensive. Last week, Motorola introduced the P935, a model aimed at the BlackBerry's core corporate market.

But for now, the BlackBerry is at the forefront of a shift in communications reminiscent of the introduction of the cellular phone in the early 1980's, except that it is happening much faster, and with an added dimension. Wireless e-mail changes the nature of e-mail itself, making for a shorter, jerkier exchange not unlike a typical cell phone call. But it also alters communication as a whole, because people can now choose to send e-mail all the time rather than call.

Already, there is a BlackBerry backlash. The devices are banned at the staff meetings of Loudcloud, an Internet company based in Sunnyvale, Calif. "Staff meetings are not worth holding if everybody is there thumb-typing," said Ben Horowitz, Loudcloud's chief executive.

Hoai Ta, the senior director of information technology at Broadvision, a Silicon Valley company that offers BlackBerrys to all employees, said he took his with him even on weekend fishing trips.

"Every so often I pull it out, to see, do I have a message from my boss?" Mr. Ta said. "Being in touch, staying on top of things is better for me. Otherwise I have to deal with the problem later on anyway, and there's the perception that you're not acting fast enough."

Not everybody considers that a good trade-off. Kim Smith, 32, said her fiancé, Jonathan Guerster, an avid BlackBerry user, sometimes "almost crashes when we're driving."

"There's definitely a lack-of-focus issue," she added. For instance, during conversations about getting married and buying a house, Mr. Guerster "may from time to time decide to start doing e-mails," Ms. Smith said. "It's annoying."

On the way to Nantucket, Mass., where the couple recently bought a house, Mr. Guerster sends e-mail from the nine-seater plane until the BlackBerry stops working. On the way back, he holds it in his lap waiting for his connection to click in, Ms. Smith said.

Mr. Guerster, a venture capitalist, conceded a certain BlackBerry addiction, but he said the ability to send e-mail as thoughts popped into his head had made him more productive and more focused because he no longer had to keep lists in his head.

Still, he said, he is glad the BlackBerry doesn't work on Nantucket. "I like to be able to get out of range," he said.

How long that will last, however, is unclear. Ms. Smith had heard that Mr. Scott, among others, had begun to petition RIM to extend its coverage area to the island. "I hope it doesn't work," she said.

Apple Introduces What It Calls an Easier to Use Portable Music Player

BY MATT RICHTEL

CUPERTINO, CALIF, OCT. 23—Apple Computer introduced a portable music player today and declared that the new gadget, called the iPod, was so much easier to use that it would broaden a nascent market in the way the Macintosh once helped make the personal computer accessible to a more general audience.

But while industry analysts said the device appeared to be as consumer friendly as the company said it was, they also pointed to its relatively limited potential audience, around seven million owners of the latest Macintosh computers. Apple said it had not yet decided whether to introduce a version of the music player for computers with the Windows operating system, which is used by more than 90 percent of personal computer users.

"It's a nice feature for Macintosh users," said P. J. McNealy, a senior analyst for Gartner G2, an e-commerce research group. "But to the rest of the Windows world, it doesn't make any difference."

Steven P. Jobs, Apple's chief executive, disputed the concern that the market was limited, and said the company might have trouble meeting holiday demand. He predicted that the improvement in technology he said the iPod represented would inspire consumers to buy Macintosh computers so they could use an iPod.

There are several categories of digital music devices, including players that use flash memory, which are small but expensive. Another competing player relies on magnetic hard drives, which are typically larger in both capacity and size, and thus are enclosed in larger gadgets. The market for all such devices is growing and is expected to be around 18 million units by 2005, according to IDC, a market research firm.

The iPod, which will sell for $399 when it becomes available on Nov. 10, is something of a hybrid of existing products. At 4 inches by just under 2.5 inches and just over three-quarters of an inch thick, it is as small as flash players, but it has a 5-gigabyte hard drive, large enough to store 1,000 songs.

Among the features being promoted, the device uses an Apple technology called Firewire to permit songs to be transferred from a computer onto the gadget at a rate of around 1 second a song, substantially faster than other portable players, the company said.

Mr. Jobs said other major advances were its ease of use and a rechargeable lithium battery that runs for 10 hours, making it the most sophisticated battery in any Apple computer or device.

But just how easy MP3 players are to use is a matter of some concern to the record industry. The industry has expressed concern that songs encoded in the MP3 format—a popular digital format into which songs can be converted and stored—can be easily pirated or traded freely, as on services like Napster.

Mr. Jobs said the company had taken some steps to protect against piracy in its device. For instance, he said, songs loaded onto the iPod from a Macintosh computer, cannot then be loaded from the device to a different Macintosh computer, a step he said would make it difficult for people to distribute music they own to other users.

The Recording Industry Association of America, which represents the major record labels, declined to comment on the iPod.

Susan Kevorkian, a digital music industry analyst with IDC, praised the new iPod design, saying the combination of its ease of use, portability and big storage space would influence competitors. "This raises the bar," she said.

In 1942, the economist Joseph Schumpeter coined the term *creative destruction* to describe the never-ending dynamism of capitalism. He went on to define this process as one that "revolutionizes the economic structure *from within,* incessantly destroying the old one, incessantly creating a new one."[1] Few moments in the last fifty years have seen the gales of creative destruction move so fast and forcefully across the landscape as that ushered in by the financial crisis of 2008. Beginning in the United States, this crisis took the capital markets and the larger global banking system to the edge of collapse, ushering in a far-reaching economic downturn that was felt around the world.

As some of the dust from this extraordinary moment begins to settle, we can see that it has cleared away a range of old products, organizations, structures, perspectives, and behaviors. As this book is being published, consumers, investors, lenders, government actors, and business leaders from virtually every industry are scrambling to make sense of what has happened in the past year and of what this means for their respective paths ahead. Almost every individual and organization, from the poorest citizen to the wealthiest socialite, from Wal-Mart to Harvard University, have been touched by the powerful winds of change.

Widespread recessions are not new, of course. The United States, like most other industrial countries, has been buffeted by business cycles in different forms and to different degrees since the late eighteenth century. (The last thirty years, for example, have witnessed at least four recessions). What is distinct about this time, our time, is the breadth and magnitude of change—political, demographic, and technological—that is unfolding in and around large-scale economic shifts.

Politically, the election of Barack Hussein Obama as the forty-fourth president of the United States in late 2008 unleashed a current of collective idealism that washed across the planet. At the same time, the intensifying economic crisis created much larger roles for government intervention in global markets. This, in turn, realigned the balance of political power in many countries, including the United States.

Meanwhile, in companies, colleges, traditional villages, and elsewhere, a new cohort of young people born between 1978 and 1991 grew into adulthood. Many of these "Millenials" or "Generation Yers," saw themselves as citizens of the world, linked by a common destiny, shared challenges, and overlapping aspirations. One of the most important priorities of this vocal, active, and technologically accomplished cohort was to work for a company (or other organization) committed to positive social change.

At the same time, an older generation, the Baby Boomers, born between 1946 and 1964, struggled to define the next phase of their lives. For many, this meant dealing with the large—sometimes-crippling—losses to their retirement savings wrought by the financial crisis. These losses, in tandem with ever-increasing life spans (an average of seventy-eight years in the United States), promised to the keep the Boomers active in the workforce long past age sixty-five. This development, as well as the growing importance of Millenials, promised to reshape the workplace and institutional objectives of the early twenty-first century.

In the midst of economic, political, and demographic transition, the Information Revolution—begun some thirty years ago—accelerated and took a firm hold. All over the world, individuals and organizations worked to understand and use the wide-ranging power of the Internet. Much like the railroad did, more than 140 years ago, the Internet and the transmission technologies that fueled its growth and its impact began to transform markets, products, and companies—not to mention collective perspectives of distance and time—in lasting ways. From music shopping to trading stocks to the business of health care, just about every aspect of out lives was affected by breakthroughs in information technology.

Underlying the possibility and challenge of all this creative destruction were two larger systems: the global financial system and the Earth's environment. In the opportunity of this moment, would leaders from all walks of life and from organizations of all kinds find the direction, energy, consensus, and talent to build a stable, sustainable financial system and at the same time shepherd the earth's natural resources with an eye to sustainability and justice?

At the end of the first decade of a young century, these were pressing questions. The answers were critical to our collective future, and they were not certain. What *was* clear was that this was not the first time that men and women have confronted astounding, high-stakes change. The past 150 years of American history have encompassed other important inflection points. The end of the Civil War was one. The onset of the Great Depression was another. So, too, was the close of World War II. In each of these instances, American business has played a central role in moving the nation and, in some ways, the world, forward into the future. Understanding these stories offers vital perspective on our own hopeful, anxious, and, at times, exhausting moment. The past is where we came from. We cannot afford to ignore it.

TIMELINE

MAJOR EVENTS IN AMERICAN BUSINESS

This enhanced version of the timelines found throughout the book gives more detail about the key events surrounding the articles in each chapter.

Chapter 1
The Rise of Big Business

1802 French immigrant E. I. du Pont establishes a gunpowder mill in Delaware. By 1812, du Pont will operate the largest industrial enterprise in the United States.

1826 In New York City, Samuel Lord and George Washington Taylor found a dry-goods store. Their enterprise will evolve into the Lord & Taylor department store chain.

1837 William Procter and James Gamble found a consumer-goods company in Cincinnati.

1859 The Great American Tea Company, later renamed the Great Atlantic & Pacific Tea Company (A&P), is founded in New York by George F. Gilman. By 1903, the chain will number two hundred stores, selling groceries in addition to teas and spices. In 1930, A&P will operate more than fifteen thousand stores nationwide.

1871 Aaron Montgomery Ward founds a retail business in Chicago. The company's first mail-order catalogue will start circulation the next year.

1875 Gustavus Swift, founder of the meatpacking firm Swift & Co., opens a business in Chicago. In 1881, he will introduce a refrigerated railroad car capable of shipping dressed beef from Chicago to Boston.

1886 In Atlanta, Georgia, pharmacist John Stith Pemberton invents the stimulating but nonalcoholic Coca-Cola beverage.

1895 Salesman C. W. Post starts a cereal company. He will introduce Grape-Nuts two years later. In 1929, the company will be reorganized as General Foods.

1909 James L. Kraft, cheese merchant, incorporates the J. L. Kraft & Bros. Co. in Chicago. In 1916, he will patent a method for making processed cheese.

1917 The United States enters World War I.

1923 Following a bankruptcy in Kansas City, cartoonist Walt Disney moves to Hollywood. With his brother, Roy, he founds the Disney Brothers Studio.

1926 James O. McKinsey, formerly a professor of accounting at the University of Chicago, founds a management consulting firm.

1933 Franklin Delano Roosevelt is inaugurated and initiates a host of legislation to address the economic, social, and political consequences of the Great Depression.

1941 The United States enters World War II.

1950 In Quincy, Massachusetts, William Rosenberg opens the first Dunkin' Donuts.

Chapter 2
Wall Street: Its Origins, Influence, and Evolution

1791 Congress charters the First Bank of the United States.

1873 A financial panic follows the bankruptcy of Jay Cooke & Co., a private banking firm.

1882 Charles Dow, Edward Jones, and Charles Bergstresser found Dow, Jones & Company, delivering daily bulletins to Wall Street subscribers.

1893 Foreign investors begin to sell off American securities for gold, triggering the Panic of 1893.

1913 Congress passes the Federal Reserve Act, establishing the Federal Reserve System and creating the central bank of the United States.

1929 The stock market collapses on Tuesday, October 29, helping precipitate a worldwide depression.

1933 Congress, under Franklin Roosevelt's leadership, passes the Securities Act, which aims "to provide full and fair disclosure of the character of securities sold in interstate and foreign commerce and through the mails, and to prevent frauds in the sale thereof," and the Banking Act of 1933, known as Glass-Steagall, which separates commercial and investment banking. The next year, Congress passes the Securities Exchange Act, which creates the Securities and Exchange Commission (SEC).

1944 Representatives from forty-four nations attend a conference at Bretton Woods, New Hampshire, that becomes the basis for the International Monetary Fund and the International Bank for Reconstruction and Development (precursor to the World Bank). These institutions are intended to help stabilize the global economic system and prevent shocks as severe as the depression of the 1930s.

1956 The Dow Jones Industrial Average closes above 500 for the first time.

1967 Muriel Siebert becomes the first woman member of the NYSE.

1987 Junk-bond pioneer Michael Milken earns $550 million this year at the investment-banking firm Drexel Burnham Lambert.

2001 Terrorist attacks in New York City, Washington D.C., and Pennsylvania destroy the World Trade Center and part of the Pentagon.

2001 Energy firm Enron, at one time the seventh-largest company in the United States, collapses amid charges of financial and ethical abuse. In the following years, Enron founder Kenneth Lay and former chief executive Jeffrey Skilling will be found guilty of fraud. Former chief financial officer Andrew Fastow will plead guilty to two counts of wire and securities fraud.

2001 The dot-com stock market bubble bursts, ending a period of intense speculation in Internet-based firms. The Dow Jones Industrial Average, which had approached 12,000 the year before, falls to less than 9,000.

2008 A global financial crisis becomes a rapid, far-reaching economic downturn. Uncertainty in credit, product, and labor markets mounts as housing, equity, and other asset values decline.

Chapter 3
Merger Mania

1882 The Standard Oil Trust is formed.

1890 The American Tobacco Company is formed in a merger of five rival tobacco manufacturers.

1890 Congress passes the Sherman Antitrust Act, declaring "every contract, combination in the form of trust or otherwise, or conspiracy, in restraint of trade or commerce" to be illegal.

1901   Vice President Theodore Roosevelt, then forty-two, becomes the youngest president of the United States when William McKinley is assassinated, and remains in office until 1909. His domestic policies, called the "Square Deal," include strong moves toward antitrust regulation.

1901   J. P. Morgan engineers the acquisition of the Carnegie Steel Company, merging it with other smaller companies to create U.S. Steel, the world's first billion-dollar corporation. An unsuccessful antitrust legal suit is filed against the company in 1911.

1911   A Supreme Court decision breaks the Standard Oil Trust into thirty-four separate companies. The Court breaks up the American Tobacco Company the same year.

1914   The Federal Trade Commission is established to regulate the increasing power of big business. The same year, Congress passes the Clayton Act, which aims to thwart monopolies by banning price discriminations, mergers, stock acquisitions, and interlocking directorships between competing firms.

1960s   A wave of conglomerate mergers gathers momentum. The federal government concludes that such mergers can add efficiency and value to the marketplace and adapts its antitrust policy.

1973   The Organization of Petroleum Exporting Countries (OPEC) increases the price of oil, triggering a crisis in the financial markets, widespread inflation, and long waits at gasoline stations in the United States.

1984   The Bell System is broken up into a new AT&T, which retains the functions of telephone manufacturing, long-distance service, and R&D, and seven regional Bell operating companies.

1988   Kohlberg Kravis Roberts & Co. (KKR) engineers the takeover of conglomerate RJR Nabisco with a bid of $25 billion. At the time, it is the largest leveraged buyout in history.

2000   Internet firm AOL announces plans to merge with media giant Time Warner. The deal will be completed the following year.

Chapter 4
Leadership, Past and Present

1810   Sixteen-year-old Cornelius Vanderbilt purchases his own two-masted boat to begin a ferry business between New York City and Staten Island.

1848   John Jacob Astor, the wealthiest man in America, dies. Astor's fortune, built on international trade and real-estate investments, totals between $20 million and $30 million at the time of his death.

1870   John D. Rockefeller monopolizes his oil-refining and -distribution business as the Standard Oil Company. At the time, Standard Oil controlled more than 80 percent of the refining capacity in the United States.

1871   J. P. Morgan establishes Drexel, Morgan & Company on Wall Street in New York City and is soon earning over half a million dollars a year.

1906   Sarah Breedlove, who was born to slave parents and who takes the professional name Madam C.J. Walker, develops a hair product for African American women. The hair and cosmetics company she founds will make her a millionaire and provide employment to hundreds of other African American women.

1914   Henry Ford announces that workers for the Ford Motor Company will be paid $5 a day and have a shortened workday (down to eight hours from nine). The new wage more than doubles an average worker's salary.

1923   Alfred Sloan is named president of General Motors.

1954   Ray Kroc becomes the first franchise agent for a drive-in hamburger business in San Bernadino, California, founded by brothers Dick and Mac McDonald. Kroc opens the first franchise of the new McDonald's restaurant in Des Plaines, Illinois, the following year. He will buy out the McDonald brothers' stake in 1961 and quickly ramp up expansion, creating one of the world's largest food-service businesses.

1956   Returning to Nebraska after earning a master's in economics at Columbia University, Warren Buffett founds an investment firm called the Buffett Partnership. His skills will later earn him the moniker "the Oracle of Omaha." He will also later become the primary stockholder in milling and textile company Berkshire Hathway. By 1985, the enterprise is no longer in the textile business and has becomes an investment company.

1962   Sam Walton opens the first Wal-Mart discount store in Rogers, Arkansas. The same year, discount retailers Target and Kmart (a venture of the S.S. Kresge Corporation) open their first stores, in Roseville, Minnesota, and Garden City, Michigan, respectively.

1979   Andy Grove—born András Gróf, a Hungarian Jew who managed to evade Hitler as a boy and immigrated to the United States in 1967—becomes the president of Intel.

1980   Twenty-seven-year-old college dropout John Mackey merges a natural food store called SaferWay with Clarksville Natural Grocery and calls the new company Whole Foods Market.

1980   Ted Turner founds the Cable News Network. CNN is the first station to offer twenty-four-hour news coverage.

1987   Howard Shultz acquires a Seattle coffee company called Starbucks.

2003   Oprah Winfrey becomes the first African American woman to make the annual *Forbes* magazine list of billionaires.

2008   Steve Jobs takes a leave of absence from his CEO position at Apple, prompting debate about how the company—or any company whose brand relies strongly on association with a particular individual—will be able to weather his absence.

Chapter 5
From Farm to Factory

1793   Eli Whitney develops the cotton gin. U.S. cotton production increases from about 10,000 bales in this year to 126,000 ten years later. Much of this output is initially sent to Great Britain, where textile production is fast becoming an important industry.

1823   The Merrimack Manufacturing Company, a venture financed by Francis Cabot Lowell and other investors, begins textile production in a mill on the Merrimack River north of Boston, jump-starting what will become the Industrial Revolution in the United States. The company uses farm girls as factory operatives and provides them with education and housing in a highly structured, supervised environment.

1834   Virginia inventor Cyrus McCormick patents a horse-drawn mechanical reaper destined to have enormous impact on farm productivity.

1836   Massachusetts is the first state to pass a law restricting child labor.

1882   At Midvale Steel, engineer Frederick W. Taylor performs time studies. This work will help lay the foundation of scientific management: a tightly structured organization of labor, based on its division into precise parts, that aims to achieve greater efficiency.

1886   The American Federation of Labor (A.F. of L.) is founded in Columbus, Ohio.

1892   A confrontation between labor and management at the Homestead Works of Carnegie Steel in Pittsburgh turns violent; ten people are killed and several more are injured.

1905   Milton Hershey opens a plant in Hershey, Pennsylvania, for the mass production of milk chocolate candy. During the next decade, Hershey will build a town around his factory designed to provide workers with all the benefits of welfare capitalism.

1908   Henry Ford introduces the Model T car. During the next ten years, his assembly-line production of this automobile will be widely copied and will drive production costs down, creating an increasingly affordable mode of transportation and helping to popularize car ownership among the American middle class. By 1927, the company he founded will have manufactured 15 million Model T cars.

1910   A.F. of L. membership tops 1.5 million. By 1919, this number will climb to more than 3.2 million.

1933   As the Great Depression deepens, unemployment climbs to nearly 25 percent, or about 13 million people.

1936   In December, the United Auto Workers (UAW) and Committee for Industrial Organization (CIO) initiate a sit-down strike against General Motors in Flint, Michigan. The strike ends less than two months later, in February 1937, with GM agreeing to recognize the UAW as the sole bargaining unit for the corporation.

1964   The Civil Rights Act provides for the desegregation of public schools and prohibits discrimination in public places. It also bans discrimination by employers on the basis of "race, color, religion, sex, or national origin."

1974   Congress passes the Employee Retirement Income Security Act (ERISA), providing for the regulation of most pension and health funds established by private employers.

Chapter 6
The Fruits of Our Labor

1853   Levi Strauss, a dry-goods merchant born in Bavaria, sails to California. He plans to sell fabric and other supplies to gold rush prospectors there. In 1873, he and Jacob Davis, a tailor, patent a process for creating riveted work pants—the precursor to today's blue jeans.

1879   First demonstration of Thomas Edison's incandescent electric light bulb.

1899   Sociologist and economist Thorstein Veblen publishes *The Theory of the Leisure Class*, introducing the term *conspicuous consumption*.

1902   The first permanent movie theater opens in Los Angeles. The following year, Hollywood officially becomes an incorporated city.

1914   Russian immigrant Max Faktor (later Max Factor, thanks to officials at Ellis Island) creates makeup especially for film actors; soon both they and the public start wearing it off-screen as well.

1915   In Indiana, Alfred Mellowes invents an electric refrigerator. The company that produces his invention will be purchased by General Motors in 1918 and renamed Frigidaire.

1918   William and Ida Rosenthal move to Manhattan, where Ida will soon enter the dressmaking business with partner Enid Bissett. As flapper dresses become fashionable, Bissett and the Rosenthals develop a brassiere to help women dress comfortably. By 1922, they will register the name "Maiden Form."

1919   The Radio Corporation of America (RCA) is established following the end of World War I.

1927   While mowing rows of hay in Idaho in 1921, a fourteen-year-old Mormon farm boy comes up with the idea of an electronic beam scanning and reproducing an image. Six years later, Philo T. Farnsworth, now twenty, invents the television.

1949   Albert and Meyer Bernstein found Frozen Dinners, Inc., which produces prepackaged frozen meals with separate compartments for the different food groups (meat, vegetables, and potatoes). In 1954, trying to offload a huge inventory of unsold meat from Thanksgiving, poultry supplier C.A. Swanson & Sons creates a frozen and compartmentalized meal of turkey, peas, and potatoes, and launches the "TV Dinner."

1958   American Express offers its first credit card. The same year, Bank of America launches BankAmericard (later renamed Visa). Master Charge, later called MasterCard, follows in 1967.

1960   The U.S. Food and Drug Administration approves Envoid, the first (and 100 percent effective) birth control pill. However, subsequent research concludes that the dose is ten times higher than necessary. The lower-dose birth control pills hit the market in the 1980s.

1981   IBM launches its first personal computers (PCs). Apple starts work on what will become its Macintosh computer the same year.

1997   New home sales pass 800,000 for the first time in ten years; the Dow tops 7,000 points for the first time.

2006   Sales for private jets hit an all-time high of $9 billion. The average starting price for a private jet ranges from $3 million for a small carrier to $17 million for a large jet.

2008   The gravely overleveraged housing market collapses, pulling the similarly overleveraged stock market (and a lot of pension funds) down with it. A global credit crisis ensues that gives way to a broader global recession.

Chapter 7
The Changing Workplace

1844   The female factory operatives at Massachusetts' Lowell Mill form the Lowell Female Labor Reform Association (LFLRA) to seek improved working conditions and compensation—the first organization of professional working women in the United States.

1870   The Fifteenth Amendment prohibits restrictions on voting based on "race, color, or previous condition of servitude."

1906   Upton Sinclair publishes *The Jungle*, detailing gruesome conditions in the Chicago meatpacking industry. Congress passes the Pure Food and Drug Act and the Meat Inspection Act the same year.

1920   The Nineteenth Amendment grants equal voting rights to women.

1942   The United States enters World War II after the December 1941 bombing of Pearl Harbor.

1943   "Rosie the Riveter," a fictional woman meant to personify the surge of female workers during World War II, appears on the cover of the *Saturday Evening Post* in the form of the now-iconic image by Norman Rockwell. At the beginning of the war, 12 million women comprised 25 percent of the workforce; by the end, 18 million women comprise one-third of the workforce.

1944   Union membership rises to 14,146,000, up from 8,717,000 members in 1940.

1946   The Employment Act of 1946 sets forth a policy of promoting "maximum employment, production, and purchasing power."

1956   White-collar workers become the majority of the workforce for the first time, as the number of service jobs surpasses those involved in producing goods.

1973 The Health Maintenance Organization (HMO) Act provides $375 million for the development of managed health care.

1975 In June, the unemployment rate reaches 9.2 percent, the highest in thirty-three years.

2007 Higher education becomes increasingly important as a qualification for work. In this year, nearly 29 percent of Americans over age twenty-five have completed four years of college, up from about 20 percent in 1987, 10 percent in 1967, and 5 percent in 1947.

2001 According to one estimate, the ratio of average pay between a CEO and an average production (that is, nonmanagement) worker is 525:1. In 1982, this ratio was calculated as 42:1.

2009 Unemployment across the United States rises to 9.5 percent as a recession takes hold. The jobless number more than 14.7 million. Hardest hit are those without college degrees. More than three-quarters of job losses are among men, stirring speculation about whether women will soon became the majority of the workforce.

Chapter 8
The Transportation Revolution

1817 The New York State Legislature approves plans to finance the Erie Canal, which is to cost $7 million and run 363 miles from Buffalo on Lake Erie to Albany on the Hudson River. Construction will begin one year later.

1862 President Abraham Lincoln authorizes the building of the transcontinental railroad by signing the Pacific Railway Act.

1869 The transcontinental railroad, connecting the Central Pacific and Union Pacific railroads, is completed as the last rail is secured by the famous "Golden Spike," driven in at Promontory, Utah, on May 10. The project connects 1,776 miles of railroad across the country.

1881 Financial speculator Jay Gould controls the largest network of railroads in the nation.

1887 Congress passes the Interstate Commerce Act, providing for federal regulation of the railroads. The act also establishes an enforcement agency, the Interstate Commerce Commission.

1903 Orville and Wilbur Wright conduct the first successful airplane flight at Kitty Hawk, North Carolina.

1908 Henry Ford introduces the Model T for $950. By 1927, his company's mass-production techniques will be capable of manufacturing a Model T in twenty-four seconds.

1916 The Federal Aid Road Act establishes state highway departments.

1927 Charles Lindbergh takes off from Long Island, New York, and lands 33½ hours later in Paris, completing the first solo nonstop flight across the Atlantic Ocean.

1944 Lockheed Aircraft employs 93,000 people, up from about 2,500 before the outbreak of World War II. Wartime production of aircraft and engines will lay the foundations for the modern airline industry.

1956 Congress passes the Federal-Aid Highway Act, providing for the creation of a national interstate highway system.

1958 In the United States, airlines carry more passengers than railroads or buses for the first time.

1968 A Japanese car company called Toyota introduces the first generation of a new car: the Corolla. The Corolla goes on to be one of the best-selling cars in the world.

1971 A small new airline company from Texas begins flying between San Antonio, Houston, and Dallas. It calls itself, appropriately, Southwest Airlines.

Chapter 9
Communications

1844 Samuel Morse sends the first electric telegraph message from Washington, D.C., to Baltimore, Maryland: "WHAT HATH GOD WROUGHT."

1876 Alexander Graham Bell files a patent for the telephone.

1896 First commercial motion picture is exhibited in the United States.

1922 RCA (Radio Corporation of America) advertises personal radios, proclaiming, "Radio Enters the Home."

1934 Established as part of the Communications Act of 1934, the Federal Communications Commission (FCC) is charged with regulating non-federal government use of radio and interstate communications. Within a year, two-thirds of American homes have radio sets and can listen to twenty-four different AM channels (four national, twenty regional) twenty-four hours a day.

1939 In California, engineers William Hewlett and David Packard start a business in Packard's garage. Their first product is an audio oscillator, a device that generates pure frequencies and is used to produce machines such as telephones and radios.

1946 The Electronic Numerical Integrator and Computer (ENIAC), one of the world's first digital computers, is unveiled at the University of Pennsylvania.

1941 NBC broadcasts the first television advertisement.

1954 RCA begins mass production of color televisions.

1971 Marcian E. "Ted" Hoff invents the microprocessor, a silicon chip that acts as a central processing unit for electronic calculators, computers, and other machines.

1974 Using the 8080 Intel microprocessor, Ed Roberts develops the first personal computer (PC), which he dubs the Altair.

1977 Steve Wozniak, Steve Jobs, and Mike Markkula introduce the Apple II, a user-friendly PC that quickly enjoys widespread popularity.

1981 IBM launches its first PC. It licenses the operating system from a young Seattle company called Microsoft, founded by a Harvard dropout named Bill Gates and his partner, a Washington State University dropout named Paul Allen.

1992 The World Wide Web is introduced, and Internet use explodes in popularity.

2005 College dropout Mark Zuckerberg changes the name of the social networking application he created while at Harvard from "thefacebook" to "Facebook." By 2009, it is the second-largest social networking site on the Internet.

2007 An estimated 80 percent of adults report that they use the Internet.

Introduction

1. Theodore Dreiser, *A Book About Myself* (New York: Boni and Liverright, 1922), 20.

Chapter One

1. Richard S. Tedlow, *The Rise of the American Business Corporation*, from the series *Fundamentals of Pure and Applied Economics*, eds. P. David and M. Lévy-Leboyer (Chur, Switzerland: Harwood Academic Publishers, 1991), 12.

2. Thomas McCraw, "American Capitalism," in *Creating Modern Capitalism: How Entrepreneurs, Companies, and Countries Triumphed in Three Industrial Revolutions,* ed. Thomas McCraw (Cambridge, MA: Harvard University Press, 1997), 321.

3. McCraw, "American Capitalism," 321.

4. Tedlow, *Rise of the American Business Corporation*, 13–24.

5. Alfred D. Chandler, Jr., "The Standard Oil Company—Combination, Consolidation, and Integration," in *Management Past and Present,* eds. Alfred D. Chandler, Jr., Thomas K. McCraw, and Richard S. Tedlow (Cincinnati, OH: South-Western College Publishing, 2000), 3–51.

6. Tedlow, *Rise of the American Business Corporation*, 39–41.

7. Evans Clark, "Big Business Now Sweeps Retail Trade," *The New York Times*, July 8, 1928, 109.

8. For grocery chain statistics, see Clark, "Big Business," 109.

9. Thomas McCraw, *American Business, 1920–2000: How It Worked* (Wheeling, IL: Harlan Davidson, 2000), 13–14.

10. The Ford Runabout Model T was advertised in *The Youth's Companion* and *American Boy* in May and June in 1924 for the price of $265, with "demountable rims and starter $85 extra." The Henry Ford Museum, "Advertising," http://www.the henryford.org/exhibits/showroom/1908/ads.html.

11. Tedlow, *Rise of the American Business Corporation*, 57.

12. Ibid., 60.

13. The Sherman Antitrust Act, July 2, 1890 (*U.S. Statutes at Large*, Vol. XXVI, 209), excerpted in Thomas K. McCraw, "Antitrust: Perceptions and Reality in Coping with Big Business," in *Management Past and Present* (see note 5), 5–12.

14. McCraw, *American Business*, 93–94.

15. Procter & Gamble built its first international manufacturing site in Canada in 1915 and acquired its first overseas subsidiary, in England, in 1930. The company sold two hundred branded items around the world by the 1930s. See McCraw, *American Business*, 44, and Procter & Gamble, "Our History," http://www.pg.com/company/who_we_are/ourhistory_2.jhtml;jsessionid= DJXOKXEDF2AHBQFIAJ1XKYWAVABIIM3MK

16. Alfred D. Chandler, Jr., "Rise and Evolution of Big Business," in *Encyclopedia of American Economic History*, vol. 2, ed. Glenn Porter (New York: Charles Scribner's Sons, 1980), 636.

17. McCraw, "American Capitalism," 323.

18. IBM, *2006 Annual Report*, http://www.ibm.com/annualreport.

Chapter Two

1. Walter Werner and Steven T. Smith, *Wall Street* (New York: Columbia University Press, 1991), 12–14.

2. Charles R. Geisst, *Wall Street: A History* (New York: Oxford University Press, 1997), 11. See also Robert Sobel, "Exchanges," in *Encyclopedia of American Economic History*, vol. 2, ed. Glenn Porter (New York: Charles Scribner's Sons, 1980), 696.

3. Geisst, *Wall Street*, 10.

4. Ibid., 10.

5. Ibid., 10. See also Sobel, "Exchanges," 697.

6. Werner and Smith, *Wall Street*, 17; and Geisst, *Wall Street*, 13.

7. Geisst, *Wall Street*, 13.

8. Sobel, "Exchanges," 697.

9. Ibid., 697.

10. Geisst, *Wall Street*, 14.

11. Werner and Smith, *Wall Street*, 133–135. See also Geisst, *Wall Street*, 35.

12. Charles Morris, *The Tycoons* (New York: Times Books, 2005), 61. See also Alfred D. Chandler, Jr., "Jay Gould and the Coming of Railroad Consolidation," in *Management Past and Present*, eds. Alfred D. Chandler, Jr., Thomas K. McCraw, and Richard S. Tedlow (Cincinnati: South-Western College Publishing, 2000), 2-38–2-42.

13. Geisst, *Wall Street*, 60–61, and Morris, *Tycoons*, 74.

14. Morris, *Tycoons*, 246–248. Greenbacks were the first printed currency issued by the U.S. Department of the Treasury. U.S. Treasury, "Duties and Functions: Bureau of Engraving and Printing," http://www.ustreas.gov/education/duties/bureaus/engraving-printing.shtml.

15. Geisst, *Wall Street*, 119.

16. Ibid., 134.

17. Ibid., 127.

18. Ibid., 187–189.

19. John M. Blum, William S. McFeely, Edmund S. Morgan, Arthur M. Schlesinger, Jr., Kenneth M. Stampp, and C. Vann Woodward, *The National Experience: A History of the United States Since 1865*, vol. 2 (San Diego: Harcourt Brace Jovanovich, 1989), 602.

20. Sobel, "Exchanges," 703.

21. Thomas K. McCraw, *American Business, 1920–2000: How It Worked* (Wheeling, IL: Harlan Davidson, 2000), 70.

22. Geisst, *Wall Street*, 229–234.

23. Ibid., 234.

24. Ibid., 703.

25. Sobel, "Exchanges," 703.

26. Harley Shaiken, "Unions, the Economy, and Employee Free Choice," Agenda for Shared Prosperity, Economic Policy Institute, http://www.shared prosperity.org/bp181.html. In the postwar period, as many as one in three workers belonged to a union. See also Geisst, *Wall Street*, 274, 290.

27. Geisst, *Wall Street*, 290. During the 1950s, the mutual fund sector grew by a factor of 10.

28. Sobel, "Exchanges," 703.

29. Geisst, *Wall Street*, 316.

30. McCraw, *American Business*, 35.

31. Ibid., 35.

32. Investment Company Institute, "2005 Facts at a Glance," http://www.icifactbook.org/06_fb_facts.html.

33. McCraw, *American Business*, 31–32. The amount of money available to fund managers soon exceeded the amount that could be invested in low-risk investment-grade bonds, a condition that helped lead to the popularity of junk bonds later in the decade.

34. Peter Waldman and George Anders, "KKR Completes Buy-Out of RJR Without Fanfare—Sound of No Corks Popping Greets History's Largest Corporate Acquisition," *The Wall Street Journal*, February 10, 1989, http://global.factiva.com/ha/default.aspx.

35. Nancy F. Koehn and Rowena Olegario, "Michael Milken," in *Management Past and Present* (see note 12), 6–33.

36. Ibid.

37. McCraw, *American Business*, 36.

38. Ibid., 36.

39. Ibid., 37.

40. In 2002, in response to corporate governance and accounting scandals such as Enron's, Congress passed the Sarbanes-Oxley Act. The law established the first federal board to oversee the accounting industry.

Chapter Three

1. Leslie Hannah, "Mergers," *Encyclopedia of American Economic History*, vol. 2, ed. Glenn Porter (New York: Charles Scribner's Sons, 1980), 639.

2. Ibid., 642.

3. Ibid., 646.

4. Ibid.

5. Simon J. Evenett, "The Cross Border Mergers and Acquisitions Wave of the Late 1990s," working paper 9655, National Bureau of Economic Research, April 2003; Christopher Farrell, "Is Today's Merger Wave Sweeping Away Good Sense?" *BusinessWeek*, January 21, 2000; Devra L. Golbe and Lawrence J. White, "Catch a Wave: The Time Series Behavior of Mergers," *Review of Economics and Statistics* 75, no. 3 (1993): 493; Hannah, "Mergers," 639.

6. Alfred D. Chandler, Jr., "Rise and Evolution of Big Business," in *Encyclopedia of American Economic History* (see note 1), 619.

7. Thomas McCraw, *American Business, 1920–2000: How It Worked* (Wheeling, IL: Harlan Davidson, 2000), 42.

8. Hannah, "Mergers," 641.

9. Chandler, "Rise and Evolution of Big Business," 620.

10. Charles Morris, *The Tycoons* (New York: Henry Holt and Company, 2005), 60–78, 141–150.

11. Alfred D. Chandler, Jr., "The Standard Oil Company—Combination, Consolidation, and Integration," in *Management Past and Present,* eds. Alfred D. Chandler, Jr., Thomas K. McCraw, and Richard S. Tedlow (Cincinnati, OH: Southwestern College Publishing, 2000), 3–51.

12. Morris, *Tycoons*, 193. See also Hannah, "Mergers," 641, and Chandler, "The Standard Oil Company."

13. Morris, *Tycoons*, 252. See also Hannah, "Mergers," 642.

14. Morris, *Tycoons*, 253.

15. Hannah, "Mergers," 641.

16. Morris, *Tycoons*, 256–262. In today's dollars, Morgan paid about $11 billion for Carnegie Company.

17. Morris, *Tycoons*, 265.

18. Hannah, "Mergers," 641. Although business consolidation concentrated economic power, it often divided ownership among shareholders so that fewer large firms were controlled by families or founders, and more were run by professional managers. Management skills became more standardized and transferable across various industries, and professional associations, journals, and graduate schools of business grew up to serve a growing managerial class (see Chandler, "Rise and Evolution of Big Business," 643–647).

19. George David Smith and Richard Sylla, "Capital Markets," in *Encyclopedia of the United States in the Twentieth Century*, ed. Stanley I. Kutler (New York: Charles Scribner's Sons, 1995), 1219.

20. U.S. Department of Justice, "Antitrust Enforcement and the Consumer," http://www.usdoj.gov/atr/public/div_stats/211491.htm.

21. Hannah, "Mergers," 644. See also Naomi R. Lamoreaux, "Mergers in Manufacturing and Mining—Entities, Capitalization, and Type: 1895–1930," Table Ch416-421 in *Historical Statistics of the United States Millennial Edition Online,* eds. Susan B. Carter, Scott Sigmund Gartner, Michael R. Haines, Alan L. Olmstead, Richard Sutch, and Gavin Wright (Cambridge: Cambridge University Press, 2006).

22. Hannah, "Mergers," 644.

23. Ibid., 645.

24. Chandler, "Rise and Evolution of Big Business," 634, and Hannah, "Mergers," 645.

25. National Labor Relations Board, "National Industrial Recovery Act," in *The First Sixty Years: The Story of the National Labor Relations Board 1935–1995* (Washington, DC: American Bar Association, 1995), 5, http://www.nlrb.gov/nlrb/shared_files/brochures/60yrs_05-08.pdf.

26. McCraw, *American Business*, 129. At that time, AT&T controlled a greater amount of wealth than twenty U.S. states combined (Adolph Berle and Gardiner Means, *The Modern Corporation and Private Property*, quoted in Charles R. Geisst, *Wall Street: A History* [New York: Oxford University Press, 1997], 257).

27. Federal Aviation Administration, "History," http://www.faa.gov/about/history/brief_history/.

28. Hannah, "Mergers," 646.

29. C. Eis, "The 1919–1930 Merger Movement in American Industry," 294, quoted in Hannah, "Mergers," 646.

30. Ibid.

31. Hannah, "Mergers," 647.

32. Chandler, "Rise and Evolution of Big Business," 636.

33. Ibid.

34. Geisst, *Wall Street*, 284.

35. R. Hewitt Pate, "Antitrust Law in the U.S. Supreme Court" (address presented at British Institute of International and Comparative Law Conference, London, England, May 11, 2004), http://www.usdoj.gov/atr/public/speeches/204136.htm.

36. Geisst, *Wall Street*, 287. See also the Clorox Company, "Company History," http://www.theclorox company.com/company/history/history3.html.

37. Geisst, *Wall Street*, 286.

38. Ibid., 304.

39. Consumer Price Index calculator, Federal Reserve Bank of Minneapolis, http://minneapolisfed. org/research/data/us/calc/. See also Thomas B. Leary, "The Essential Stability of Merger Policy in the United States" (address presented at the Joint U.S./E.U. Conference, Guidelines for Merger Remedies: Prospects and Principles, Berkeley, CA, January 17, 2002), http://www.ftc.gov/speeches/leary/learyuseu.shtm. In current dollars, the value was $43.6 billion in 1968 and $11.8 billion in 1975.

40. Smith and Sylla, "Capital Markets," 1235.

41. Consumer Price Index calculator, Federal Reserve Bank of Minneapolis. See also Leary, "Essential Stability of Merger Policy in the United States." In current dollars, the value was $246.90 billion.

42. Smith and Sylla, "Capital Markets," 1236.

43. Consumer Price Index calculator, Federal Reserve Bank of Minneapolis. See also Leary, "Essential Stability of Merger Policy in the United States." The real value of mergers in 1980 was $110 billion.

44. Louis Uchitelle, "Uneasy Pieces in an Era of Mergers; Who's Afraid Now That Big Is No Longer Bad?" *The New York Times*, November 5, 2000.

45. Evenett, "Cross Border Mergers and Acquisitions Wave of the Late 1990s," 4.

46. Uchitelle, "Uneasy Pieces."

47. Ibid. See also Steve Lohr, "Technology; Court Lets Settlement Stand In Microsoft Antitrust Case," *The New York Times*, July 1, 2004.

48. Leary, "Essential Stability of Merger Policy in the United States."

49. Conrad De Aenlle, "Market Values; If It's a Merger, 2nd Thoughts Should Follow," *The New York Times*, April 14, 2007.

50. Tom Sullivan, "Current Yield: Mergers: The New Reign of Terror," *Barron's*, November 27, 2006.

51. Rik Kirkland, "Private Money," *Fortune*, March 5, 2007.

52. Emily Thornton, with Dean Foust, Gail Edmondson, and Tom Lowry, "Unsolicited Aggression: A Barrage of Hostile Bidding, Fueled by Mountains of Cash, Is Sweeping the Globe," *BusinessWeek*, December 25, 2006.

Chapter Four

1. Howard H. Stevenson, "A Perspective on Entrepreneurship," in *New Business Ventures and the Entrepreneur*, eds. H. H. Stevenson, Michael J. Roberts, and H. Irving Grousbeck (Homewood, IL: Richard D. Irwin, 1985), 2–15. See also William A. Sahlman, Howard H. Stevenson, Michael J. Roberts, and Amar Bhidé, eds., *The Entrepreneurial Venture* (Boston: Harvard Business School Press, 1999), 1.

2. See Anthony Mayo and Nitin Nohria, *In Their Time: The Greatest Business Leaders of the Twentieth Century* (Boston: Harvard Business School Press, 2005), xxi–xxv.

3. On management, see Mayo and Nohria, *In Their Time*, xxiii–xxiv.

4. Charles R. Morris, *The Tycoons* (New York: Times Books, 2005), 15, 262. Price indices are from the Federal Reserve Bank of Minneapolis, http://www.minneapolisfed.org/research/data/us/calc/ hist1800.cfm, and U.S. Department of Commerce, *Historical Statistics of the United States: Colonial Times to 1970*, vol. 1 (Washington, DC: U.S. Government Printing Office, 1976), 211, 199.

5. For the relative size of Rockefeller's wealth, see Louis Uchitelle, "Age of Riches: The Richest of the Rich, Proud of a New Gilded Age," *The New York Times*, July 15, 2007.

6. Nancy F. Koehn, "Estée Lauder: Self-Definition and the Modern Cosmetics Market," in *Beauty and Business: Commerce, Gender, and Culture in Modern America*, ed. Philip Scranton (New York: Routledge, 2001), 237.

7. Nancy F. Koehn, *Brand New* (Boston: Harvard Business School Press, 2001), 45–92.

8. Nancy F. Koehn and Erica Helms, "Candy Land: The Utopian Vision of Milton Hershey," Case 805-066 (Boston: Harvard Business School, 2005), 4.

9. Ibid., 9–10.

10. Price indices are from the Federal Reserve Bank of Minneapolis, http://www.minneapolisfed.org/research/data/us/calc/hist1800.cfm, and U.S. Department of Commerce, *Historical Statistics of the United States: Colonial Times to 1970*, vol. 1 (Washington, DC: U.S. Government Printing Office, 1976), 211.

11. Koehn and Helms, "Candy Land," 17, 27. See also Hershey Entertainment & Resorts, "Hersheypark History," http://www.hersheypa.com/town_of_hershey/history/hersheypark.html.

12. H. W. Brands, "Sweating Burgers," in *Masters of Enterprise* (New York: The Free Press, 1999), 211–222.

13. Thomas K. McCraw, *American Business, 1920–2000: How It Worked* (Wheeling, IL: Harlan Davidson, 2000), 169, 186.

14. Ibid., 186.

15. Matt Kranz, "Ousting CEOs Often Boosts Stock Price," *USA Today*, February 10, 2005, http://www.usatoday.com/money/companies/management/2005-02-10-departing-ceos-usat_x.htm.

Chapter Five

1. On real wage trends, see Robert A. Margo, "Wages and Wage Inequality," in *Historical Statistics of the United States, Millennial Edition Online*, eds. Susan B. Carter, Scott Sigmund Gartner, Michael R. Haines, Alan L. Olmstead, Richard Sutch, and Gavin Wright (Cambridge: Cambridge University Press, 2006), 2-40–2-46. On working hours, see William A. Sundstrom, "Hours and Working Conditions," Figure Ba-P in *Historical Statistics of the United States*, 2-46–2-54.

2. Susan B. Carter, "Labor," in *Historical Statistics of the United States* (see note 1), 2-5–2-10.

3. Ibid., 2-10.

4. Ibid., 2-10.

5. See the arguments of Robert Steinfeld and Peter Way, quoted in Carter, "Labor," 2-11.

6. Susan B. Carter, "Labor Force," in *Historical Statistics of the United States* (see note 1), 2-18–2-19. See also Clarence H. Danhof, "Agriculture in the North and West," in *Encyclopedia of American Economic History*, vol. 1, ed. Glenn Porter (New York: Charles Scribner's Sons, 1980), 364–365.

7. Richard A. Easterlin, "Population," in *Encyclopedia of American Economic History* (see note 6), 170.

8. Forty-nine percent lived in rural areas in 1920. Easterlin, "Population," 170.

9. Carter, "Labor Force," 2-19.

10. Carter, "Labor," 2-11. "Stanley Lebergott estimates that as late as 1900, hired labor accounted for only a little more than half (55.4 percent) of the labor force (calculated from series Ba470, Ba910, and Ba918). The continuing importance of owner-operated farms and small retail and service establishments limited the extent of hired labor economy wide."

11. Charles R. Morris, *The Tycoons* (New York: Times Books, 2005), 299–300.

12. House Special Committee to Investigate the Taylor and Other Systems of Shop Management, *Congressional Testimony on Taylor's Scientific Management*, vol. 3 of *Hearings* (Washington, DC: Government Printing Office, 1912), 1386–1389, quoted in *Management Past and Present*, eds. Alfred D. Chandler, Jr., Thomas K. McCraw, and Richard S. Tedlow (Cincinnati, OH: South-Western College Publishing, 2000), 4-61.

13. Morris, *Tycoons*, 305–318.

14. Jack Beatty, *Colossus: How the Corporation Changed America* (New York: Broadway Books, 2001), 206–208.

15. Joshua L. Rosenbloom, "Labor Unions," in *Historical Statistics of the United States* (see note 1), 2-56.

16. Kheel Center for Labor-Management Documentation and Archives, Cornell University/ILR, "The Triangle Factory Fire," http://www.ilr.cornell.edu/trianglefire/narrative1.html.

17. "The Labor Movement Between the Wars," in *Management Past and Present* (see note 12), 4-78. Parts of this case were written by the following individuals: Professor George C. Lodge, Research Associate Audrey C. Sproat under the direction of Professor Bruce R. Scott, and Professor Richard S. Tedlow.

18. Ibid.

19. T. H. Watkins, *The Great Depression* (Boston: Little, Brown and Company, 1993), 60–61.

20. Ibid., 80.

21. "The Labor Movement Between the Wars," 4-81.

22. The Wagner Act of 1935, http://www.civics online.org/library/formatted/texts/wagner_act.html.

23. Rosenbloom, "Labor Unions," 2-56.

24. Matthew Sobek, "Occupations" and Table Ba1033-1046, in *Historical Statistics of the United States* (see note 1), 2-38.

25. Ibid., 2-38.

26. Carter, "Labor," 2-11.

27. Sundstrom, "Hours and Working Conditions," 2-48.

28. Carter, "Labor Force," 2-21. See also Wex, The Legal Information Institute and Cornell Law School, "Workers Compensation," http://www.law.cornell.edu/wex/index.php/Workers_compensation.

29. Carter, "Labor Force," 2-29.

30. Ibid., 2-26.

31. "Civil Rights Act of 1964," 88th Congress, H. R. 7152, http://usinfo.state.gov/usa/infousa/laws/majorlaw/civilr19.htm.

32. U.S. Bureau of the Census, "Table 672. Money Income of Households—Median Income in Current and Constant (2004)," http://www.census.gov/compendia/statab/income_expenditures_wealth/household_income/.

33. U.S. Bureau of the Census, "Table 602. Employed Civilians, by Occupation, Sex, Race, and Hispanic Origin, 2005," http://www.census.gov/compendia/statab/labor_force_employment_earnings/employed_persons/.

34. Carter, "Labor Force," 2-22.

35. Ibid.

36. U.S. Bureau of the Census, "Table 679. Money Income of Families—Distribution by Family Characteristics and Income Level: 2003," http://www.census.gov/hhes/income/histinc/hstchg.html.

37. Ibid.

Chapter Six

1. Federal Reserve Statistical Release, "Consumer Credit, July 2007," September 10, 2007, http://federalreserve.gov/releases/g19/20070910/.

2. Lawrence B. Glickman, "Born to Shop? Consumer History and American History," in *Consumer Society in American History: A Reader*, ed. Lawrence B. Glickman (Ithaca: Cornell University Press, 1999).

3. Susan J. Matt, *Keeping Up with the Joneses: Envy in American Consumer Society, 1890–1930* (Philadelphia: University of Pennsylvania Press, 2003), 18.

4. Thomas K. McCraw, "Henry Ford, Alfred Sloan, and the Three Phases of Marketing," in *Creating Modern Capitalism: How Entrepreneurs, Companies, and Countries Triumphed in Three Industrial Revolutions* (Cambridge, MA: Harvard University Press, 1997), 266–302. Illustration courtesy of General Motors Corporation/Historical Collections, Baker Library, Harvard Business School.

5. Nancy F. Koehn, *Brand New* (Boston: Harvard Business School Press, 2001), 93.

6. Ibid., 4–5.

7. The John W. Hartman Center for Sales, Advertising, and Marketing History, Duke University Libraries, "J. Walter Thompson Company (JWT) History," http://library.duke.edu/specialcollections/hartman/guides/jwt-history.html.

8. Daniel M. G. Raff, "Table De482-515. Advertising Expenditures, by Medium: 1867–1998," in *Historical Statistics of the United States, Millennial Edition Online*, eds. Susan B. Carter, Scott Sigmund Gartner, Michael R. Haines, Alan L. Olmstead, Richard Sutch, and Gavin Wright (Cambridge: Cambridge University Press, 2006).

9. U.S. Department of Commerce, *Historical Statistics of the United States, Colonial Times to 1970*, vol. 1 (Washington, DC: U.S. Government Printing Office, 1976), 224; U.S. Bureau of Labor Statistics, Inflation Calculator, http://146.142.4.24/cgi-bin/cpicalc.pl.

10. Matt, *Keeping Up with the Joneses*, 77–78.

11. Ibid., 45.

12. Martha L. Olney, *Buy Now Pay Later: Advertising, Credit, and Consumer Durables in the 1920s* (Chapel Hill, NC: The University of North Carolina Press, 1991), 3, 6–8.

13. Matt, *Keeping Up with the Joneses,* 26–29.

14. Dana Thomas, *Deluxe: How Luxury Lost Its Luster* (New York: Penguin Press, 2007).

15. Matt, *Keeping Up with the Joneses,* 34–35.

16. Thorstein Veblen, "Conspicuous Consumption," 68–101, from *The Theory of the Leisure Class* by Thorstein Veblen (New York: Dutton Signet, 1953), reprinted in *The Consumer Society Reader*, eds. Juliet B. Schor and Douglas B. Holt (New York: The New Press, 2000), 195.

17. Koehn, *Brand New*, 93–97, 114–129.

18. Glickman, "Born to Shop?" 12. See also Rachel Bowlby, quoted in John Fiske, "Shopping for Pleasure: Malls, Power, and Resistance," in *The Consumer Society Reader* (see note 16), 313.

19. See Kathy Peiss, *Hope in a Jar: The Making of America's Beauty Culture* (New York: Metropolitan Books, 1998).

20. Thomas K. McCraw, *American Business 1920–2000: How It Worked* (Wheeling, IL: Harlan Davidson, 2000) 47, 52–53.

21. Matt, *Keeping Up with the Joneses,* 41.

22. Ibid., 44–45.

23. Thomas Weiss, "Table Dh298-308. Personal Consumption Expenditures for Recreational Goods: 1909–1963" and "Table Dh309-318. Personal Consumption Expenditures for Recreational Services, 1909–1963," in *Historical Statistics of the United States, Millennial Edition Online* (*see* note 8), 4-1107–4-1108.

24. Ibid., 4-1108.

25. McCraw, *American Business*, 41.

26. Koehn, *Brand New*, 167.

27. The percentage of income consumers spent on food, alcohol, and tobacco dropped from about 45 percent in 1900 to less than 30 percent in 1960. Lee A. Craig, "Figure Cd-A. Consumption Expenditures on Food, Alcohol, and Tobacco—Per Capita and as a Percentage of Total Expenditures: 1900–1999," in *Historical Statistics of the United States, Millennial Edition Online* (see note 8).

28. Glickman, "Born to Shop?" 5.

29. McCraw, *American Business*, 111.

30. "According to a study [in 2006] by the Kaiser Family Foundation and Hewitt Associates, healthcare premiums have jumped 87% since 2000." Bob Tedeschi, "Other Reasons Borrowers Falter," *The New York Times*, May 6, 2007.

31. Thomas A. Durkin, "Consumers and Credit Disclosures: Credit Cards and Credit Insurance," *Federal Reserve Bulletin*, April 2002, 2.

32. The Federal Reserve Board, "Report to the Congress on the Profitability of Credit Card Operations of Depository Institutions," July 2007, http://www.federalreserve.gov/boarddocs/rptcongress/creditcard/2007/default.htm.

33. "Credit Card Buyer Beware," *The New York Times*, July 31, 2007. See also Cate Terwilliger, "Halting the Drop into Debt," *Denver Post*, July 23, 2000.

34. James Twitchell, "Two Cheers for Materialism," in *The Consumer Society Reader* (see note 16), 283–284.

35. Glickman, "Born to Shop?" 3.

Chapter Seven

1. Louis Uchitelle, *The Disposable American* (New York: Alfred A. Knopf, 2006), 29.

2. Ibid., 30.

3. T. H. Watkins, *The Great Depression* (Boston: Little, Brown and Company, 1993), 144–145, 148.

4. Thomas K. McCraw, *American Business, 1920–2000: How It Worked* (Wheeling, IL: Harlan Davidson, 2000), 89.

5. "Paint Field Faces Supply Problems: Key Material Shortages Face Producers, Who Look for

Record Demands," *The New York Times*, December 10, 1945; "Furniture Output to Show 50% Rise: Forecast for Case Goods is Based on Gradual Easing of Industry Bottlenecks," *The New York Times*, January 15, 1946; Herbert Koshetz, "Full Nylon Output is Seen Year Away: Artcraft Hosiery Head Holds Inability to Get Machines Is Largely to Blame," *The New York Times*, February 24, 1946; Jacob Deschin, "Supplies: More Materials Are Now Coming on the Markct," *The New York Times*, September 22, 1946; "Acute Shortage In Soap Reported: Lack of Fats and Oils Blamed— Women Who Ignore Salvage Called 'Free Riders,'" *The New York Times*, September 28, 1946; "Scarcity of Steel, Iron Blamed For Appliance Output Slowdown: Parsons Tells Manufacturers' Group Housing Priorities Also Are Factor—Sees No Relief Until Middle of 1947," *The New York Times*, October 29, 1946; "Electrical Units Much in Demand: Needs of Consumers for Items from Radios to Sinks Far Exceeds the Supply," *The New York Times*, January 4, 1947.

6. Uchitelle, *Disposable American,* 36–37.

7. Ibid., 46–47.

8. Ibid.

9. Ibid., 133–135.

10. Ibid., 24.

11. Louis Uchitelle and N. R. Kleinfield, "On the Battlefields of Business, Millions of Casualties," *The New York Times*, March 3, 1996.

12. Uchitelle, *Disposable American,* 209.

13. The rate for blue-collar workers was 7.3 percent; for white-collar workers, 2.6 percent. Bureau of Labor Statistics, "Displacement Rates for Blue-Collar and White-Collar Workers More Similar in Recent Years," September 16, 1999, http://www.bls.gov/opub/ted/1999/Sept/wk3/art04.htm.

14. The rate for blue-collar workers was 3.5 percent; for white-collar workers, it was 2.9 percent. Bureau of Labor Statistics, "Displacement Rates for Blue-Collar and White-Collar Workers More Similar in Recent Years."

15. According to economist Henry S. Farber, college-educated workers who lost their jobs between 1997 and 1999 suffered a drop in earnings of about 20 percent. Henry S. Farber, "Job Loss in the United States, 1981–2001," working paper 9707, National Bureau of Economic Research, Cambridge, MA, May 2003, http://www.nber.org/papers/w9707.

16. Uchitelle, *Disposable American*, 144.

17. Ibid., 144.

18. Eric Schlosser, *Fast Food Nation* (New York: Houghton Mifflin Books, 2001), 73.

19. "Table B-2. Real Gross Domestic Product, 1959–2007" and "Table B-49. Productivity and Related Data, Business and Nonfarm Business Sectors, 1959–2008," in *Economic Report of the President* (Washington, DC: U.S. Government Printing Office, 2008), http://www.gpoaccess.gov/eop/tables08.html.

20. Jack Beatty, *Colossus: How the Corporation Changed America* (New York: Broadway Books, 2001), 411

21. Ibid., 411.

22. Working Life, "Wages and Benefits: Real Wages (1964–2004)," http://www.workinglife.org/wiki/Wages+and+Benefits:+Real+Wages+(1964-2004). See also Beatty, *Colossus*, 411.

23. For example, in the mid-twentieth century, real wages had grown (above inflation) by nearly 2.5 percent per year. Earlier periods saw gains of about 1 percent per year. See Donald R. Adams, Jr., "Prices and Wages," in *Encyclopedia of American Economic History*, vol. 1, ed. Glenn Porter (New York: Charles Scribner's Sons, 1980), 245. From 1959 to 1970, productivity increased on average by 2.7 percent per year. See "Table B-50. Changes in Productivity and Related Data, Business and Nonfarm Business Sectors, 1959–2007," in *Economic Report of the President*, 2008, http://www.gpoaccess.gov/eop/tables08.html.

24. Thomas Piketty and Emmanuel Saez, quoted in Daniel Gross, "Income Inequality, Writ Larger," *The New York Times*, June 10, 2007.

25. In 2004, the top 20 percent of Americans controlled nearly 85 percent of the nation's wealth, while the bottom 40 percent controlled just 0.2 percent. Edward N. Wolff, "Recent Trends in Household Wealth in the United States: Rising Debt and the Middle-Class Squeeze," working paper 502, The Levy Economics Institute of Bard College, Annandale-on-Hudson, NY, June 2007.

26. Bureau of Labor Statistics, "*Women in the Labor Force: A Databook* Updated and Available on the Internet," May 13, 2005, http://www.bls.gov/bls/databooknews2005.pdf.

27. Ibid.

28. Ibid.

29. Anita Borg Institute for Women and Technology, "The State of Representation of Technical Women in Industry," 2007, http://anitaborg.org/files/stateofwomenhightechindustry.pdf, 3.

30. Ibid., 2.

31. Ibid.

32. Elizabeth Warren and Amelia Warren Tyagi, *The Two-Income Trap: Why Middle-Class Mothers and Fathers Are Going Broke* (New York: Basic Books, 2003), 51.

33. Bureau of Labor Statistics, "Workers on Flexible and Shift Schedules in May 2004," July 1, 2005, http://www.bls.gov/news.release/pdf/flex.pdf.

34. Juliet B. Schor, *The Overworked American* (New York: Basic Books, 1991), 1–2

35. Or 163 hours per year. Schor, *Overworked American*, 29.

36. Kimberly Fisher et al., "Gender Convergence in the American Heritage Time Use Study (AHTUS)," working paper 2006-25, Institute for Social and Economic Research (ISER), Essex, England, 32.

37. Ibid., 32.

38. Ibid.

39. W. Bentley MacCleod, Thomas Lemieux, and Daniel Parent, quoted in Gross, "Income Inequality, Writ Larger" (see note 24).

40. Arlie Russel Hochschild, *The Time Bind: When Work Becomes Home and Home Becomes Work* (New York: Metropolitan Books, 1997), 200.

41. Ibid.

Chapter Eight

1. Louis P. Cain, "Transportation," Chapter Df in *Historical Statistics of the United States, Millennial Edition Online*, eds. Susan B. Carter, Scott Sigmund Gartner, Michael R. Haines, Alan L. Olmstead, Richard Sutch, and Gavin Wright (Cambridge: Cambridge University Press, 2006), 4-762. See also Stephen B. Goddard, *Getting There: The Epic Struggle Between Road and Rail in the American Century* (New York: Basic Books, 1994).

2. That is, forty miles by land and a trans-Atlantic journey were roughly the same in price. Peter D. McClelland, "Transportation," in *Encyclopedia of American Economic History*, vol. 1, ed. Glenn Porter (New York: Charles Scribner's Sons, 1980), 310.

3. Cain, "Transportation," 4-763.

4. John M. Blum, William S. McFeely, Edmund S. Morgan, Arthur M. Schlesinger, Jr., Kenneth M. Stampp, and C. Vann Woodward, *The National Experience: A History of the United States*, vol. 1 (New York: Harcourt Brace Jovanovich, 1989), 190.

5. Cain, "Transportation," 4-764.

6. McClelland, "Transportation," 310.

7. Cain, "Transportation," 4-764.

8. Richard S. Tedlow, "The Coming of the Railroads," in *Management Past and Present: A Casebook on the History of American Business*, eds. Alfred D. Chandler, Jr., Thomas K. McCraw, and Richard S. Tedlow (Cincinnati, OH: South-Western College Publishing, 2000), 2–7.

9. McClelland, "Transportation," 314.

10. Cain, "Transportation," 4-766–4-767.

11. McClelland, "Transportation," 311.

12. Tedlow, "Coming of the Railroads," 2–8.

13. McClelland, "Transportation," 311–312. See also Christine MacLeod, "Britain as Workshop of the World," BBC History, http://www.bbc.co.uk/history/trail/victorian_britain/industry_invention/britain_workshop_world_05.shtml.

14. Cain, "Transportation," 4-762, 4-767.

15. Ibid.

16. Louis P. Cain, "Table Df667-678. Average Speeds and Travel Times for Steamboat, Keelboat, and Railroad: 1815–1855," in *Historical Statistics of the United States* (see note 1), 4-880.

17. McClelland, "Transportation," 312. For passengers in 1855, a steamboat traveling a trunk route cost $0.27 per mile (upstream); a keelboat moving upstream cost $2.22 per mile (Cain, "Table Df659-666. Passenger Fares for Steamboat, Keelboat, and

Railroad: 1815–1855," in *Historical Statistics of the United States* [see note 1], 4-880).

18. Tedlow, "The Coming of the Railroads," 2-9–2-10. See also Cain, "Transportation," 4-762.

19. Tedlow, "The Coming of the Railroads," 2-10; McClelland, "Transportation," 314–315.

20. Between 1850 and 1871, the government granted the railroads 131 million acres. Illinois State Museum, "The Land Grant Act of 1850," http://www.museum.state.il.us/RiverWeb/landings/Ambot/SOCIETY/SOC13.htm. For European investment, see Jack Beatty, *Colossus: How the Corporation Changed America* (New York: Broadway Books, 2001), 106.

21. Blum et al., *The National Experience*, vol. 2, 419.

22. Henry Adams, The *Education of Henry Adams: An Autobiography* (Boston: Houghton Mifflin, 1918), 240.

23. Beatty, *Colossus*, 93.

24. Ibid., 93–94.

25. Goddard, *Getting There*, 14.

26. Laura Ingalls Wilder, *By the Shores of Silver Lake* (New York: HarperCollins, 2004), 21–22.

27. Albro Martin, *Railroads Triumphant: The Growth, Rejection, and Rebirth of a Vital American Force* (New York: Oxford University Press, 1992), 122.

28. Walt Whitman, "To a Locomotive in Winter," quoted in Goddard, *Getting There*, 8.

29. Goddard, *Getting There*, 65–66.

30. Ibid, 66.

31. Ibid., 67–68.

32. Ibid., 75–77.

33. Ibid., 44.

34. Ibid., 48.

35. Ibid., 22–23, 44–45.

36. Ibid., 49.

37. "By 1910, nearly a half-million motor vehicles were on American roads, 187,000 of them produced in that year alone" (Goddard, *Getting There*, 57).

38. Ibid., 60–63.

39. Ibid., 63.

40. Cain, "Transportation," 4-764. See also Richard F. Weingroff, "From Names to Numbers: The Origins of the U.S. Numbered Highway System," U.S. Department of Transportation, http://www.cf.fhwa.dot.gov/infrastructure/numbers.html.

41. Cain, "Transportation," 4-765.

42. UPS, "Messenger Service," http://www.ups.com/content/corp/about/history/1929.html.

43. Louis P. Cain, "Table Df48-58. Domestic Inter-city Freight Traffic—Volume and Percentage, by Type of Transportation: 1939–1996," in *Historical Statistics of the United States* (see note 1), 4-786–4-787.

44. 1.64 million versus 1.52 million. James W. Cortada, *The Digital Hand: How Computers Changed the Work of American Manufacturing, Transportation, and Retail Industries* (Oxford: Oxford University Press, 2004), 232.

45. Goddard, *Getting There*, 129.

46. Ibid., 129–134.

47. Ibid.

48. Ibid., 134–135.

49. Chevrolet, Ford, and Oldsmobile, respectively.

50. Louis P. Cain, "Table Df330-338. Automobile Ownership and Financing," in *Historical Statistics of the United States* (see note 1), 4-829.

51. U.S. Department of Energy, "Retail Gasoline Historical Prices," http://www.eia.doe.gov/oil_gas/petroleum/data_publications/wrgp/mogas_history.html.

52. Richard F. Weingroff, "Highway History: The Greatest Decade, 1956–1966," U.S. Department of Transportation, http://www.fhwa.dot.gov/infrastructure/50interstate.cfm.

53. Thomas K. McCraw, *American Business, 1920–2000: How It Worked* (Wheeling, IL: Harlan Davidson, 2000), 157.

54. Jeffrey R. Bernstein, "Toyoda Automatic Looms and Toyota Automobiles," in *Creating Modern Capitalism: How Entrepreneurs, Companies, and Countries Triumphed in Three Industrial Revolutions*, ed. Thomas K. McCraw (Cambridge, MA: Harvard University Press, 1997), 429–430.

55. Ibid., 430.

56. Ibid.

57. Ibid., 430–431.

58. Ibid., 429 (figure 11.2).

59. Ibid., 431.

60. "Japan Overtakes U.S. as World's Largest Vehicle Producer," *The Japan Times*, May 9, 2007, www.japantimes.co.jp; "Toyota Boss Fears US Trade Fury," *BBC News*, April 26, 2005, www.bbc.co.uk.

61. Cain, "Transportation," 4-763.

62. Cain, "Table Df1165-1176: Aircraft Production and Exports," in *Historical Statistics of the United States* (see note 1), 4-963–4-964.

63. Obaid Younossi, Mark V. Arena, and Richard Moore, "An Overview of Military Jet Engine History," in *Military Jet Engine Acquisition* (Santa Monica, CA: Rand Corporation, 2002), 97.

64. Ibid., 104–106; and Peter Lyth, "Book Reviews," *Journal of Transport History* 20, no. 1 (1999): 75–76.

65. Cain, "Transportation," 4-763. See also National Aeronautics and Space Administration, "25th Anniversary of Apollo 11: 1969–1994," http://nssdc.gsfc.nasa.gov/planetary/lunar/apollo11.html.

66. U.S. Centennial of Flight Commission, "Deregulation and Its Consequences," http://www.centennialofflight.gov/essay/Commercial_Aviation/Dereg/Tran8.htm.

67. Cain, "Table Df1112-1125. Scheduled Domestic Air Transportation," in *Historical Statistics of the United States* (see note 1), 4-954–4-956.

68. U.S. Department of Transportation, Research and Innovative Technology Administration, Bureau of Transportation Statistics, National Transportation Statistics, Section B, "Table 1-11. Number of U.S. Aircraft, Vehicles, Vessels, and Other Conveyances," updated December 2007, http://www.bts.gov/publications/national_transportation_statistics/.

69. U.S. Department of Transportation, Research and Innovative Technology Administration, Bureau of Transportation Statistics, National Transportation Statistics, Section B, "Table 1-37. U.S. Passenger Miles (Millions)," updated December 2007, http://www.bts.gov/publications/national_transportation_statistics/.

Chapter Nine

1. Quoted in James H. Madison, "Communications," in *Encyclopedia of American Economic History*, vol. 1, ed. Glenn Porter (New York: Charles Scribner's Sons, 1980), 338.

2. U.S. Constitution, Article I, Section 8; Alexander J. Field, "Communications," Chapter Dg in *Historical Statistics of the United States*, *Millennial Edition Online*, eds. Susan B. Carter, Scott Sigmund Gartner, Michael R. Haines, Alan L. Olmstead, Richard Sutch, and Gavin Wright (Cambridge: Cambridge University Press, 2006), 4-981.

3. Alexander J. Field, "Table Dg181-189. U.S. Postal Service," in *Historical Statistics of the United States* (see note 2), 4-1038.

4. Madison, "Communications," 336.

5. In 1831, there were 8,764 postmasters, and the federal army numbered 6,332. Richard John, *Spreading the News: The American Postal System from Franklin to Morse* (Boston: Harvard University Press, 1995) 3.

6. Tom Standage, "The Mother of All Networks," in *The Victorian Internet: The Remarkable Story of the Telegraph and the Nineteenth Century's On-Line Pioneers* (New York: Walker and Company, 1998), 41–56; Field, "Communications," 4-985.

7. Standage, "Mother of All Networks," 42–43.

8. Ibid., 46.

9. Ibid., 48.

10. Madison, "Communications," 338.

11. Ibid., 338.

12. Ibid., 338–339; Field, "Communications," 4-977; The Associated Press, "AP History," http://www.ap.org/pages/about/history/history_FIRST.html.

13. A *caveat* was a document with descriptions and the intent to patent, similar to a provisional patent, Field, "Communications," 4-988–4-989. Alan Stone, *How America Got On-Line: Politics, Markets, and the Revolution in Telecommunications* (Armonk, NY: M.E. Sharpe, 1997), 21.

14. Madison, "Communications," 341.

15. Field, "Communications," 4-989; Madison, "Communications," 341.

16. Field, "Communications," 4-988, 4-990.

17. Alexander J. Field, "Table Dg34-35. Telephone industry," in *Historical Statistics of the United States* (see note 1), 4-1008–4-1012.

18. Stone, *How America Got On-Line*, 21, 25.

19. Field, "Communications," 4-993; Madison, "Communications," 341.

20. Field, "Communications," 4-993.

21. Tom Lewis, *Empire of the Air* (New York: HarperCollins, 1991), 121, 142.

22. Ibid., 142.

23. Ibid., 142–143. See also Thomas K. McCraw, *American Business, 1920–2000: How It Worked* (Wheeling, IL: Harlan Davidson, 2000), 120.

24. McCraw, *American Business,* 117.

25. Ibid., 121.

26. Alexander J. Field, "Table Dg117-130. Radio and Television," in *Historical Statistics of the United States* (see note 1), 4-1027–4-1030.

27. Reproduced in Susan Smulyan, *Selling Radio: The Commercialization of American Broadcasting 1920–1934* (Washington, DC: Smithsonian Institution Press, 1994).

28. Lewis, *Empire of the Air*, 224.

29. McCraw, *American Business*, 116, 124–126, 133.

30. Ibid., 116.

31. David E. Brown, *Inventing Modern America* (Cambridge, MA: MIT Press, 2002), 58–61.

32. Field, "Communications," 4-995; Field, "Table Dg117-130. Radio and Television," in *Historical Statistics of the United States* (see note 1), 4-1027–4-1028.

33. Field, "Table Dg117-130. Radio and Television," in *Historical Statistics of the United States* (see note 1), 4-1027–4-1028; U.S. Department of Commerce, *Historical Statistics of the United States: Colonial Times to 1970,* vol. 1 (Washington, DC: U.S. Government Printing Office, 1975), 41.

34. TV History, "Number of TV Households in America," http://www.tvhistory.tv/Annual_TV_Households_50-78.JPG.

35. Nancy F. Koehn, *Brand New: How Entrepreneurs Earned Customers' Trust from Wedgwood to Dell* (Boston: Harvard Business School Press, 2001), 263.

36. Ibid., 262–263.

37. Field, "Communications," 4-996.

38. Koehn, *Brand New*, 266.

39. Ibid.

40. Ibid.

41. Ibid., 264, 268–269.

42. Ibid., 269–270.

43. Ibid, 270.

44. U.S. Census Bureau, "Computer and Internet Use in the United States: 2003," October 2005, http://www.census.gov/prod/2005pubs/p23-208.pdf; Leichtman Research Group, "Over Half of U.S. Households Subscribe to Broadband Internet," www.leichtmanresearch.com/press/060707release.html. See also Alex Moskalyuk, "In 2008, 80 Mln US Households Will Have a PC, 46 Mln Will Have Two or More," IT Facts, March 19, 2005, http://blogs.zdnet.com/ITFacts/?p=7380.

45. Field, "Communications," 4-997.

46. Ibid., 4-997.

47. CERN, "Welcome to info.cern.ch, the Website of the World's First-Ever Web Server," http://info.cern.ch/.

48. U.S. Census Bureau, "Computer and Internet Use in the United States." See also National Telecommunications and Information Administration, "Households Using the Internet In and Outside the Home, by Selected Characteristics: Total, Urban, Rural, Principal City, 2007," http://www.ntia.doc.gov/reports/2008/table_householdinternet2007.pdf.

Epilogue

1. Joseph A. Schumpeter, *Capitalism, Socialism and Democracy* (New York: Harper & Row, 1942, 1950), 82.

INDEX

An *i* after a page number indicates an image. A *t* indicates a timeline entry.

NANCY F. KOEHN is a historian at the Harvard Business School where she holds the James E. Robison chair of Business Administration. Koehn's research focuses on entrepreneurial leadership and how leaders, past and present, craft lives of purpose, worth, and impact. She is currently working on a book about the most important leadership lessons from Abraham Lincoln's journey and another on social entrepreneurs.

Koehn is the author of *Brand New: How Entrepreneurs Earned Consumers' Trust from Wedgwood to Dell* (2001) and *The Power of Commerce: Economy and Governance in the First British Empire* (1994), as well as a contributor to *Creative Capitalism: A Conversation with Bill Gates, Warren Buffett and other Economic Leaders* (2008); *Remember Who You Are: Life Stories That Inspire the Heart and Mind* (2004); *Beauty and Business (2000)*; *The Intellectual Venture Capitalist: John H. McArthur and the Work of the Harvard Business School, 1980–1995* (1999); *Creating Modern Capitalism: How Entrepreneurs, Companies, and Countries Triumphed in Three Industrial Revolutions* (1997); and *Management Past and Present: A Casebook on American Business History* (1995). She has written and supervised cases on Bono and U2, Oprah Winfrey, Whole Foods, Starbucks Coffee Company, Ernest Shackleton, Wedgwood, Estée Lauder, Henry Heinz, Milton Hershey, Celeste Walker, Marshall Field, Dell Computer, and other leaders and organizations.

At the Harvard Business School, she teaches the MBA elective Entrepreneurial Leadership in Turbulent Times. For many years she taught The Coming of Managerial Capitalism, one of the school's most popular courses.

Before coming to HBS, Koehn was a member of Harvard University's Faculty of Arts and Sciences, first as a graduate student in history and then as a lecturer in the History and Literature concentration and the Department of Economics. A Phi Beta Kappa graduate of Stanford University, Koehn earned a Master of Public Policy from Harvard's Kennedy School of Government before taking her MA and PhD in History from Harvard.

Koehn lives outside Boston and is an avid equestrian.